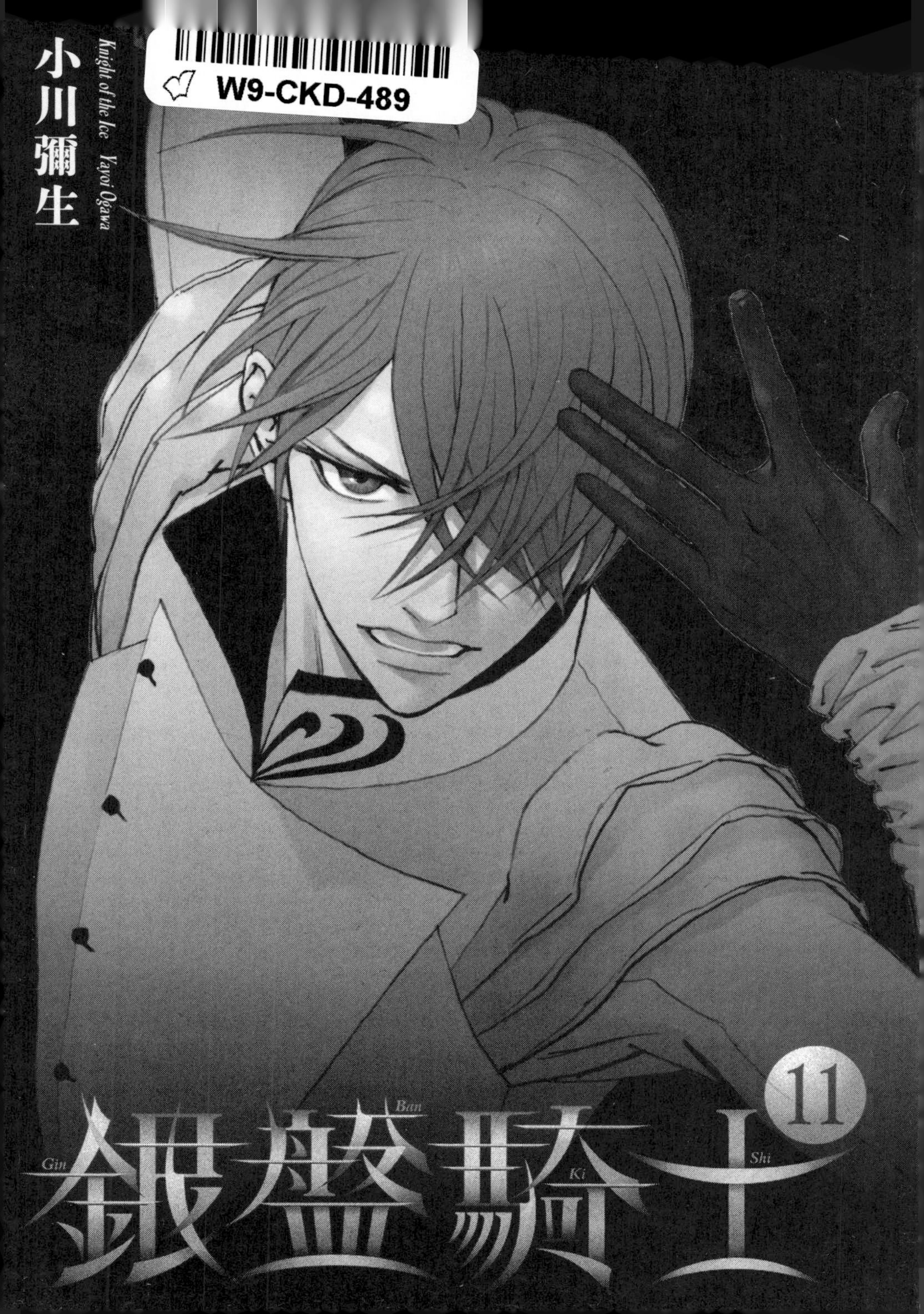
小川彌生
Knight of the Ice Yayoi Ogawa
11
Gin Ban Ki Shi
銀盤騎士

Characters

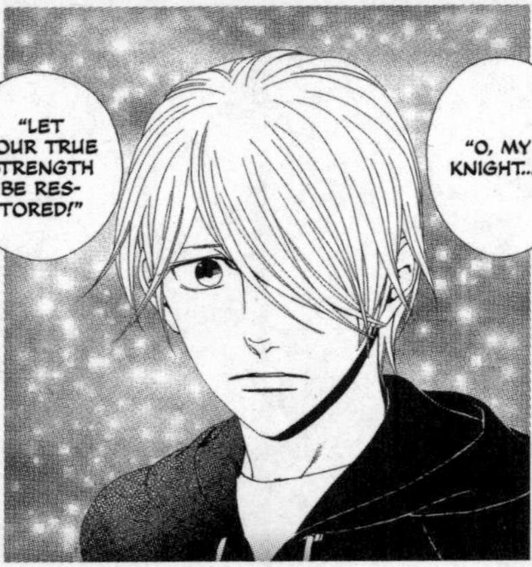
"LET YOUR TRUE STRENGTH BE RESTORED!"
"O, MY KNIGHT..."

Kokoro Kijinami

Japan's top men's figure skater. One of his greatest strengths is the beauty his height lends to his quadruple jumps. He's recovered shockingly quickly from his ankle surgery, but now he has to compete in the Sochi Olympics without the help of Chitose's magic spell.

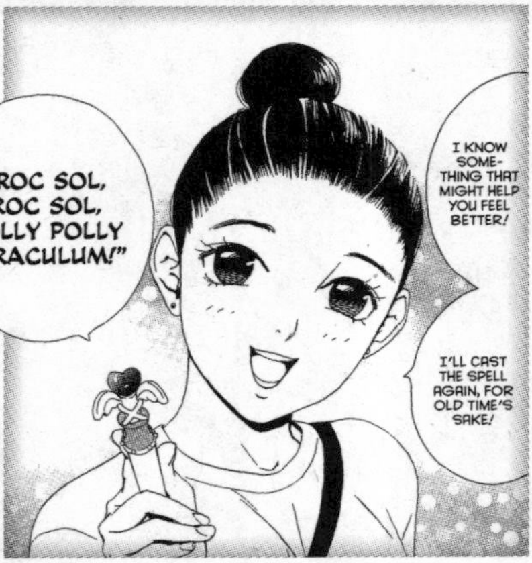
"ROC SOL, ROC SOL, POLLY POLLY MIRACULUM!"
I KNOW SOMETHING THAT MIGHT HELP YOU FEEL BETTER!
I'LL CAST THE SPELL AGAIN, FOR OLD TIME'S SAKE!

Chitose Igari

An editor for the health-and-lifestyle magazine *SASSO*. She's so short that she often gets mistaken for an elementary schooler. She's been accompanying Kokoro to competitions and pretending to be his personal trainer, but this time she has to watch from home in Japan due to her recent heart surgery.

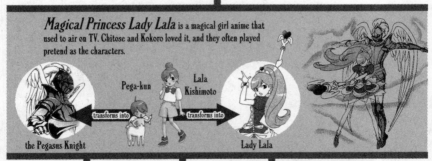

Magical Princess Lady Lala is a magical girl anime that used to air on TV. Chitose and Kokoro loved it, and they often played pretend as the characters.

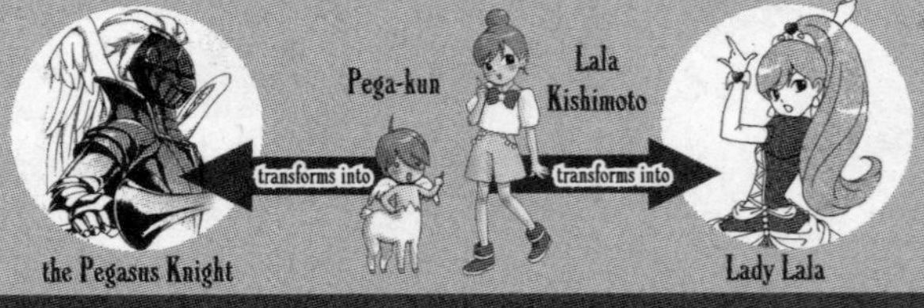
Pega-kun
Lala Kishimoto
transforms into
transforms into
the Pegasus Knight
Lady Lala

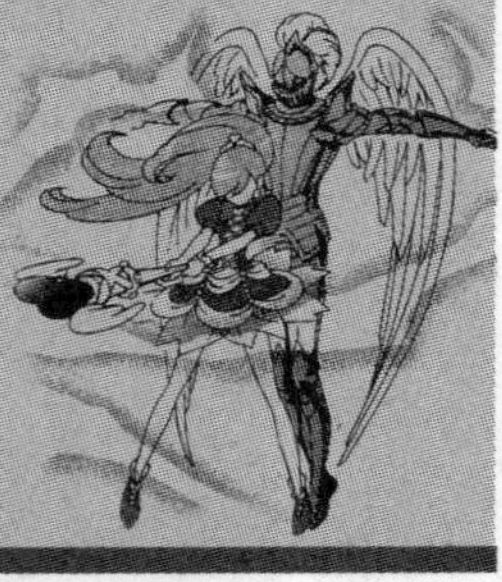

Kokoro's Father

President of the Kijinami Group, a company that runs a number of boutique ryokans.

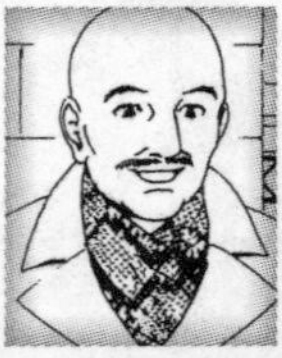

Yayoi Ogata

A manga artist. She went to the same college as Chitose and knows about her relationship with Kokoro.

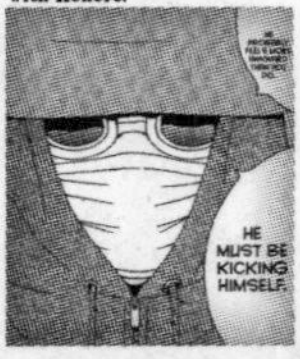
HE MUST BE KICKING HIMSELF.

Reiko Yano

An employee at Kodan Publishing who was having an affair with Sawada.

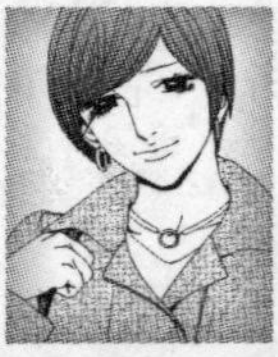

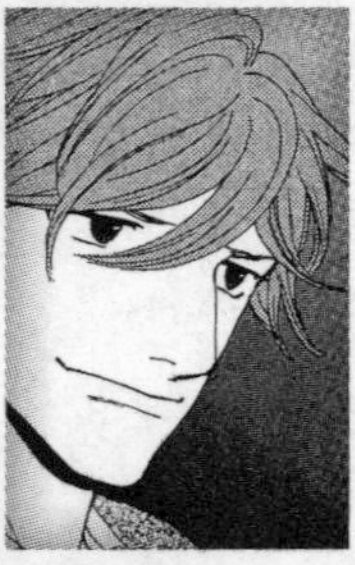

Koichi Sawada

The head of the editorial department for Kodan Publishing's magazine *SASSO*. He's good at his job, but can be somewhat lacking in delicacy...

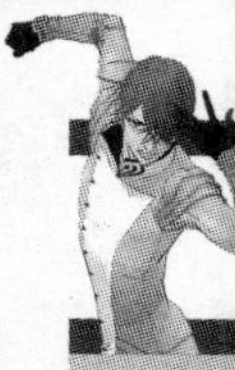

Knight of the Ice

Kokoro's Staff

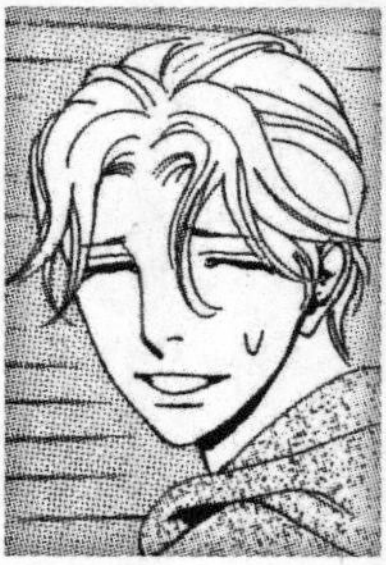

Kenzo Dominic Takiguchi

Kokoro's personal trainer.

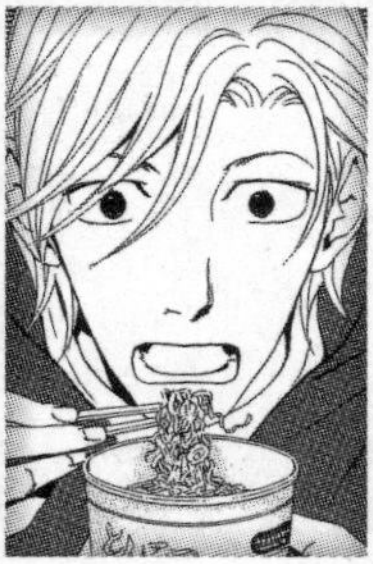

Hikaru Yomota

Kokoro's assistant coach and a former ice dancer.

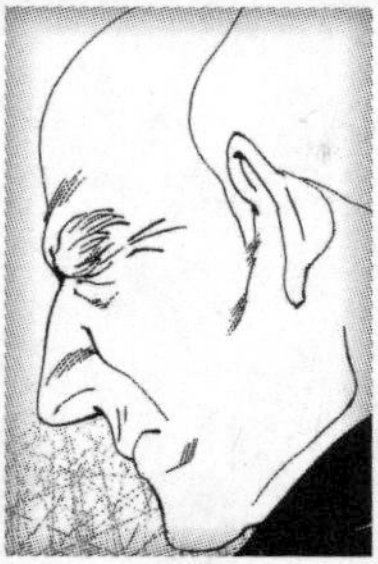

Takejiro Honda

Kokoro's coach. Due to unexpected health problems, he's had to entrust Kokoro's coaching to his longtime rival, Masato Tamura.

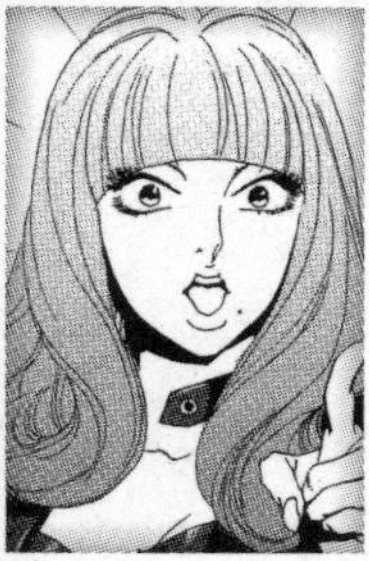

Moriyama

Kokoro's manager. She's not afraid to get a little pushy if that's what it takes to get results.

Kokoro's Rivals

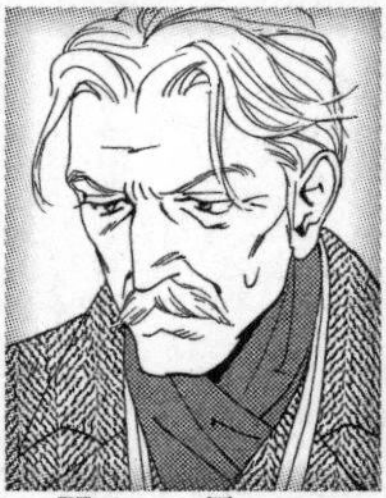

Masato Tamura

Raito Tamura's grandfather and Kokoro's temporary coach.

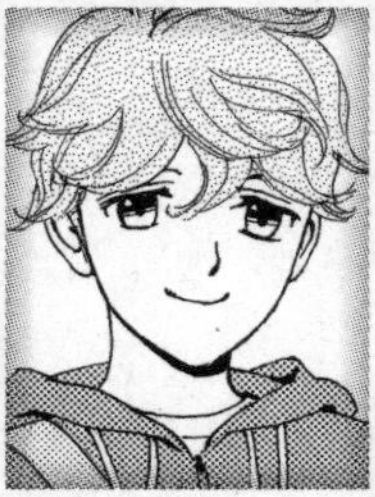

Fuuta Kumano

He can always rely on his speed and his devilish cuteness.

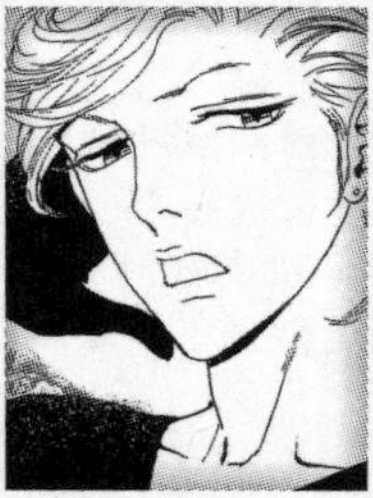

Raito Tamura

He dazzles the crowd with his passion and expressiveness.

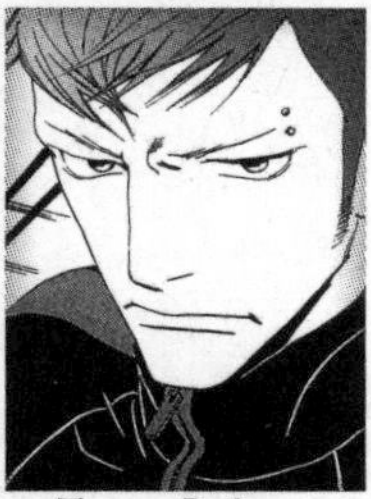

Taiga Aoki

His greatest strength is his ability to land two different quad jumps.

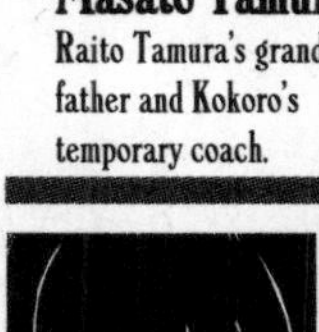

Ilia Sokurov

Russia's young top skater. He's an extreme klutz.

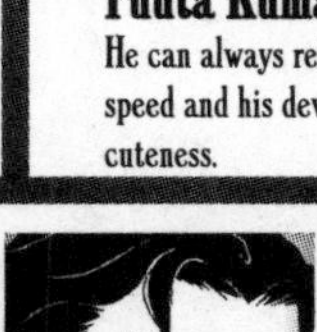

Kyle Miller

An American skater. He and Louis are dating.

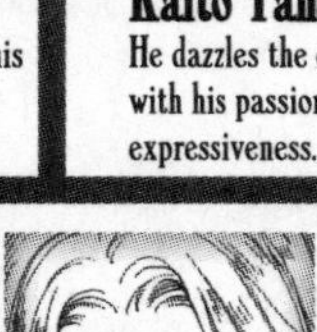

Louis Claire

A Canadian skater. He's a year younger than Kokoro and is the reigning World Champion.

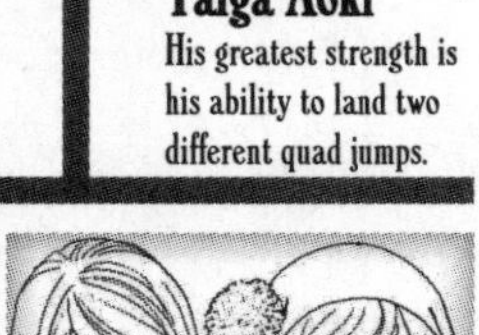

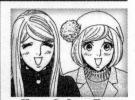

Maria & Anna Kijinami

Kokoro's younger twin sisters. Maria (right) is in a relationship with Taiga, and Anna is in a relationship with their father's personal assistant, Kanzaki.

Contents

Spell 52
The Knight Takes to the Ice
006

Spell 53
The Foe Unseen
036

Spell 54
The Star and the Pebble
066

Spell 55
My Knight
096

Spell 56
The Opening Page
128

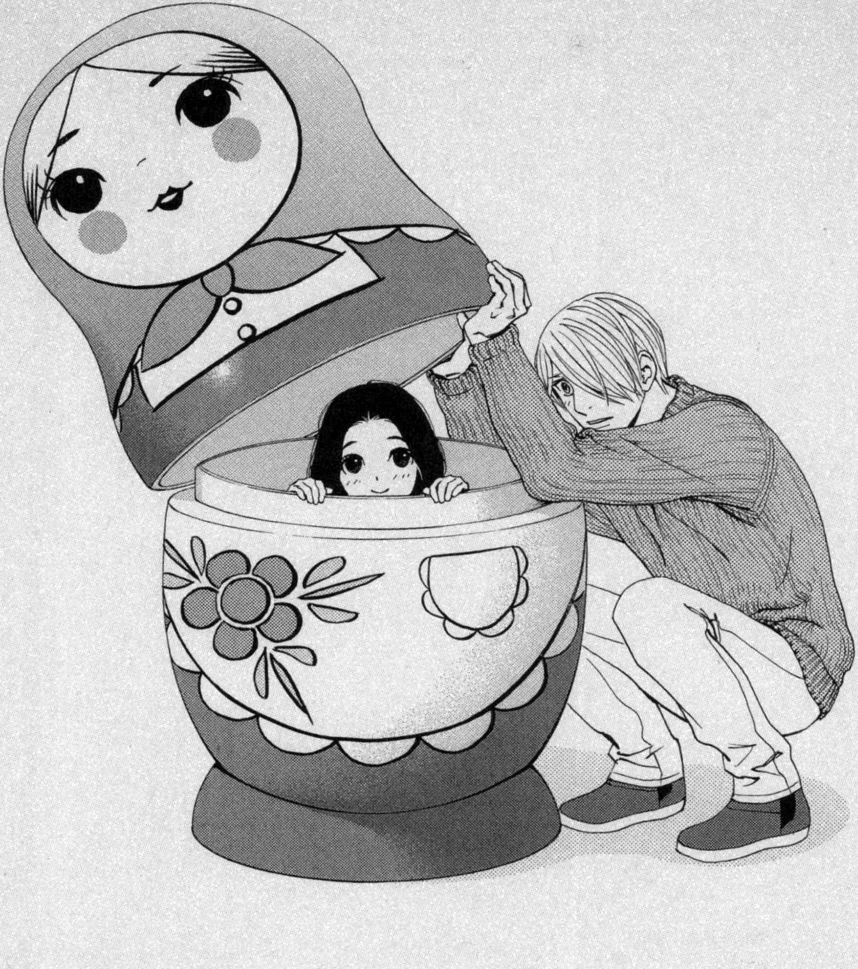

Spell 52

The Knight Takes to the Ice

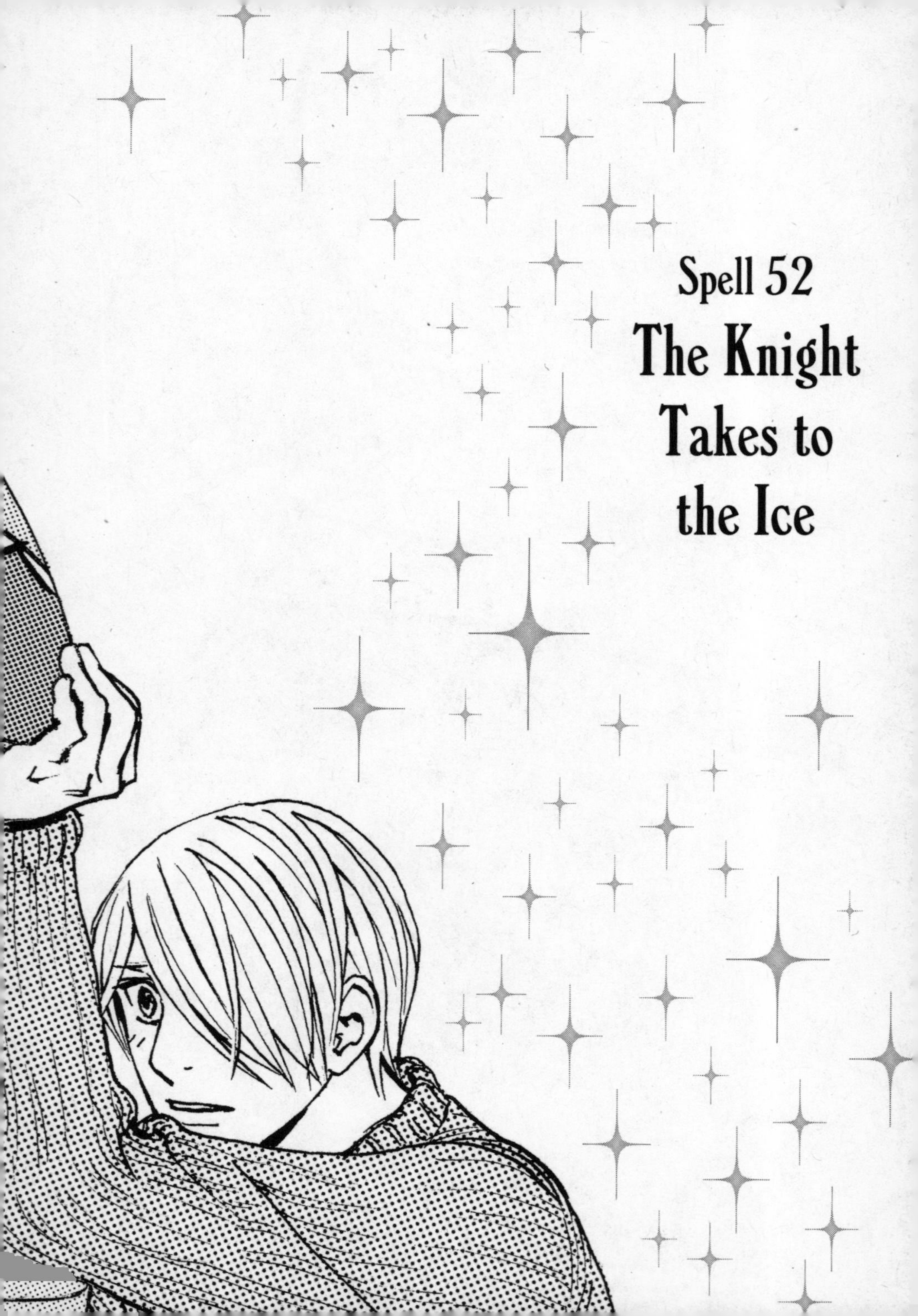

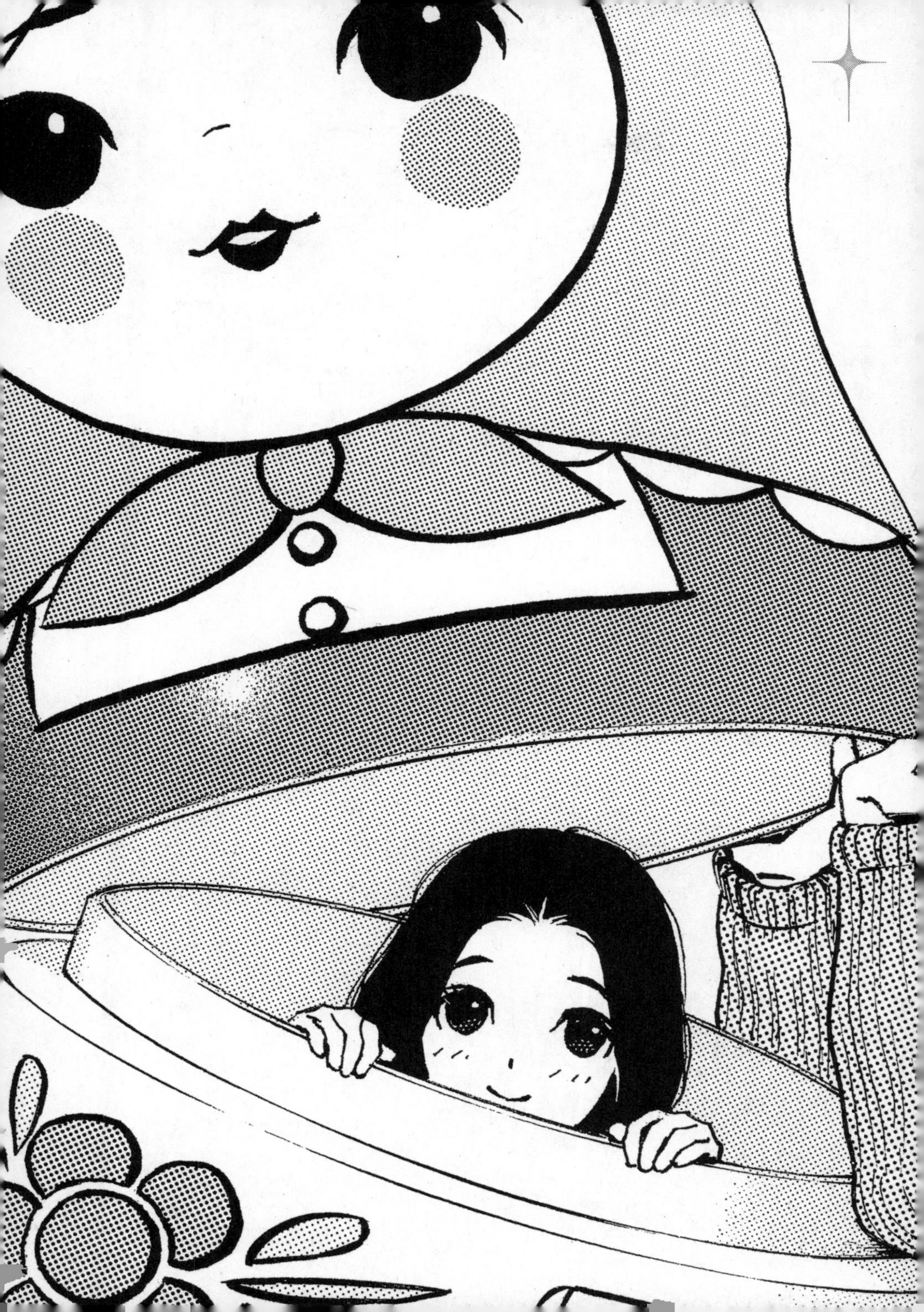

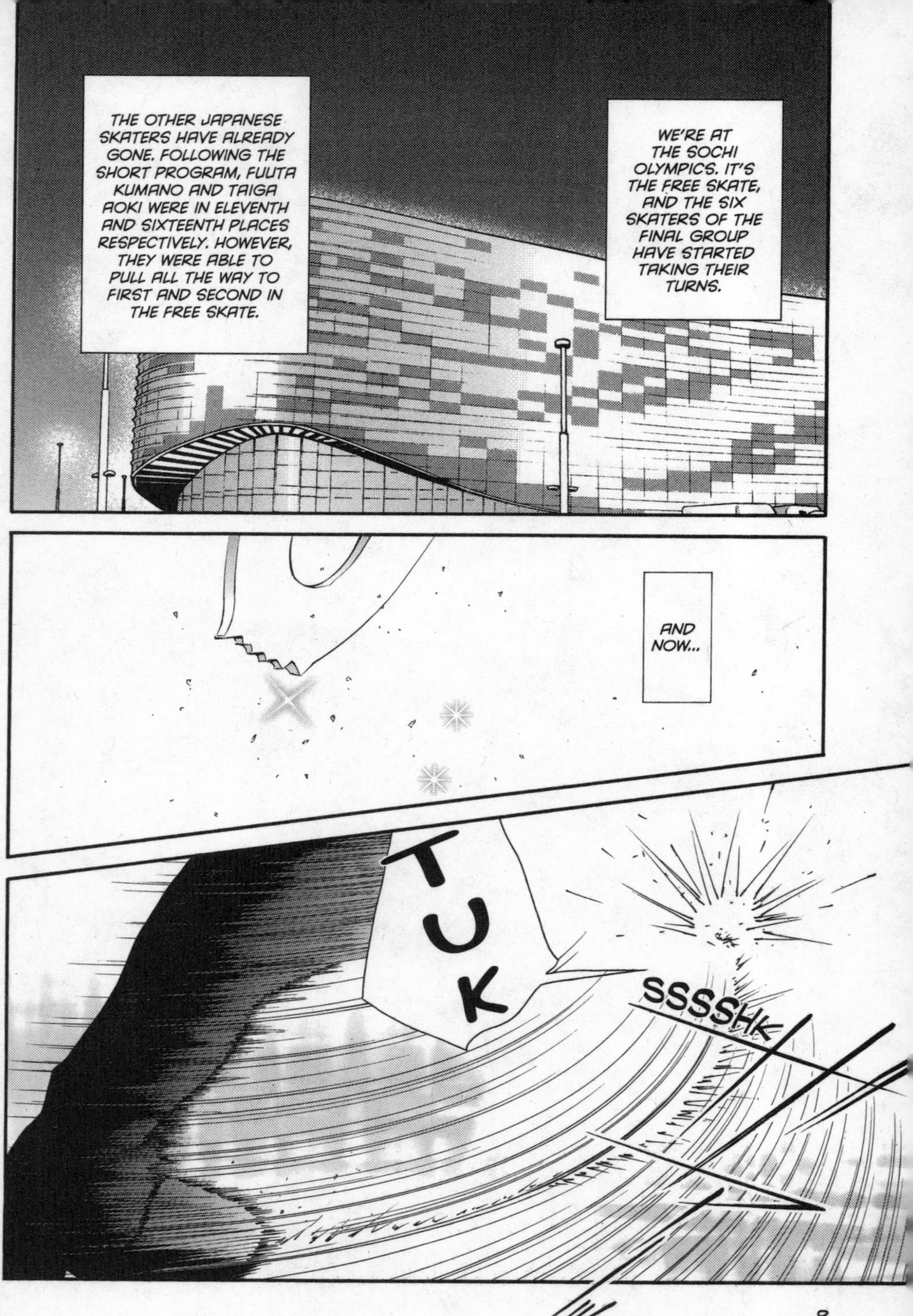
WE'RE AT THE SOCHI OLYMPICS. IT'S THE FREE SKATE, AND THE SIX SKATERS OF THE FINAL GROUP HAVE STARTED TAKING THEIR TURNS.
THE OTHER JAPANESE SKATERS HAVE ALREADY GONE. FOLLOWING THE SHORT PROGRAM, FUUTA KUMANO AND TAIGA AOKI WERE IN ELEVENTH AND SIXTEENTH PLACES RESPECTIVELY. HOWEVER, THEY WERE ABLE TO PULL ALL THE WAY TO FIRST AND SECOND IN THE FREE SKATE.
AND NOW...
TUK
SSSSHK

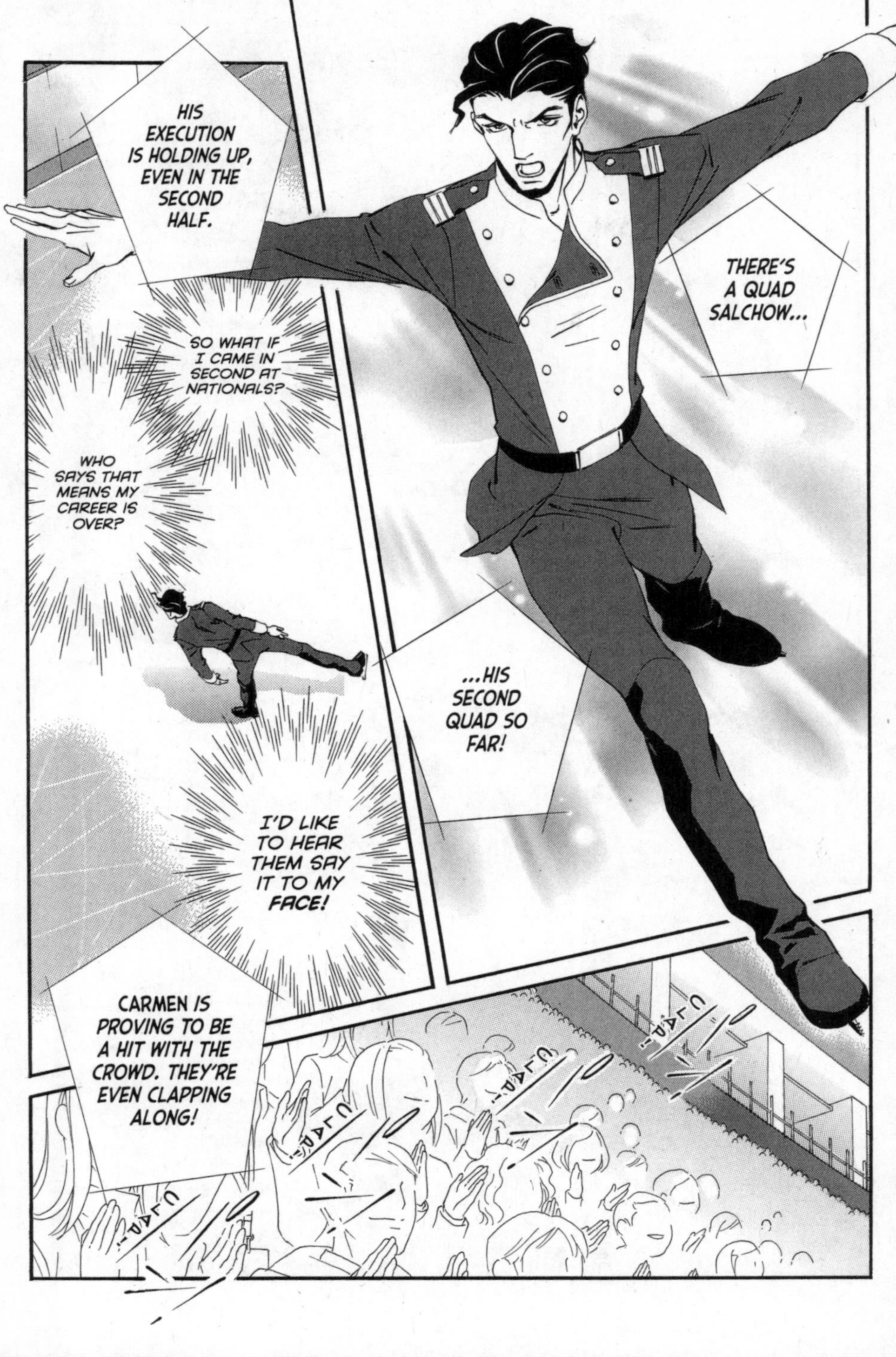
THERE'S A QUAD SALCHOW...
...HIS SECOND QUAD SO FAR!
HIS EXECUTION IS HOLDING UP, EVEN IN THE SECOND HALF.
SO WHAT IF I CAME IN SECOND AT NATIONALS?
WHO SAYS THAT MEANS MY CAREER IS OVER?
I'D LIKE TO HEAR THEM SAY IT TO MY *FACE!*
CARMEN IS PROVING TO BE A HIT WITH THE CROWD. THEY'RE EVEN CLAPPING ALONG!

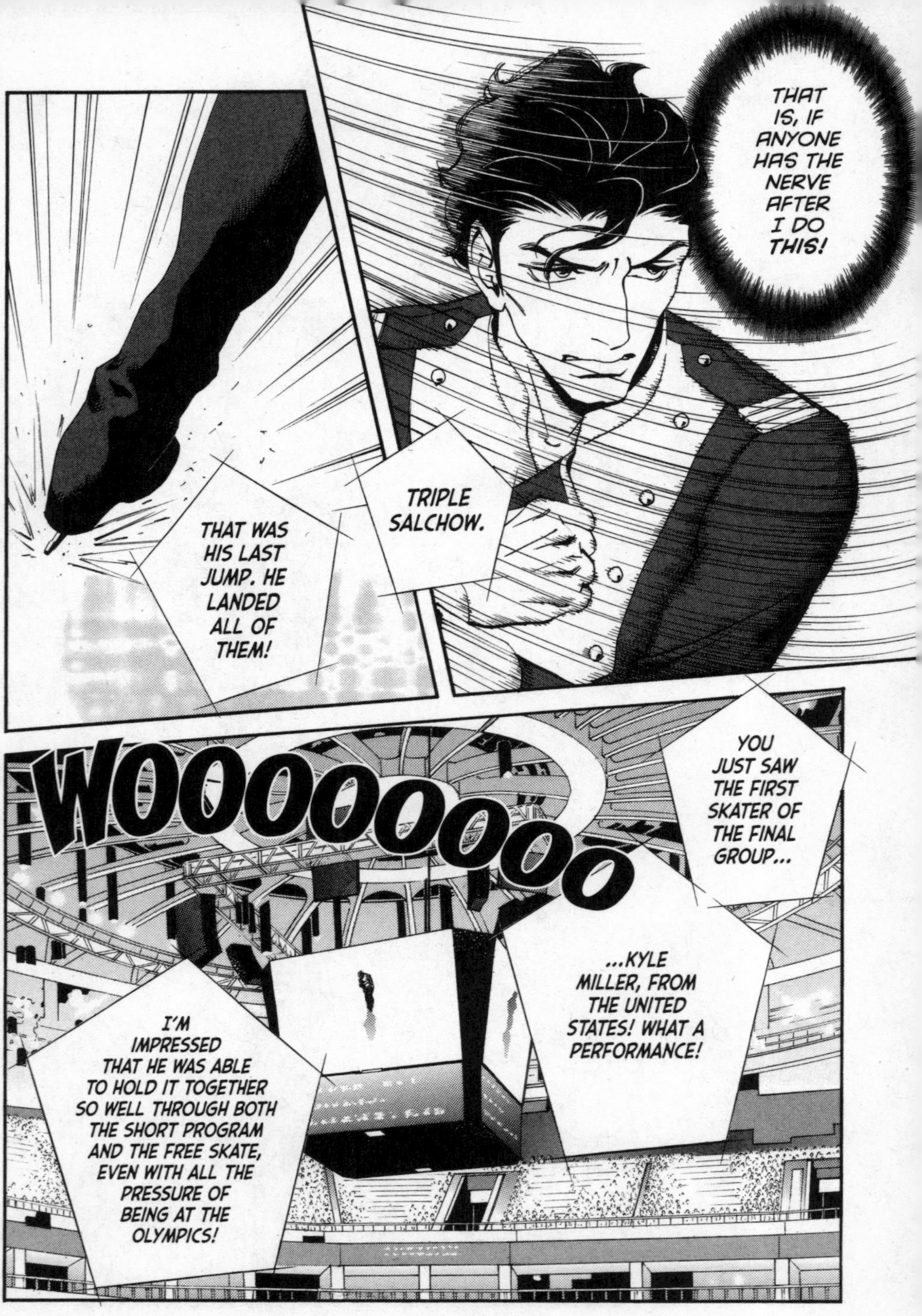
THAT IS, IF ANYONE HAS THE NERVE AFTER I DO THIS!
TRIPLE SALCHOW.
THAT WAS HIS LAST JUMP. HE LANDED ALL OF THEM!
WOOOOOOOO
YOU JUST SAW THE FIRST SKATER OF THE FINAL GROUP...
...KYLE MILLER, FROM THE UNITED STATES! WHAT A PERFORMANCE!
I'M IMPRESSED THAT HE WAS ABLE TO HOLD IT TOGETHER SO WELL THROUGH BOTH THE SHORT PROGRAM AND THE FREE SKATE, EVEN WITH ALL THE PRESSURE OF BEING AT THE OLYMPICS!

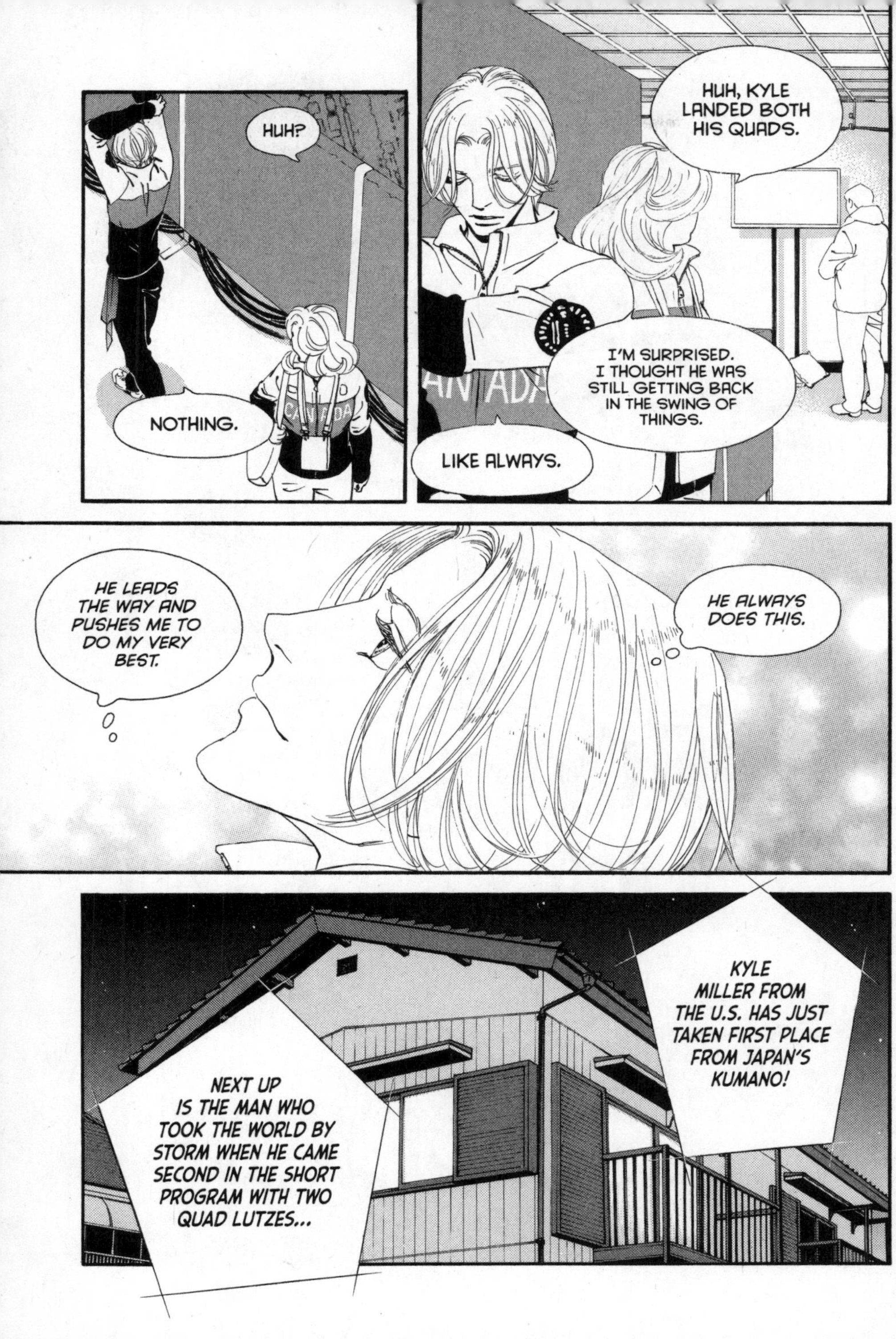
HUH, KYLE LANDED BOTH HIS QUADS.
I'M SURPRISED. I THOUGHT HE WAS STILL GETTING BACK IN THE SWING OF THINGS.
LIKE ALWAYS.
HUH?
NOTHING.
HE ALWAYS DOES THIS.
HE LEADS THE WAY AND PUSHES ME TO DO MY VERY BEST.
KYLE MILLER FROM THE U.S. HAS JUST TAKEN FIRST PLACE FROM JAPAN'S KUMANO!
NEXT UP IS THE MAN WHO TOOK THE WORLD BY STORM WHEN HE CAME SECOND IN THE SHORT PROGRAM WITH TWO QUAD LUTZES...

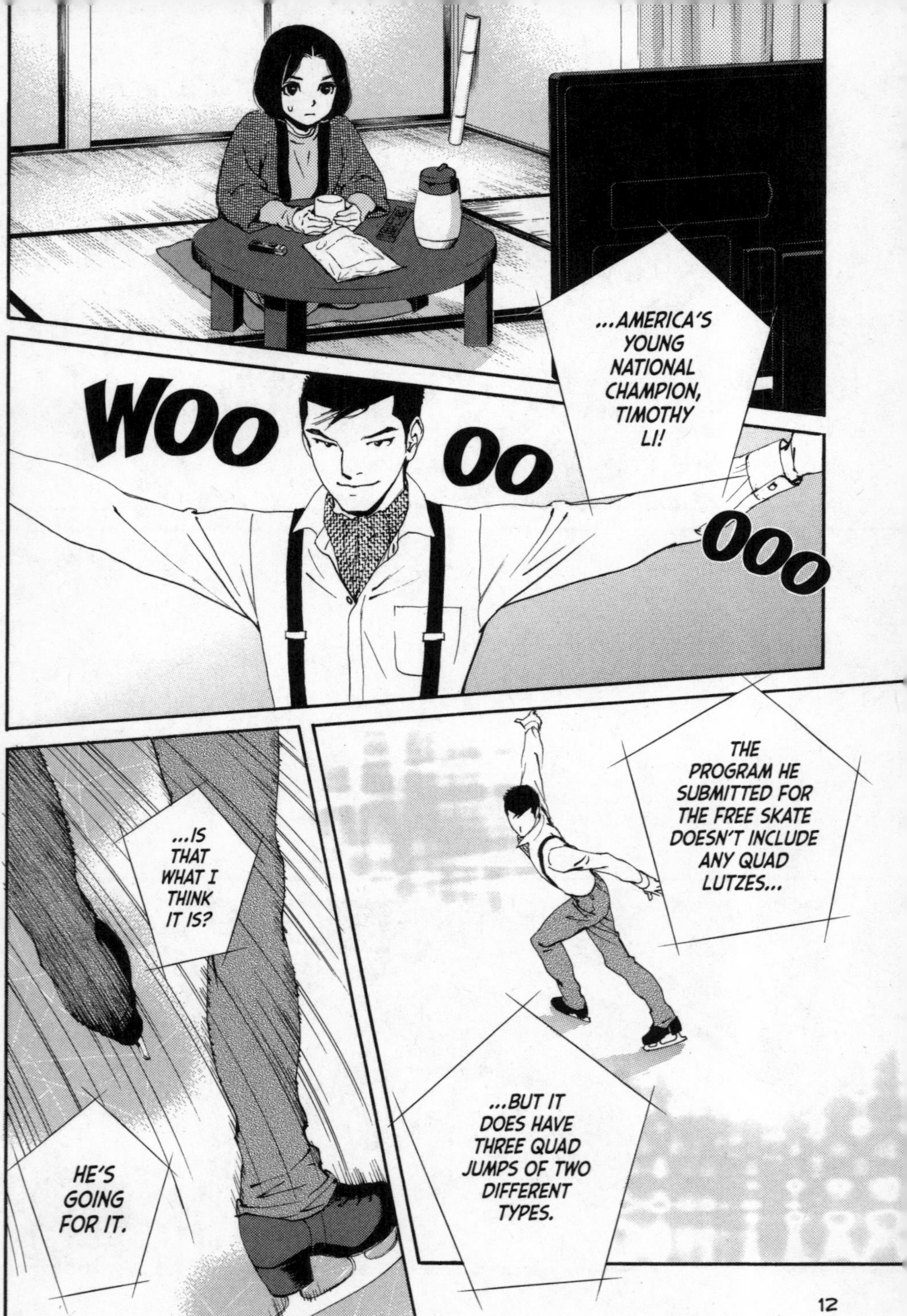
...AMERICA'S YOUNG NATIONAL CHAMPION, TIMOTHY LI!
WOO
OO
OOO
THE PROGRAM HE SUBMITTED FOR THE FREE SKATE DOESN'T INCLUDE ANY QUAD LUTZES...
...BUT IT DOES HAVE THREE QUAD JUMPS OF TWO DIFFERENT TYPES.
...IS THAT WHAT I THINK IT IS?
HE'S GOING FOR IT.

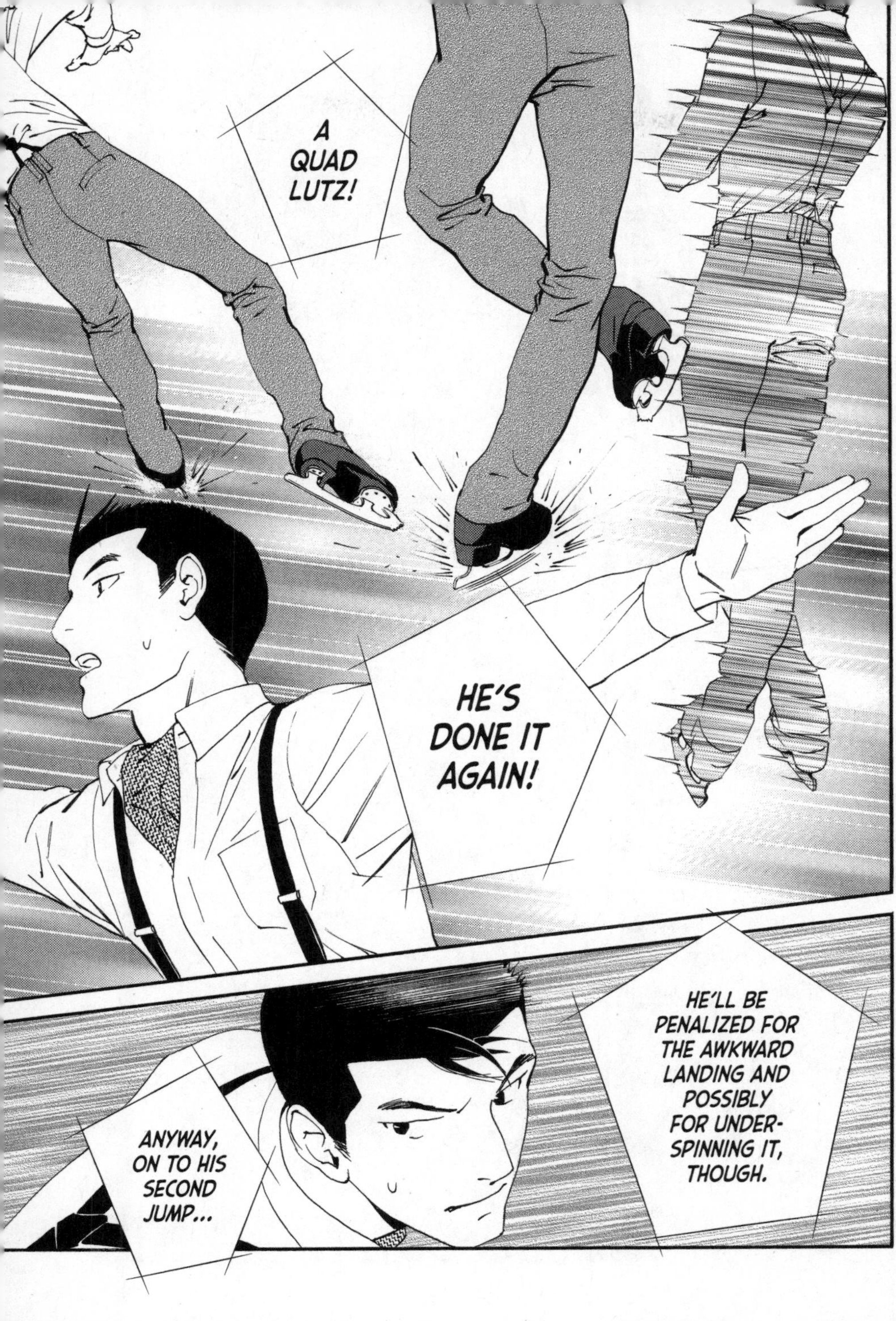
A QUAD LUTZ!
HE'S DONE IT AGAIN!
HE'LL BE PENALIZED FOR THE AWKWARD LANDING AND POSSIBLY FOR UNDER-SPINNING IT, THOUGH.
ANYWAY, ON TO HIS SECOND JUMP...

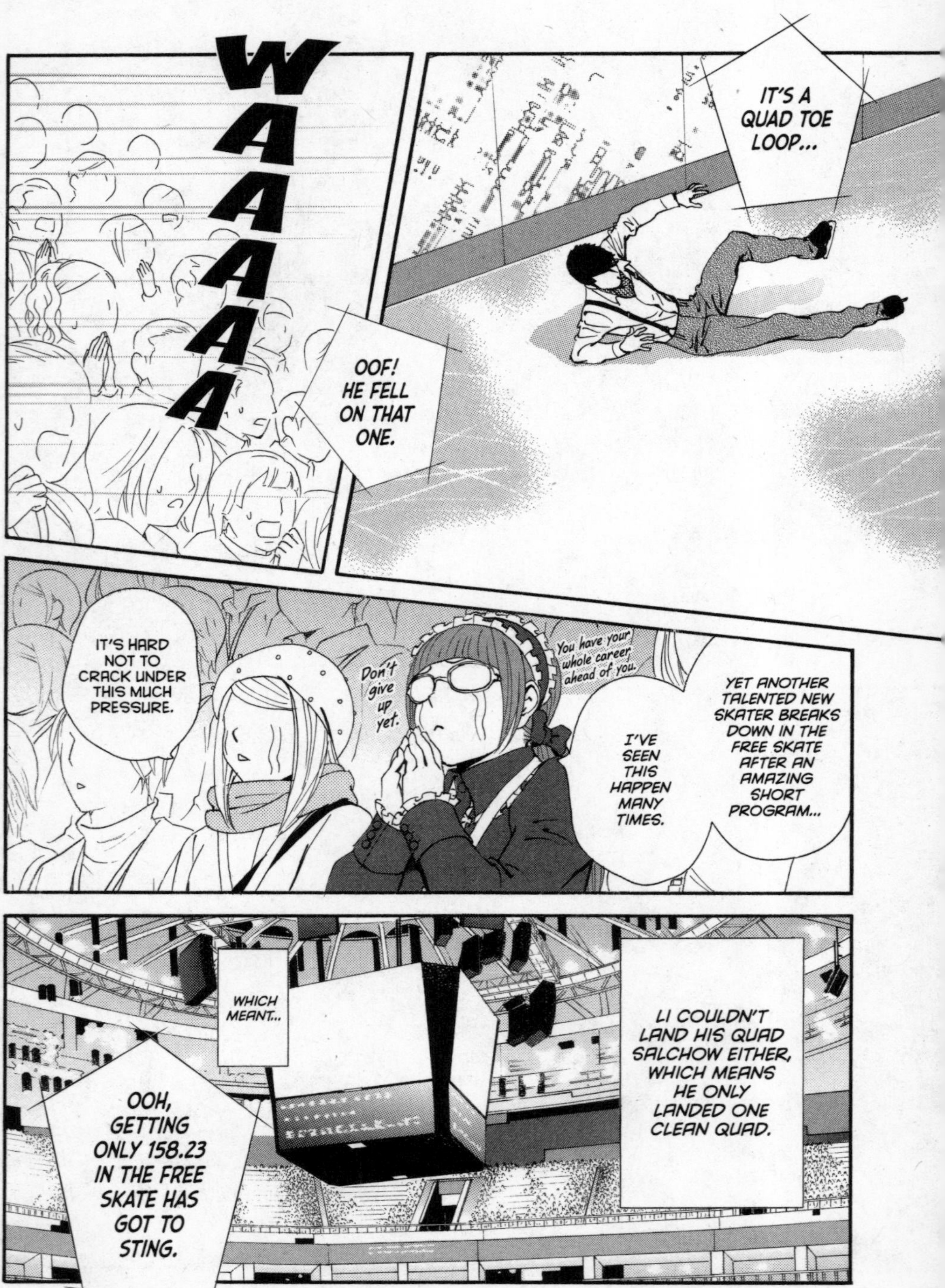
IT'S A QUAD TOE LOOP...
WAAAAAA
OOF! HE FELL ON THAT ONE.
YET ANOTHER TALENTED NEW SKATER BREAKS DOWN IN THE FREE SKATE AFTER AN AMAZING SHORT PROGRAM...
I'VE SEEN THIS HAPPEN MANY TIMES.
You have your whole career ahead of you.
Don't give up yet.
IT'S HARD NOT TO CRACK UNDER THIS MUCH PRESSURE.
LI COULDN'T LAND HIS QUAD SALCHOW EITHER, WHICH MEANS HE ONLY LANDED ONE CLEAN QUAD.
WHICH MEANT...
OOH, GETTING ONLY 158.23 IN THE FREE SKATE HAS GOT TO STING.

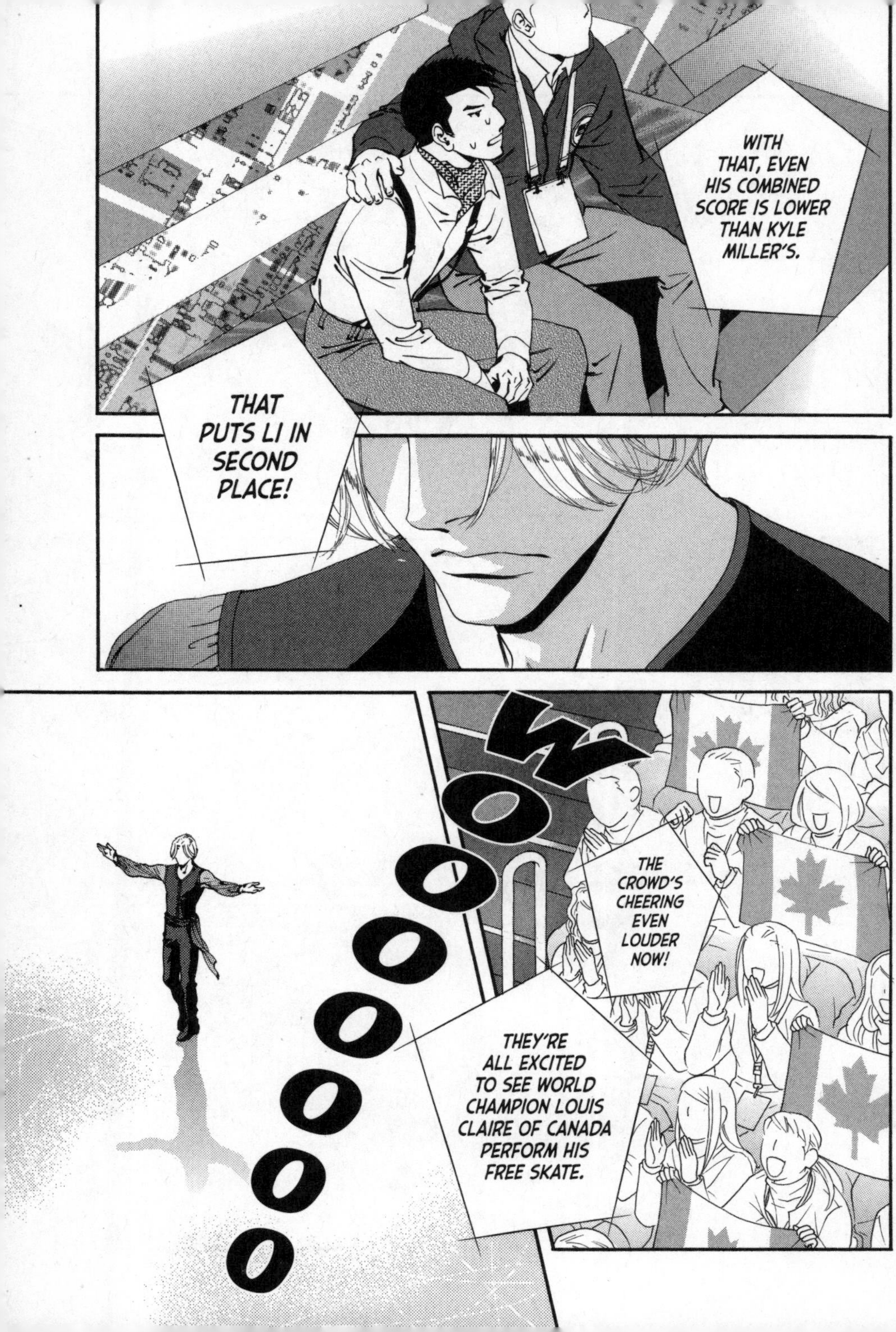
WITH THAT, EVEN HIS COMBINED SCORE IS LOWER THAN KYLE MILLER'S.
THAT PUTS LI IN SECOND PLACE!
WOOOOOOOO
THE CROWD'S CHEERING EVEN LOUDER NOW!
THEY'RE ALL EXCITED TO SEE WORLD CHAMPION LOUIS CLAIRE OF CANADA PERFORM HIS FREE SKATE.

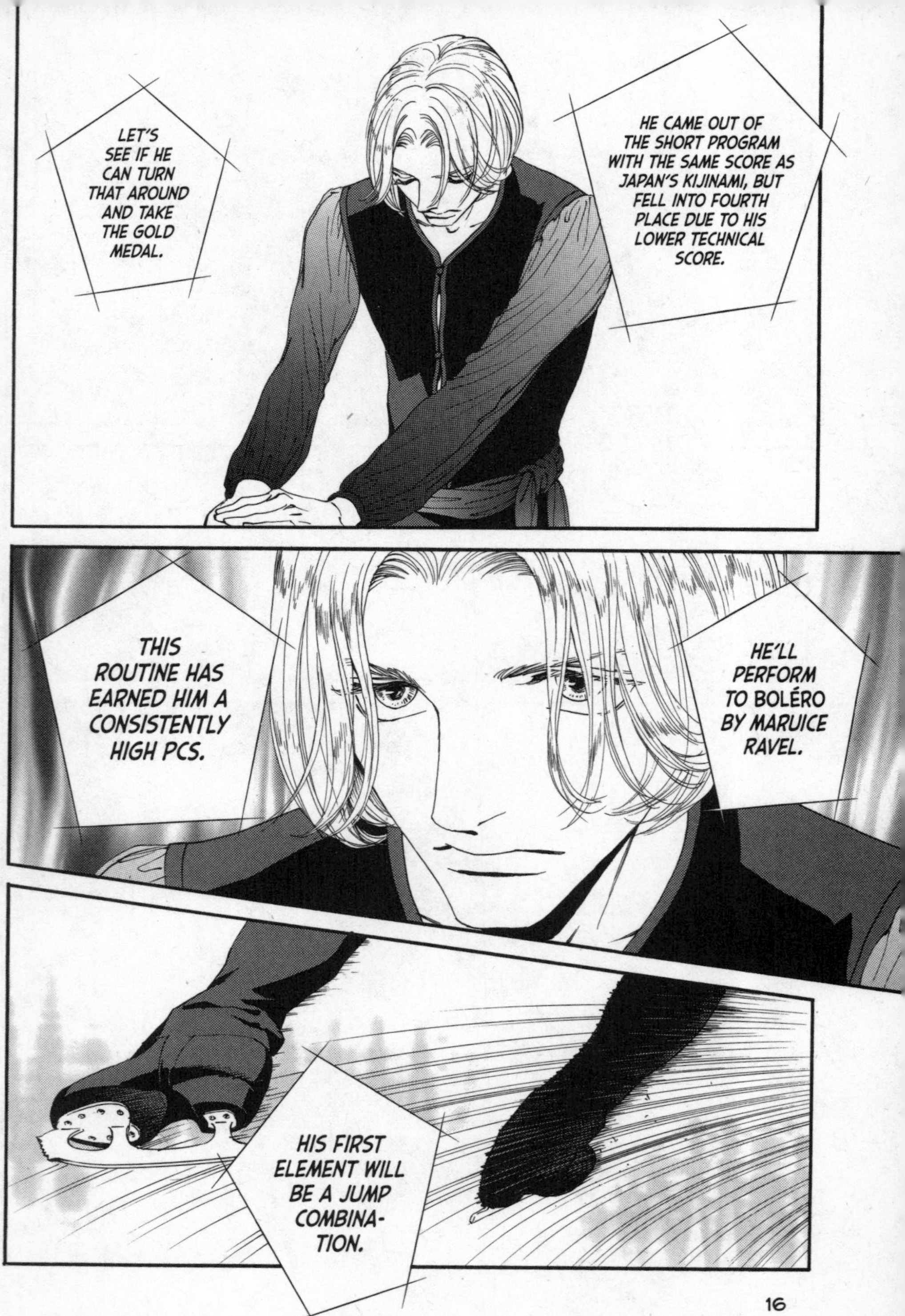
HE CAME OUT OF THE SHORT PROGRAM WITH THE SAME SCORE AS JAPAN'S KIJINAMI, BUT FELL INTO FOURTH PLACE DUE TO HIS LOWER TECHNICAL SCORE.
LET'S SEE IF HE CAN TURN THAT AROUND AND TAKE THE GOLD MEDAL.
HE'LL PERFORM TO BOLÉRO BY MARUICE RAVEL.
THIS ROUTINE HAS EARNED HIM A CONSISTENTLY HIGH PCS.
HIS FIRST ELEMENT WILL BE A JUMP COMBINA-TION.

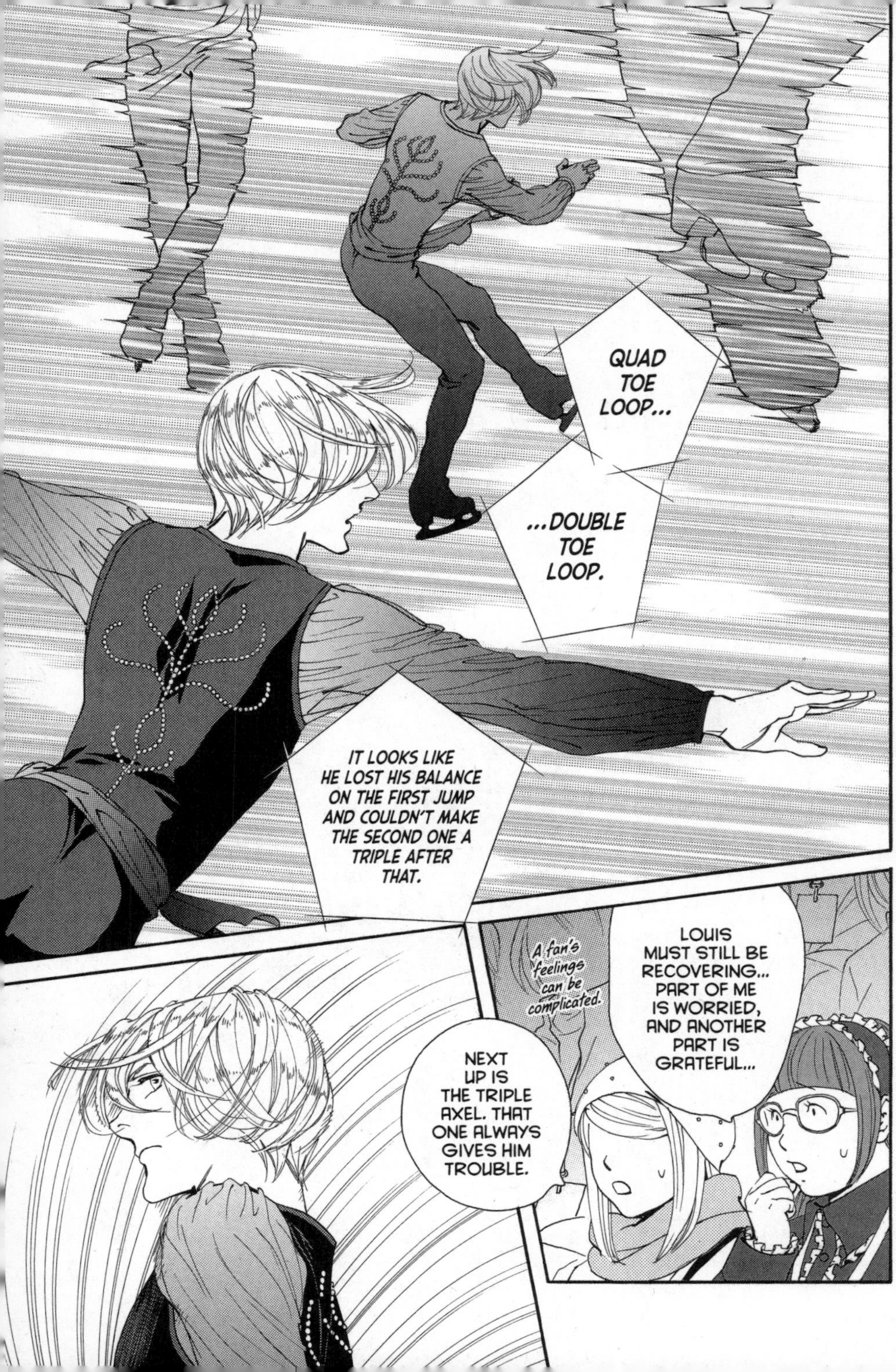
QUAD TOE LOOP...
...DOUBLE TOE LOOP.
IT LOOKS LIKE HE LOST HIS BALANCE ON THE FIRST JUMP AND COULDN'T MAKE THE SECOND ONE A TRIPLE AFTER THAT.
LOUIS MUST STILL BE RECOVERING... PART OF ME IS WORRIED, AND ANOTHER PART IS GRATEFUL...
A fan's feelings can be complicated.
NEXT UP IS THE TRIPLE AXEL. THAT ONE ALWAYS GIVES HIM TROUBLE.

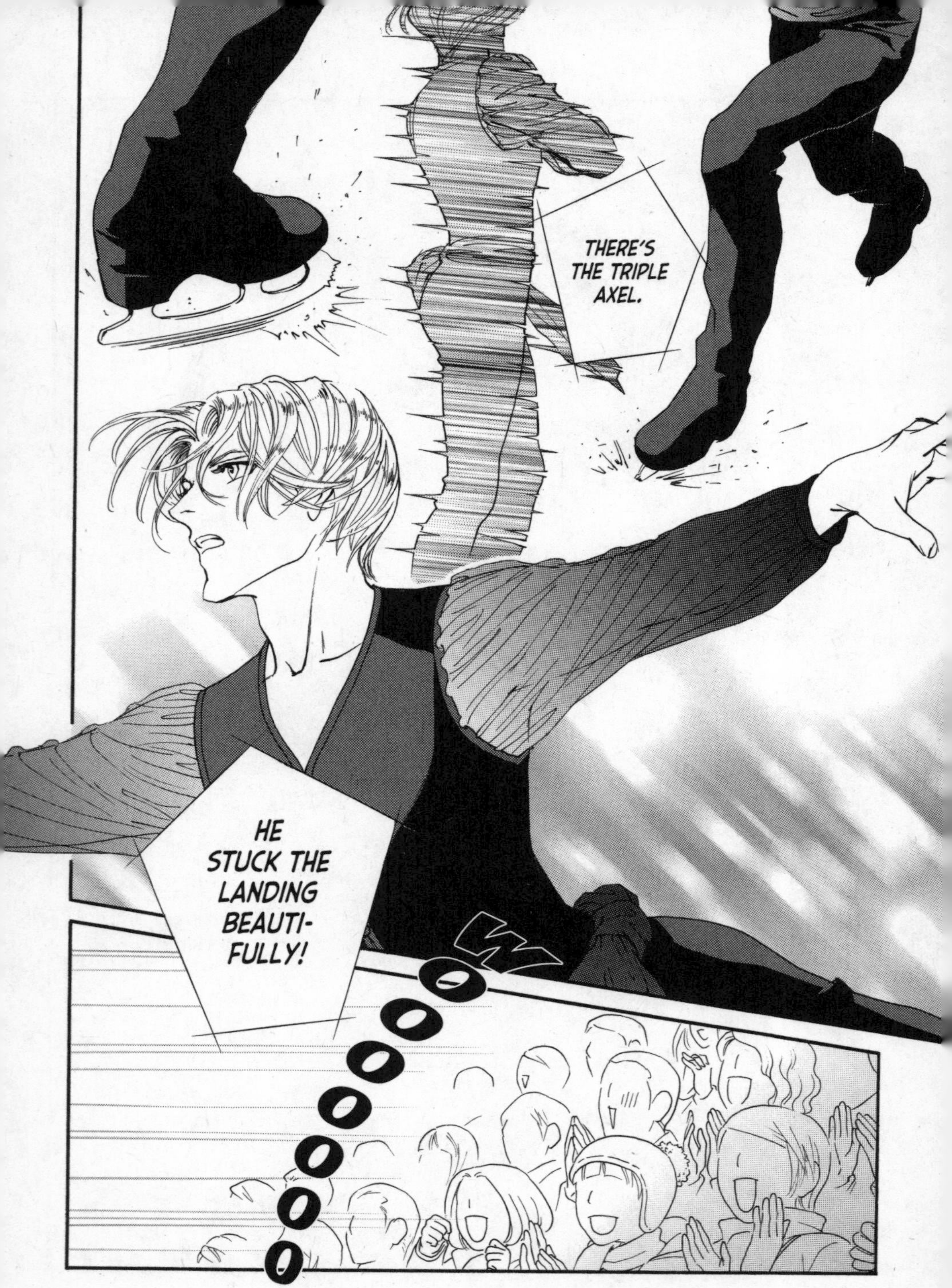
THERE'S THE TRIPLE AXEL.
HE STUCK THE LANDING BEAUTI-FULLY!
WOOOOOOOOOO

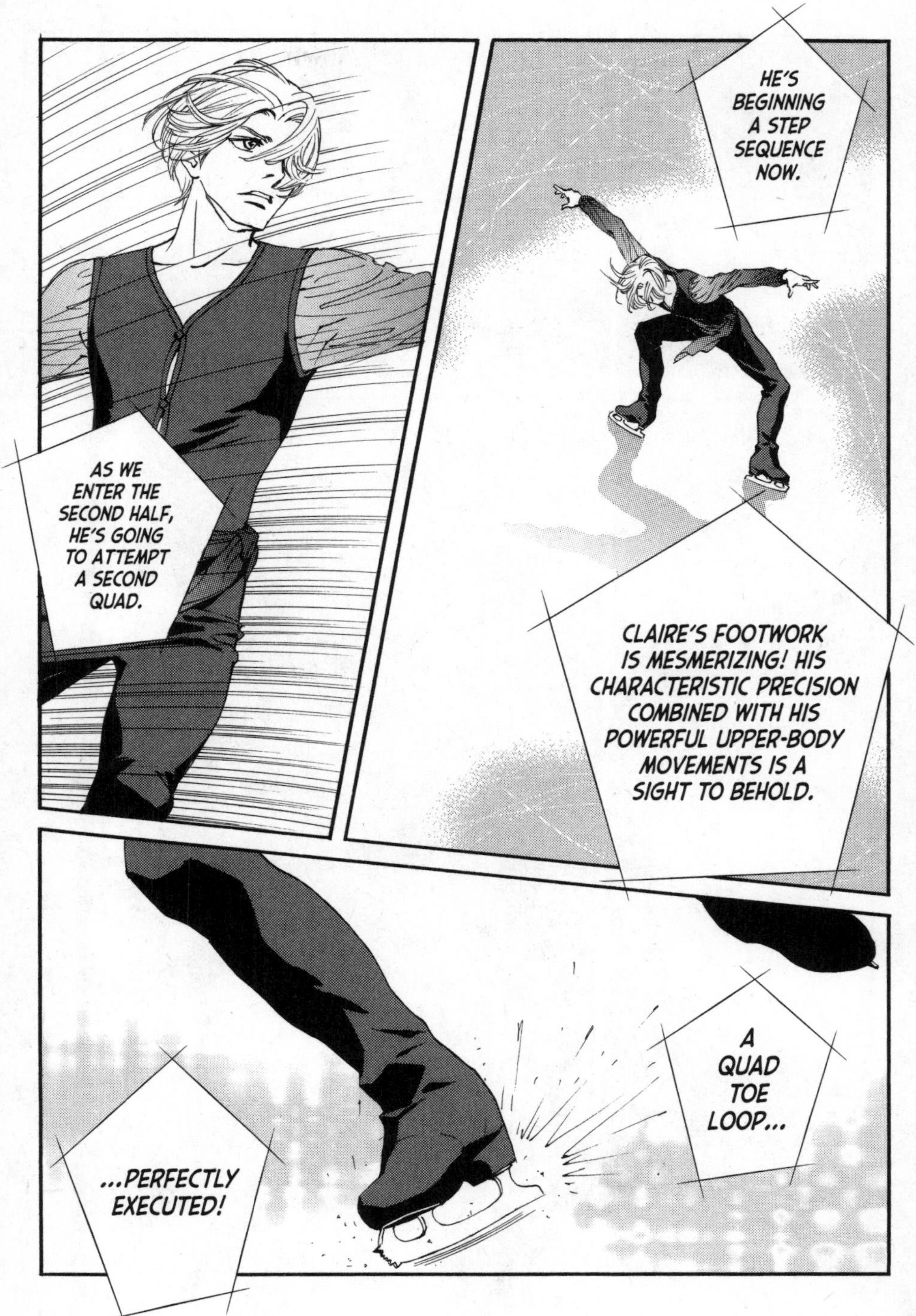
HE'S BEGINNING A STEP SEQUENCE NOW.
CLAIRE'S FOOTWORK IS MESMERIZING! HIS CHARACTERISTIC PRECISION COMBINED WITH HIS POWERFUL UPPER-BODY MOVEMENTS IS A SIGHT TO BEHOLD.
AS WE ENTER THE SECOND HALF, HE'S GOING TO ATTEMPT A SECOND QUAD.
A QUAD TOE LOOP...
...PERFECTLY EXECUTED!

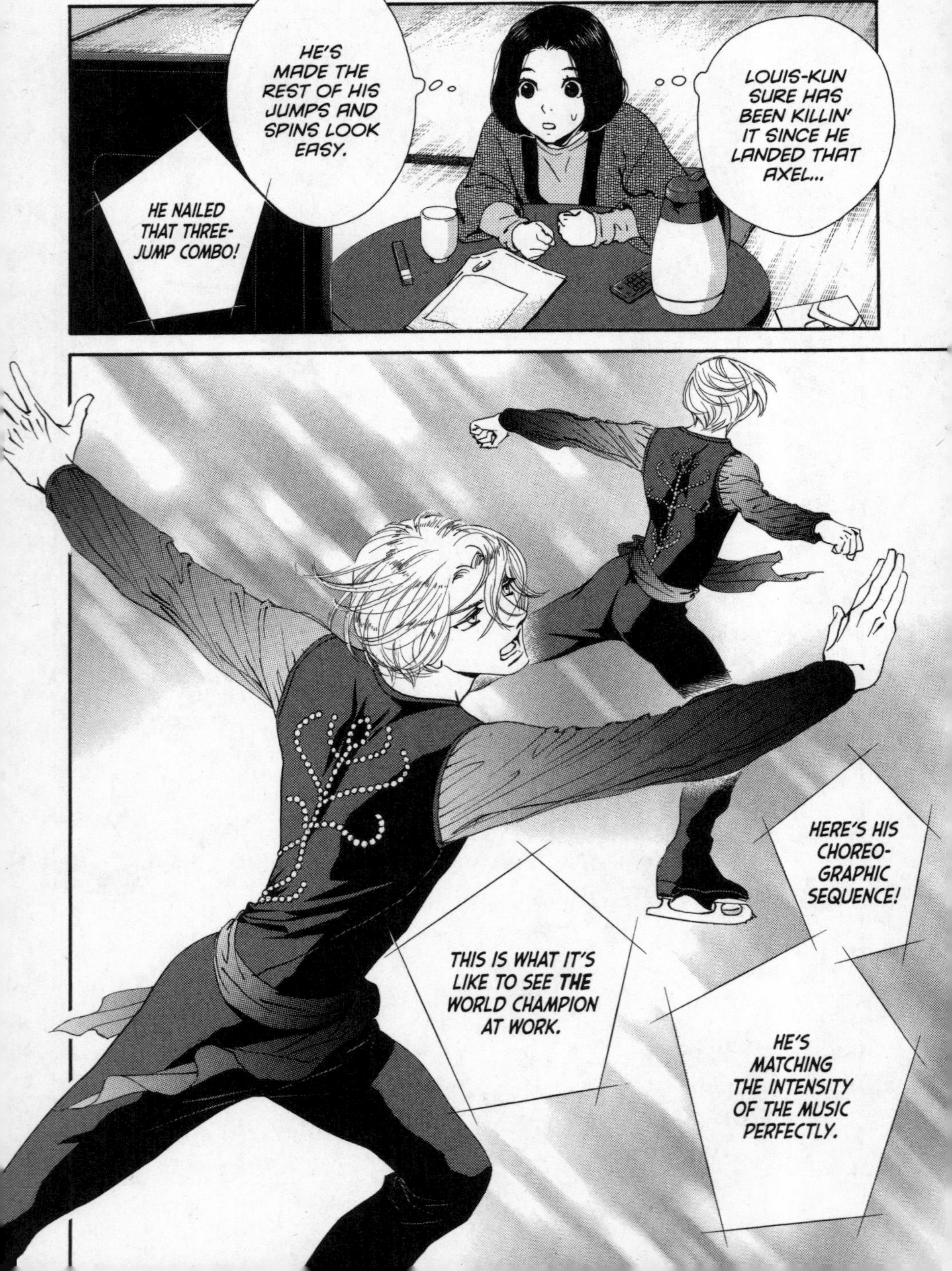
LOUIS-KUN SURE HAS BEEN KILLIN' IT SINCE HE LANDED THAT AXEL...
HE'S MADE THE REST OF HIS JUMPS AND SPINS LOOK EASY.
HE NAILED THAT THREE-JUMP COMBO!
HERE'S HIS CHOREO-GRAPHIC SEQUENCE!
THIS IS WHAT IT'S LIKE TO SEE THE WORLD CHAMPION AT WORK.
HE'S MATCHING THE INTENSITY OF THE MUSIC PERFECTLY.

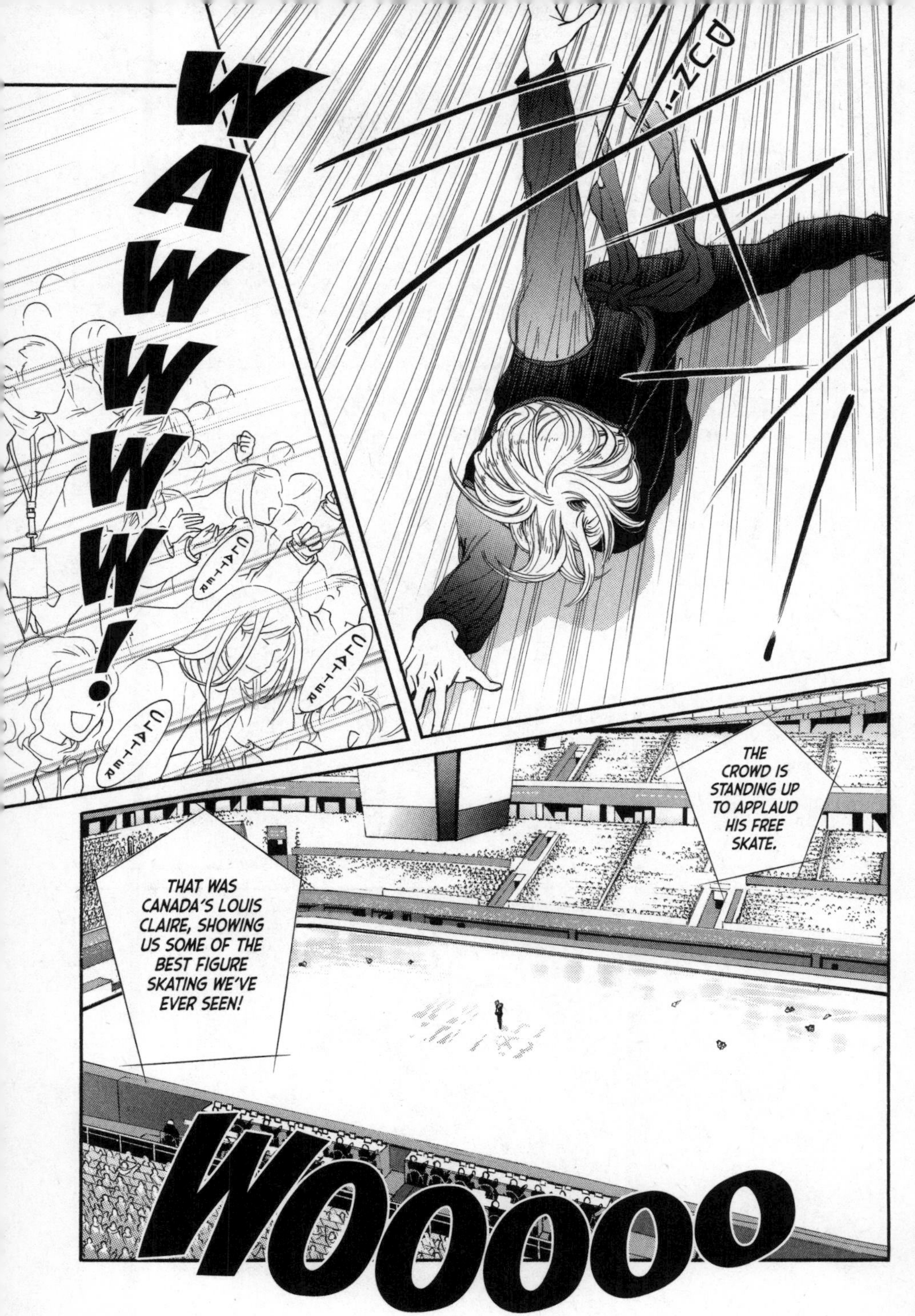
WAWWWW!
CLATTER
CLATTER
CLATTER
THE CROWD IS STANDING UP TO APPLAUD HIS FREE SKATE.
THAT WAS CANADA'S LOUIS CLAIRE, SHOWING US SOME OF THE BEST FIGURE SKATING WE'VE EVER SEEN!
WOOOOO

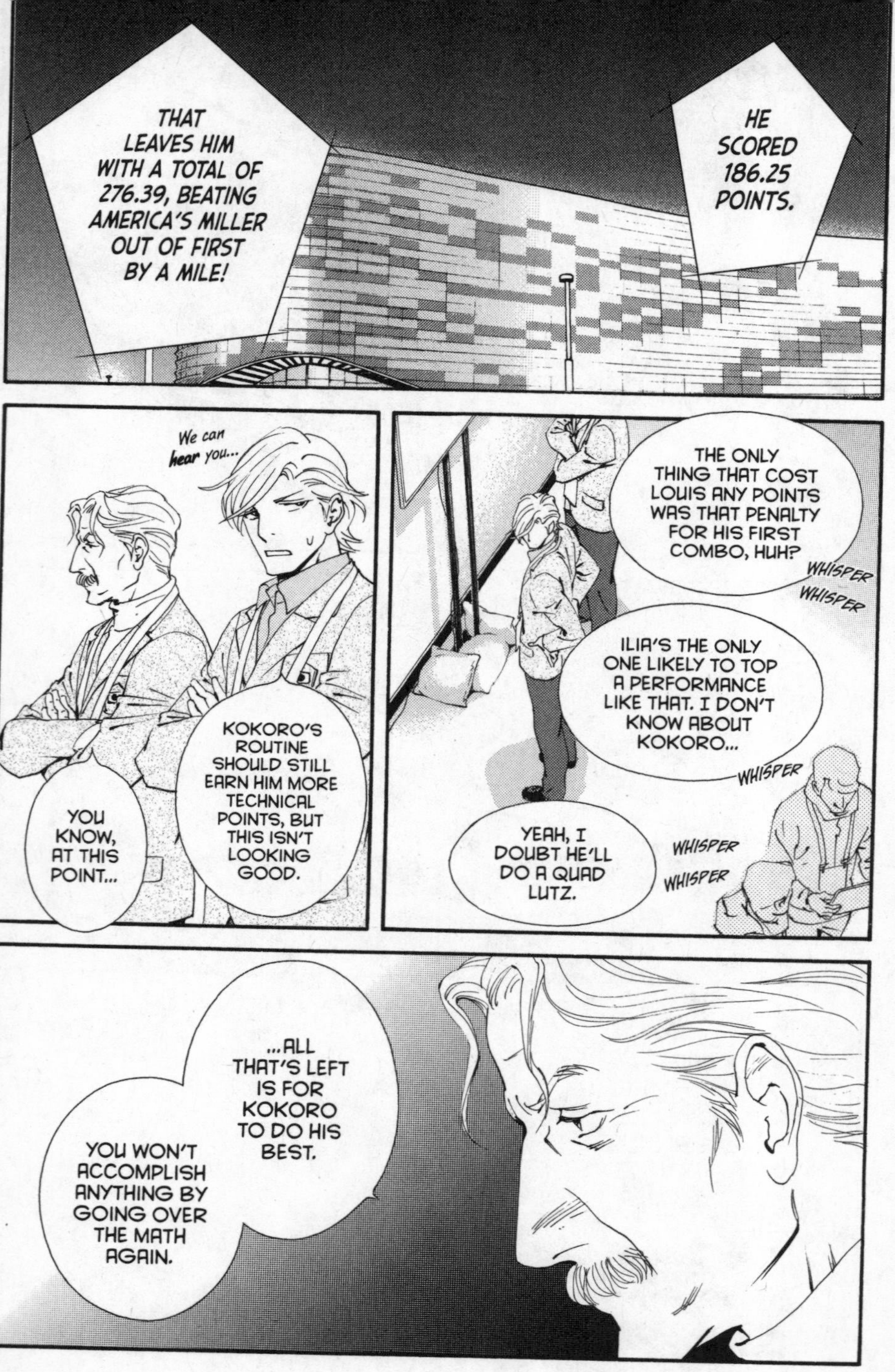
HE SCORED 186.25 POINTS.
THAT LEAVES HIM WITH A TOTAL OF 276.39, BEATING AMERICA'S MILLER OUT OF FIRST BY A MILE!
THE ONLY THING THAT COST LOUIS ANY POINTS WAS THAT PENALTY FOR HIS FIRST COMBO, HUH?
WHISPER
WHISPER
ILIA'S THE ONLY ONE LIKELY TO TOP A PERFORMANCE LIKE THAT. I DON'T KNOW ABOUT KOKORO...
WHISPER
YEAH, I DOUBT HE'LL DO A QUAD LUTZ.
WHISPER
WHISPER
We can *hear* you...
KOKORO'S ROUTINE SHOULD STILL EARN HIM MORE TECHNICAL POINTS, BUT THIS ISN'T LOOKING GOOD.
YOU KNOW, AT THIS POINT...
...ALL THAT'S LEFT IS FOR KOKORO TO DO HIS BEST.
YOU WON'T ACCOMPLISH ANYTHING BY GOING OVER THE MATH AGAIN.

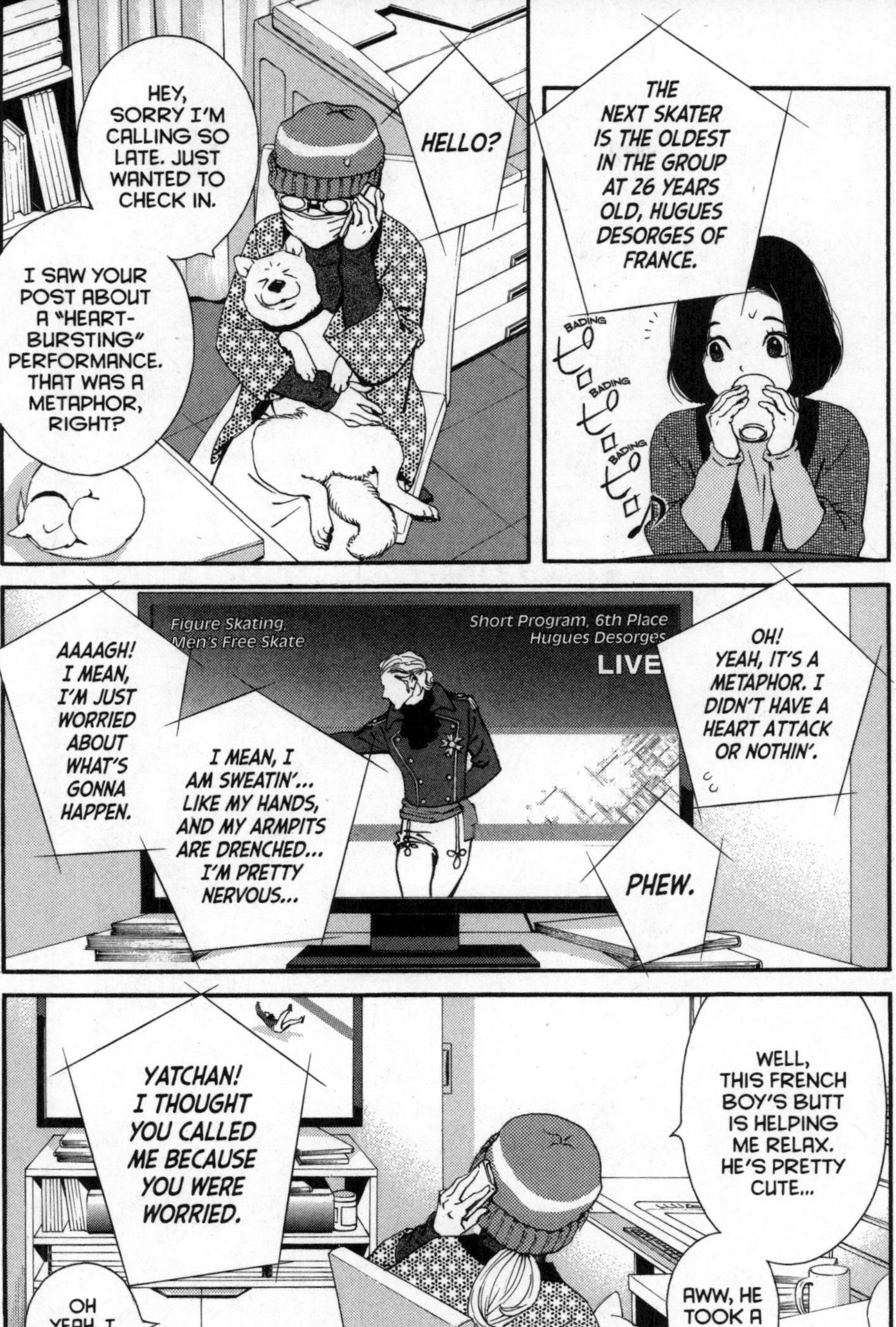
THE NEXT SKATER IS THE OLDEST IN THE GROUP AT 26 YEARS OLD, HUGUES DESORGES OF FRANCE.
BADING
BADING
BADING
HELLO?
HEY, SORRY I'M CALLING SO LATE. JUST WANTED TO CHECK IN.
I SAW YOUR POST ABOUT A "HEART-BURSTING" PERFORMANCE. THAT WAS A METAPHOR, RIGHT?
Short Program, 6th Place
Hugues Desorges
LIVE
Figure Skating,
Men's Free Skate
OH! YEAH, IT'S A METAPHOR. I DIDN'T HAVE A HEART ATTACK OR NOTHIN'.
PHEW.
AAAAGH! I MEAN, I'M JUST WORRIED ABOUT WHAT'S GONNA HAPPEN.
I MEAN, I AM SWEATIN'... LIKE MY HANDS, AND MY ARMPITS ARE DRENCHED... I'M PRETTY NERVOUS...
WELL, THIS FRENCH BOY'S BUTT IS HELPING ME RELAX. HE'S PRETTY CUTE...
AWW, HE TOOK A FALL.
YATCHAN! I THOUGHT YOU CALLED ME BECAUSE YOU WERE WORRIED.
OH YEAH, I GUESS I WAS.

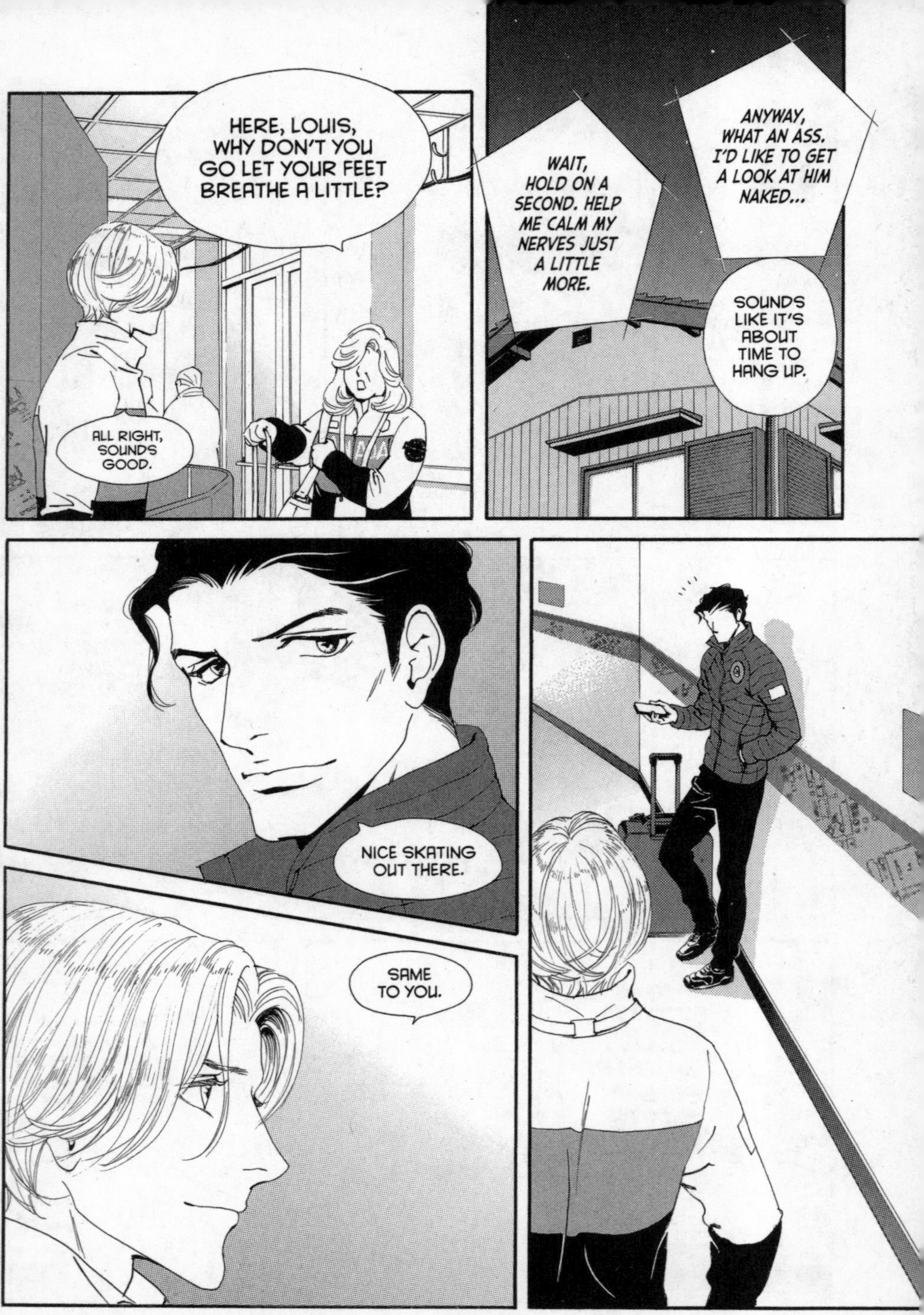
ANYWAY, WHAT AN ASS. I'D LIKE TO GET A LOOK AT HIM NAKED...
WAIT, HOLD ON A SECOND. HELP ME CALM MY NERVES JUST A LITTLE MORE.
SOUNDS LIKE IT'S ABOUT TIME TO HANG UP.
HERE, LOUIS, WHY DON'T YOU GO LET YOUR FEET BREATHE A LITTLE?
ALL RIGHT, SOUNDS GOOD.
NICE SKATING OUT THERE.
SAME TO YOU.

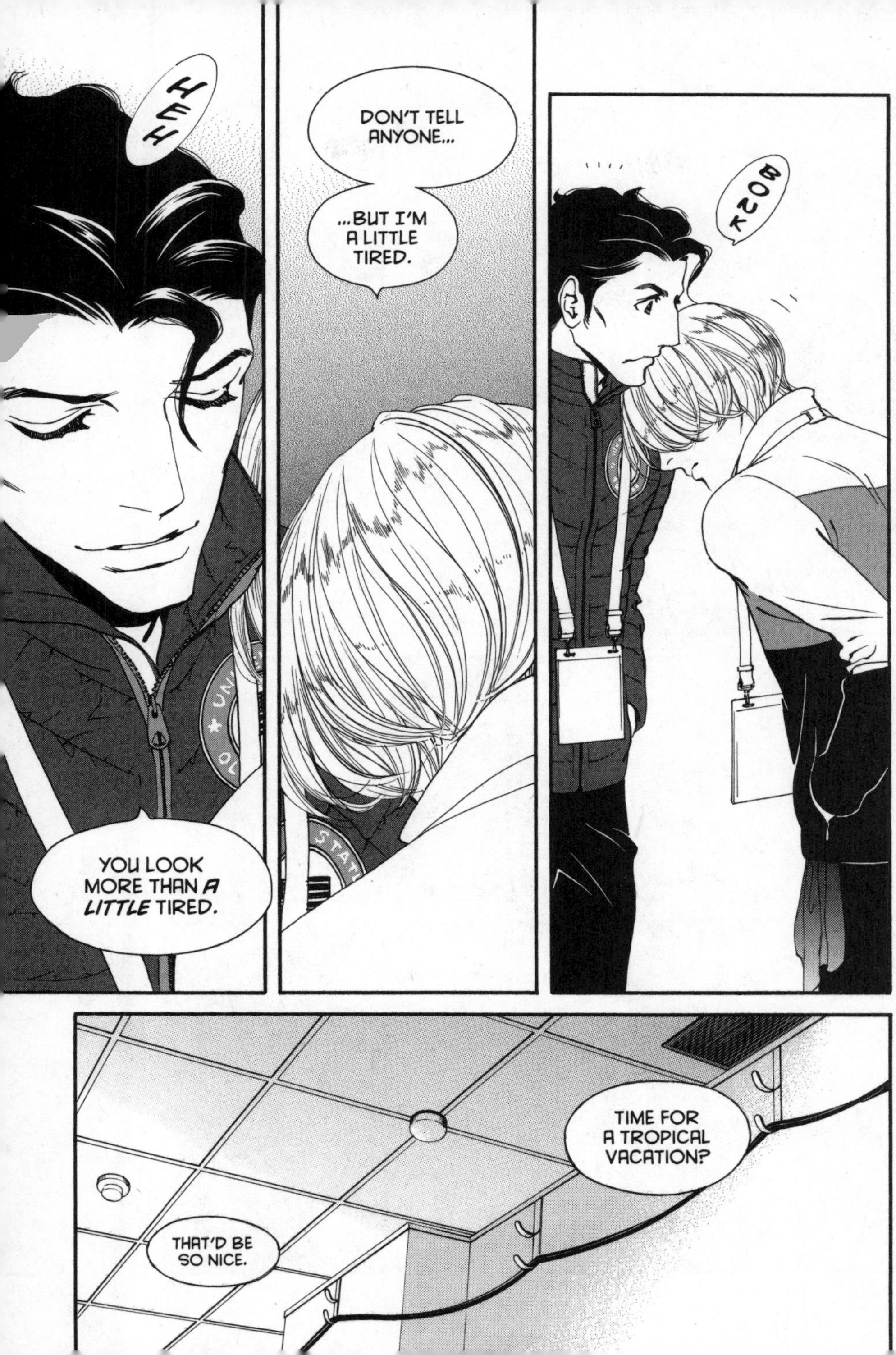
BONK
DON'T TELL ANYONE...
...BUT I'M A LITTLE TIRED.
HEH
YOU LOOK MORE THAN *A LITTLE* TIRED.
TIME FOR A TROPICAL VACATION?
THAT'D BE SO NICE.

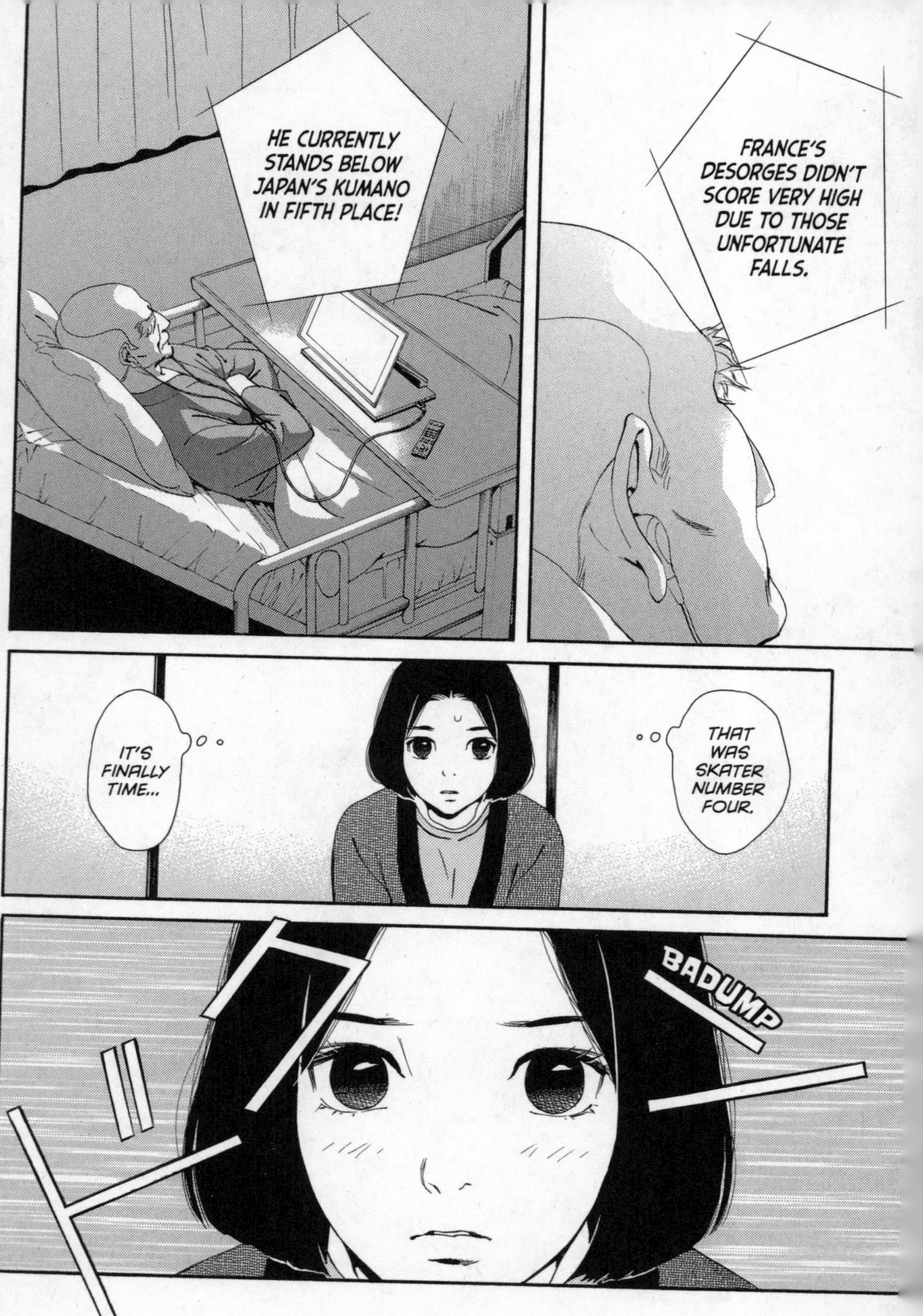
FRANCE'S DESORGES DIDN'T SCORE VERY HIGH DUE TO THOSE UNFORTUNATE FALLS.
HE CURRENTLY STANDS BELOW JAPAN'S KUMANO IN FIFTH PLACE!
THAT WAS SKATER NUMBER FOUR.
IT'S FINALLY TIME...
BADUMP

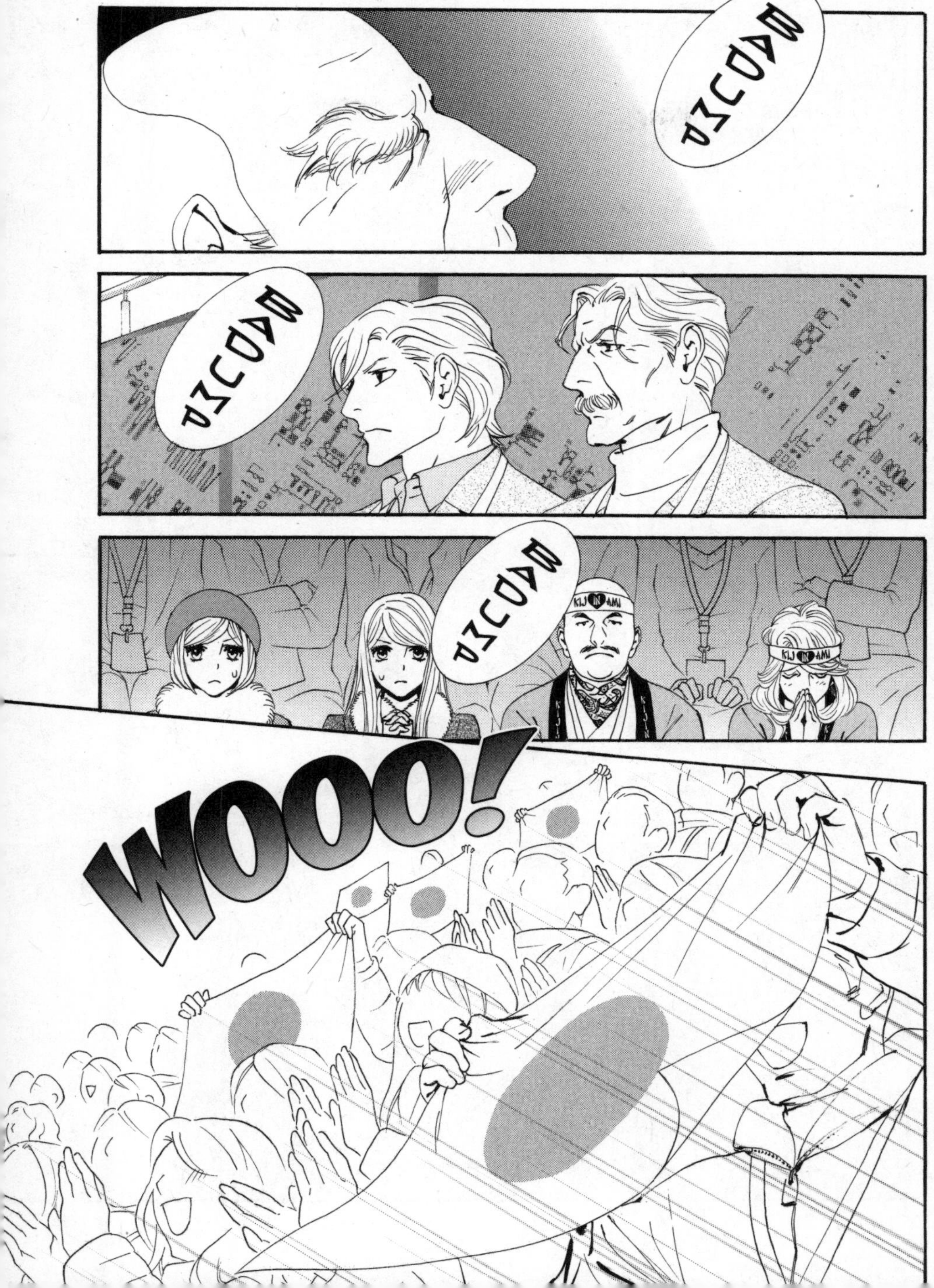
BADUMP
BADUMP
BADUMP
WOOO!

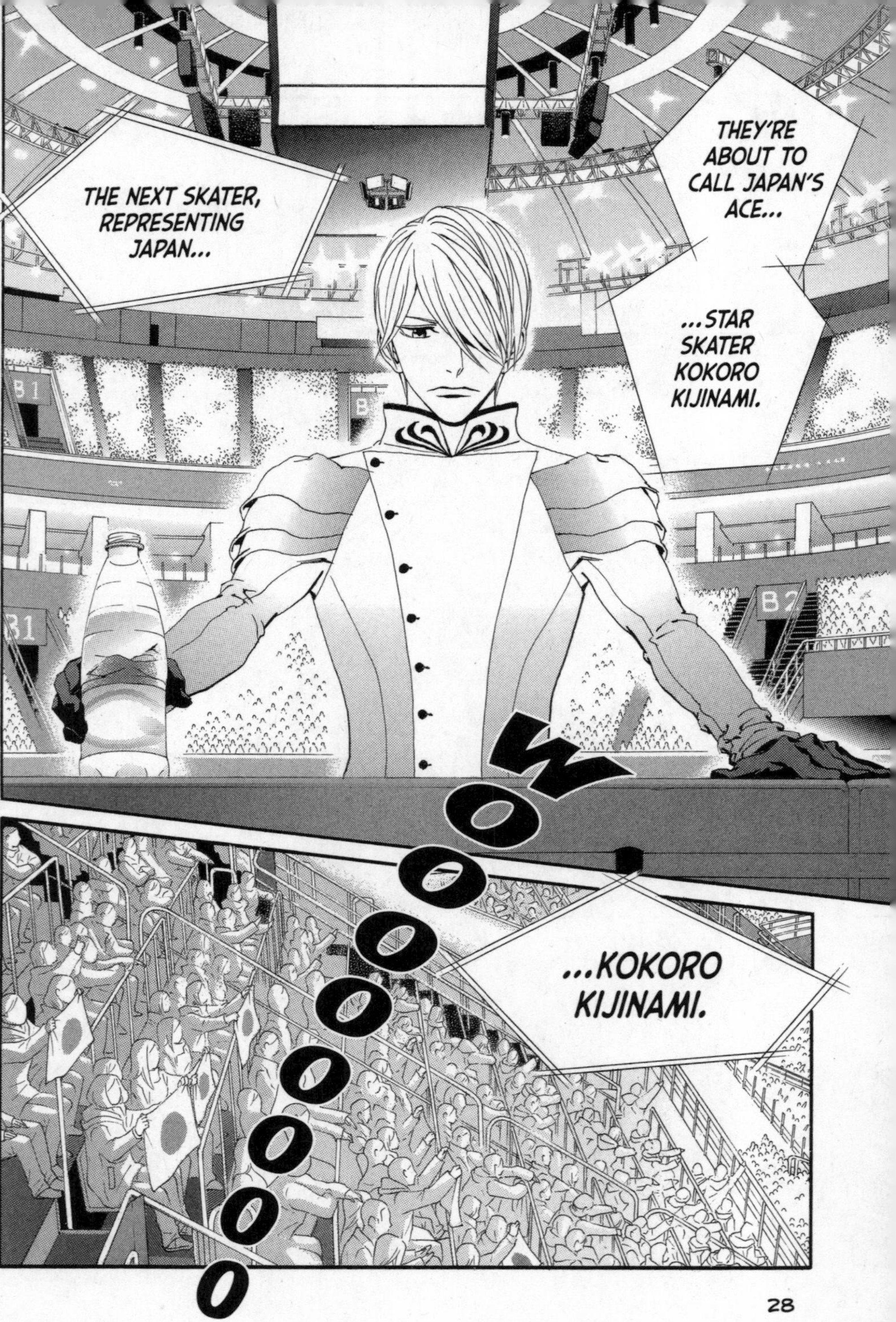
THEY'RE ABOUT TO CALL JAPAN'S ACE...
...STAR SKATER KOKORO KIJINAMI.
THE NEXT SKATER, REPRESENTING JAPAN...
WOOOOOOOO
...KOKORO KIJINAMI.

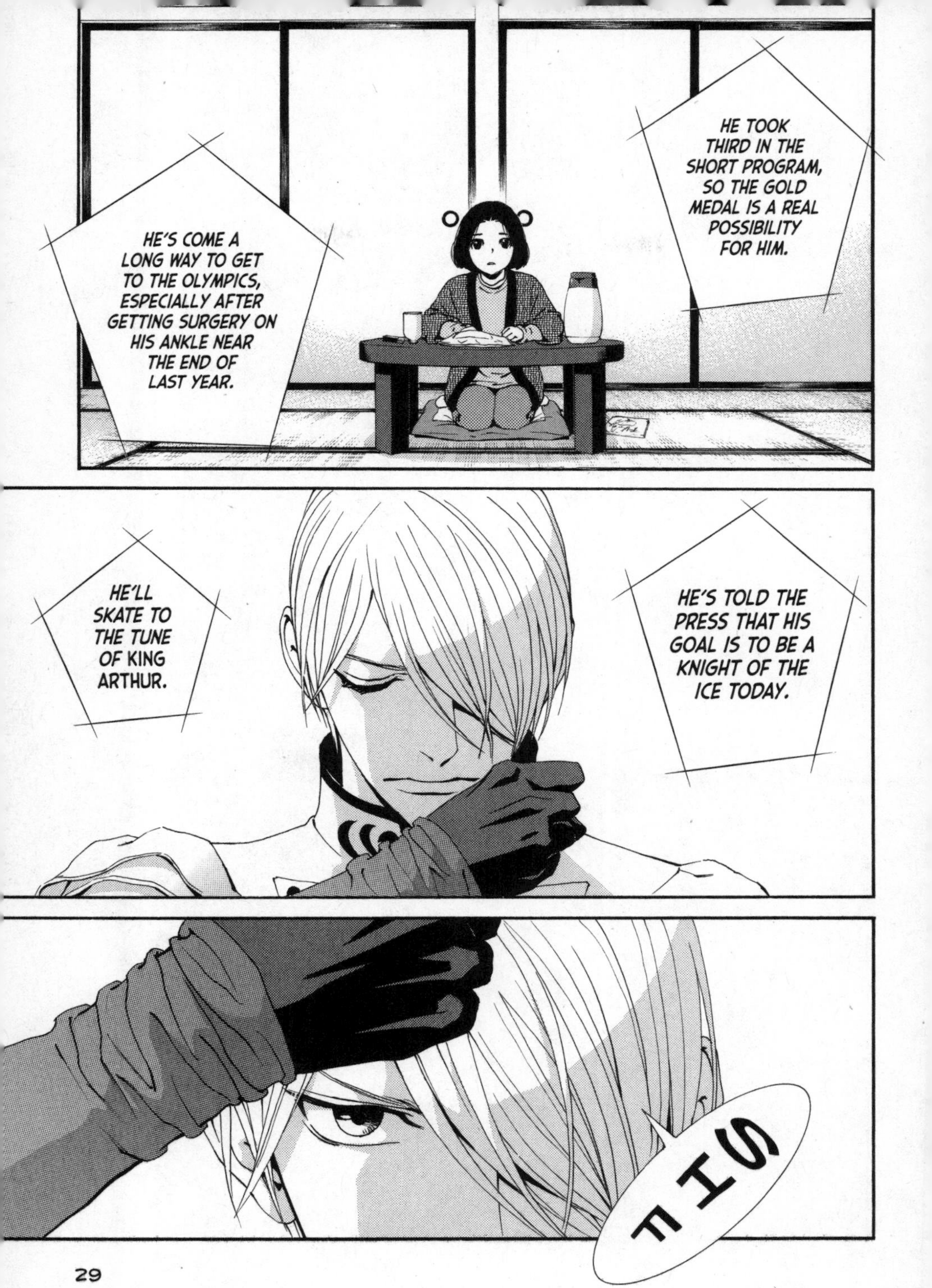
HE TOOK THIRD IN THE SHORT PROGRAM, SO THE GOLD MEDAL IS A REAL POSSIBILITY FOR HIM.
HE'S COME A LONG WAY TO GET TO THE OLYMPICS, ESPECIALLY AFTER GETTING SURGERY ON HIS ANKLE NEAR THE END OF LAST YEAR.
HE'S TOLD THE PRESS THAT HIS GOAL IS TO BE A KNIGHT OF THE ICE TODAY.
HE'LL SKATE TO THE TUNE OF KING ARTHUR.
SIF

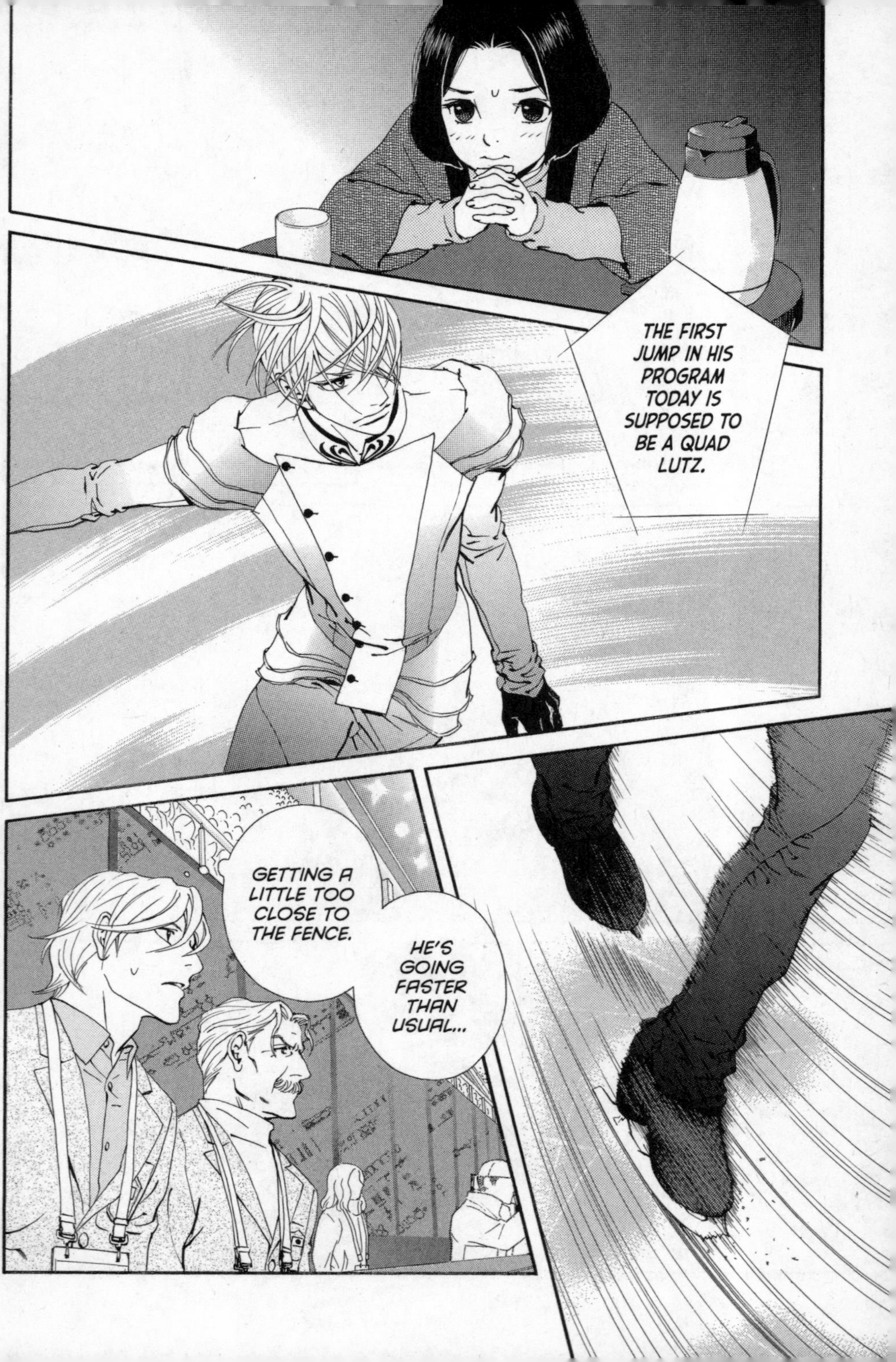
THE FIRST JUMP IN HIS PROGRAM TODAY IS SUPPOSED TO BE A QUAD LUTZ.
GETTING A LITTLE TOO CLOSE TO THE FENCE.
HE'S GOING FASTER THAN USUAL...

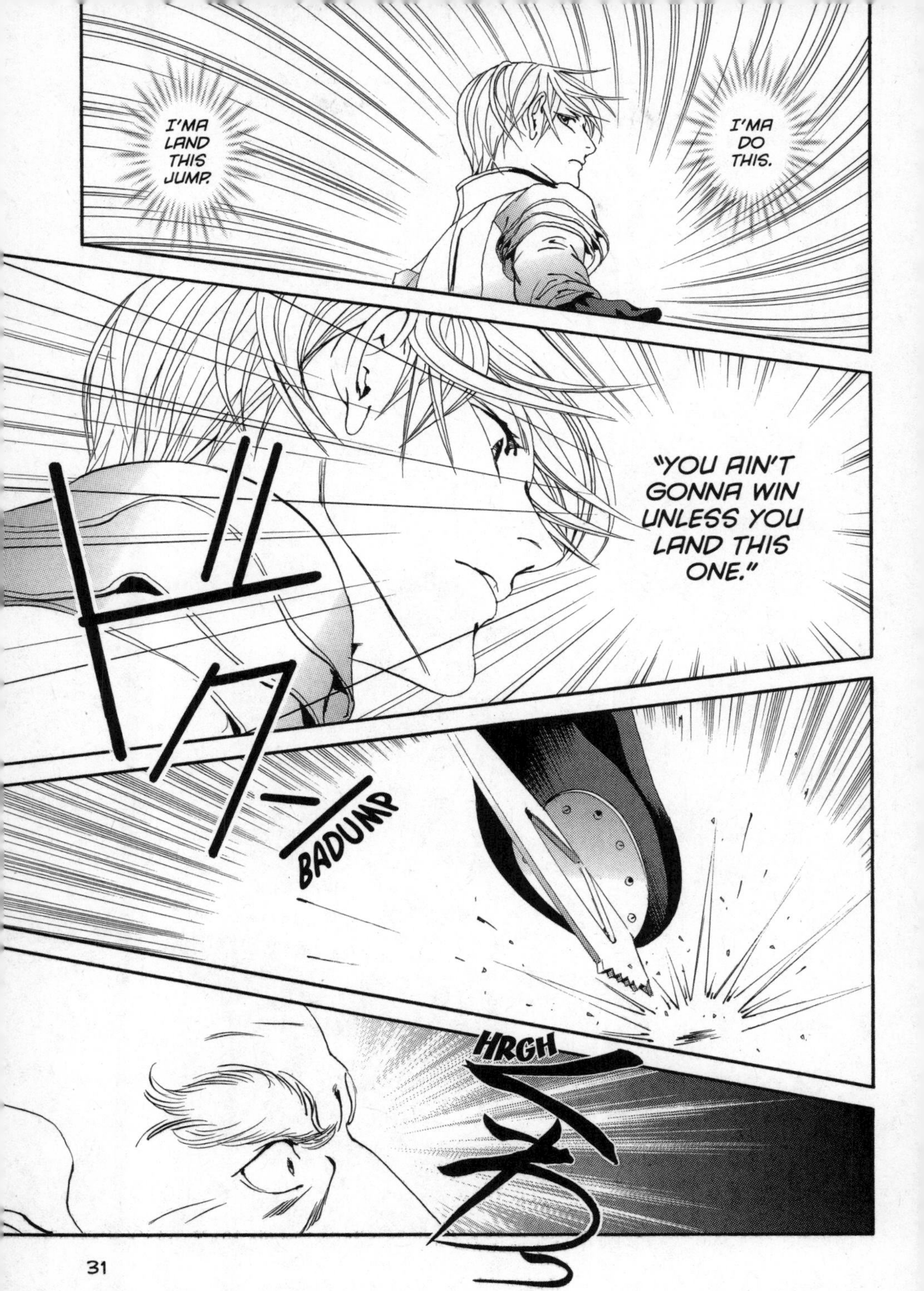
I'MA DO THIS.
I'MA LAND THIS JUMP.
"YOU AIN'T GONNA WIN UNLESS YOU LAND THIS ONE."
BADUMP
HRGH

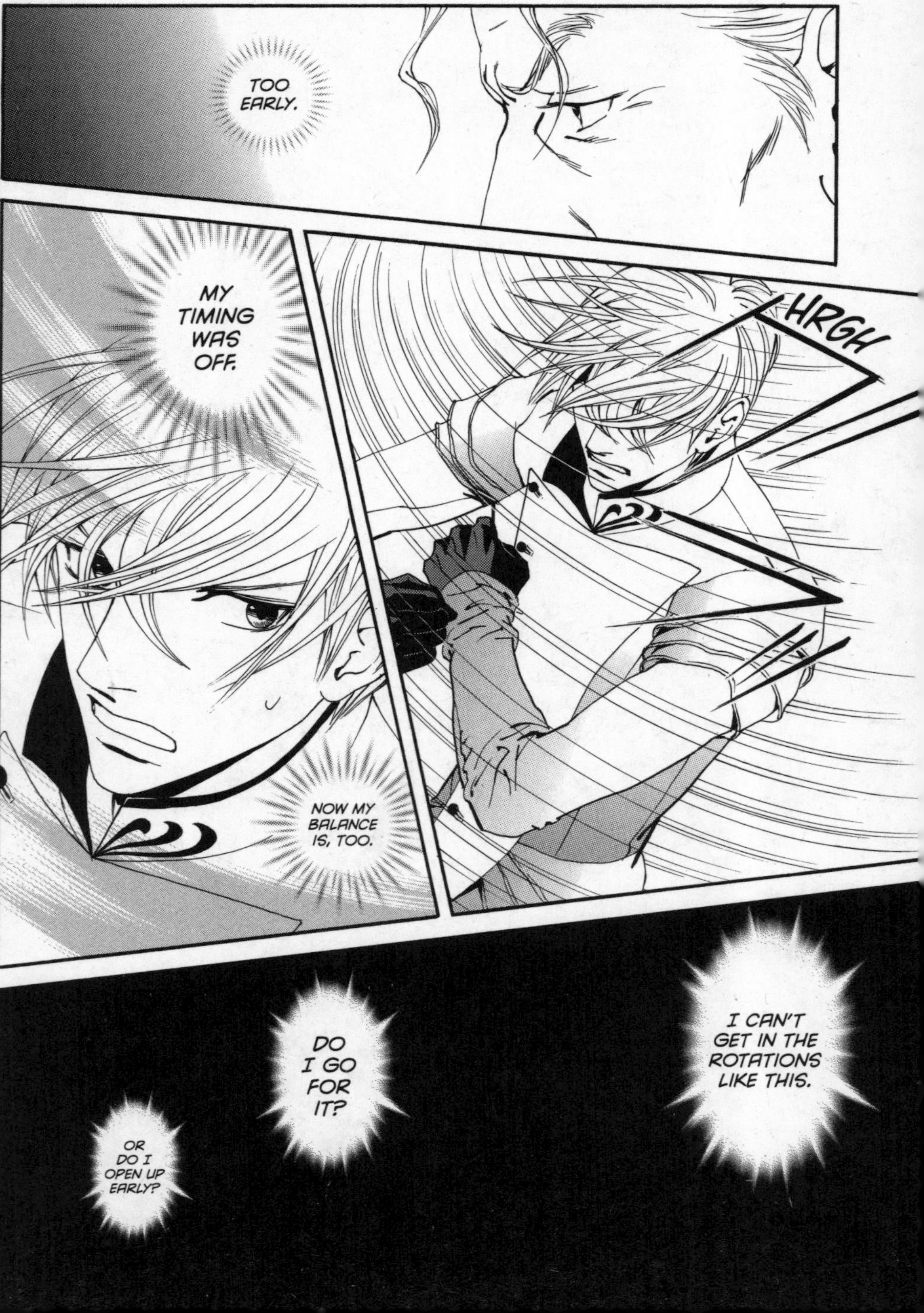
TOO EARLY.
HRGH
MY TIMING WAS OFF.
NOW MY BALANCE IS, TOO.
I CAN'T GET IN THE ROTATIONS LIKE THIS.
DO I GO FOR IT?
OR DO I OPEN UP EARLY?

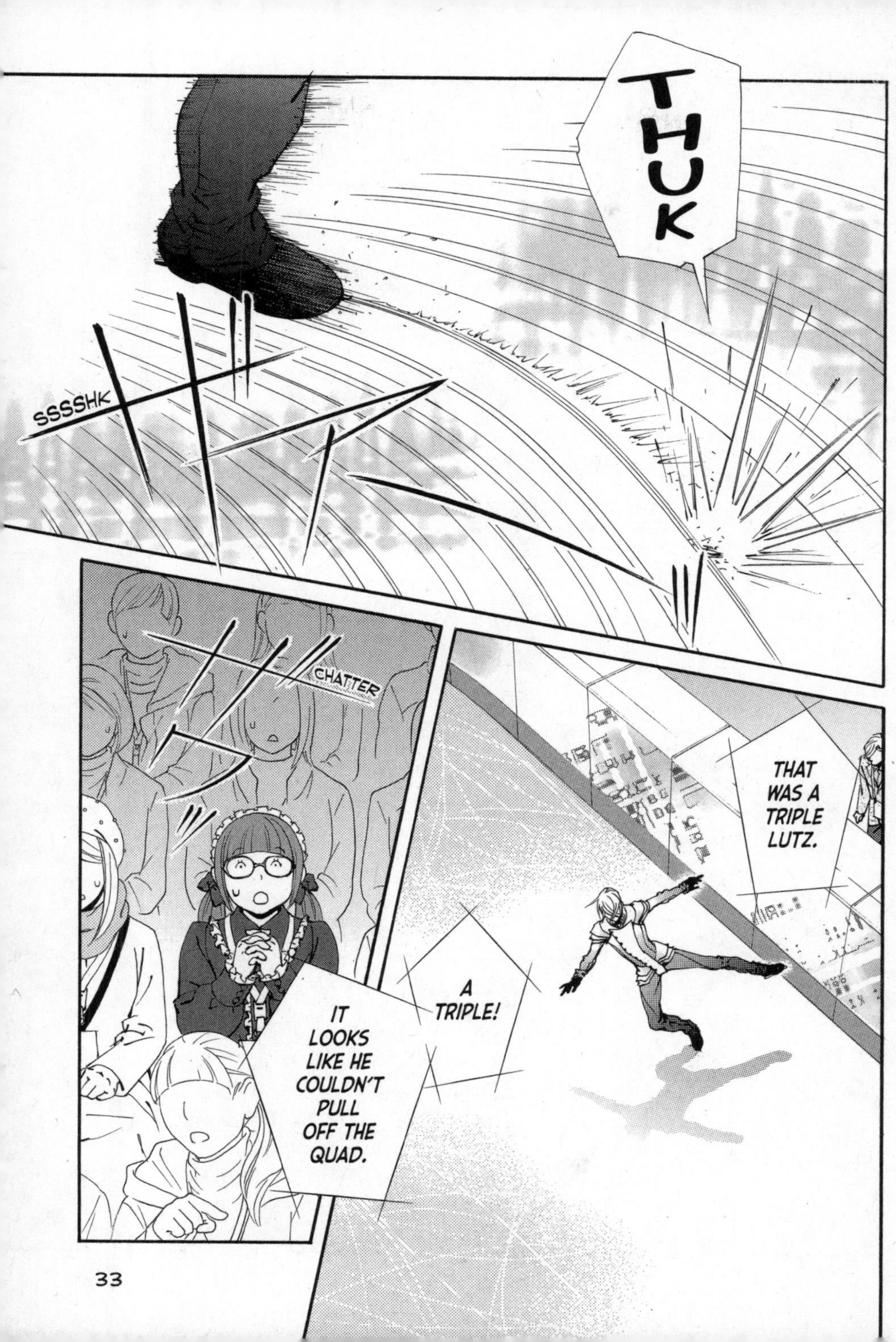
THUK
SSSSHK
THAT WAS A TRIPLE LUTZ.
A TRIPLE!
IT LOOKS LIKE HE COULDN'T PULL OFF THE QUAD.
CHATTER

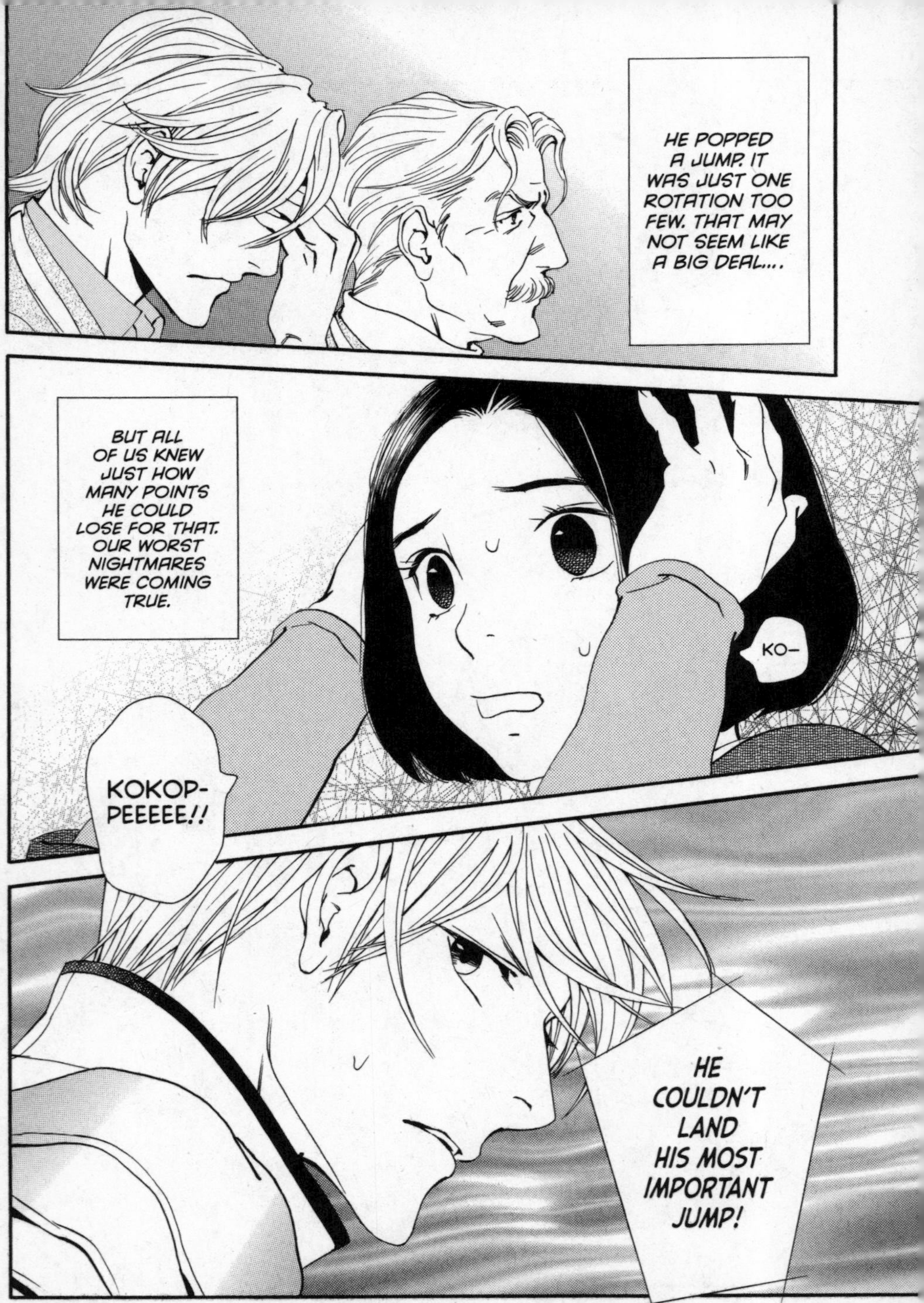
HE POPPED A JUMP. IT WAS JUST ONE ROTATION TOO FEW. THAT MAY NOT SEEM LIKE A BIG DEAL....
BUT ALL OF US KNEW JUST HOW MANY POINTS HE COULD LOSE FOR THAT. OUR WORST NIGHTMARES WERE COMING TRUE.
KO-
KOKOP-PEEEEE!!
HE COULDN'T LAND HIS MOST IMPORTANT JUMP!

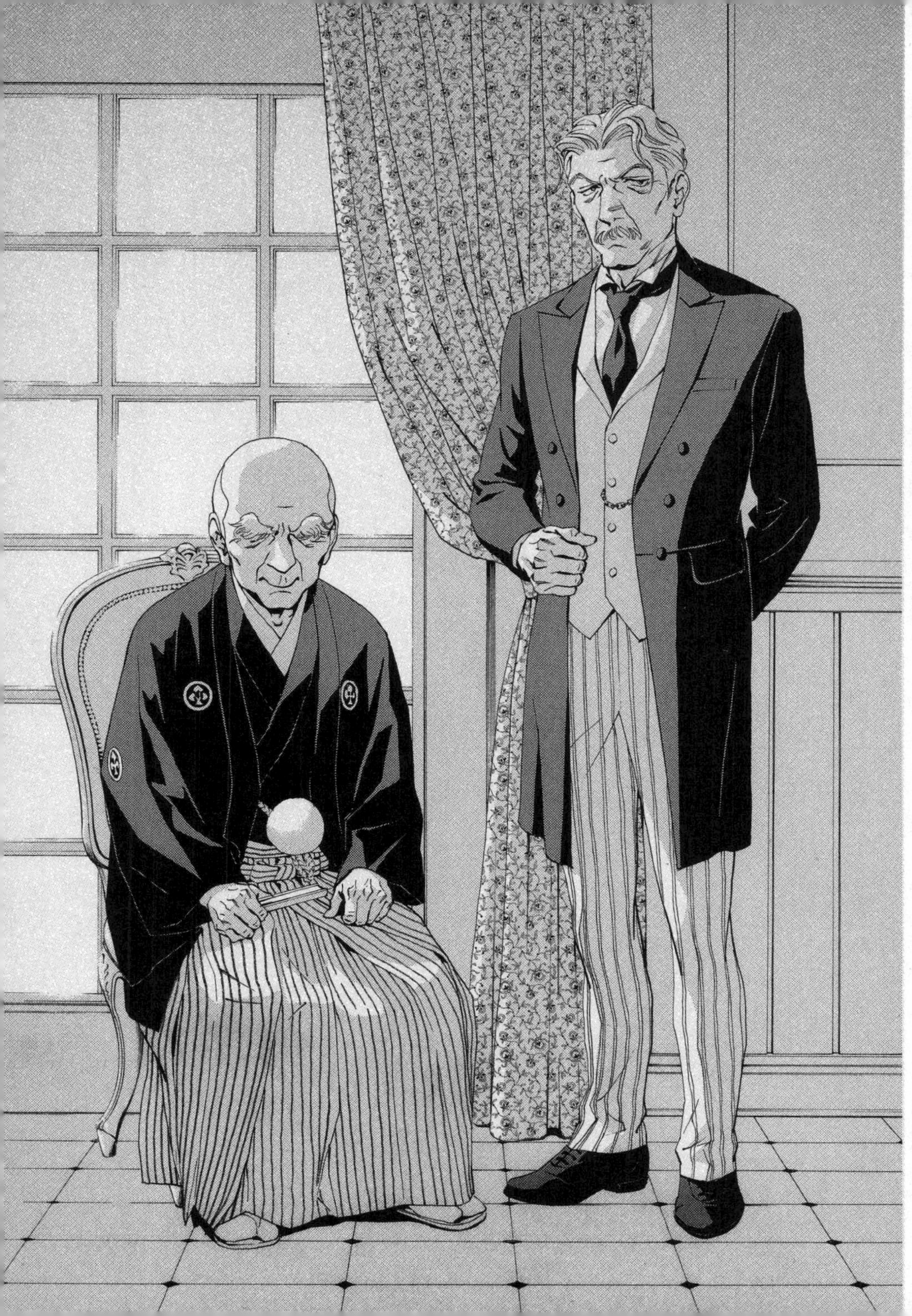

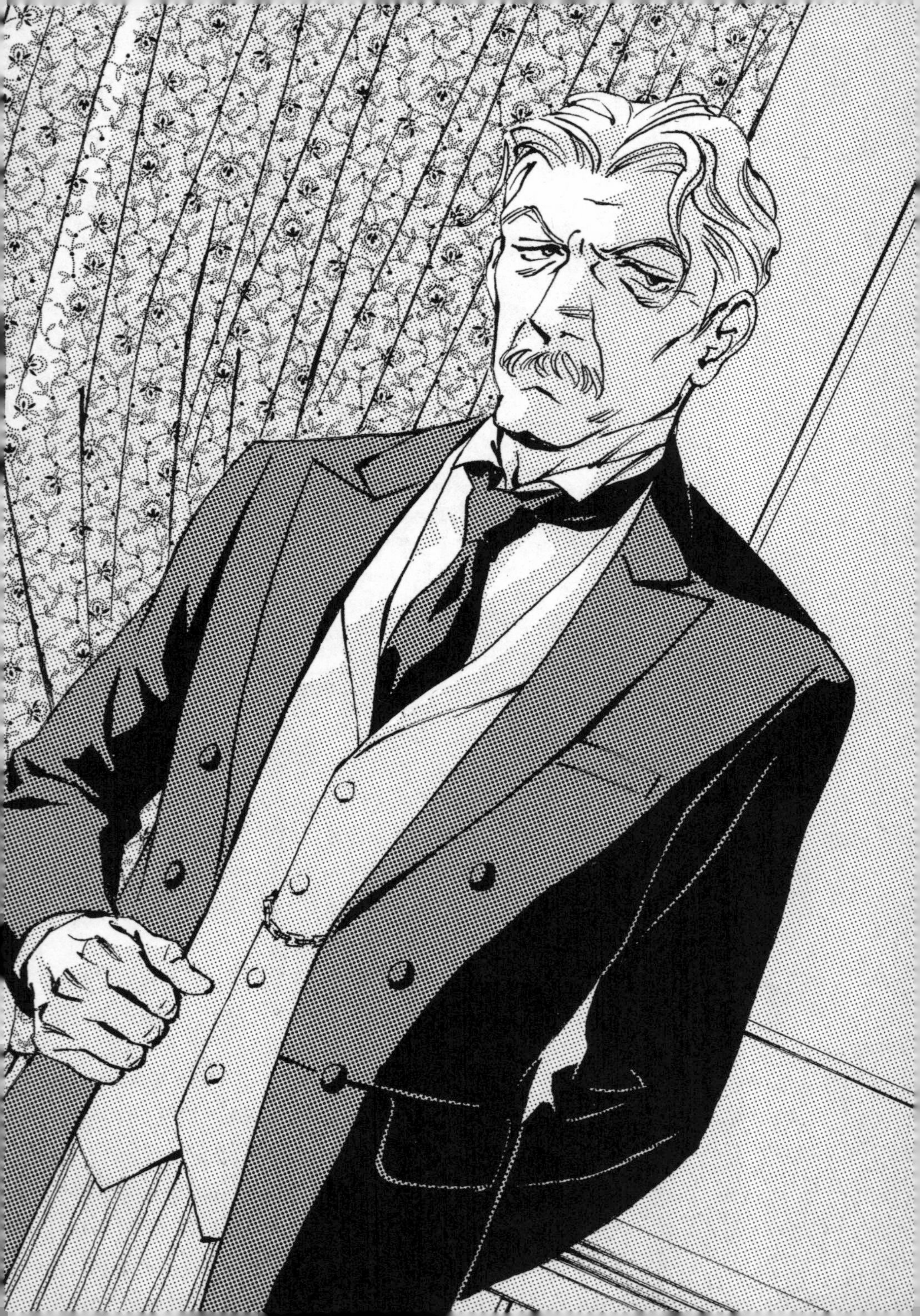

Spell 53
The Foe Unseen

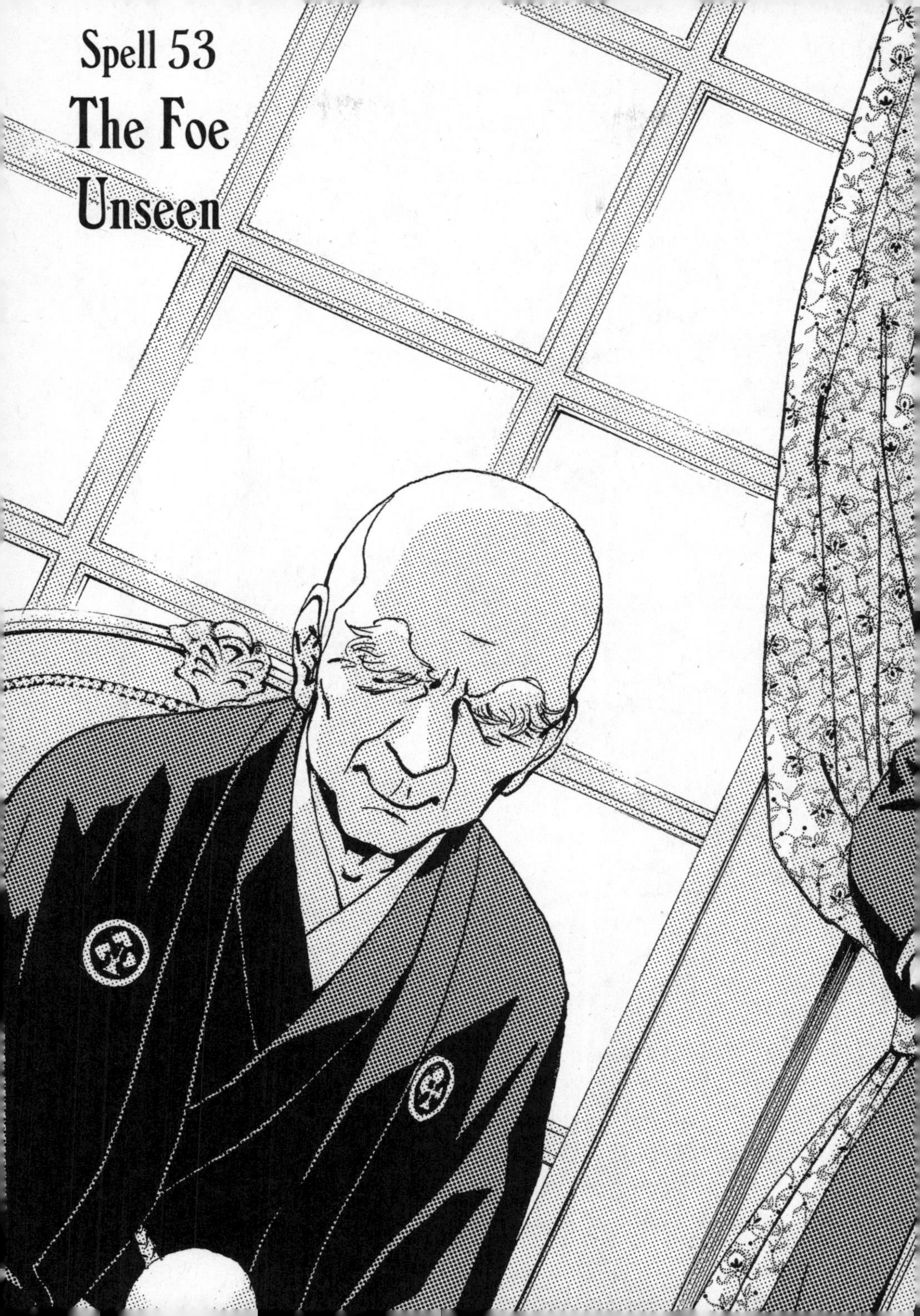

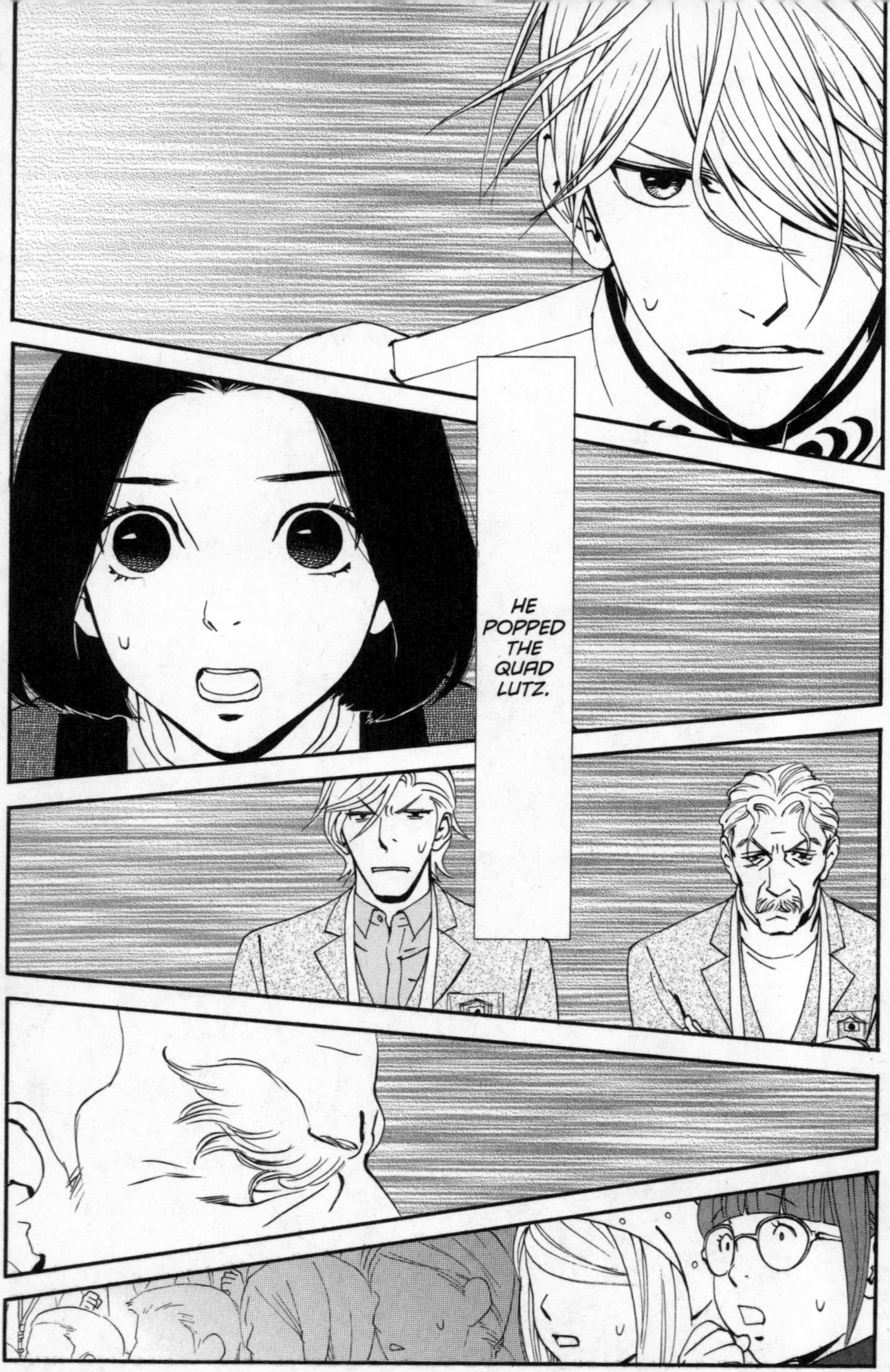
HE POPPED THE QUAD LUTZ.

PWOP
HEY, SORRY TO INTERRUPT! SO KOKOPPE DID A TRIPLE LUTZ INSTEAD OF A QUAD, RIGHT?
I THOUGHT I'D EXPLAIN JUST HOW BADLY HE SCREWED UP!
OKAY! HERE YOU'LL FIND KOKOPPE'S INTENDED FREE SKATE PROGRAM, PEGA.
PWOP
4LZ (LUTZ)
4T (TOE LOOP)
3A (AXEL)
⬇THE REST ARE WORTH 10% MORE POINTS
3A + 2T
3F (FLIP) + 3T
3LZ + 1LO (LOOP) + 3S (SALCHOW)
3LO
3LZ
WHAT'S THE BIG DEAL ABOUT THIS JUMP, YOU MAY ASK.
WELL, A QUAD LUTZ WILL NET YOU A BASE SCORE OF 13.60 POINTS, BUT A TRIPLE IS ONLY WORTH 6.0, SO HE ALREADY LOST 7.60 POINTS RIGHT THERE!
OH NO! THAT'S A LOT IN A SPORT WHERE COMPETITIONS ARE OFTEN DECIDED BY A FRACTION OF A POINT, PEGA!
REPLAY
NOT TO MENTION HIS GRADE OF EXECUTION IS GONNA TAKE A HIT FOR THAT LANDING.
BWAAA! THAT'S SO HARSH.
THERE'S MORE!
IN THE FREE SKATE, YOU'RE ONLY ALLOWED TO DO THE SAME TRIPLE OR QUAD JUMP TWICE.
KOKOPPE'S PROGRAM HAS HIM DOING TWO TRIPLE LUTZES AND TWO TRIPLE AXELS.
BUT NOW...
FLAP
FLAP
FLAP
FLAP
NOOO! HE DID AN EXTRA TRIPLE LUTZ RIGHT OUT THE GATE, PEGA!
~~4Lz~~ → 3Lz
4T
3A
3A+2T
3F+3T
3Lz+1Lo+3S
3Lo
3Lz ✕
NOW HE CAN ONLY DO ONE MORE, PEGA!
THAT'S RIGHT! ANYWAY, QUIT YOUR SCREECHING, PEGA-KUN.

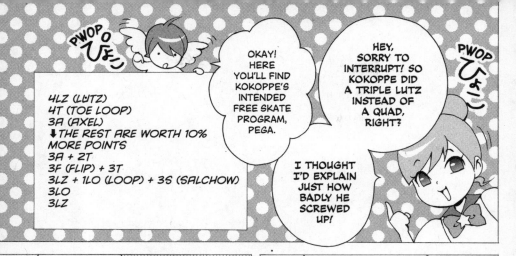

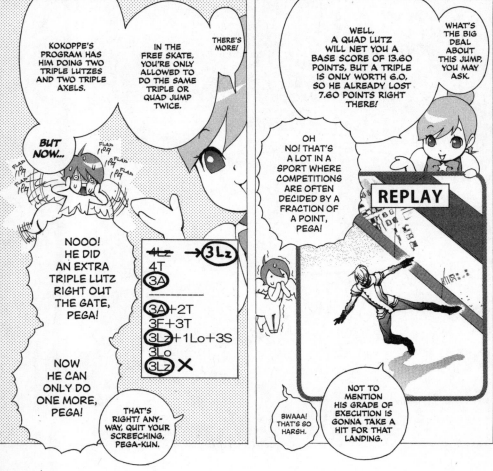

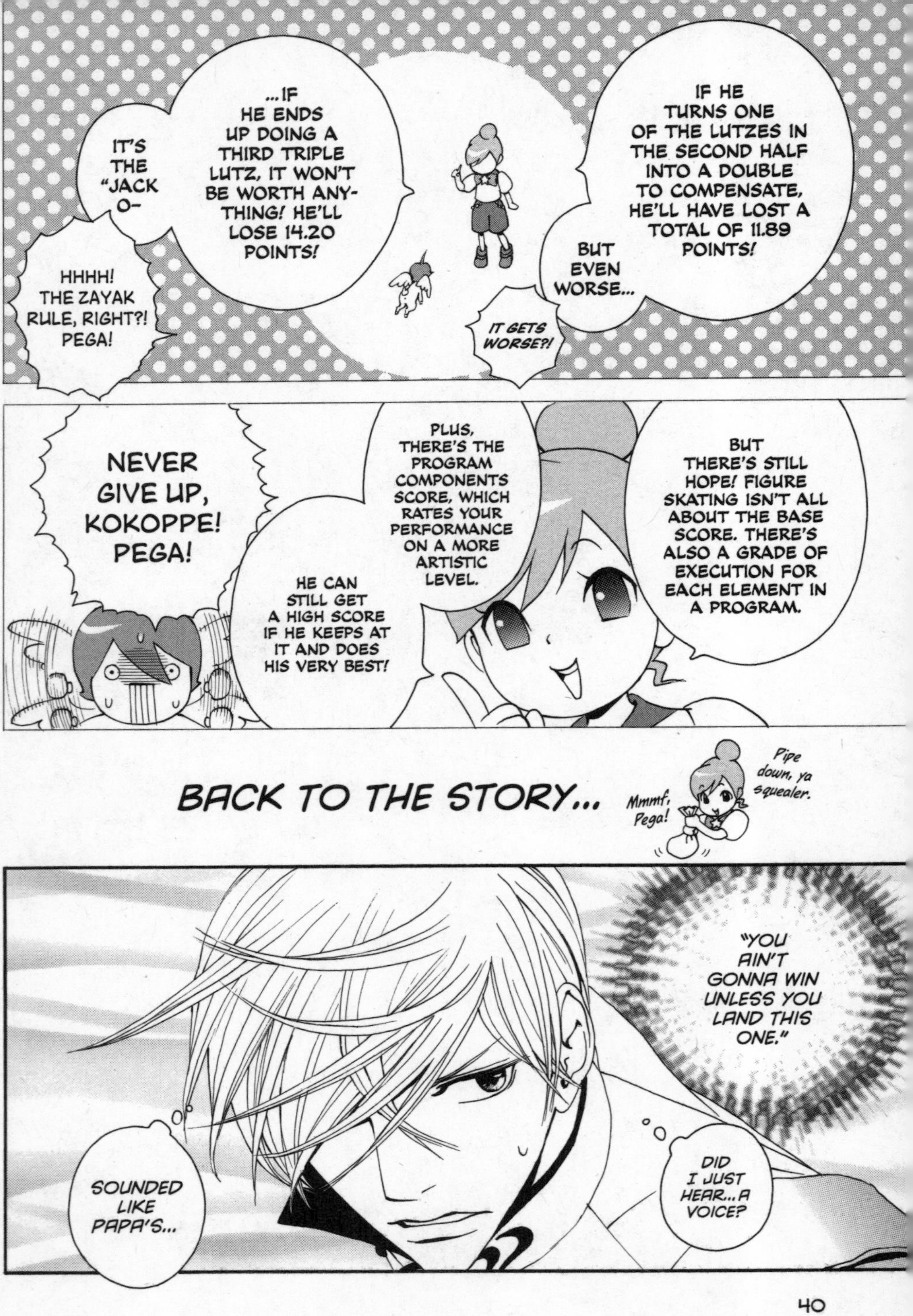
IF HE TURNS ONE OF THE LUTZES IN THE SECOND HALF INTO A DOUBLE TO COMPENSATE, HE'LL HAVE LOST A TOTAL OF 11.89 POINTS!
BUT EVEN WORSE...
IT GETS WORSE?!
...IF HE ENDS UP DOING A THIRD TRIPLE LUTZ, IT WON'T BE WORTH ANY-THING! HE'LL LOSE 14.20 POINTS!
IT'S THE "JACK O-
HHHH! THE ZAYAK RULE, RIGHT?! PEGA!
BUT THERE'S STILL HOPE! FIGURE SKATING ISN'T ALL ABOUT THE BASE SCORE. THERE'S ALSO A GRADE OF EXECUTION FOR EACH ELEMENT IN A PROGRAM.
PLUS, THERE'S THE PROGRAM COMPONENTS SCORE, WHICH RATES YOUR PERFORMANCE ON A MORE ARTISTIC LEVEL.
HE CAN STILL GET A HIGH SCORE IF HE KEEPS AT IT AND DOES HIS VERY BEST!
NEVER GIVE UP, KOKOPPE! PEGA!
BACK TO THE STORY...
Pipe down, ya squealer.
Mmmf, Pega!
"YOU AIN'T GONNA WIN UNLESS YOU LAND THIS ONE."
DID I JUST HEAR... A VOICE?
SOUNDED LIKE PAPA'S...

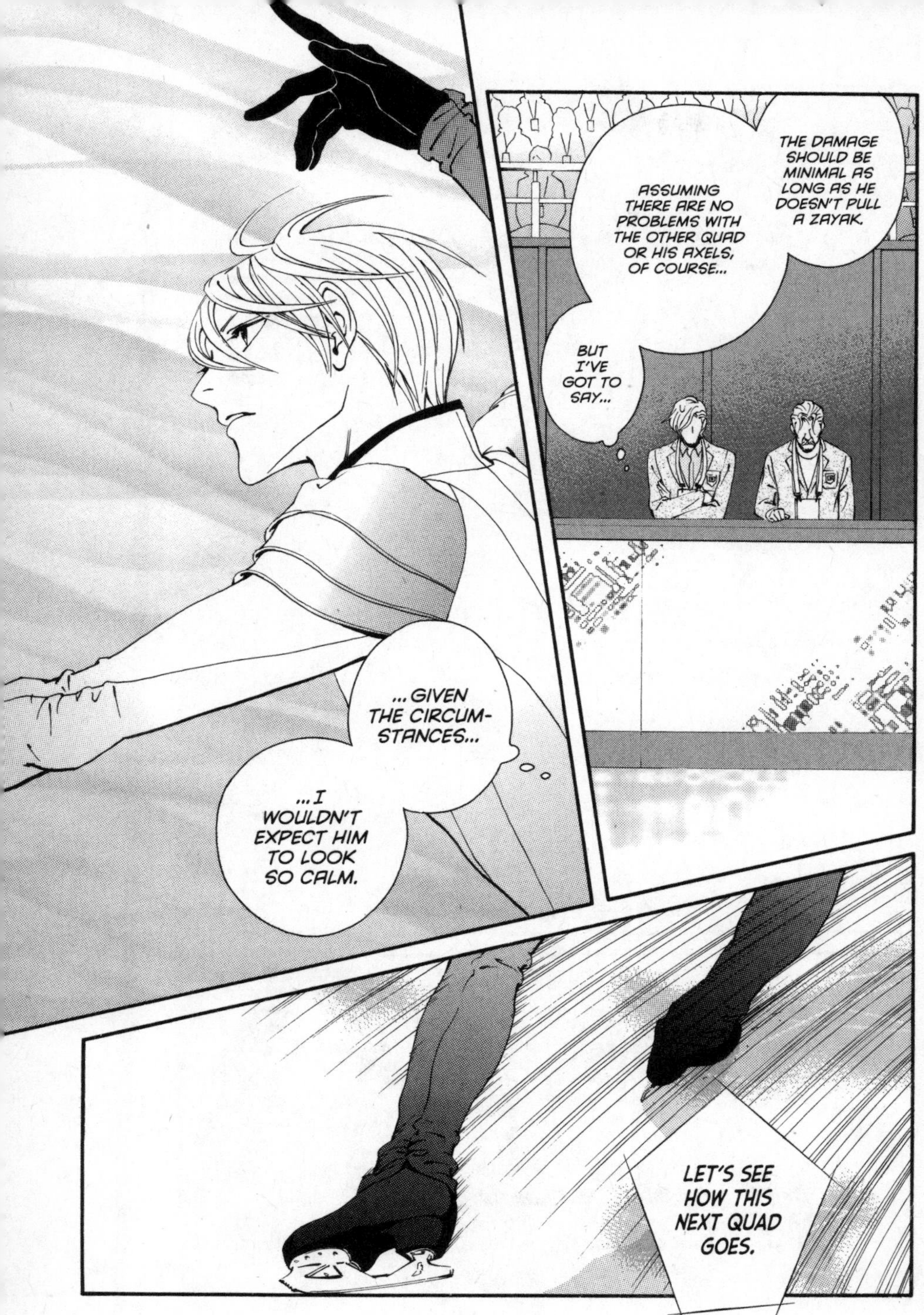
THE DAMAGE SHOULD BE MINIMAL AS LONG AS HE DOESN'T PULL A ZAYAK.
ASSUMING THERE ARE NO PROBLEMS WITH THE OTHER QUAD OR HIS AXELS, OF COURSE...
BUT I'VE GOT TO SAY...
...GIVEN THE CIRCUM-STANCES...
...I WOULDN'T EXPECT HIM TO LOOK SO CALM.
LET'S SEE HOW THIS NEXT QUAD GOES.

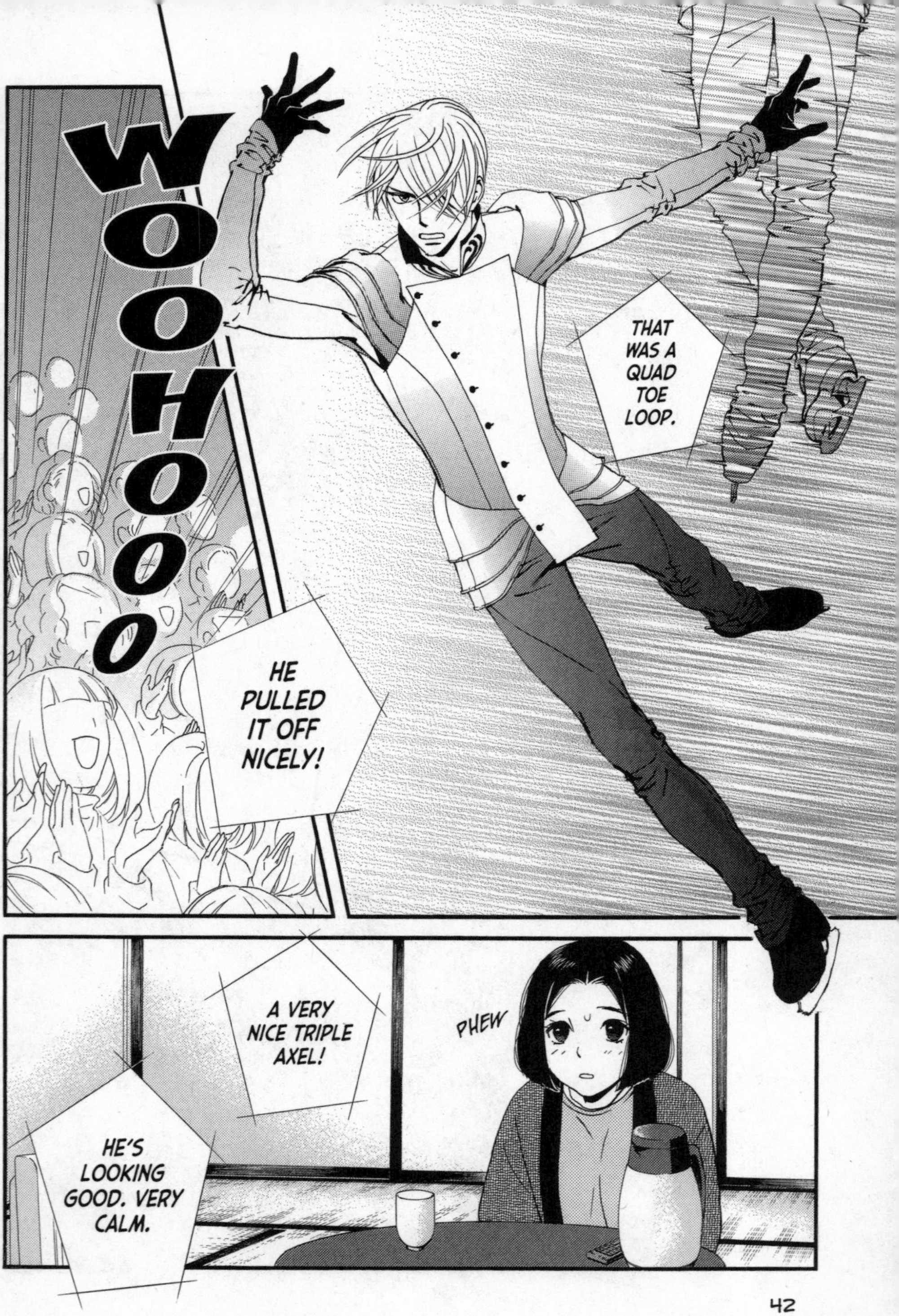
THAT WAS A QUAD TOE LOOP.
WOOHOOOO
HE PULLED IT OFF NICELY!
PHEW
A VERY NICE TRIPLE AXEL!
HE'S LOOKING GOOD. VERY CALM.

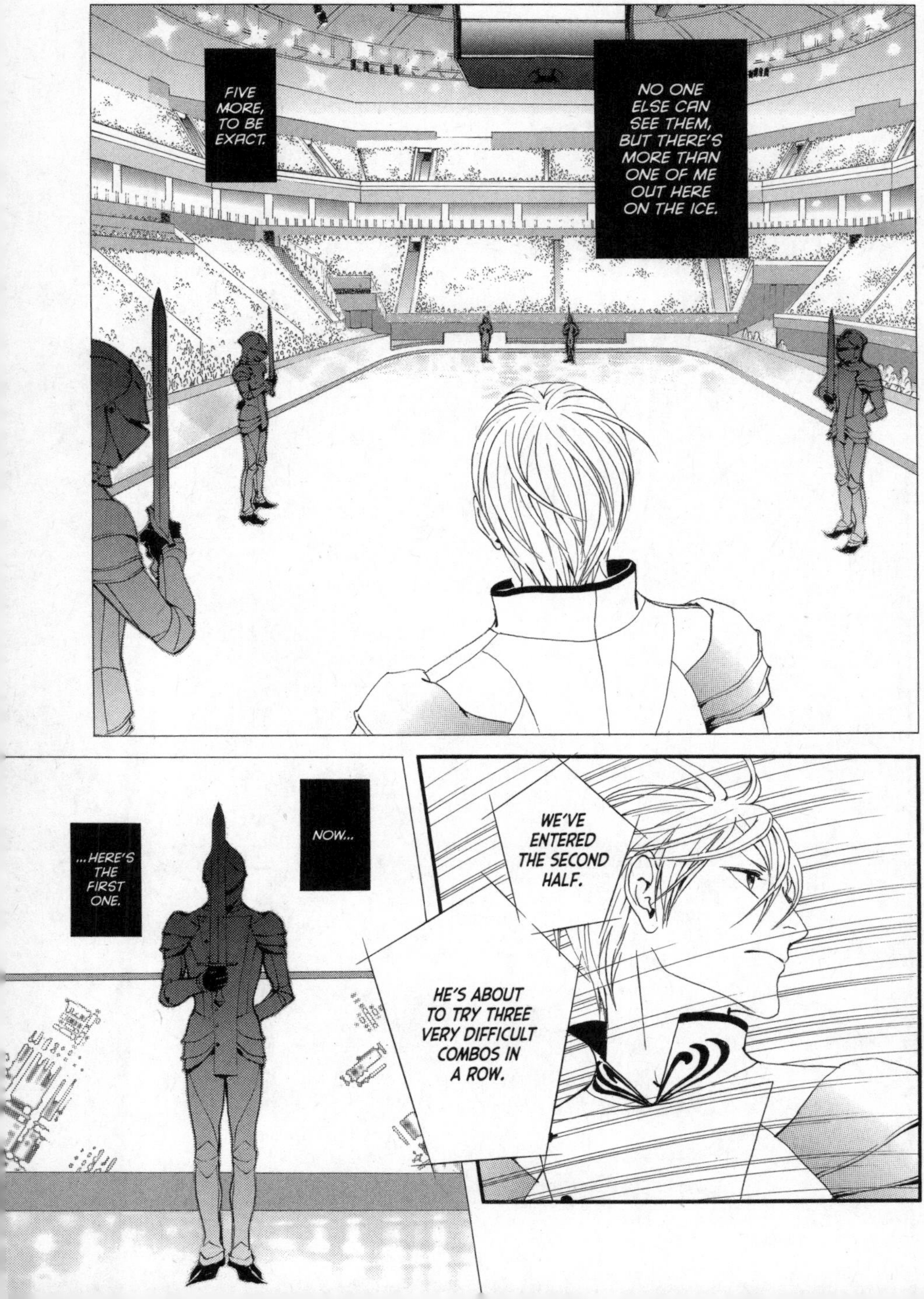
NO ONE ELSE CAN SEE THEM, BUT THERE'S MORE THAN ONE OF ME OUT HERE ON THE ICE.
FIVE MORE, TO BE EXACT.
WE'VE ENTERED THE SECOND HALF.
HE'S ABOUT TO TRY THREE VERY DIFFICULT COMBOS IN A ROW.
NOW...
...HERE'S THE FIRST ONE.

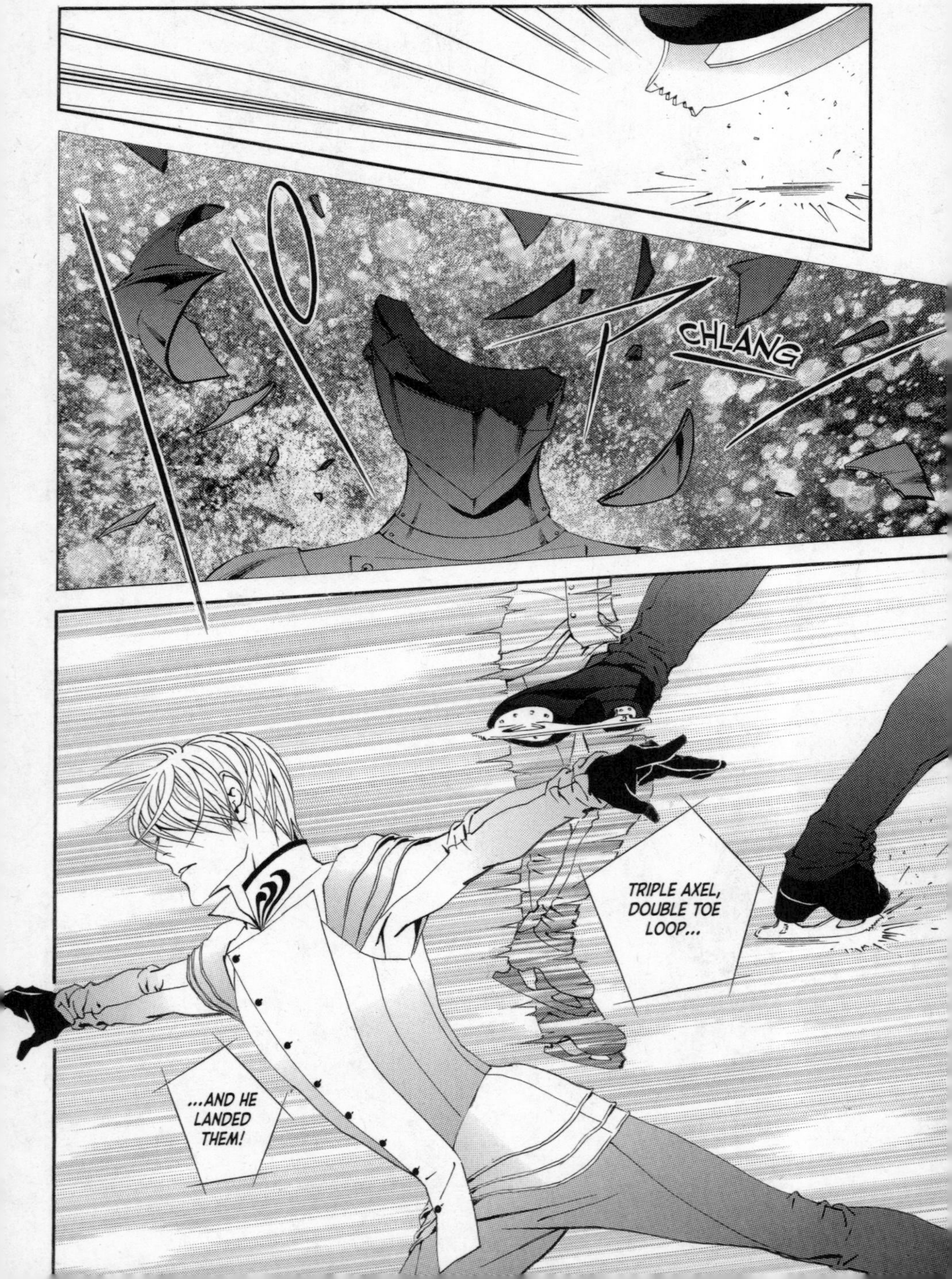
CHLANG
TRIPLE AXEL, DOUBLE TOE LOOP...
...AND HE LANDED THEM!

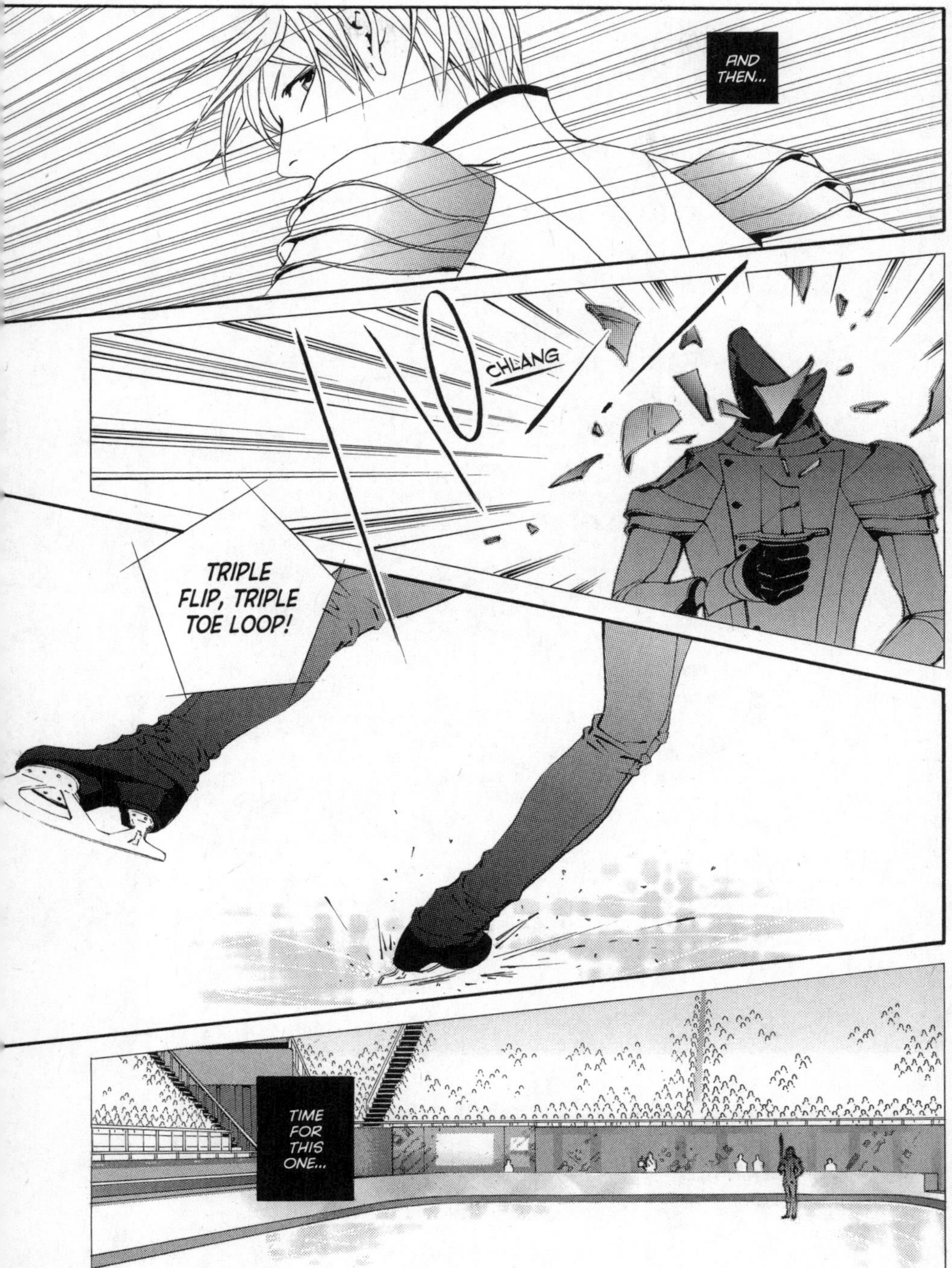
AND THEN...
CHLANG
TRIPLE FLIP, TRIPLE TOE LOOP!
TIME FOR THIS ONE...

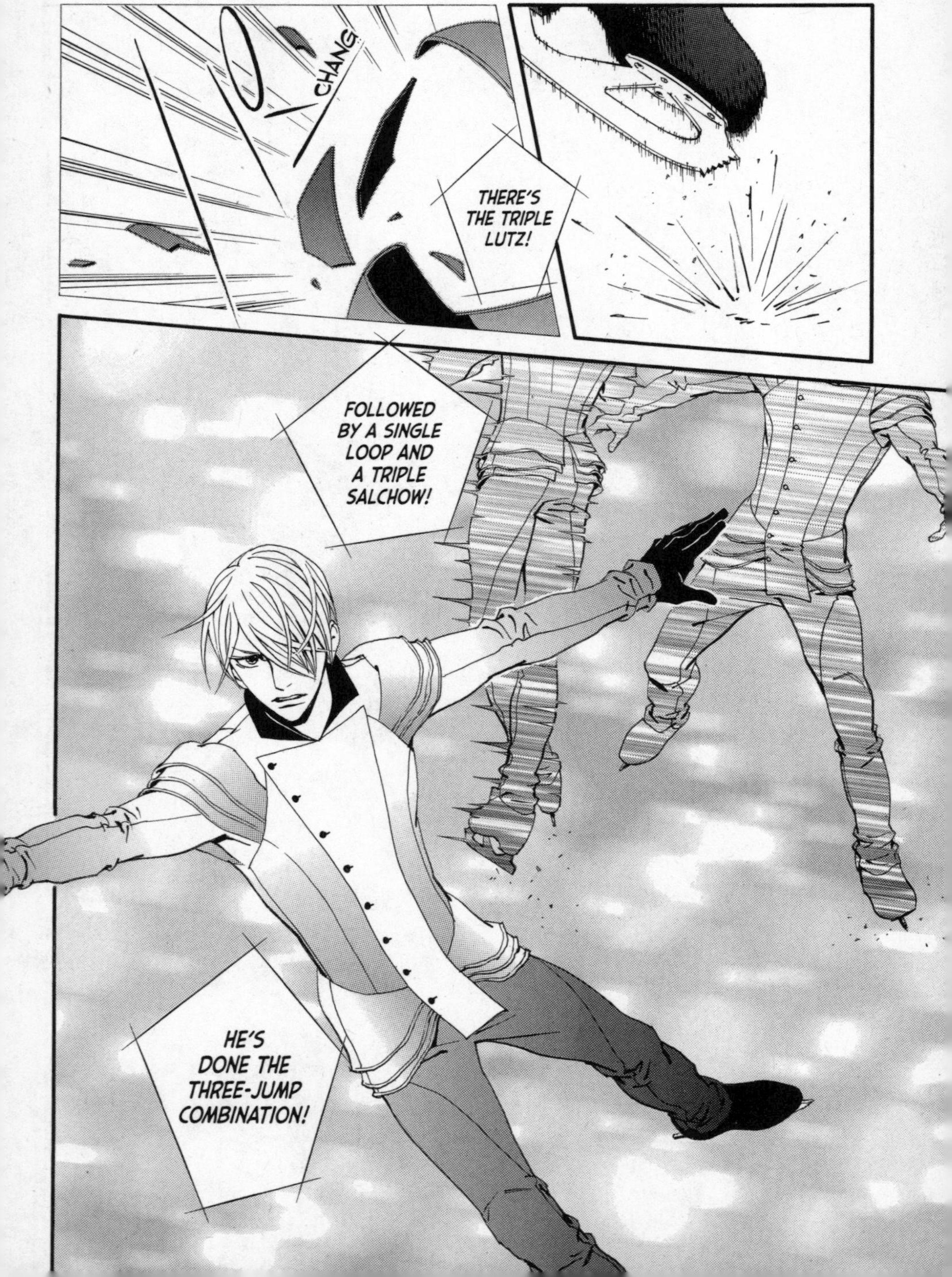
CHANG
THERE'S THE TRIPLE LUTZ!
FOLLOWED BY A SINGLE LOOP AND A TRIPLE SALCHOW!
HE'S DONE THE THREE-JUMP COMBINATION!

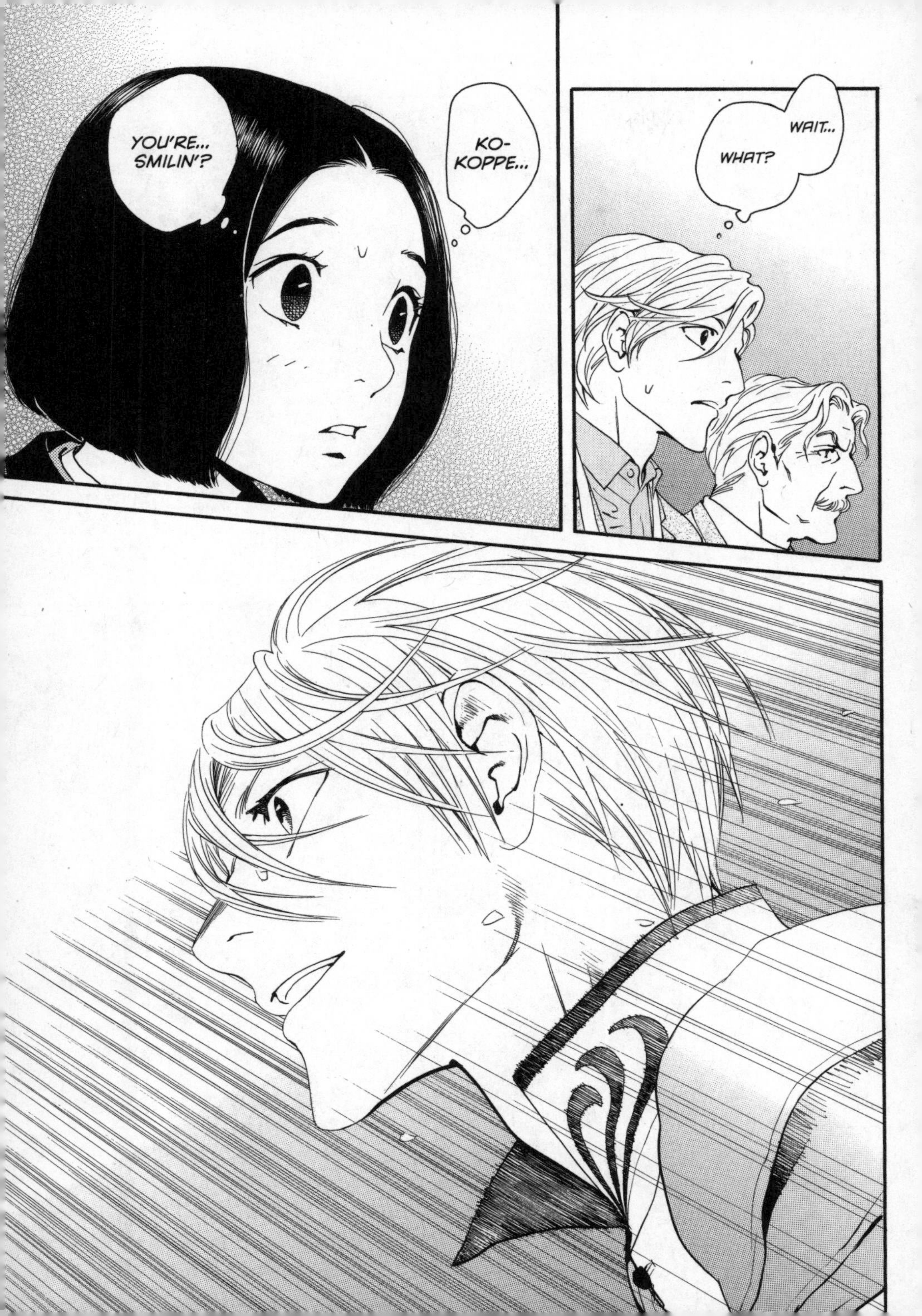
WAIT... WHAT?
KO-KOPPE...
YOU'RE... SMILIN'?

I CAN HEAR SE-CHAN'S VOICE.

I GOTTA SHOW MYSELF, TOO.

"SHOW 'EM ALL HOW BRAVE YOU ARE."

"SHOW 'EM ALL HOW BRAVE YOU ARE."

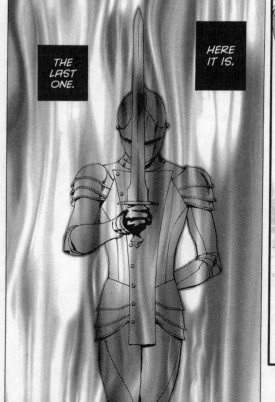

THE LAST ONE.

HERE IT IS.

A GOOD TRIPLE LOOP!

HE ONLY HAS ONE JUMP TO GO.

HIS MOTIONS ARE ALL SO SMOOTH... HE MUST REALLY BE IN THE ZONE.

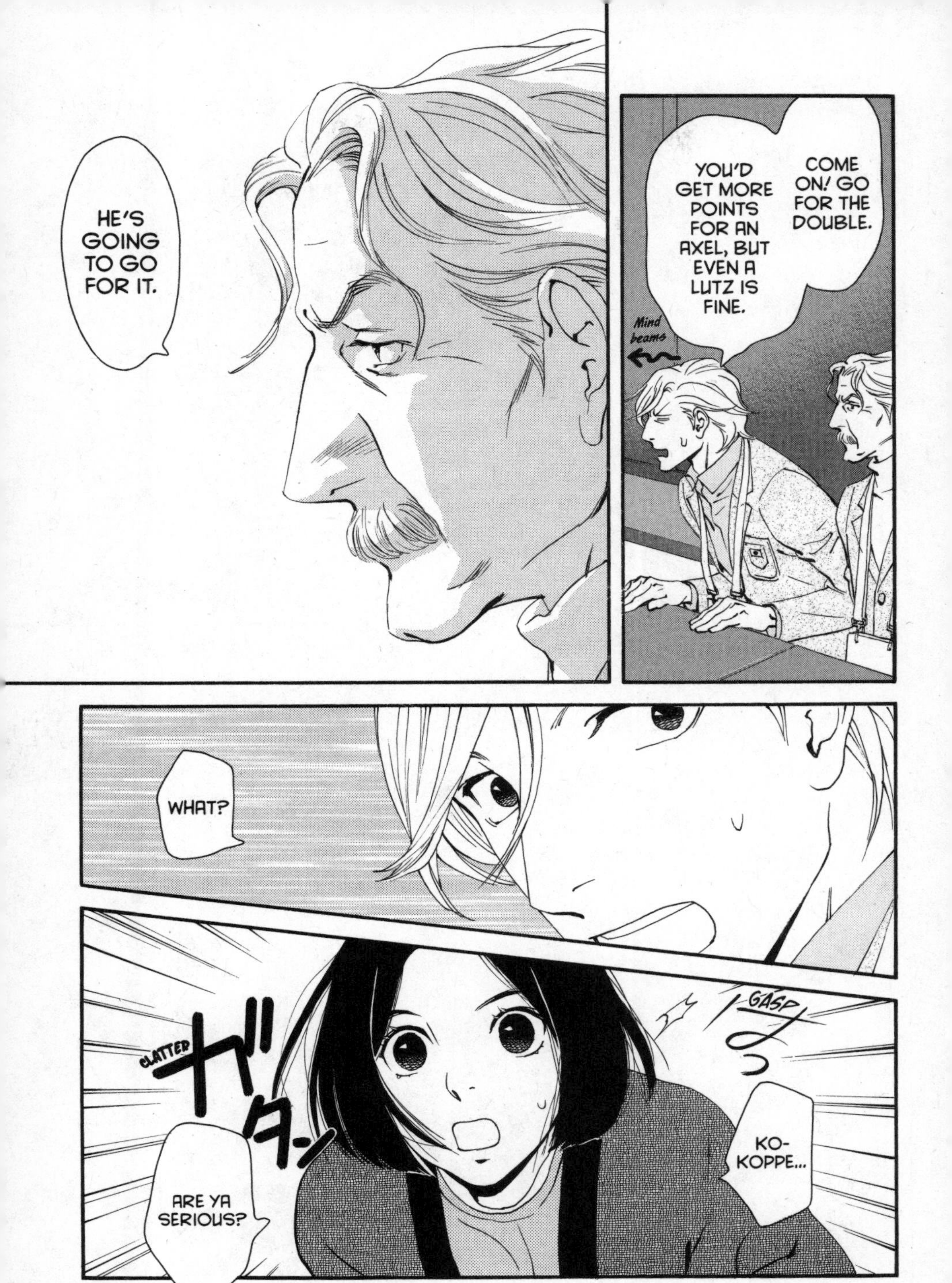
COME ON! GO FOR THE DOUBLE.
YOU'D GET MORE POINTS FOR AN AXEL, BUT EVEN A LUTZ IS FINE.
Mind beams
HE'S GOING TO GO FOR IT.
WHAT?
GASP
KO-KOPPE...
CLATTER
ARE YA SERIOUS?

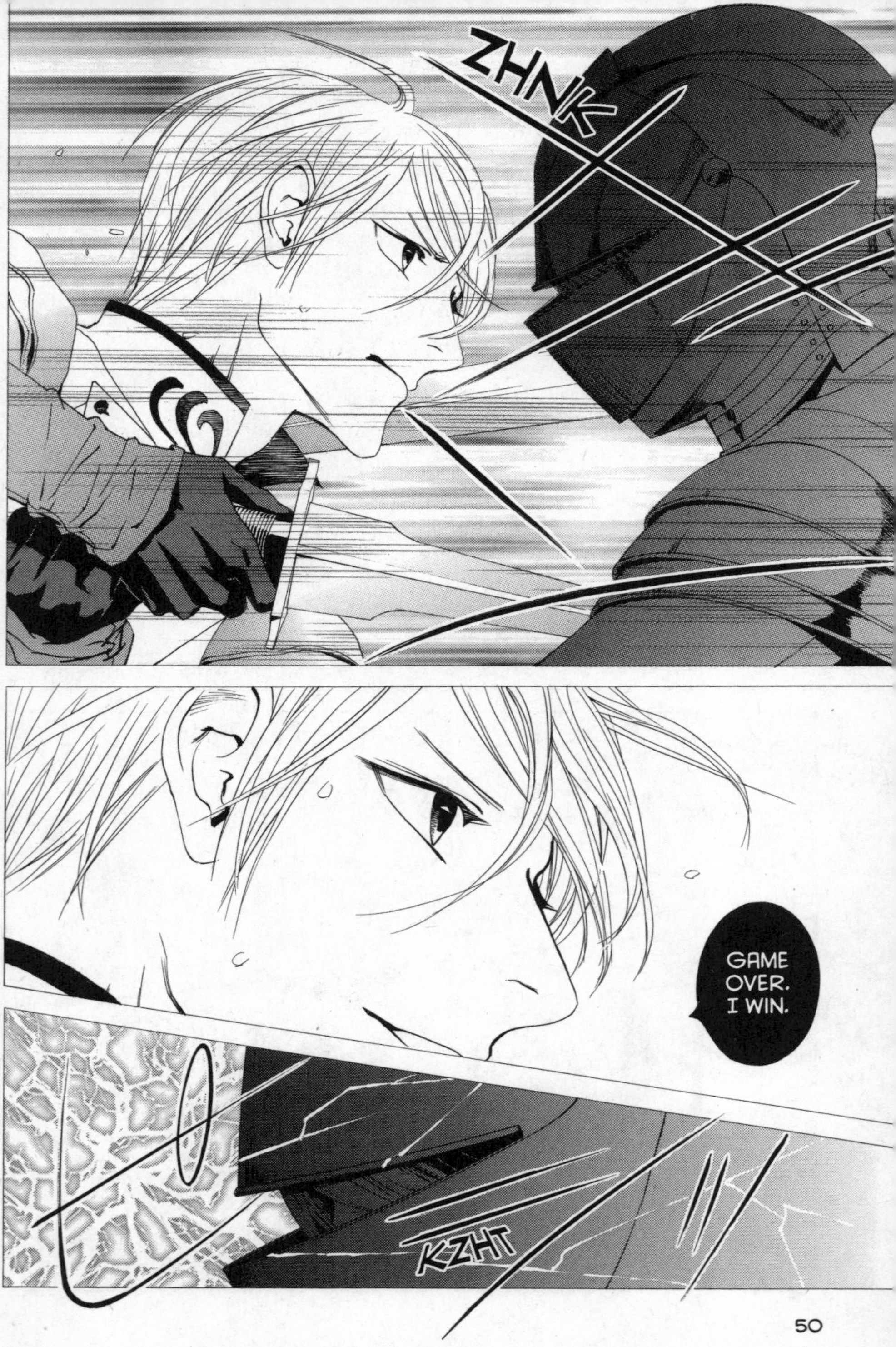
ZHNK
GAME OVER. I WIN.
KZHT

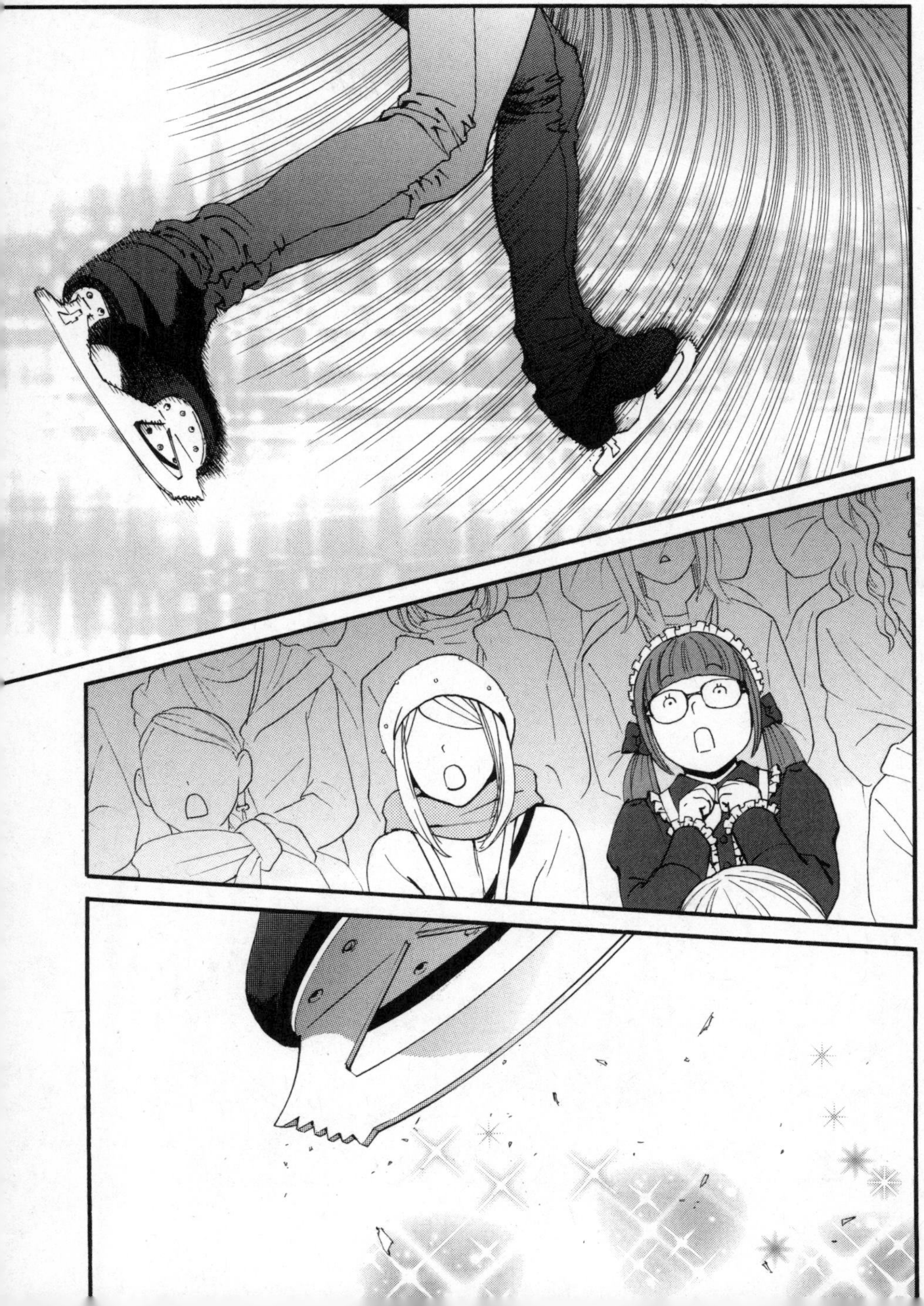

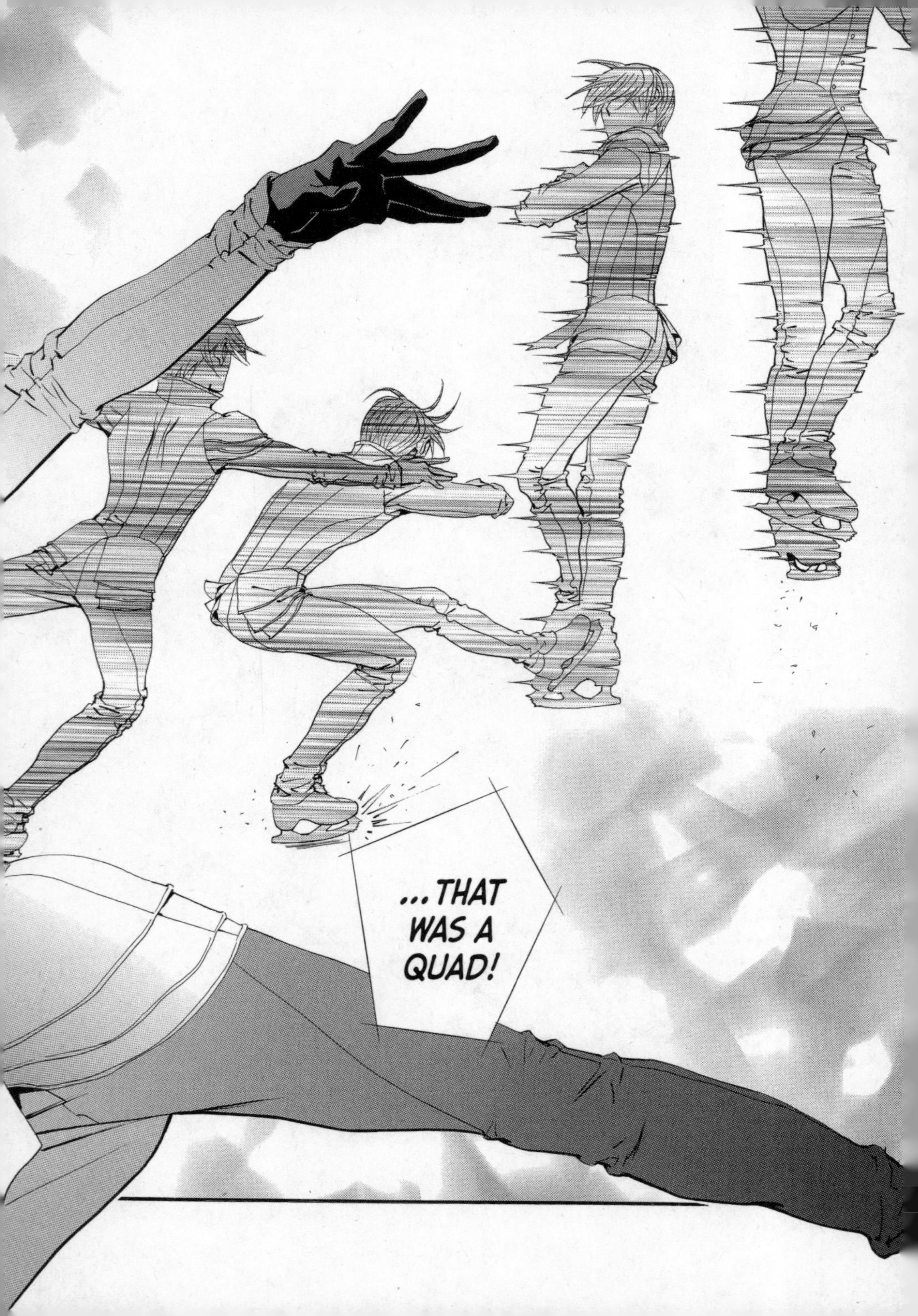
...THAT
WAS A
QUAD!

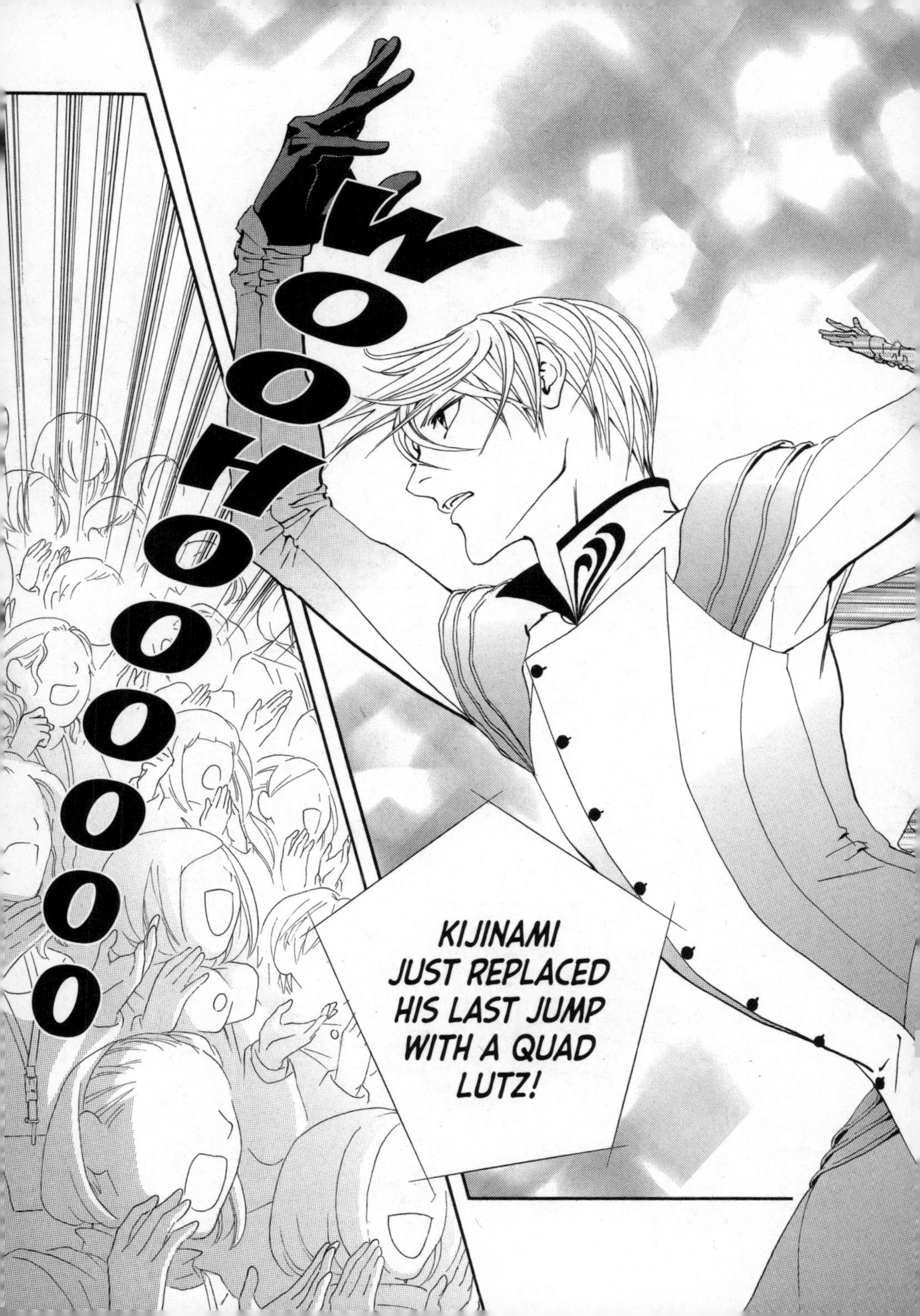
WOOHOOOOOOOO
KIJINAMI JUST REPLACED HIS LAST JUMP WITH A QUAD LUTZ!

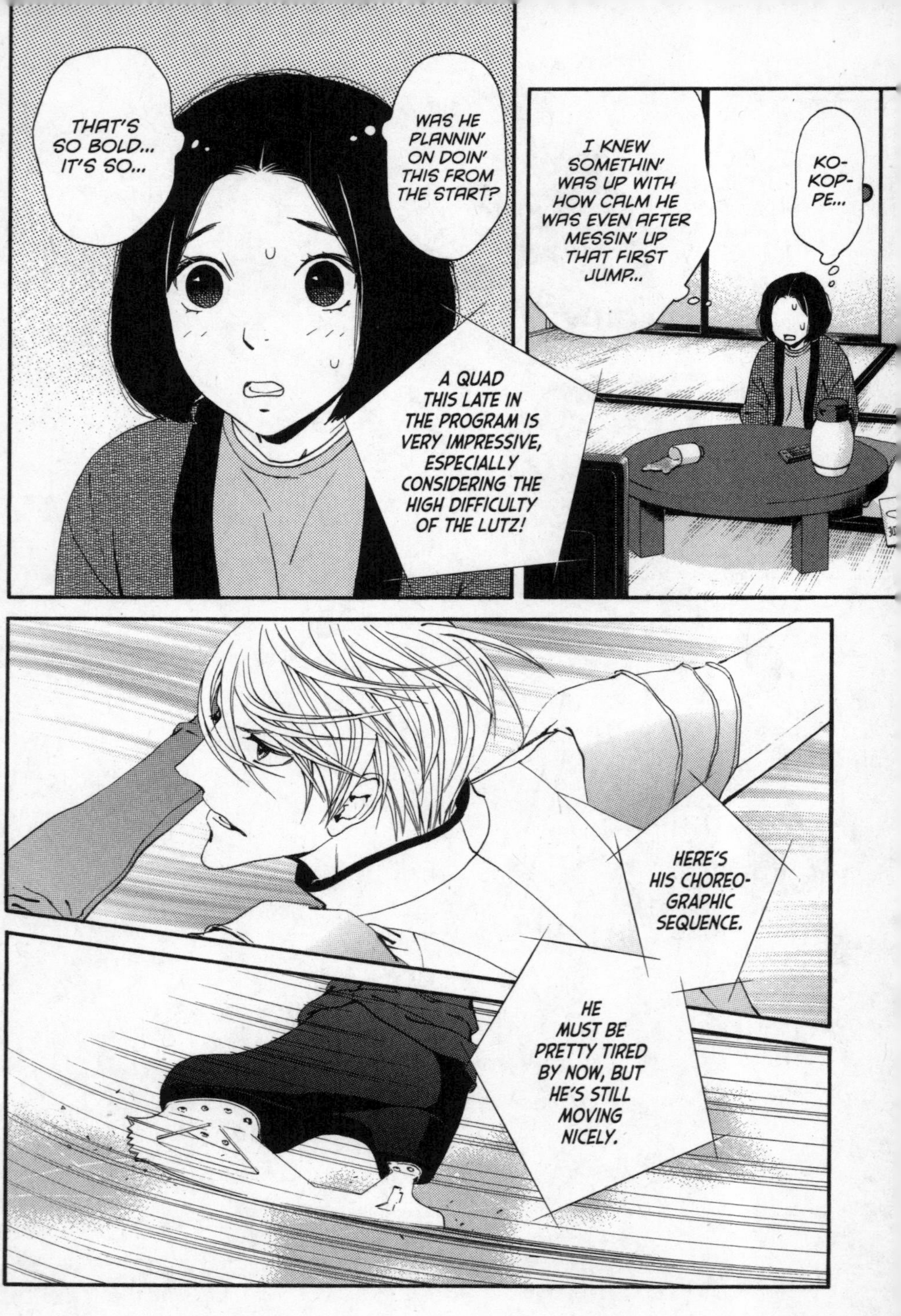
KO-KOP-PE...
I KNEW SOMETHIN' WAS UP WITH HOW CALM HE WAS EVEN AFTER MESSIN' UP THAT FIRST JUMP...
WAS HE PLANNIN' ON DOIN' THIS FROM THE START?
THAT'S SO BOLD... IT'S SO...
A QUAD THIS LATE IN THE PROGRAM IS VERY IMPRESSIVE, ESPECIALLY CONSIDERING THE HIGH DIFFICULTY OF THE LUTZ!
HERE'S HIS CHOREO-GRAPHIC SEQUENCE.
HE MUST BE PRETTY TIRED BY NOW, BUT HE'S STILL MOVING NICELY.

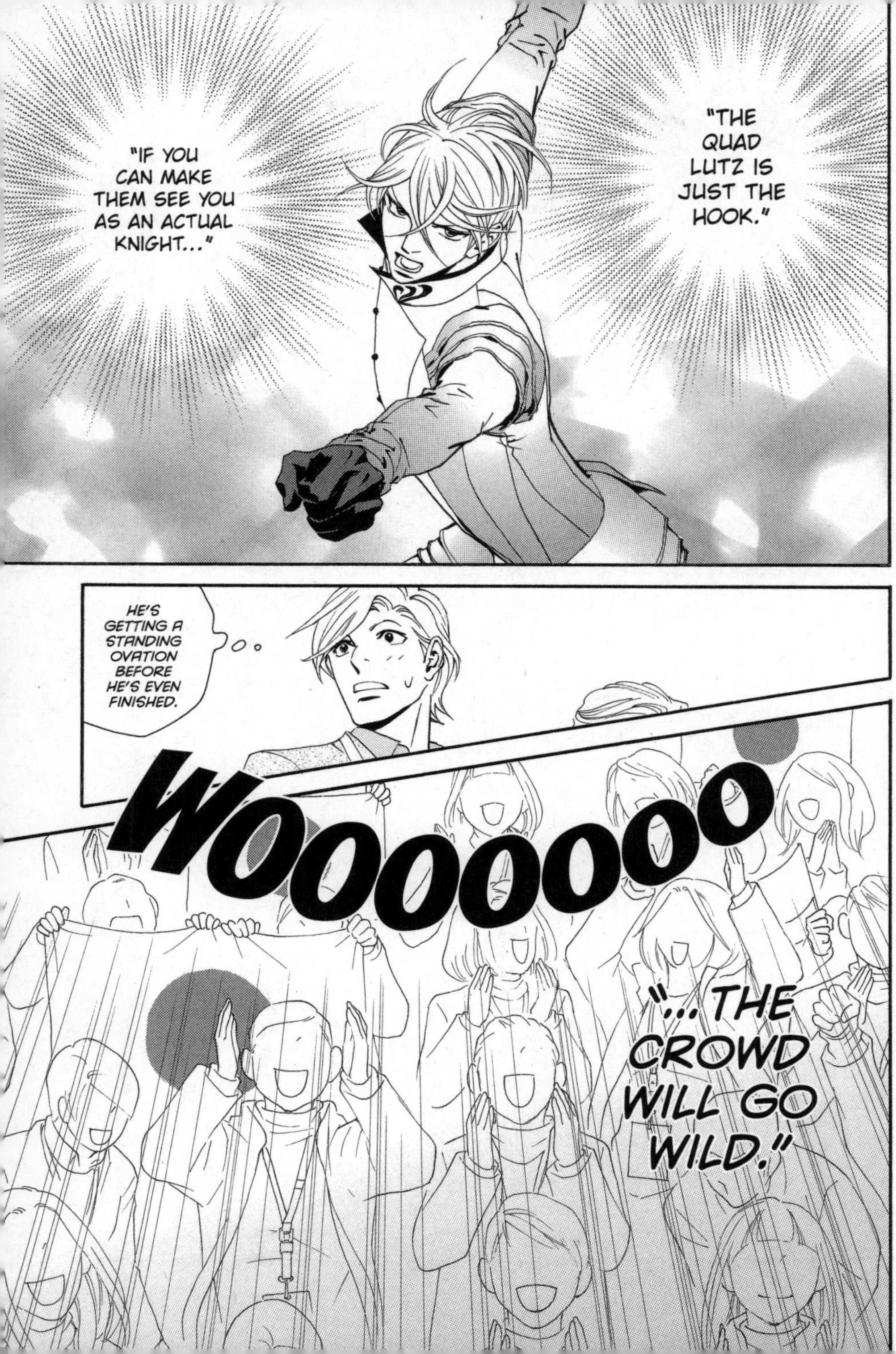
"THE QUAD LUTZ IS JUST THE HOOK."
"IF YOU CAN MAKE THEM SEE YOU AS AN ACTUAL KNIGHT..."
HE'S GETTING A STANDING OVATION BEFORE HE'S EVEN FINISHED.
WOOOOOOOO
"...THE CROWD WILL GO WILD."

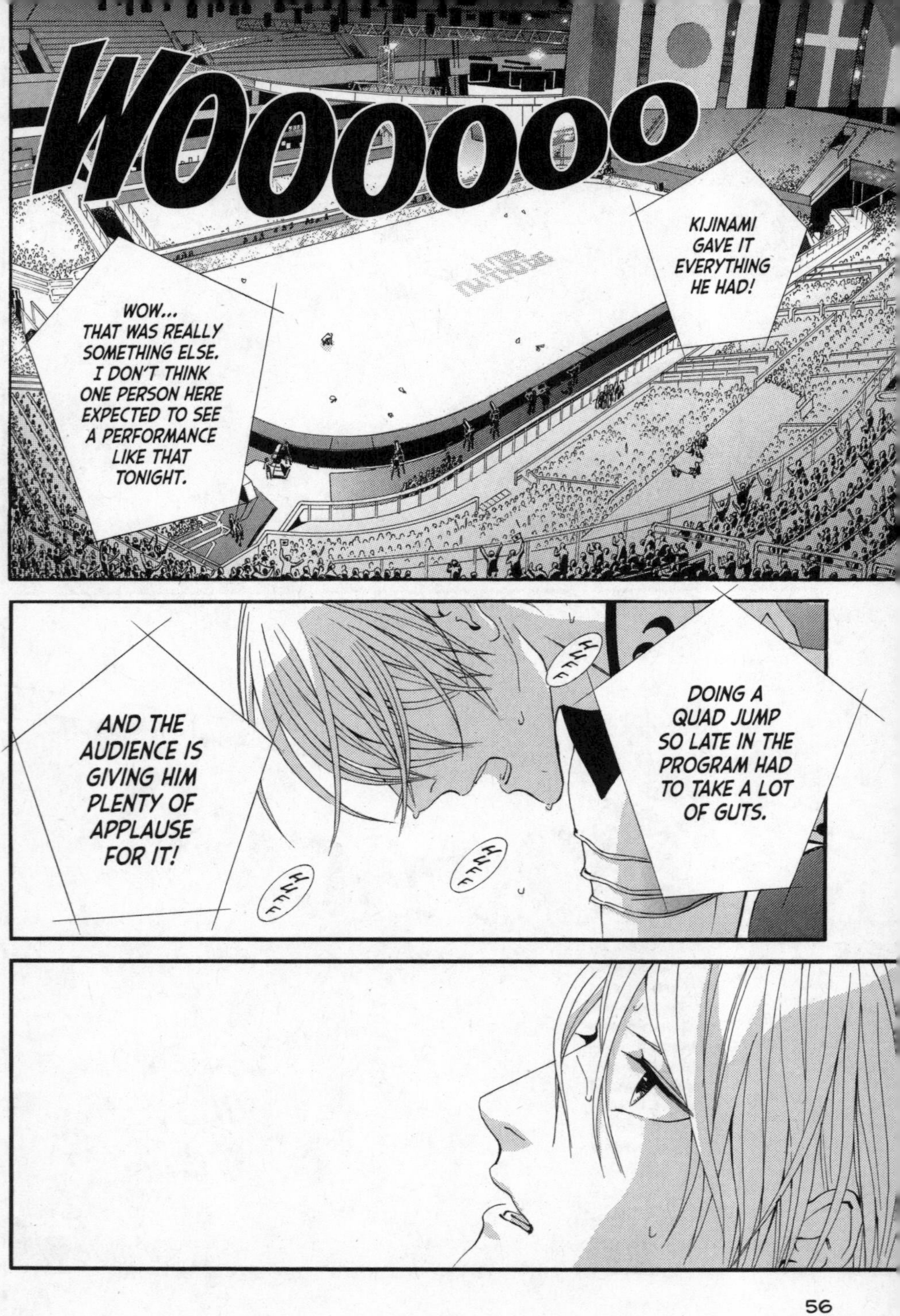
WOOOOOO
KIJINAMI GAVE IT EVERYTHING HE HAD!
WOW... THAT WAS REALLY SOMETHING ELSE. I DON'T THINK ONE PERSON HERE EXPECTED TO SEE A PERFORMANCE LIKE THAT TONIGHT.
HUFF
DOING A QUAD JUMP SO LATE IN THE PROGRAM HAD TO TAKE A LOT OF GUTS.
HUFF
HUFF
AND THE AUDIENCE IS GIVING HIM PLENTY OF APPLAUSE FOR IT!

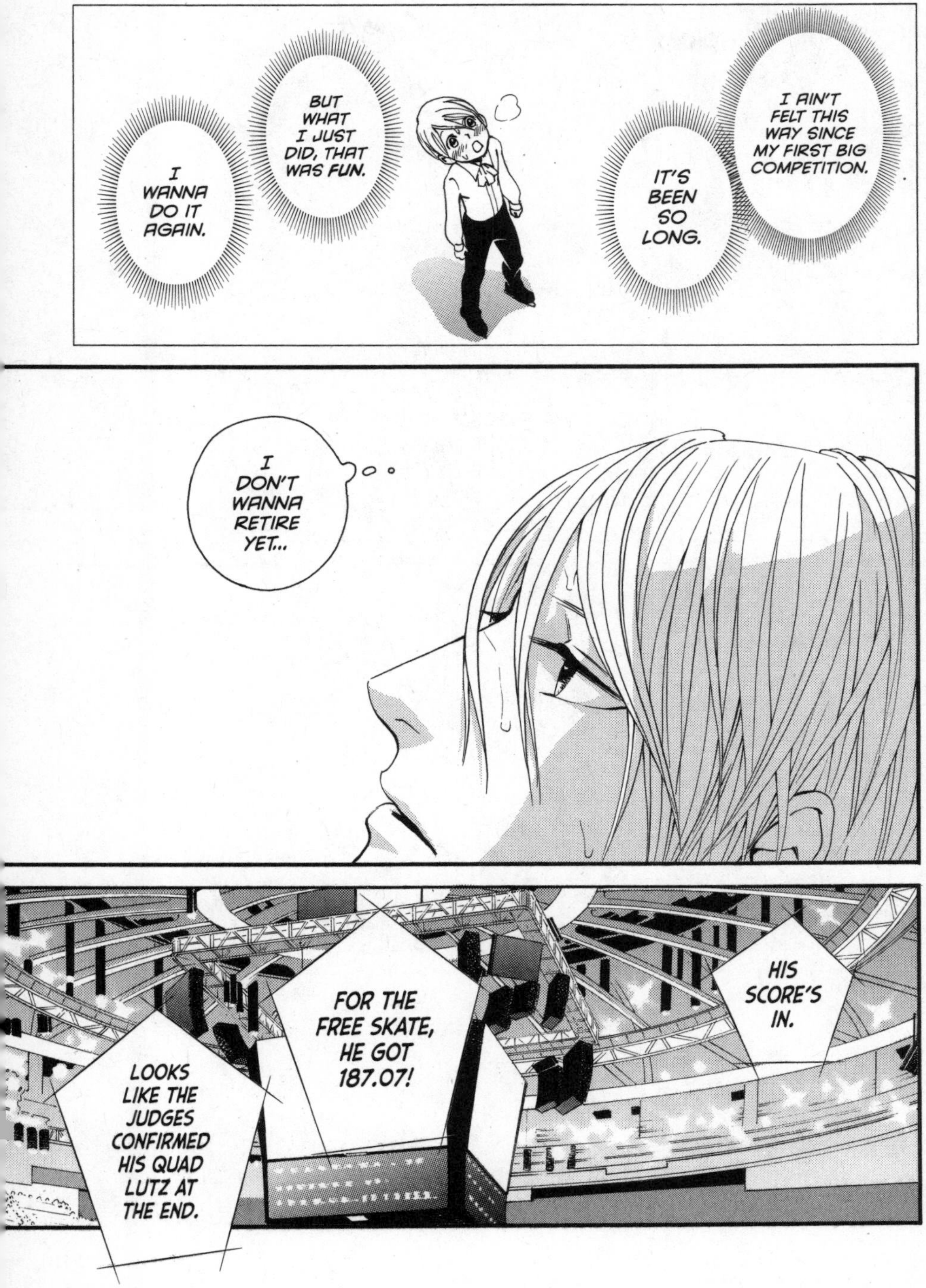
I AIN'T FELT THIS WAY SINCE MY FIRST BIG COMPETITION.
IT'S BEEN SO LONG.
BUT WHAT I JUST DID, THAT WAS FUN.
I WANNA DO IT AGAIN.
I DON'T WANNA RETIRE YET...
HIS SCORE'S IN.
FOR THE FREE SKATE, HE GOT 187.07!
LOOKS LIKE THE JUDGES CONFIRMED HIS QUAD LUTZ AT THE END.

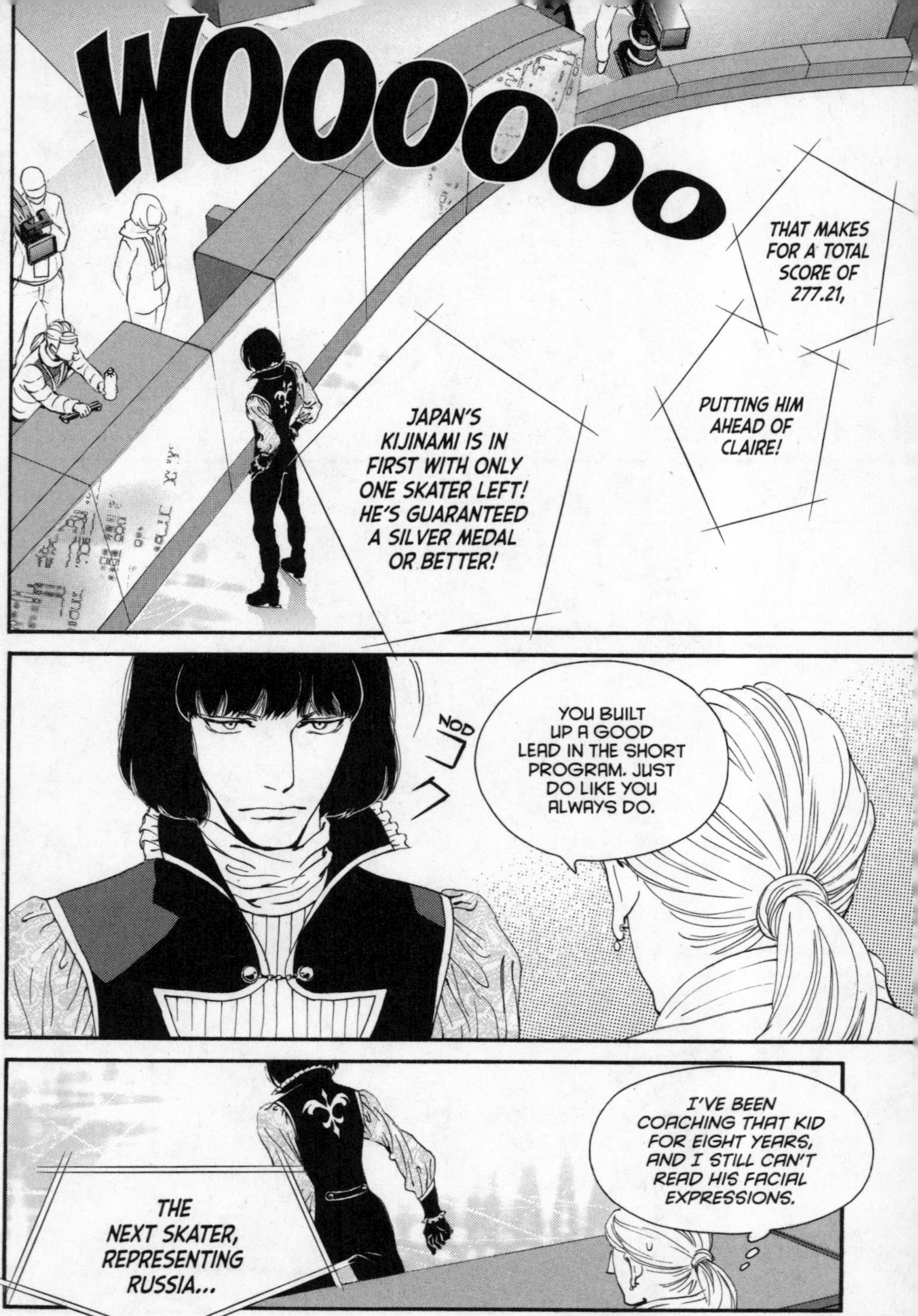
WOOOOOOO
THAT MAKES FOR A TOTAL SCORE OF 277.21,
PUTTING HIM AHEAD OF CLAIRE!
JAPAN'S KIJINAMI IS IN FIRST WITH ONLY ONE SKATER LEFT! HE'S GUARANTEED A SILVER MEDAL OR BETTER!
YOU BUILT UP A GOOD LEAD IN THE SHORT PROGRAM. JUST DO LIKE YOU ALWAYS DO.
NOD
I'VE BEEN COACHING THAT KID FOR EIGHT YEARS, AND I STILL CAN'T READ HIS FACIAL EXPRESSIONS.
THE NEXT SKATER, REPRESENTING RUSSIA...

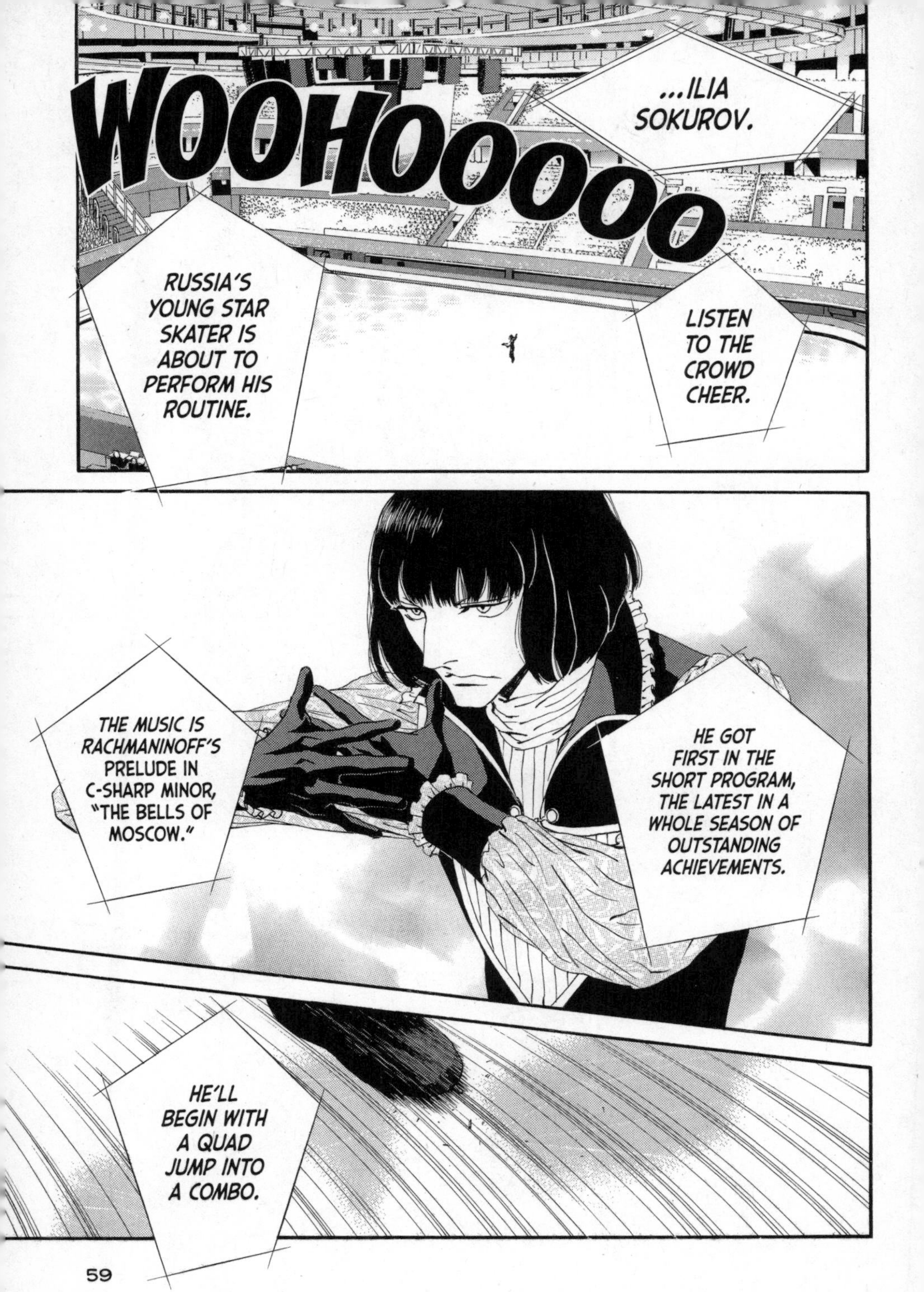
...ILIA SOKUROV.
WOOHOOOOOO
LISTEN TO THE CROWD CHEER.
RUSSIA'S YOUNG STAR SKATER IS ABOUT TO PERFORM HIS ROUTINE.
HE GOT FIRST IN THE SHORT PROGRAM, THE LATEST IN A WHOLE SEASON OF OUTSTANDING ACHIEVEMENTS.
THE MUSIC IS RACHMANINOFF'S PRELUDE IN C-SHARP MINOR, "THE BELLS OF MOSCOW."
HE'LL BEGIN WITH A QUAD JUMP INTO A COMBO.

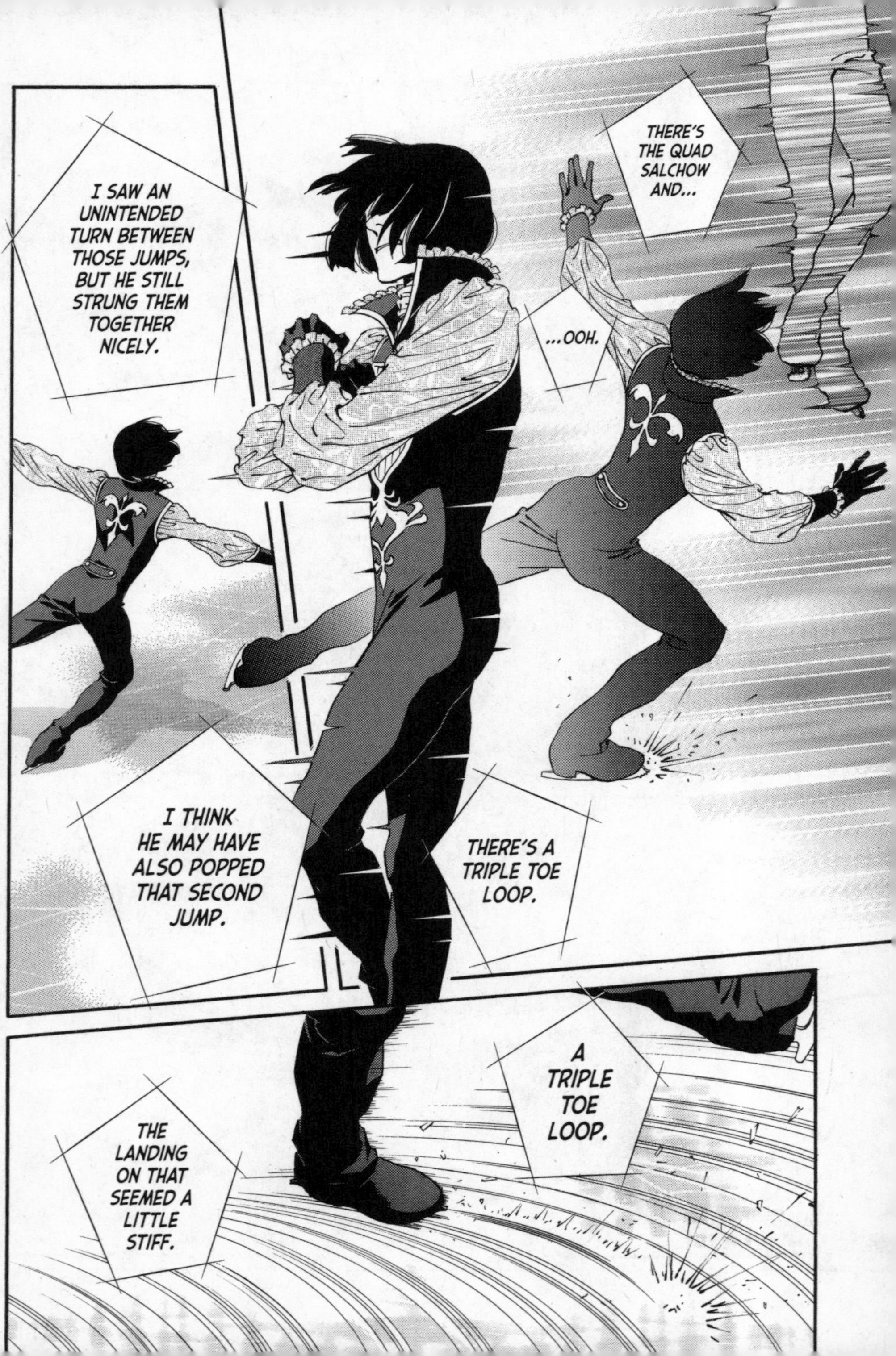
THERE'S THE QUAD SALCHOW AND...
...OOH.
I SAW AN UNINTENDED TURN BETWEEN THOSE JUMPS, BUT HE STILL STRUNG THEM TOGETHER NICELY.
THERE'S A TRIPLE TOE LOOP.
I THINK HE MAY HAVE ALSO POPPED THAT SECOND JUMP.
A TRIPLE TOE LOOP.
THE LANDING ON THAT SEEMED A LITTLE STIFF.

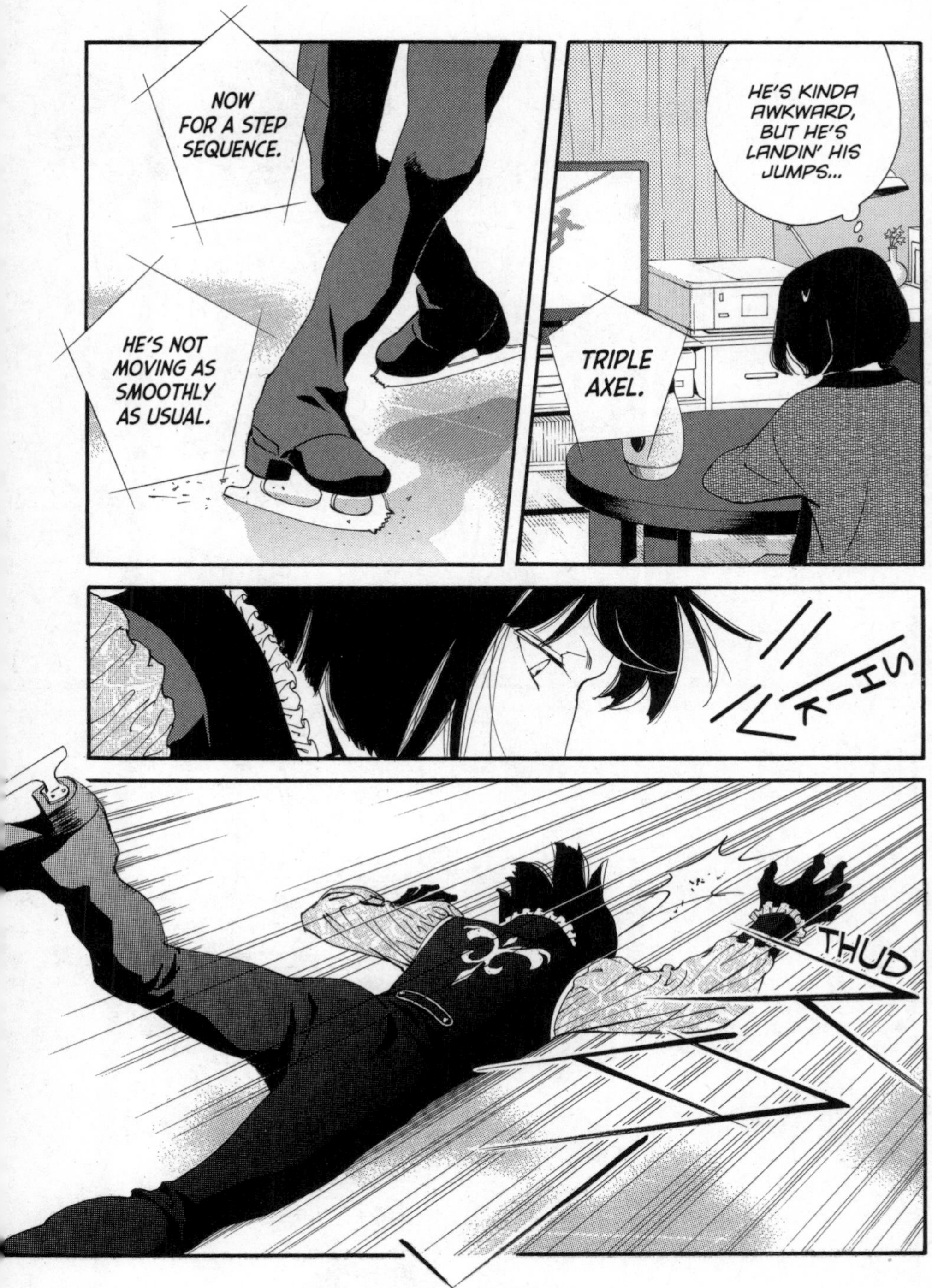
HE'S KINDA AWKWARD, BUT HE'S LANDIN' HIS JUMPS...
TRIPLE AXEL.
NOW FOR A STEP SEQUENCE.
HE'S NOT MOVING AS SMOOTHLY AS USUAL.
THUD

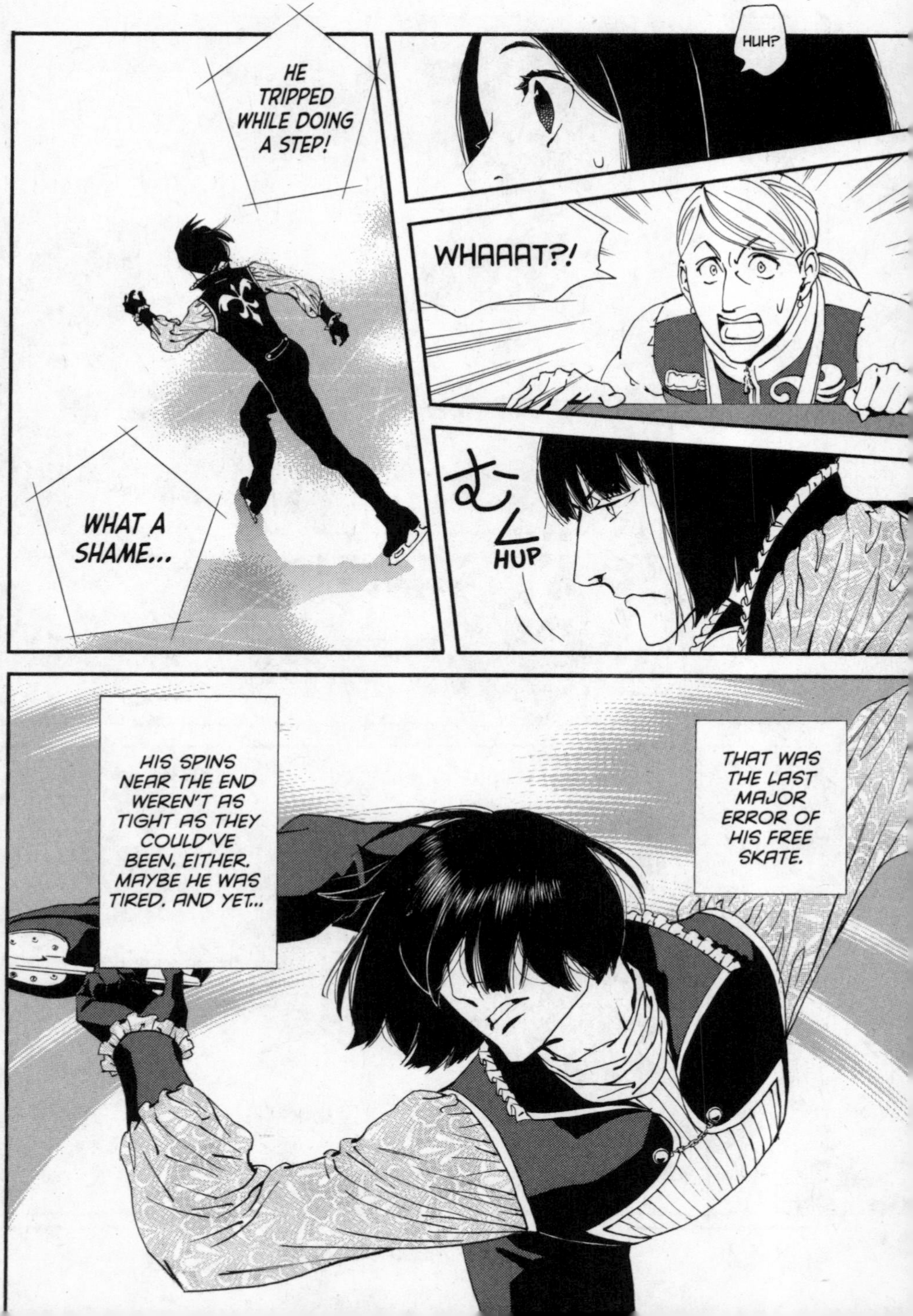
HUH?
WHAAAT?!
むく
HUP
HE TRIPPED WHILE DOING A STEP!
WHAT A SHAME...
THAT WAS THE LAST MAJOR ERROR OF HIS FREE SKATE.
HIS SPINS NEAR THE END WEREN'T AS TIGHT AS THEY COULD'VE BEEN, EITHER. MAYBE HE WAS TIRED. AND YET...

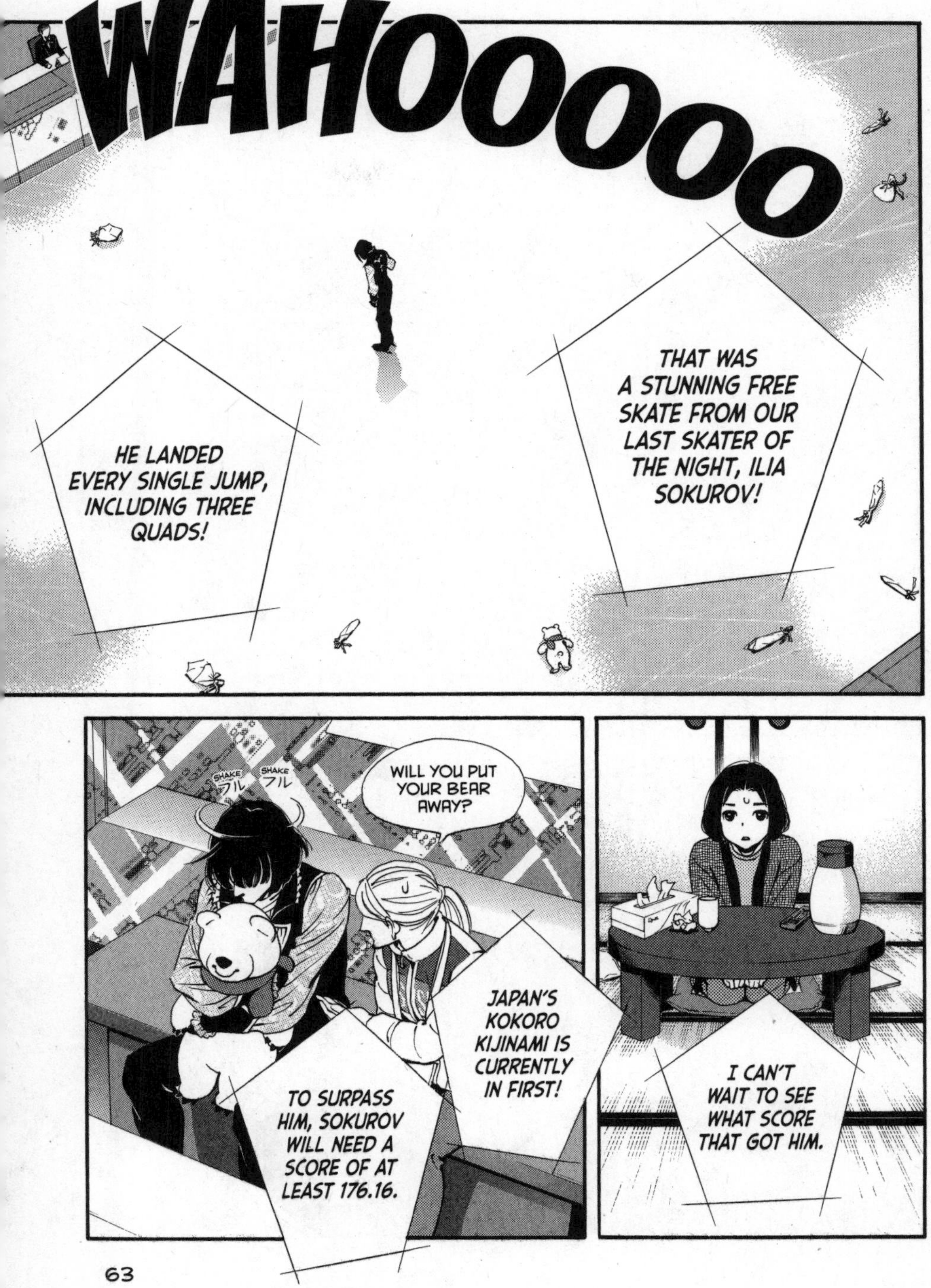
WAHOOOOOO
THAT WAS A STUNNING FREE SKATE FROM OUR LAST SKATER OF THE NIGHT, ILIA SOKUROV!
HE LANDED EVERY SINGLE JUMP, INCLUDING THREE QUADS!
I CAN'T WAIT TO SEE WHAT SCORE THAT GOT HIM.
SHAKE フル
SHAKE フル
WILL YOU PUT YOUR BEAR AWAY?
JAPAN'S KOKORO KIJINAMI IS CURRENTLY IN FIRST!
TO SURPASS HIM, SOKUROV WILL NEED A SCORE OF AT LEAST 176.16.

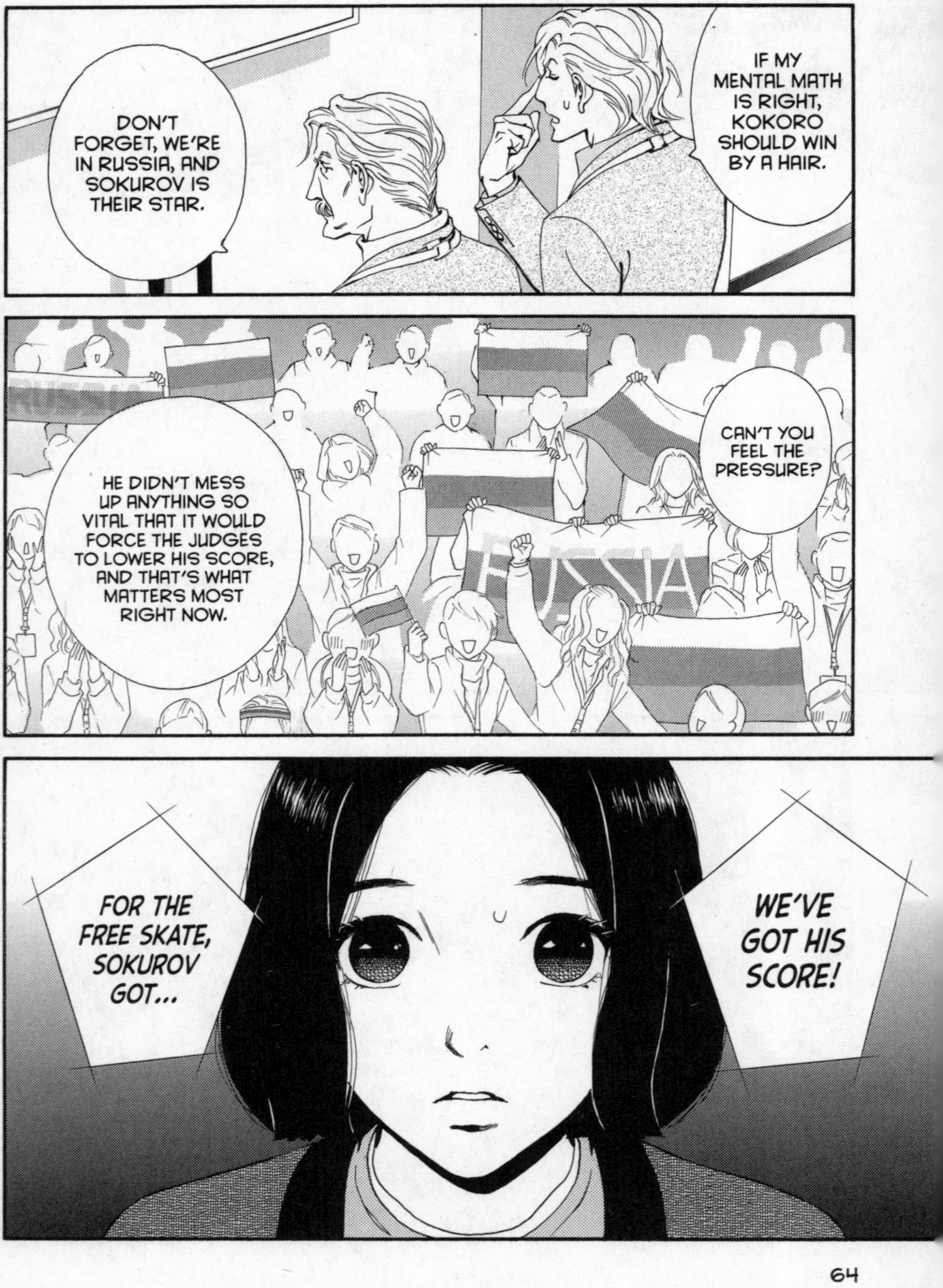
IF MY MENTAL MATH IS RIGHT, KOKORO SHOULD WIN BY A HAIR.
DON'T FORGET, WE'RE IN RUSSIA, AND SOKUROV IS THEIR STAR.
CAN'T YOU FEEL THE PRESSURE?
HE DIDN'T MESS UP ANYTHING SO VITAL THAT IT WOULD FORCE THE JUDGES TO LOWER HIS SCORE, AND THAT'S WHAT MATTERS MOST RIGHT NOW.
WE'VE GOT HIS SCORE!
FOR THE FREE SKATE, SOKUROV GOT...

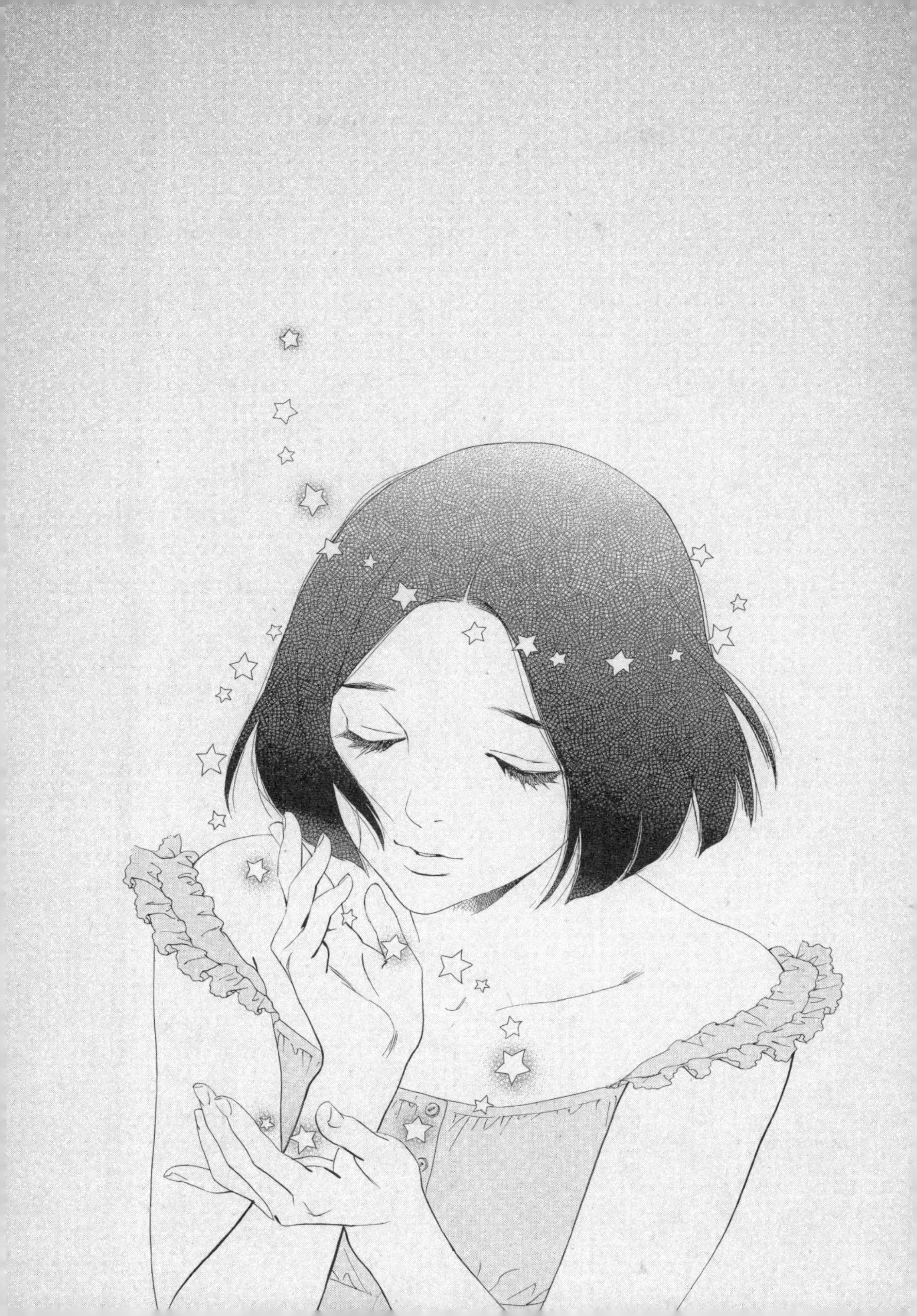

Spell 54
The Star and the Pebble

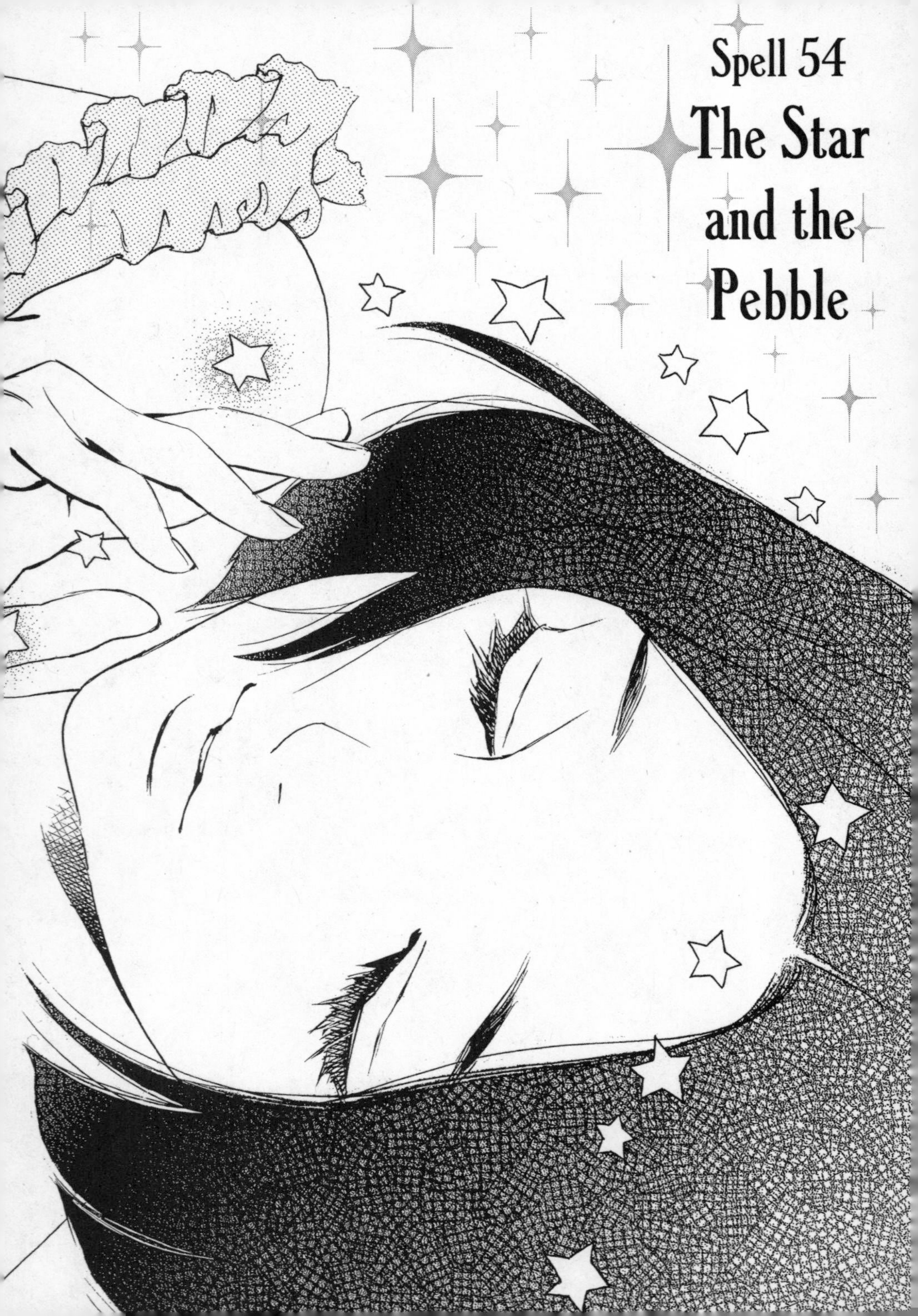

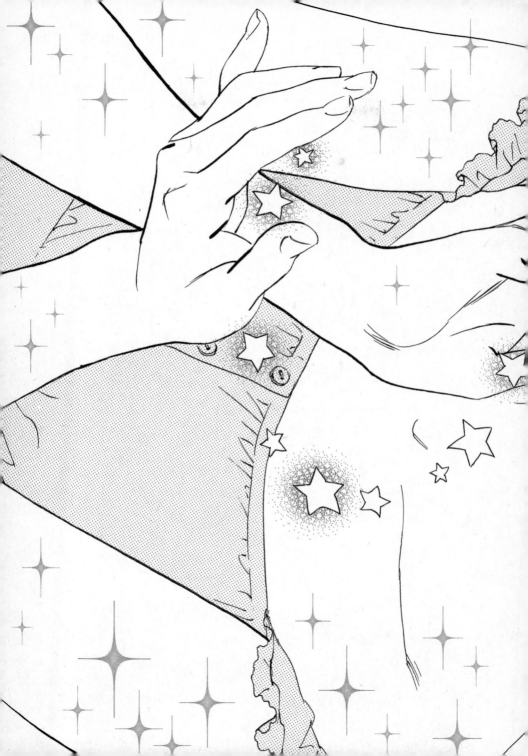

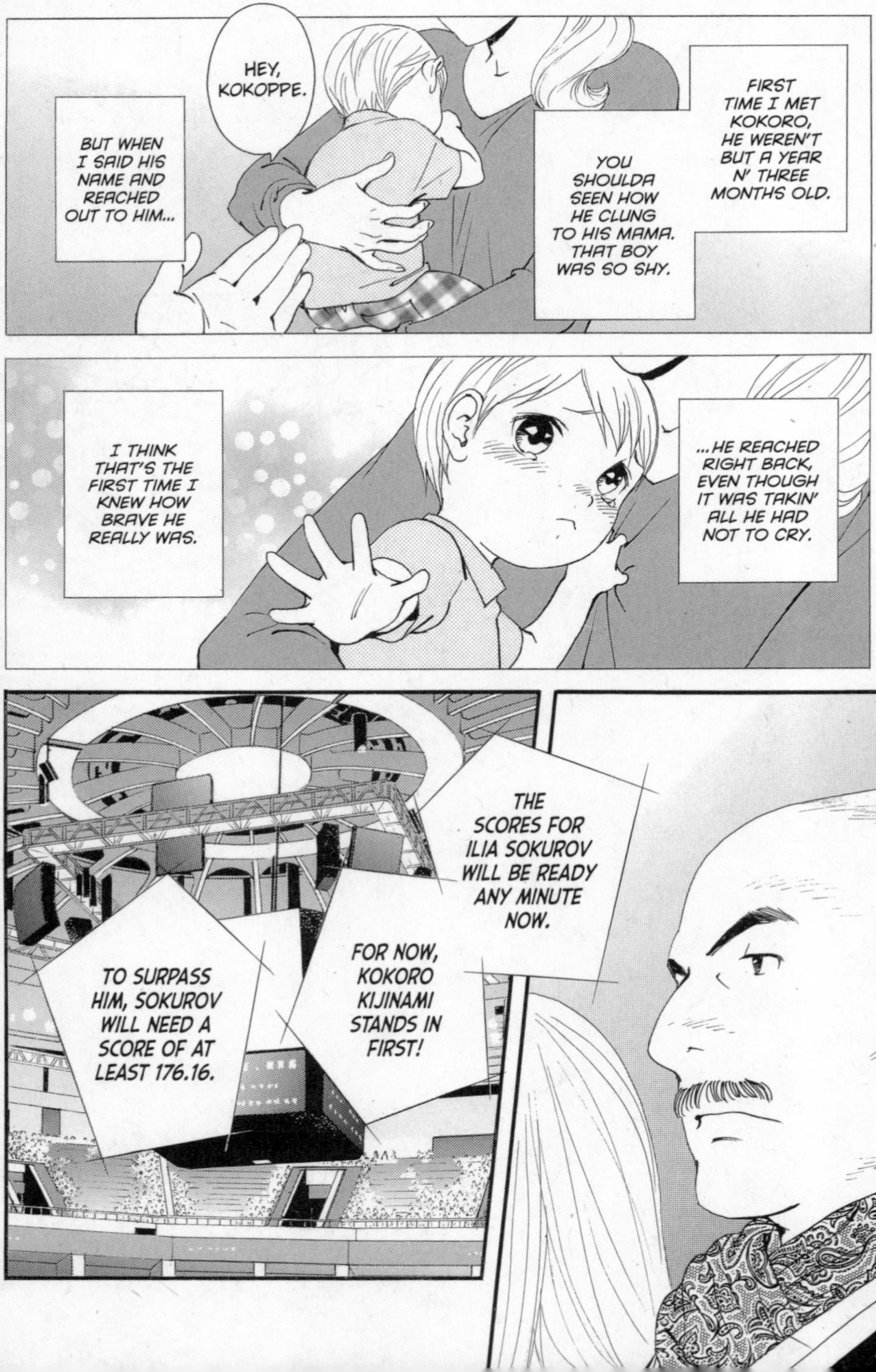
FIRST TIME I MET KOKORO, HE WEREN'T BUT A YEAR N' THREE MONTHS OLD.
YOU SHOULDA SEEN HOW HE CLUNG TO HIS MAMA. THAT BOY WAS SO SHY.
HEY, KOKOPPE.
BUT WHEN I SAID HIS NAME AND REACHED OUT TO HIM...
...HE REACHED RIGHT BACK, EVEN THOUGH IT WAS TAKIN' ALL HE HAD NOT TO CRY.
I THINK THAT'S THE FIRST TIME I KNEW HOW BRAVE HE REALLY WAS.
THE SCORES FOR ILIA SOKUROV WILL BE READY ANY MINUTE NOW.
FOR NOW, KOKORO KIJINAMI STANDS IN FIRST!
TO SURPASS HIM, SOKUROV WILL NEED A SCORE OF AT LEAST 176.16.

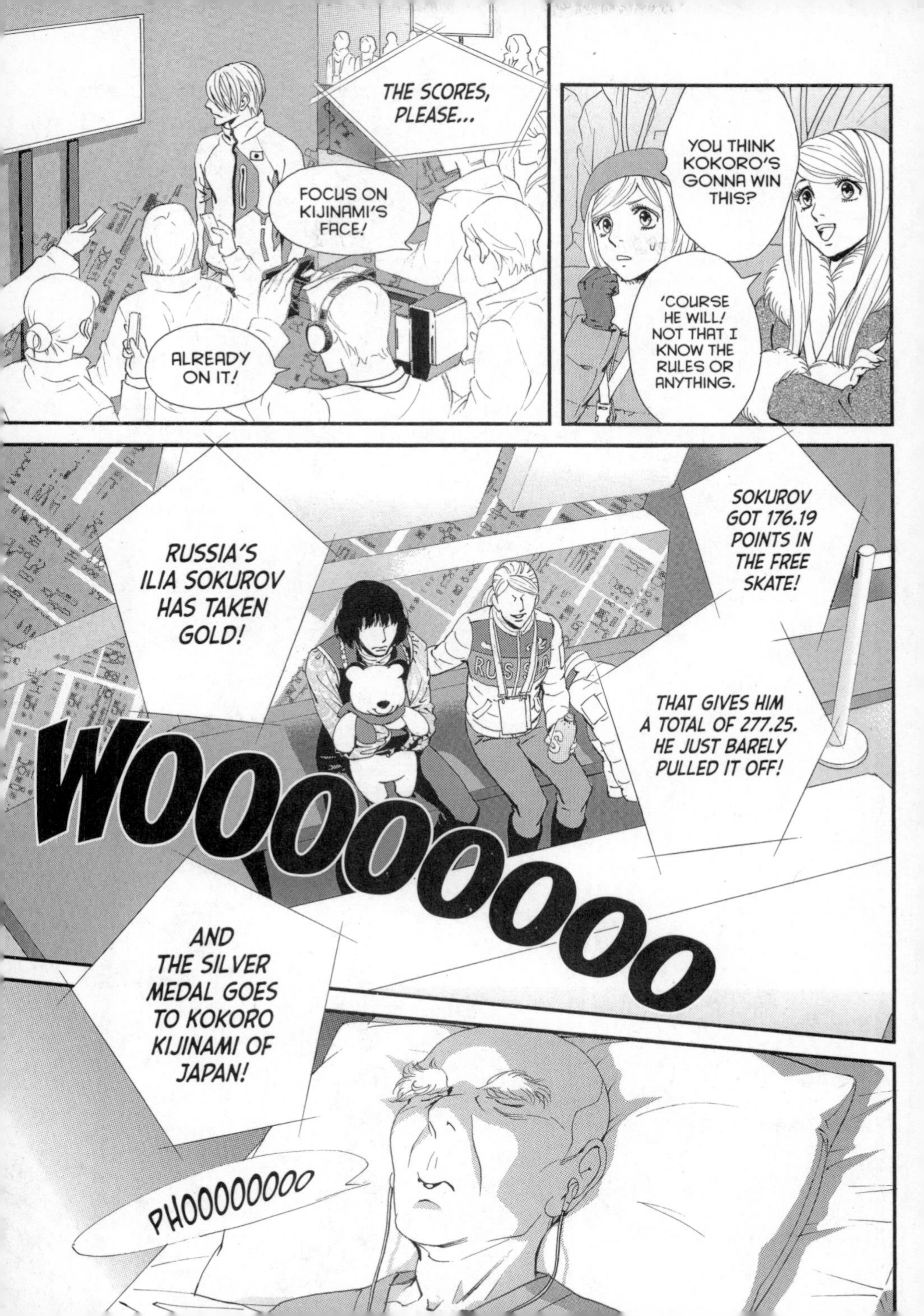
YOU THINK KOKORO'S GONNA WIN THIS?
'COURSE HE WILL! NOT THAT I KNOW THE RULES OR ANYTHING.
THE SCORES, PLEASE...
FOCUS ON KIJINAMI'S FACE!
ALREADY ON IT!
SOKUROV GOT 176.19 POINTS IN THE FREE SKATE!
RUSSIA'S ILIA SOKUROV HAS TAKEN GOLD!
THAT GIVES HIM A TOTAL OF 277.25. HE JUST BARELY PULLED IT OFF!
WOOOOOOOOOO
AND THE SILVER MEDAL GOES TO KOKORO KIJINAMI OF JAPAN!
PHOOOOOOOO

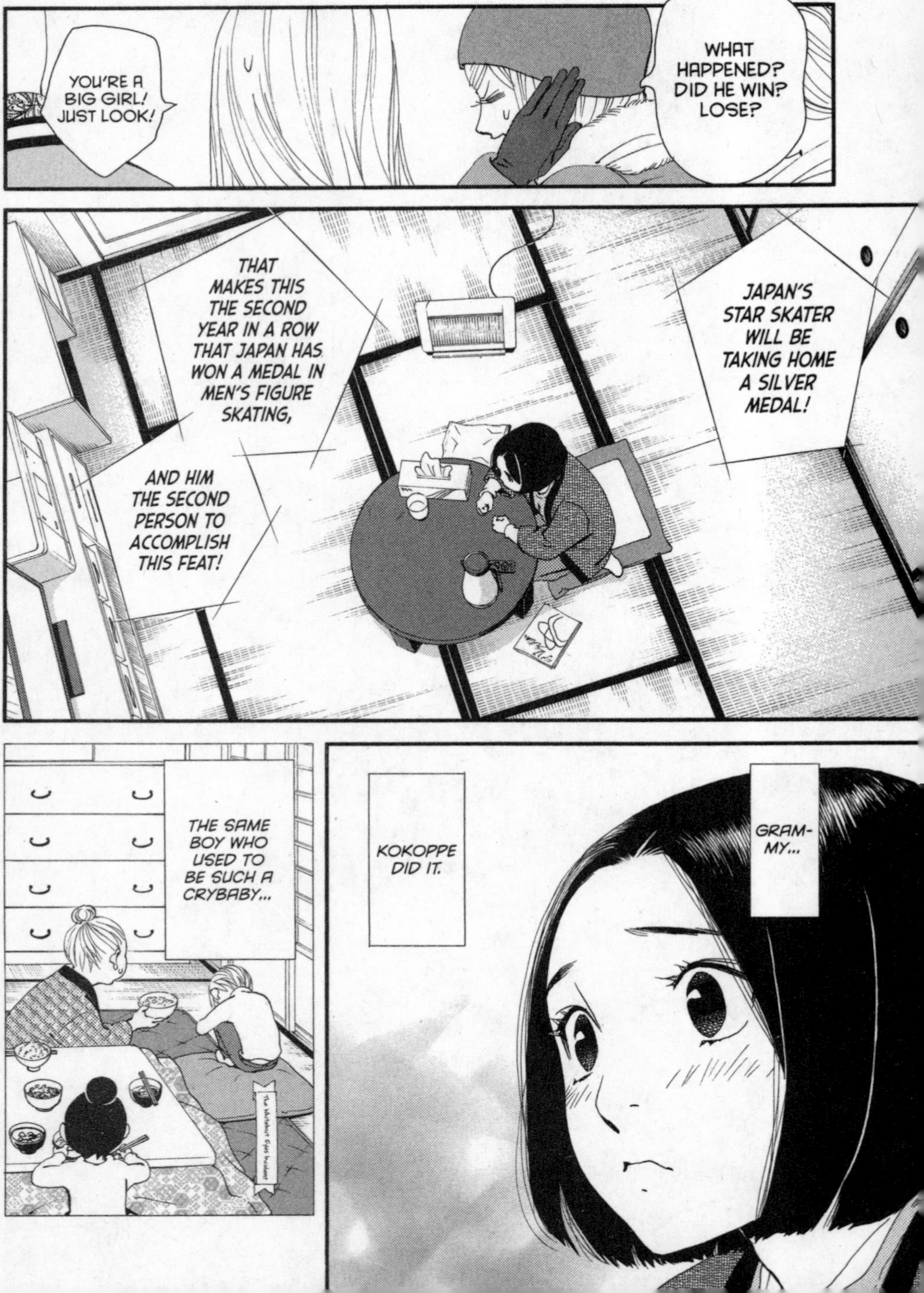
WHAT HAPPENED? DID HE WIN? LOSE?
YOU'RE A BIG GIRL! JUST LOOK!
JAPAN'S STAR SKATER WILL BE TAKING HOME A SILVER MEDAL!
THAT MAKES THIS THE SECOND YEAR IN A ROW THAT JAPAN HAS WON A MEDAL IN MEN'S FIGURE SKATING,
AND HIM THE SECOND PERSON TO ACCOMPLISH THIS FEAT!
GRAM-MY...
KOKOPPE DID IT.
THE SAME BOY WHO USED TO BE SUCH A CRYBABY...
The Whitebait Eyes Incident

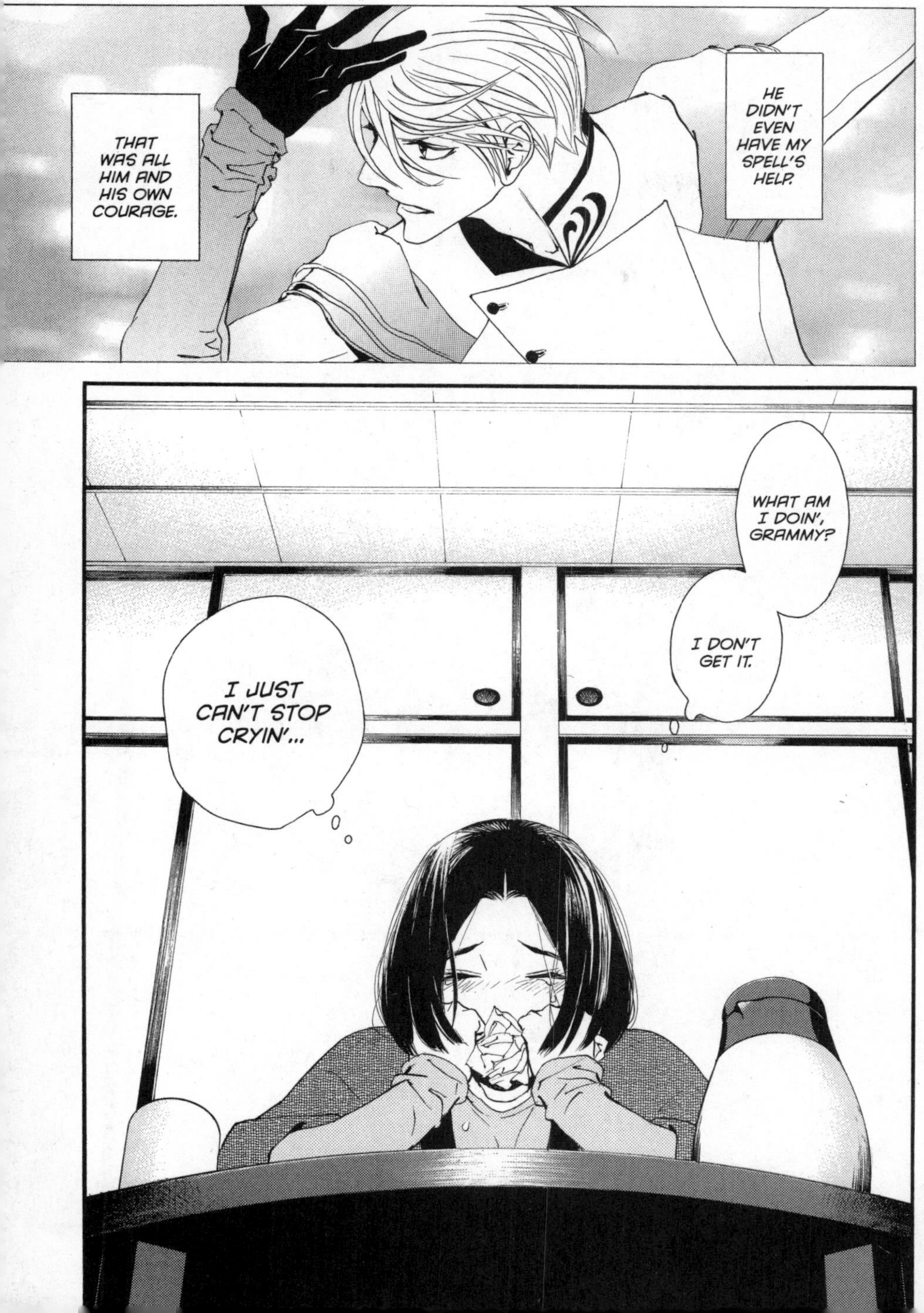
HE DIDN'T EVEN HAVE MY SPELL'S HELP.
THAT WAS ALL HIM AND HIS OWN COURAGE.
WHAT AM I DOIN', GRAMMY?
I DON'T GET IT.
I JUST CAN'T STOP CRYIN'...

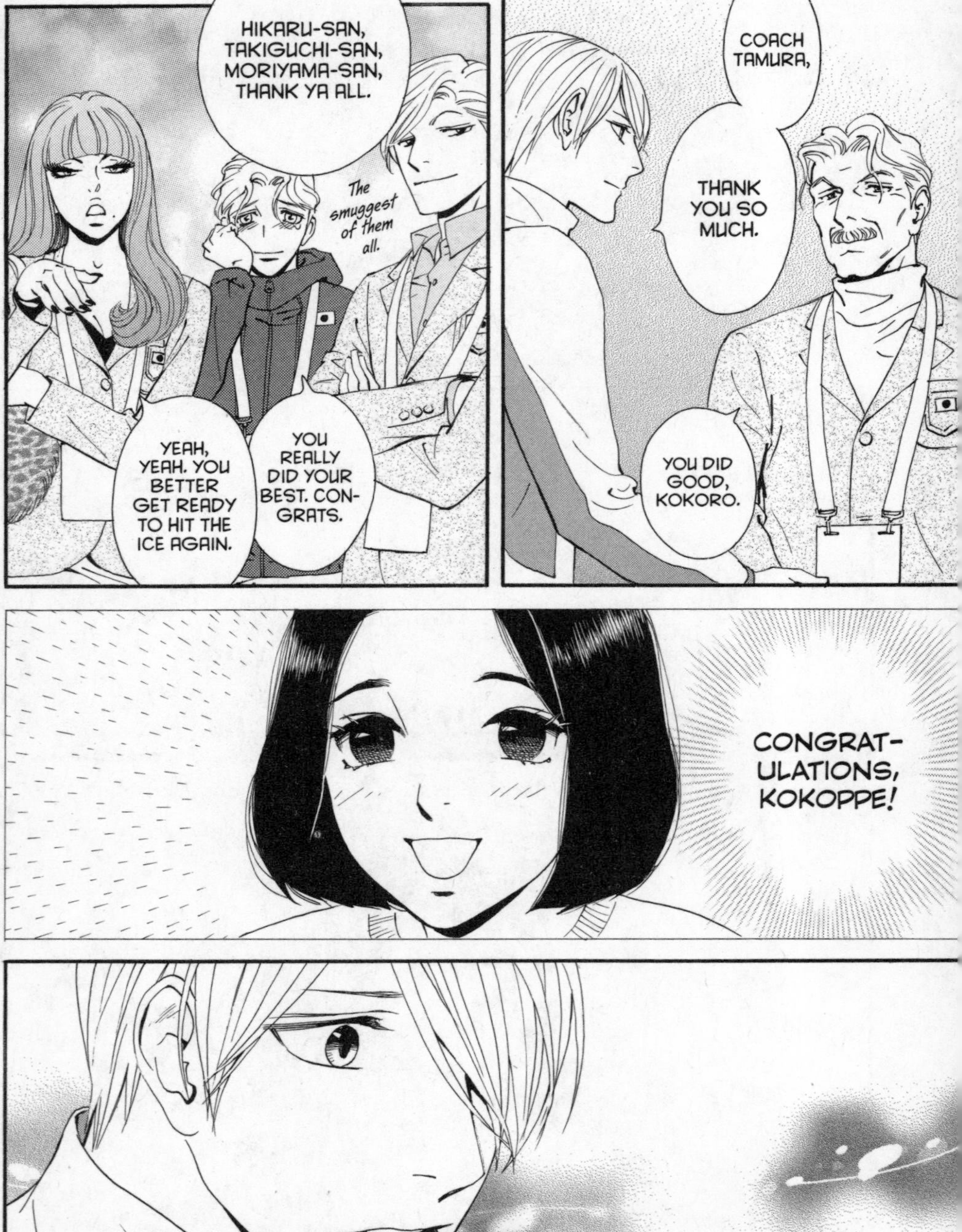
COACH TAMURA,
THANK YOU SO MUCH.
YOU DID GOOD, KOKORO.
HIKARU-SAN, TAKIGUCHI-SAN, MORIYAMA-SAN, THANK YA ALL.
The smuggest of them all.
YOU REALLY DID YOUR BEST. CON-GRATS.
YEAH, YEAH. YOU BETTER GET READY TO HIT THE ICE AGAIN.
CONGRAT-ULATIONS, KOKOPPE!

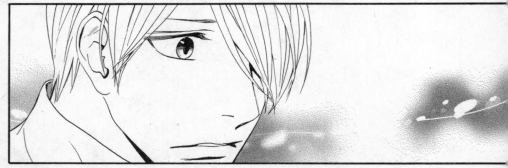

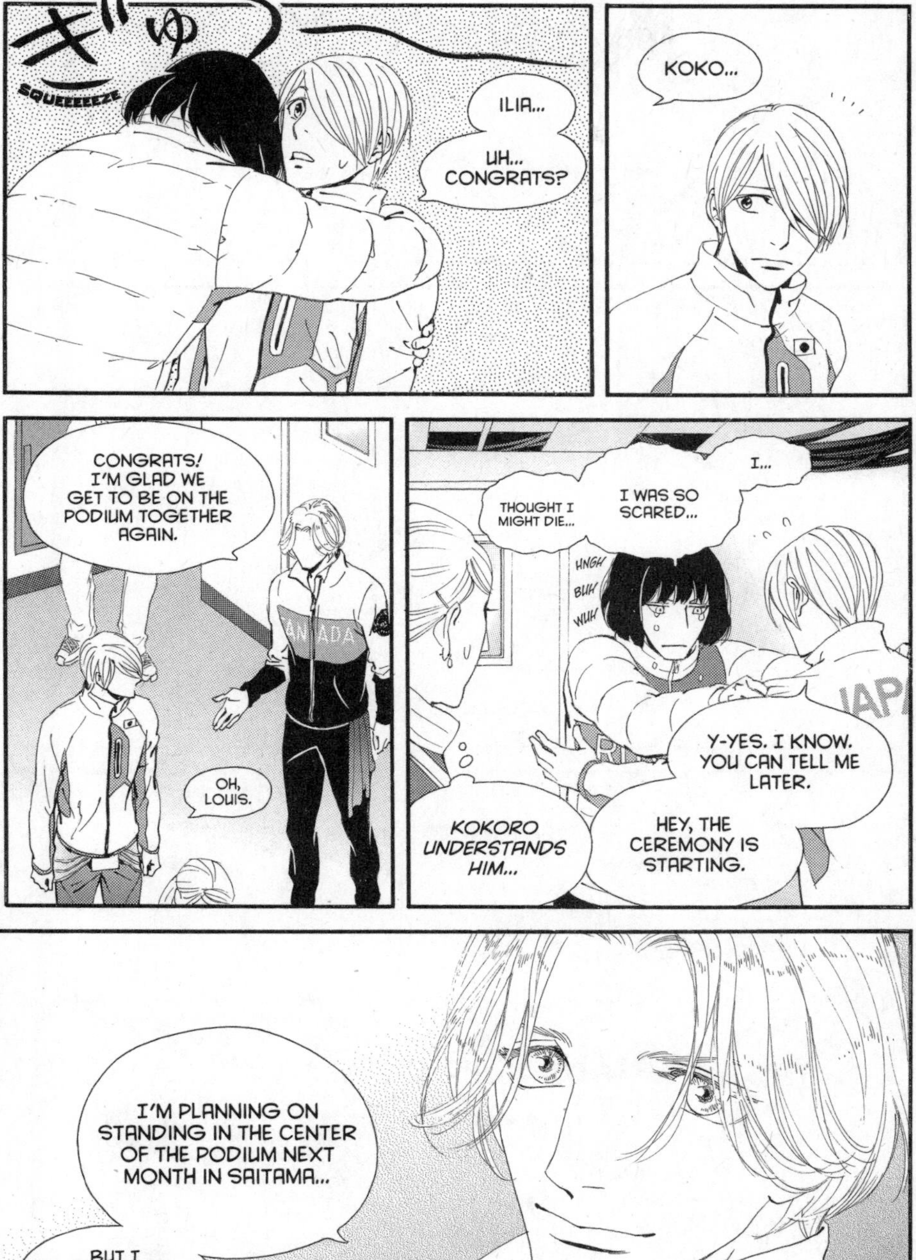
KOKO...
ぎゅう
SQUEEEEEEZE
ILIA...
UH... CONGRATS?
I...
I WAS SO SCARED...
THOUGHT I MIGHT DIE...
HNGH
BUH
WUH
Y-YES. I KNOW. YOU CAN TELL ME LATER.
HEY, THE CEREMONY IS STARTING.
KOKORO UNDERSTANDS HIM...
CONGRATS! I'M GLAD WE GET TO BE ON THE PODIUM TOGETHER AGAIN.
OH, LOUIS.
I'M PLANNING ON STANDING IN THE CENTER OF THE PODIUM NEXT MONTH IN SAITAMA...
BUT I GUESS I'LL HAVE TO GET PAST YOU FIRST, HUH?

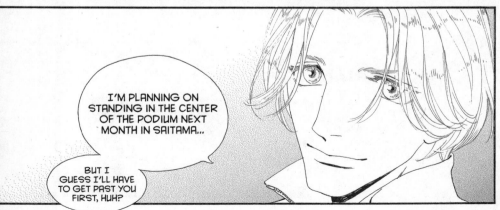

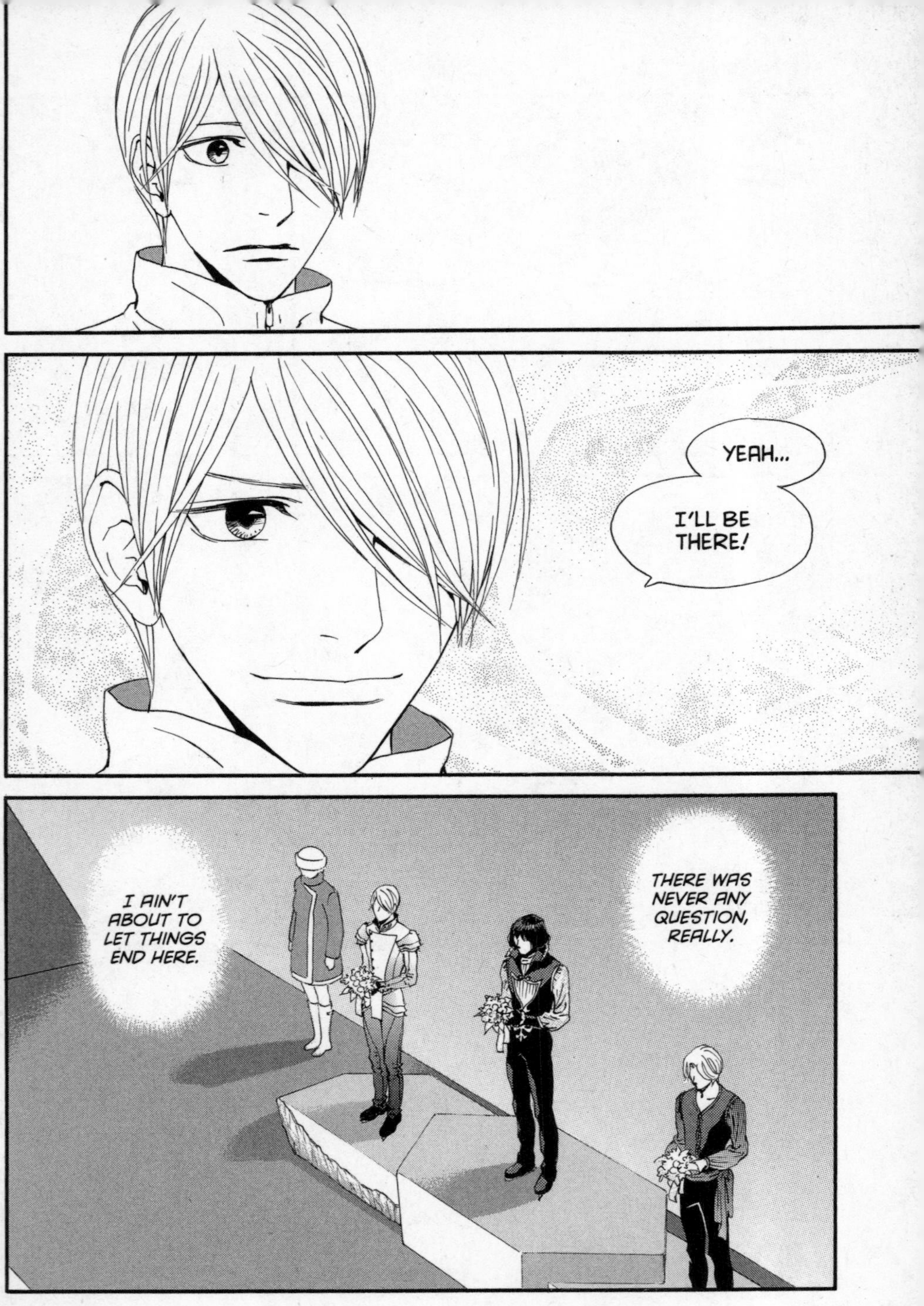
YEAH...
I'LL BE THERE!
THERE WAS NEVER ANY QUESTION, REALLY.
I AIN'T ABOUT TO LET THINGS END HERE.

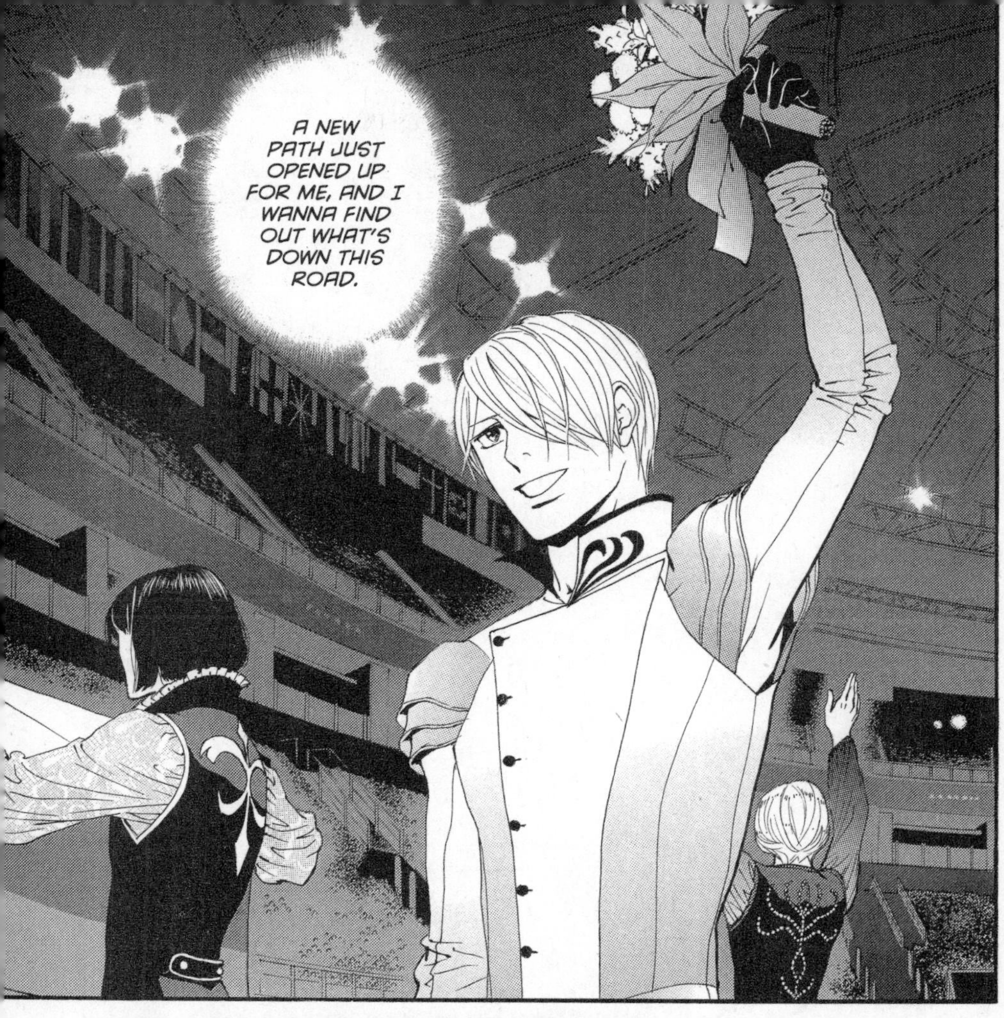
A NEW PATH JUST OPENED UP FOR ME, AND I WANNA FIND OUT WHAT'S DOWN THIS ROAD.

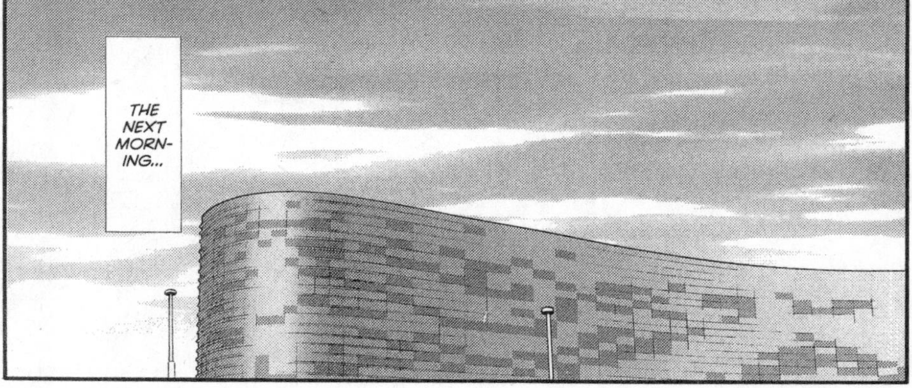
THE NEXT MORNING...

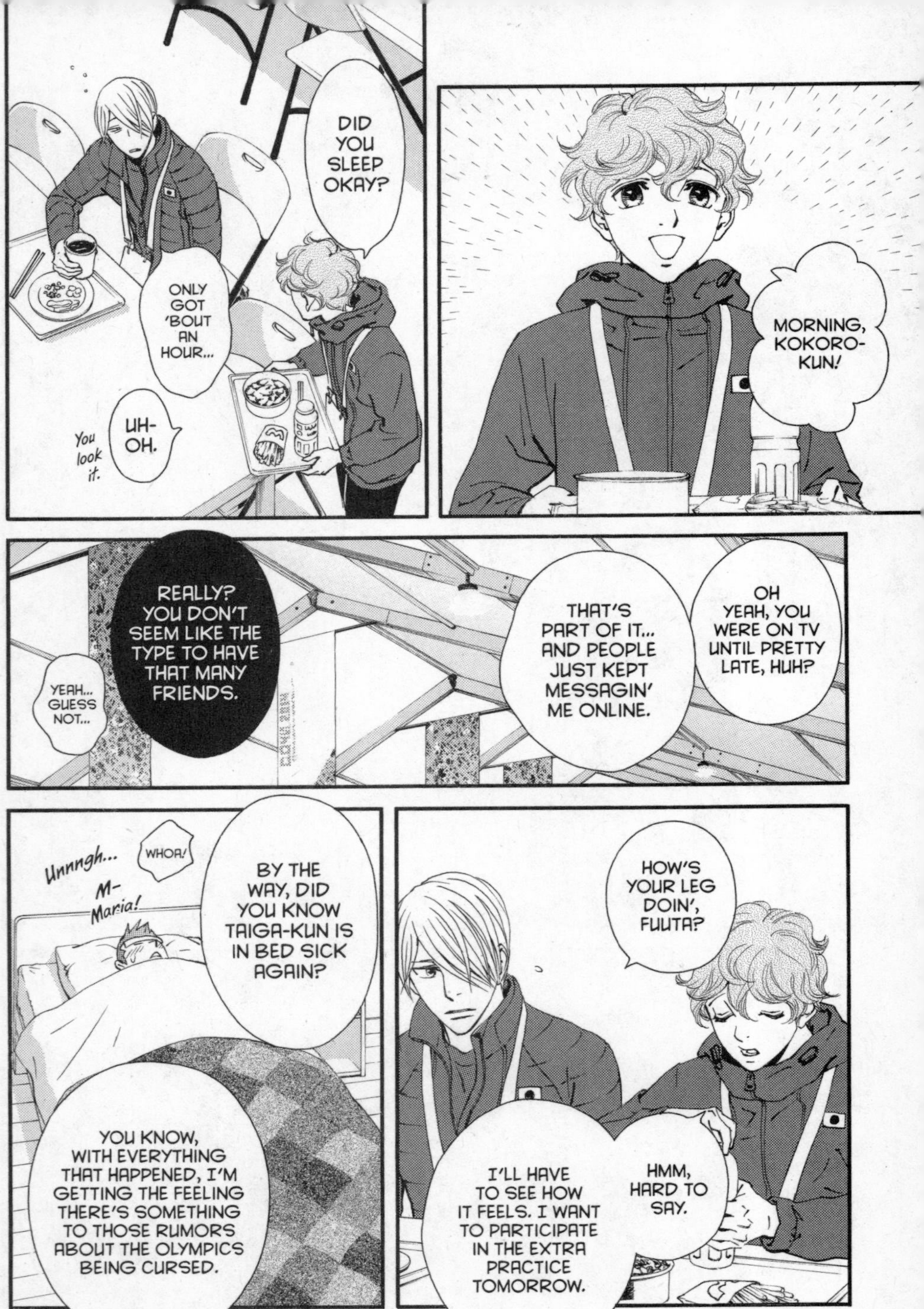
MORNING, KOKORO-KUN!
DID YOU SLEEP OKAY?
ONLY GOT 'BOUT AN HOUR...
UH-OH.
You look it.
OH YEAH, YOU WERE ON TV UNTIL PRETTY LATE, HUH?
THAT'S PART OF IT... AND PEOPLE JUST KEPT MESSAGIN' ME ONLINE.
REALLY? YOU DON'T SEEM LIKE THE TYPE TO HAVE THAT MANY FRIENDS.
YEAH... GUESS NOT...
HOW'S YOUR LEG DOIN', FUUTA?
HMM, HARD TO SAY.
I'LL HAVE TO SEE HOW IT FEELS. I WANT TO PARTICIPATE IN THE EXTRA PRACTICE TOMORROW.
BY THE WAY, DID YOU KNOW TAIGA-KUN IS IN BED SICK AGAIN?
WHOA!
Unnngh...
M-Maria!
YOU KNOW, WITH EVERYTHING THAT HAPPENED, I'M GETTING THE FEELING THERE'S SOMETHING TO THOSE RUMORS ABOUT THE OLYMPICS BEING CURSED.

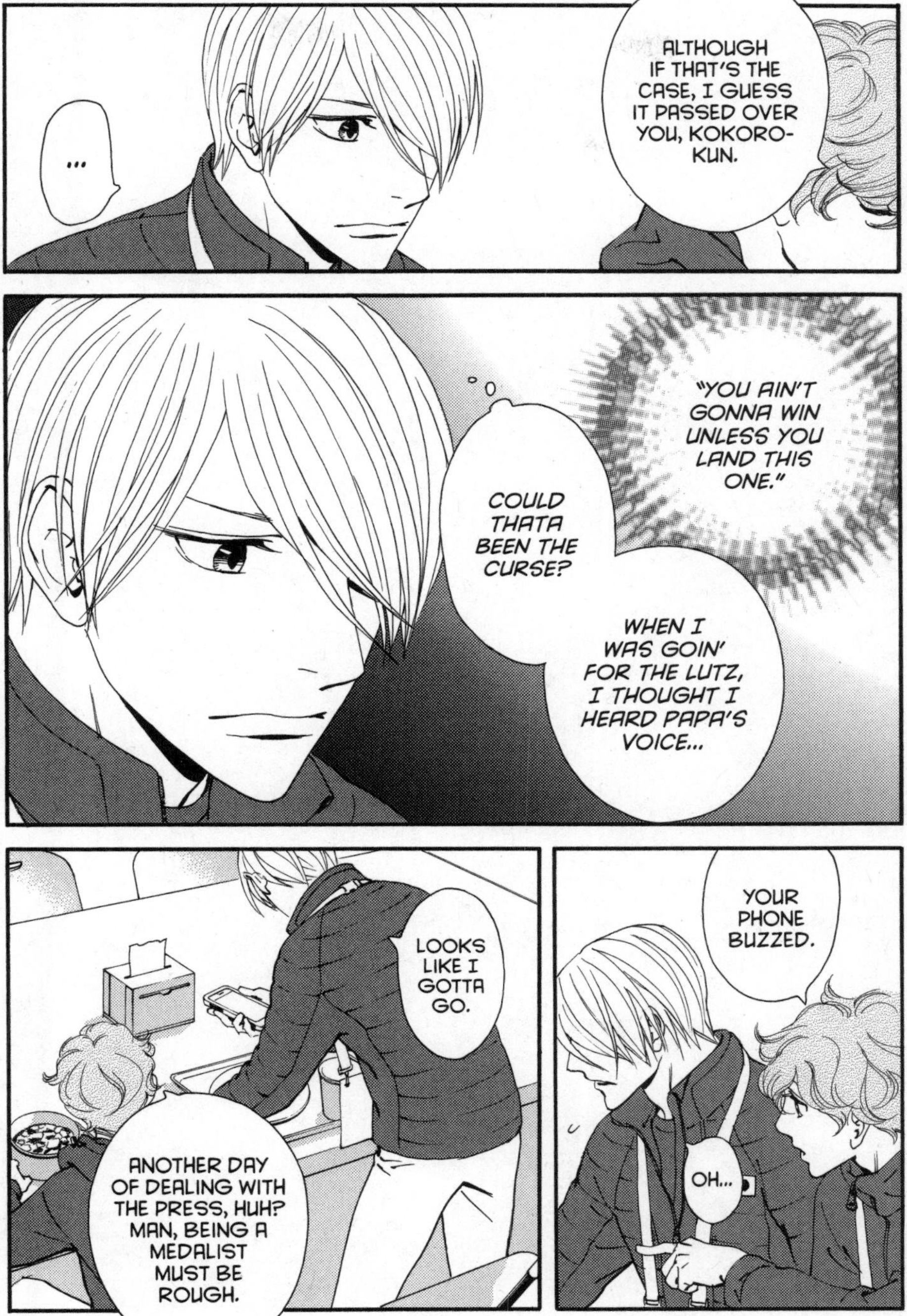
ALTHOUGH IF THAT'S THE CASE, I GUESS IT PASSED OVER YOU, KOKORO-KUN.
...
"YOU AIN'T GONNA WIN UNLESS YOU LAND THIS ONE."
COULD THATA BEEN THE CURSE?
WHEN I WAS GOIN' FOR THE LUTZ, I THOUGHT I HEARD PAPA'S VOICE...
YOUR PHONE BUZZED.
OH...
LOOKS LIKE I GOTTA GO.
ANOTHER DAY OF DEALING WITH THE PRESS, HUH? MAN, BEING A MEDALIST MUST BE ROUGH.

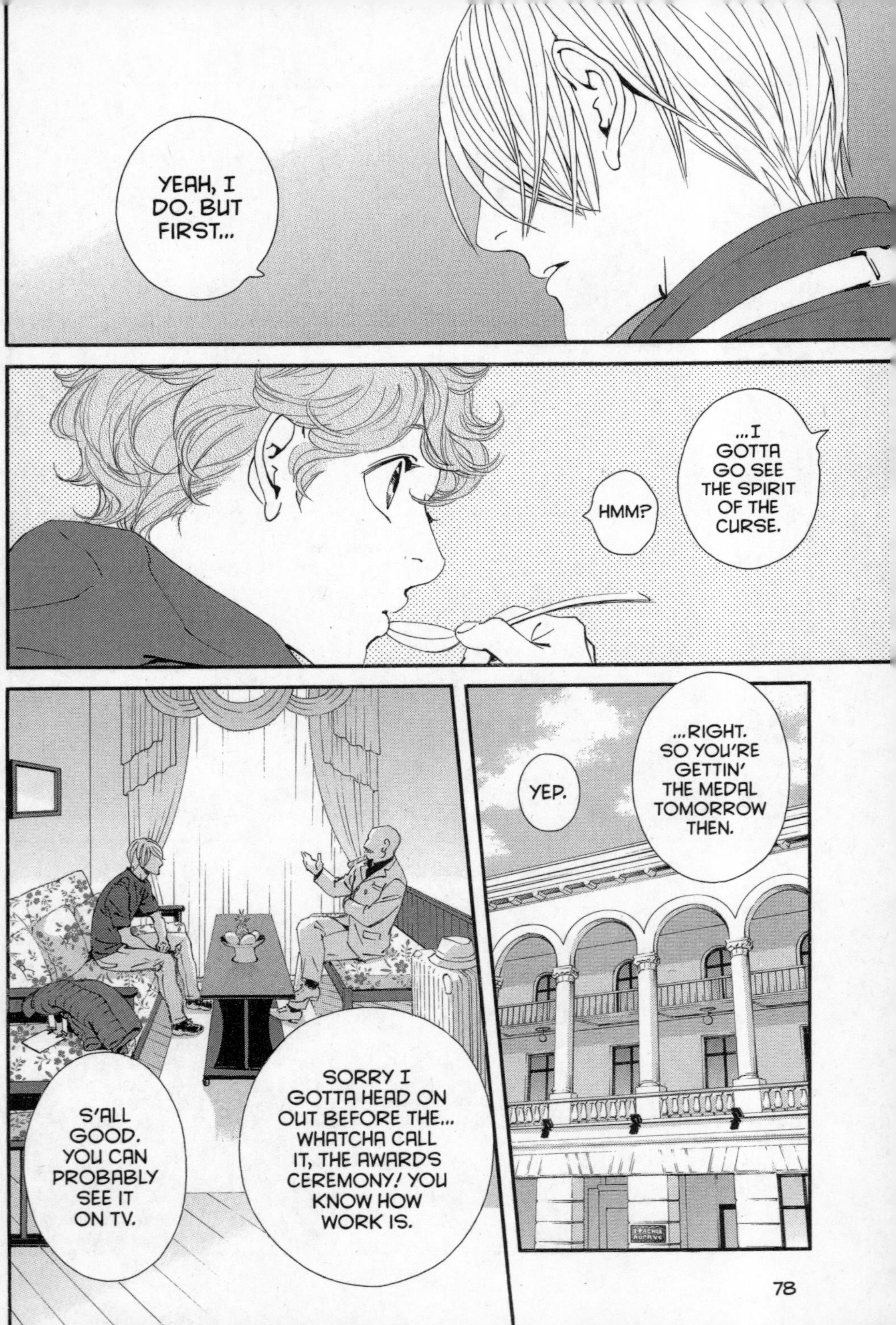
YEAH, I DO. BUT FIRST...
...I GOTTA GO SEE THE SPIRIT OF THE CURSE.
HMM?
...RIGHT. SO YOU'RE GETTIN' THE MEDAL TOMORROW THEN.
YEP.
SORRY I GOTTA HEAD ON OUT BEFORE THE... WHATCHA CALL IT, THE AWARDS CEREMONY! YOU KNOW HOW WORK IS.
S'ALL GOOD. YOU CAN PROBABLY SEE IT ON TV.

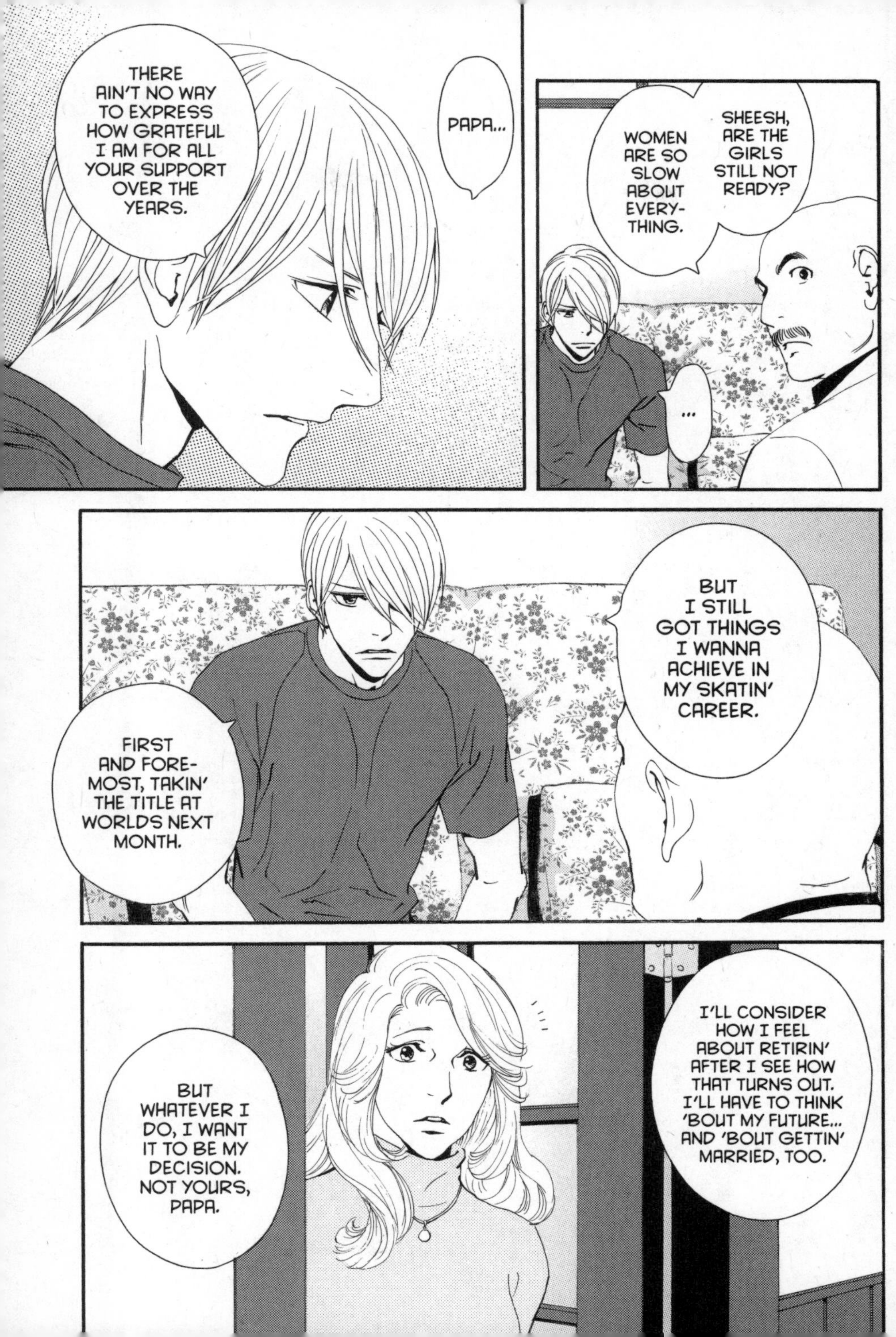
SHEESH, ARE THE GIRLS STILL NOT READY?
WOMEN ARE SO SLOW ABOUT EVERY-THING.
...
PAPA...
THERE AIN'T NO WAY TO EXPRESS HOW GRATEFUL I AM FOR ALL YOUR SUPPORT OVER THE YEARS.
BUT I STILL GOT THINGS I WANNA ACHIEVE IN MY SKATIN' CAREER.
FIRST AND FORE-MOST, TAKIN' THE TITLE AT WORLDS NEXT MONTH.
I'LL CONSIDER HOW I FEEL ABOUT RETIRIN' AFTER I SEE HOW THAT TURNS OUT. I'LL HAVE TO THINK 'BOUT MY FUTURE... AND 'BOUT GETTIN' MARRIED, TOO.
BUT WHATEVER I DO, I WANT IT TO BE MY DECISION. NOT YOURS, PAPA.

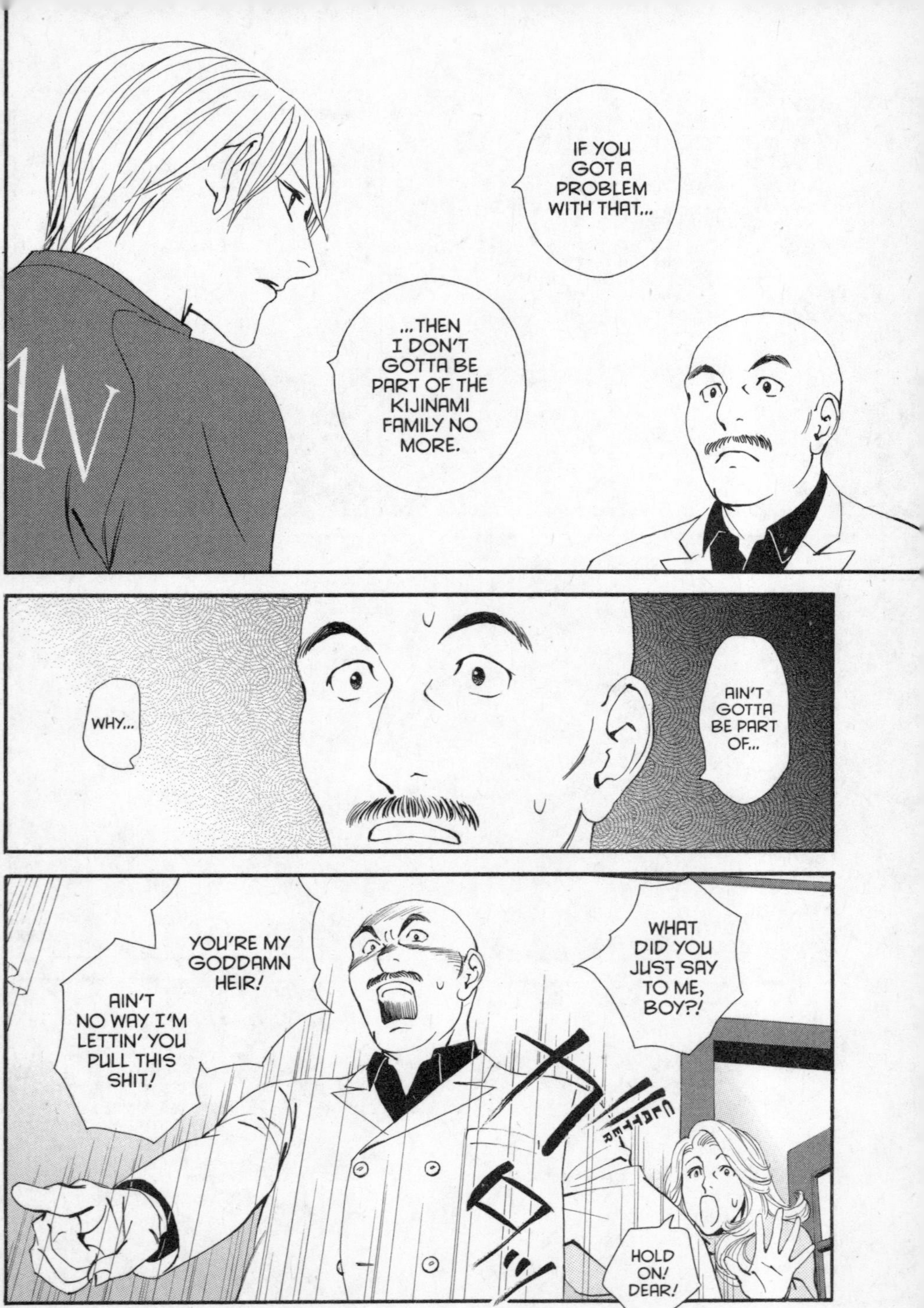
IF YOU GOT A PROBLEM WITH THAT...
...THEN I DON'T GOTTA BE PART OF THE KIJINAMI FAMILY NO MORE.
AIN'T GOTTA BE PART OF...
WHY...
WHAT DID YOU JUST SAY TO ME, BOY?!
YOU'RE MY GODDAMN HEIR!
AIN'T NO WAY I'M LETTIN' YOU PULL THIS SHIT!
HOLD ON! DEAR!

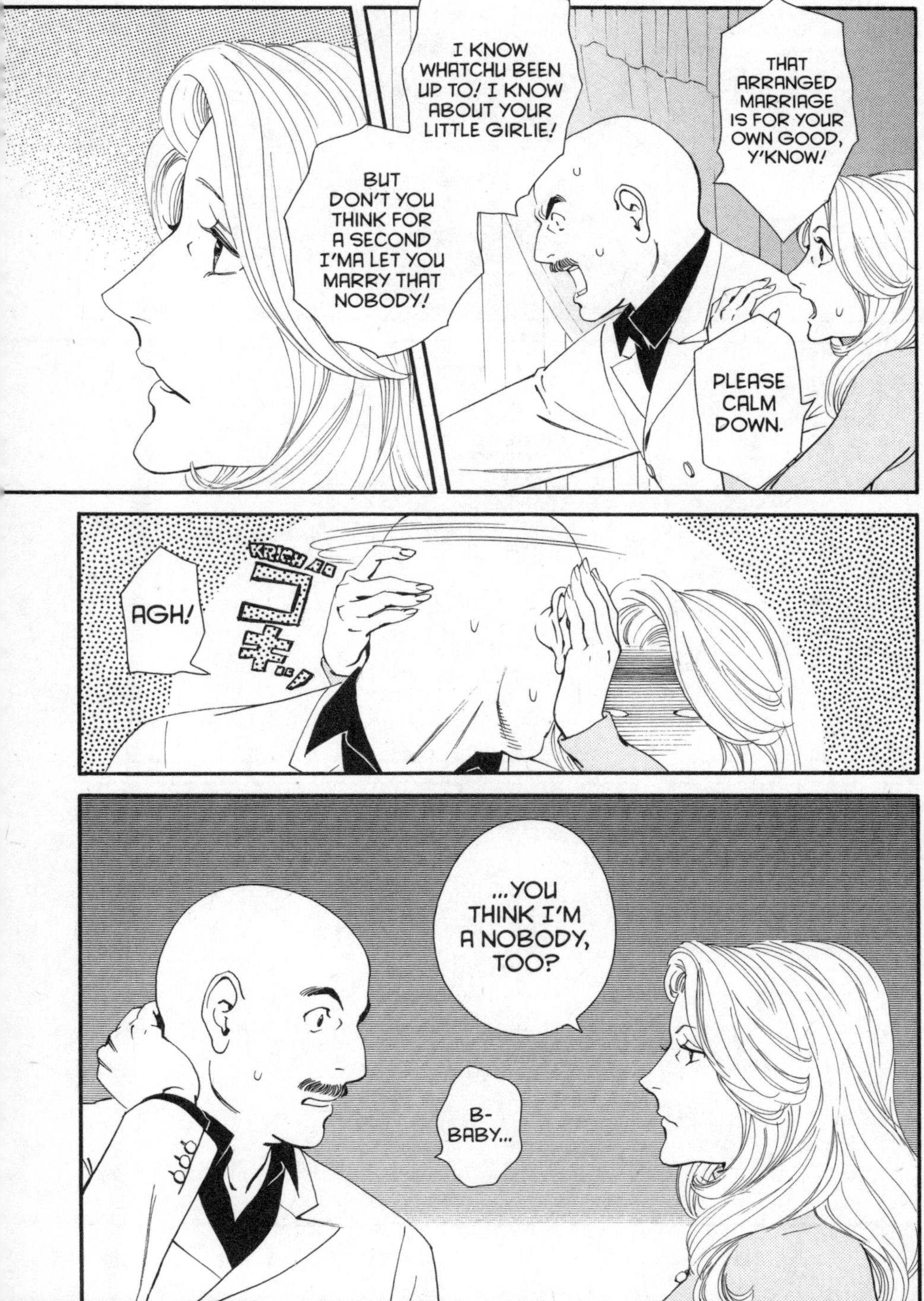
THAT ARRANGED MARRIAGE IS FOR YOUR OWN GOOD, Y'KNOW!
I KNOW WHATCHU BEEN UP TO! I KNOW ABOUT YOUR LITTLE GIRLIE!
PLEASE CALM DOWN.
BUT DON'T YOU THINK FOR A SECOND I'MA LET YOU MARRY THAT NOBODY!
KRICH
AGH!
...YOU THINK I'M A NOBODY, TOO?
B- BABY...

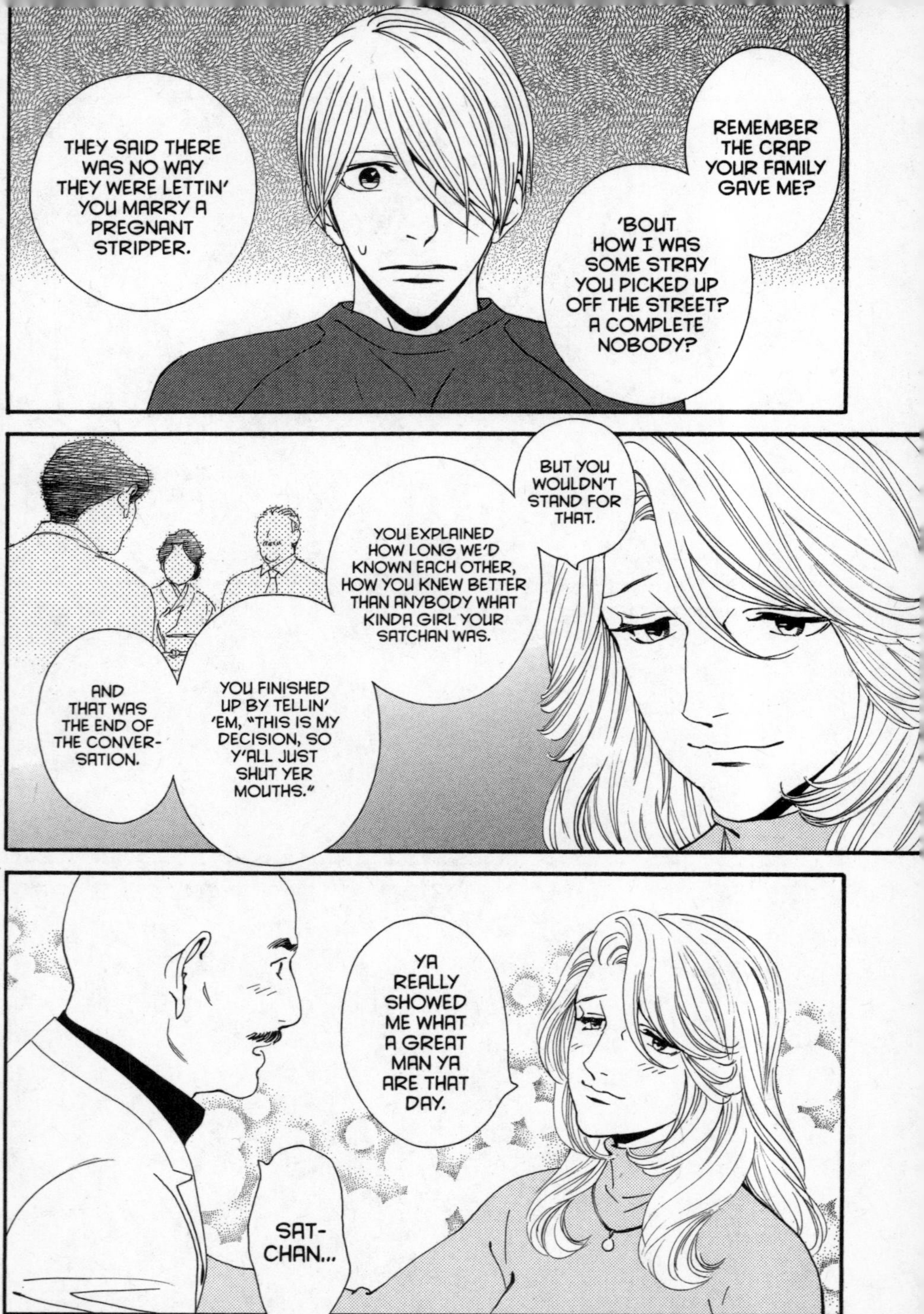
REMEMBER THE CRAP YOUR FAMILY GAVE ME?
'BOUT HOW I WAS SOME STRAY YOU PICKED UP OFF THE STREET? A COMPLETE NOBODY?
THEY SAID THERE WAS NO WAY THEY WERE LETTIN' YOU MARRY A PREGNANT STRIPPER.
BUT YOU WOULDN'T STAND FOR THAT.
YOU EXPLAINED HOW LONG WE'D KNOWN EACH OTHER, HOW YOU KNEW BETTER THAN ANYBODY WHAT KINDA GIRL YOUR SATCHAN WAS.
YOU FINISHED UP BY TELLIN' 'EM, "THIS IS MY DECISION, SO Y'ALL JUST SHUT YER MOUTHS."
AND THAT WAS THE END OF THE CONVER-SATION.
YA REALLY SHOWED ME WHAT A GREAT MAN YA ARE THAT DAY.
SAT-CHAN...

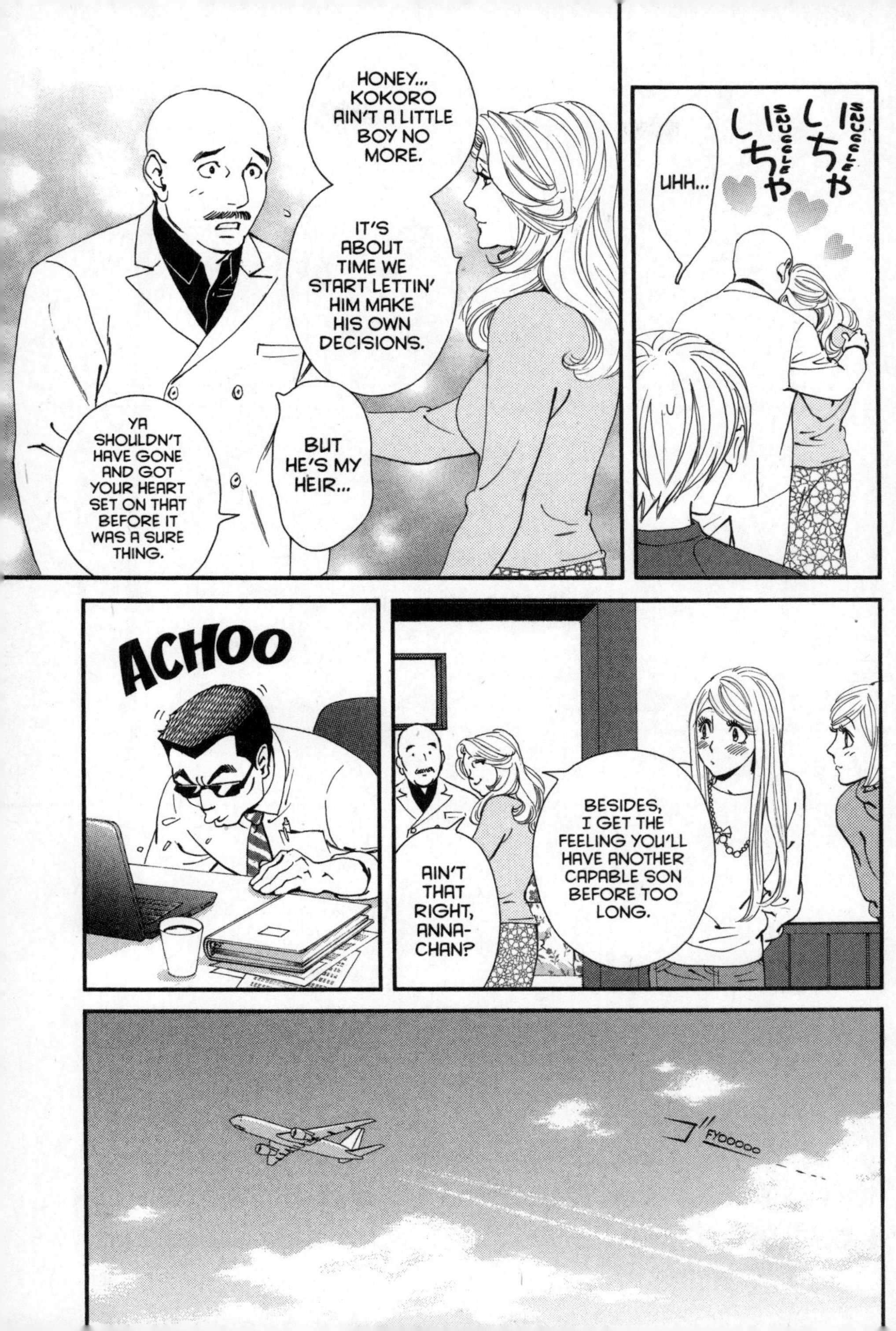

いちゃ SNUGGLE
いちゃ SNUGGLE
UHH...
HONEY... KOKORO AIN'T A LITTLE BOY NO MORE.
IT'S ABOUT TIME WE START LETTIN' HIM MAKE HIS OWN DECISIONS.
BUT HE'S MY HEIR...
YA SHOULDN'T HAVE GONE AND GOT YOUR HEART SET ON THAT BEFORE IT WAS A SURE THING.
BESIDES, I GET THE FEELING YOU'LL HAVE ANOTHER CAPABLE SON BEFORE TOO LONG.
AIN'T THAT RIGHT, ANNA-CHAN?
ACHOO
ゴ FYOOOOO

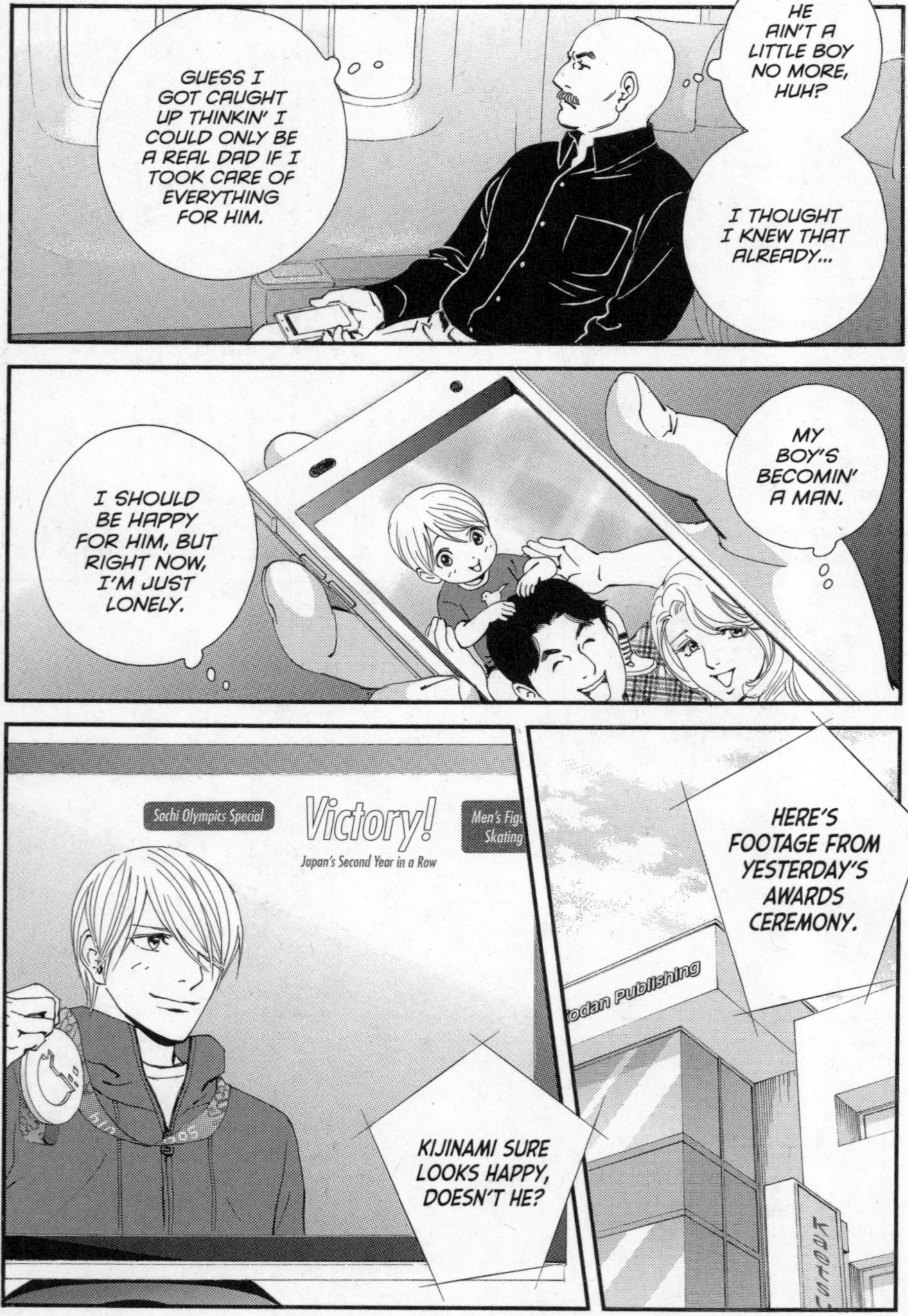
HE AIN'T A LITTLE BOY NO MORE, HUH?
I THOUGHT I KNEW THAT ALREADY...
GUESS I GOT CAUGHT UP THINKIN' I COULD ONLY BE A REAL DAD IF I TOOK CARE OF EVERYTHING FOR HIM.
MY BOY'S BECOMIN' A MAN.
I SHOULD BE HAPPY FOR HIM, BUT RIGHT NOW, I'M JUST LONELY.
HERE'S FOOTAGE FROM YESTERDAY'S AWARDS CEREMONY.
Kodan Publishing
Sochi Olympics Special
Victory!
Japan's Second Year in a Row
KIJINAMI SURE LOOKS HAPPY, DOESN'T HE?

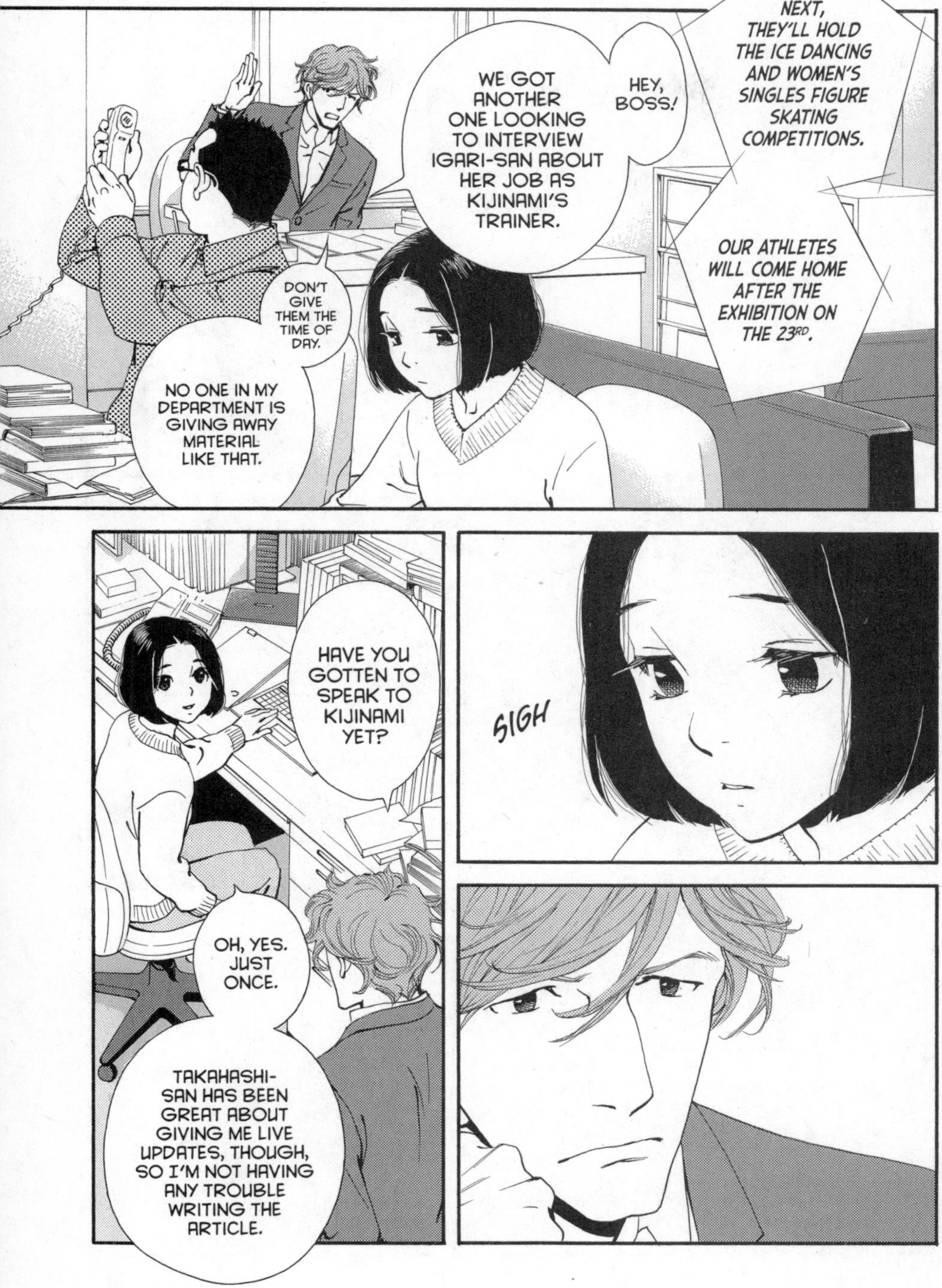
NEXT, THEY'LL HOLD THE ICE DANCING AND WOMEN'S SINGLES FIGURE SKATING COMPETITIONS.
OUR ATHLETES WILL COME HOME AFTER THE EXHIBITION ON THE 23RD.
HEY, BOSS!
WE GOT ANOTHER ONE LOOKING TO INTERVIEW IGARI-SAN ABOUT HER JOB AS KIJINAMI'S TRAINER.
DON'T GIVE THEM THE TIME OF DAY.
NO ONE IN MY DEPARTMENT IS GIVING AWAY MATERIAL LIKE THAT.
SIGH
HAVE YOU GOTTEN TO SPEAK TO KIJINAMI YET?
OH, YES. JUST ONCE.
TAKAHASHI-SAN HAS BEEN GREAT ABOUT GIVING ME LIVE UPDATES, THOUGH, SO I'M NOT HAVING ANY TROUBLE WRITING THE ARTICLE.

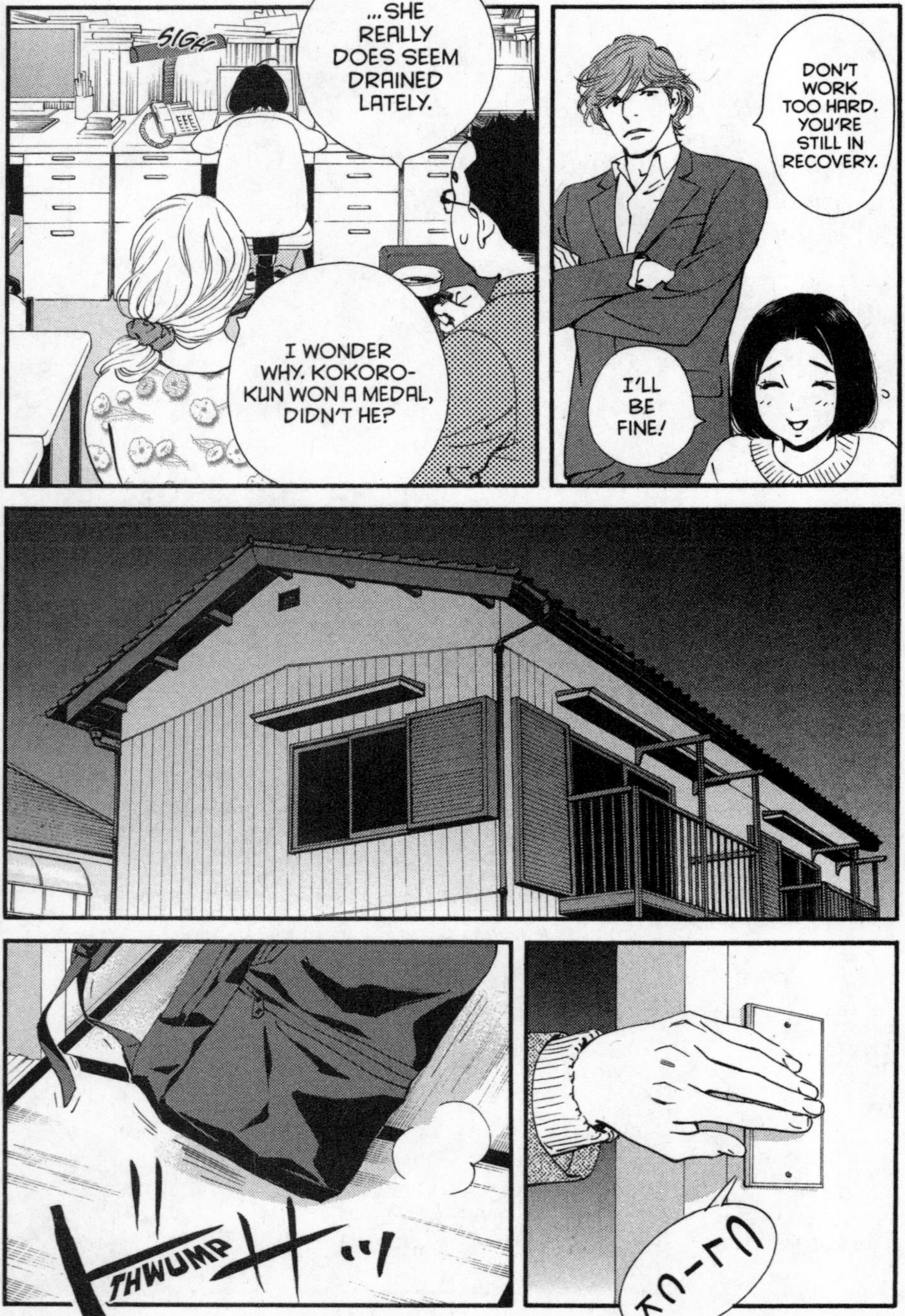
DON'T WORK TOO HARD. YOU'RE STILL IN RECOVERY.
I'LL BE FINE!
SIGH
...SHE REALLY DOES SEEM DRAINED LATELY.
I WONDER WHY. KOKORO-KUN WON A MEDAL, DIDN'T HE?
THWUMP

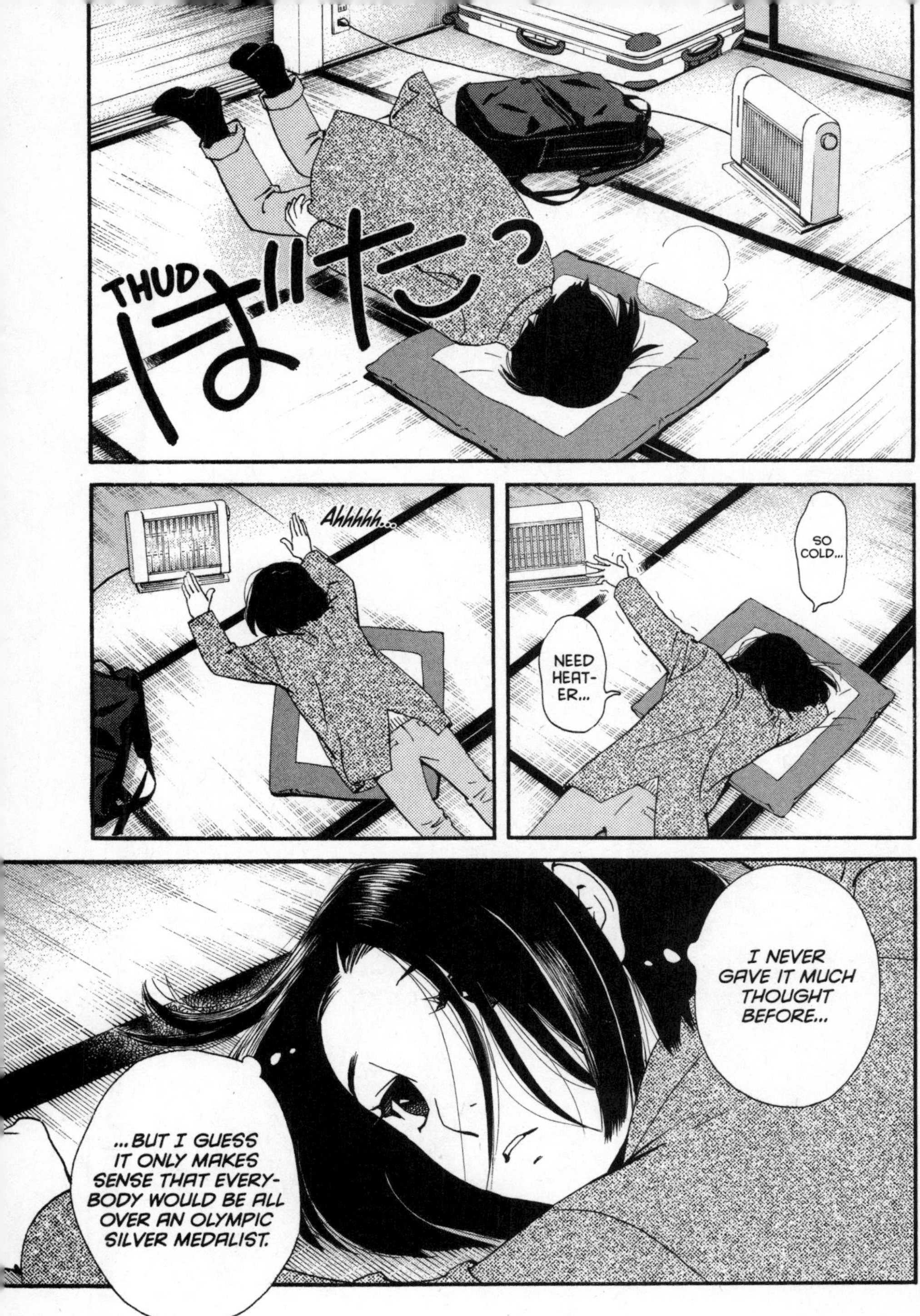
THUD
ばたっ
SO COLD...
NEED HEAT-ER...
Ahhhhh...
I NEVER GAVE IT MUCH THOUGHT BEFORE...
...BUT I GUESS IT ONLY MAKES SENSE THAT EVERY-BODY WOULD BE ALL OVER AN OLYMPIC SILVER MEDALIST.

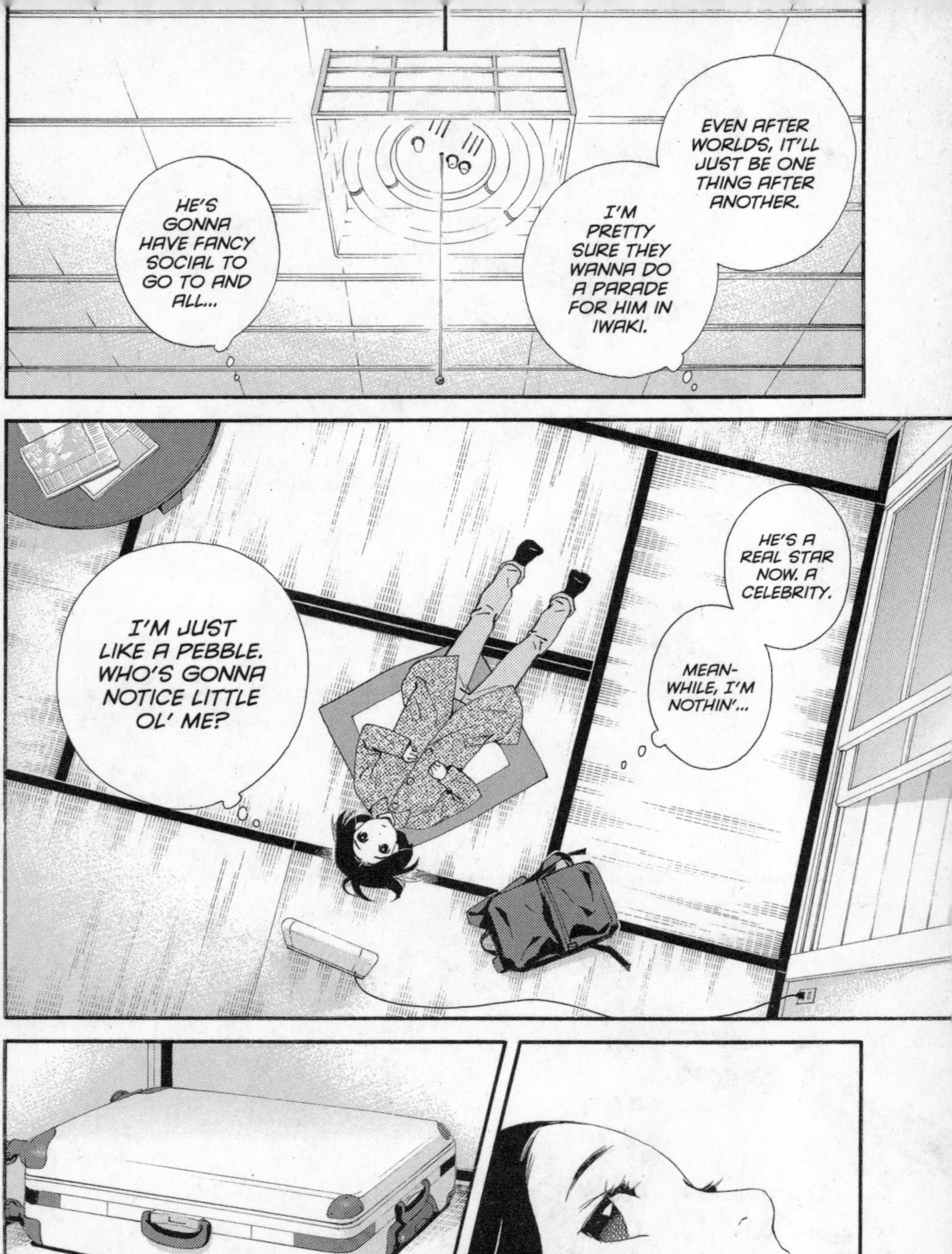
EVEN AFTER WORLDS, IT'LL JUST BE ONE THING AFTER ANOTHER.
I'M PRETTY SURE THEY WANNA DO A PARADE FOR HIM IN IWAKI.
HE'S GONNA HAVE FANCY SOCIAL TO GO TO AND ALL...
HE'S A REAL STAR NOW. A CELEBRITY.
MEAN-WHILE, I'M NOTHIN'...
I'M JUST LIKE A PEBBLE. WHO'S GONNA NOTICE LITTLE OL' ME?

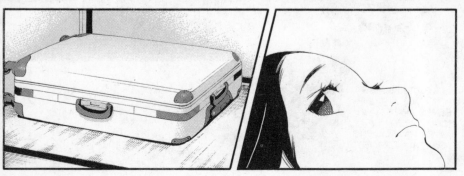

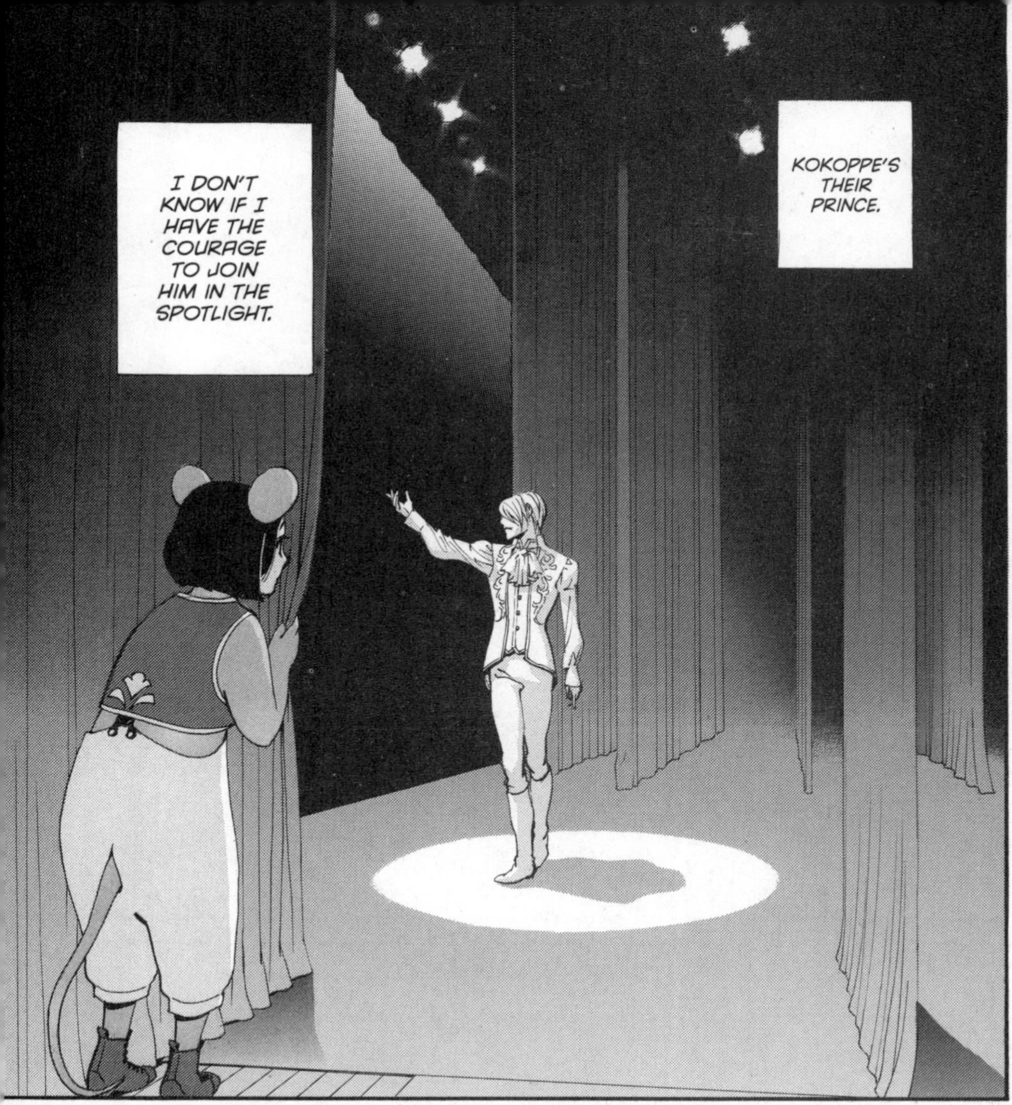
KOKOPPE'S THEIR PRINCE.
I DON'T KNOW IF I HAVE THE COURAGE TO JOIN HIM IN THE SPOTLIGHT.

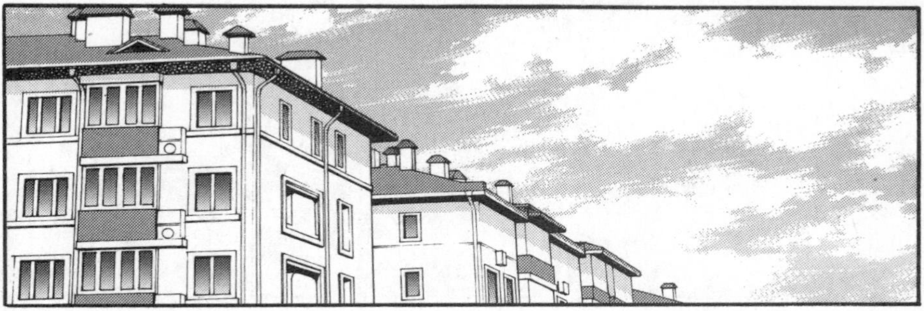

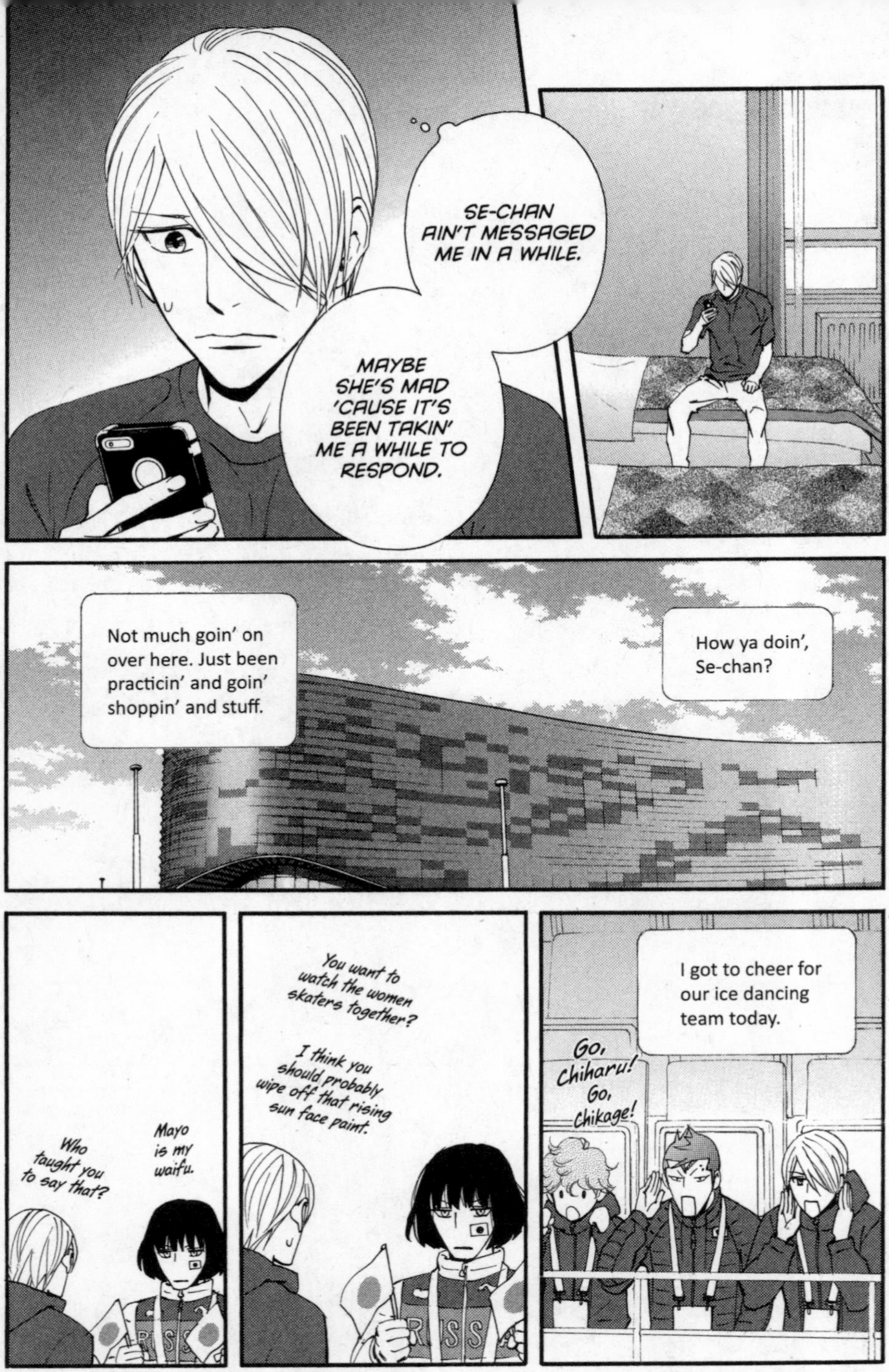
SE-CHAN AIN'T MESSAGED ME IN A WHILE.
MAYBE SHE'S MAD 'CAUSE IT'S BEEN TAKIN' ME A WHILE TO RESPOND.
How ya doin', Se-chan?
Not much goin' on over here. Just been practicin' and goin' shoppin' and stuff.
I got to cheer for our ice dancing team today.
Go, Chiharu! Go, Chikage!
You want to watch the women skaters together?
I think you should probably wipe off that rising sun face paint.
Mayo is my waifu.
Who taught you to say that?

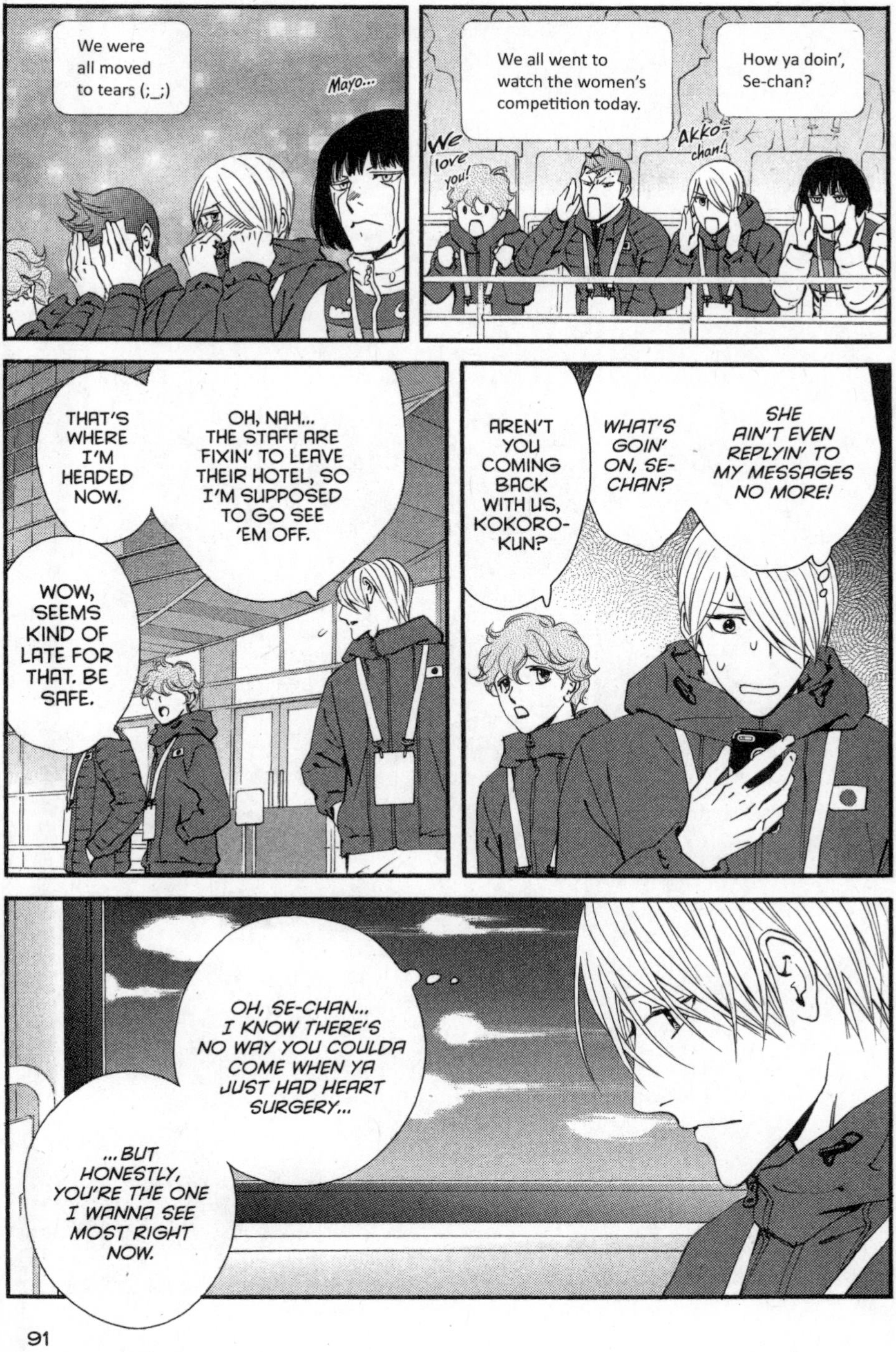
How ya doin', Se-chan?
We all went to watch the women's competition today.
Akko-chan!
We love you!
Mayo...
We were all moved to tears (;_;)
SHE AIN'T EVEN REPLYIN' TO MY MESSAGES NO MORE!
WHAT'S GOIN' ON, SE-CHAN?
AREN'T YOU COMING BACK WITH US, KOKORO-KUN?
OH, NAH... THE STAFF ARE FIXIN' TO LEAVE THEIR HOTEL, SO I'M SUPPOSED TO GO SEE 'EM OFF.
THAT'S WHERE I'M HEADED NOW.
WOW, SEEMS KIND OF LATE FOR THAT. BE SAFE.
OH, SE-CHAN... I KNOW THERE'S NO WAY YOU COULDA COME WHEN YA JUST HAD HEART SURGERY...
...BUT HONESTLY, YOU'RE THE ONE I WANNA SEE MOST RIGHT NOW.

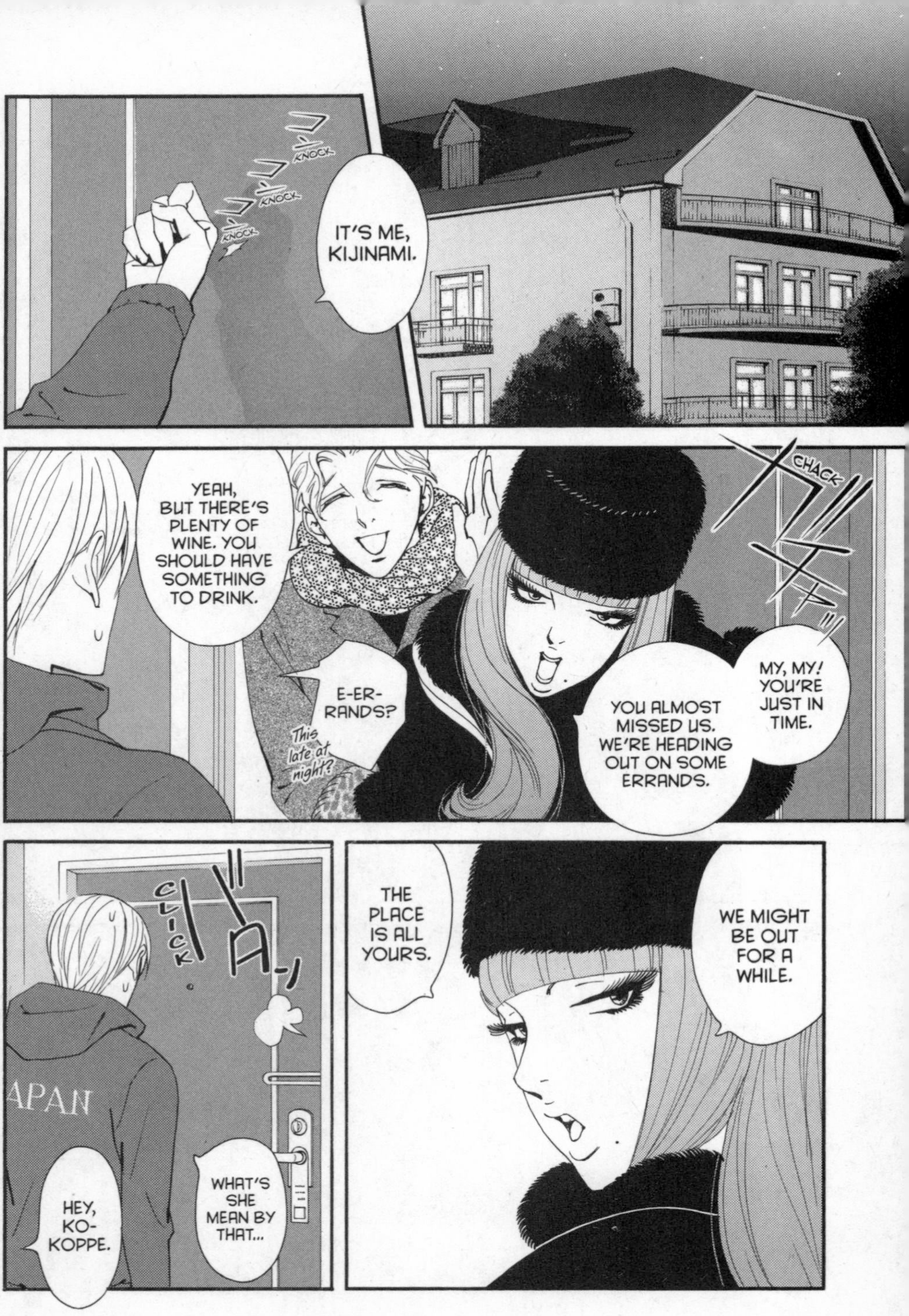
KNOCK
KNOCK
KNOCK
IT'S ME, KIJINAMI.
CHACK
MY, MY! YOU'RE JUST IN TIME.
YOU ALMOST MISSED US. WE'RE HEADING OUT ON SOME ERRANDS.
YEAH, BUT THERE'S PLENTY OF WINE. YOU SHOULD HAVE SOMETHING TO DRINK.
E-ER-RANDS?
This late at night?
WE MIGHT BE OUT FOR A WHILE.
THE PLACE IS ALL YOURS.
CLICK
APAN
WHAT'S SHE MEAN BY THAT...
HEY, KO-KOPPE.

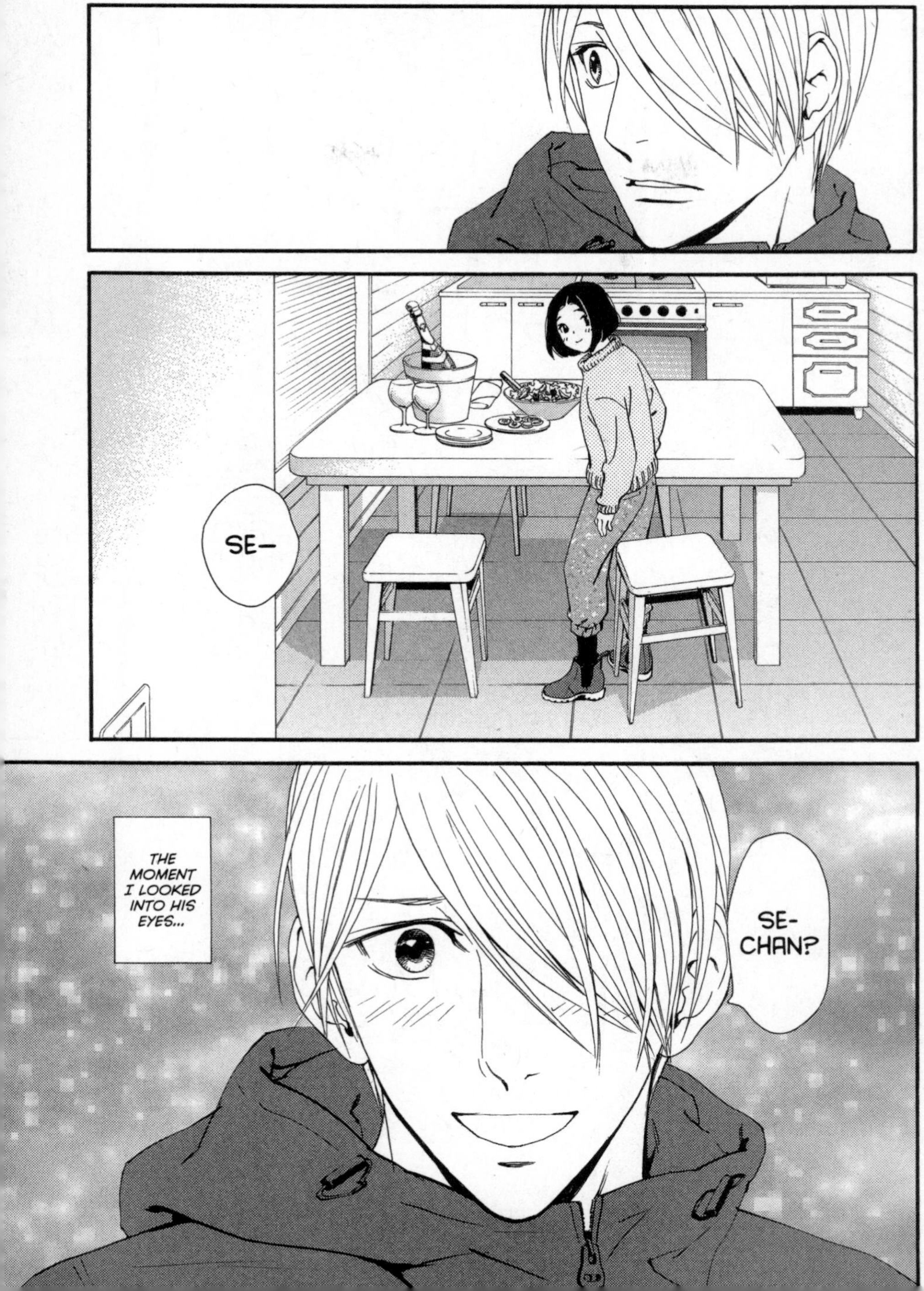
SE–
SE-CHAN?
THE MOMENT I LOOKED INTO HIS EYES...

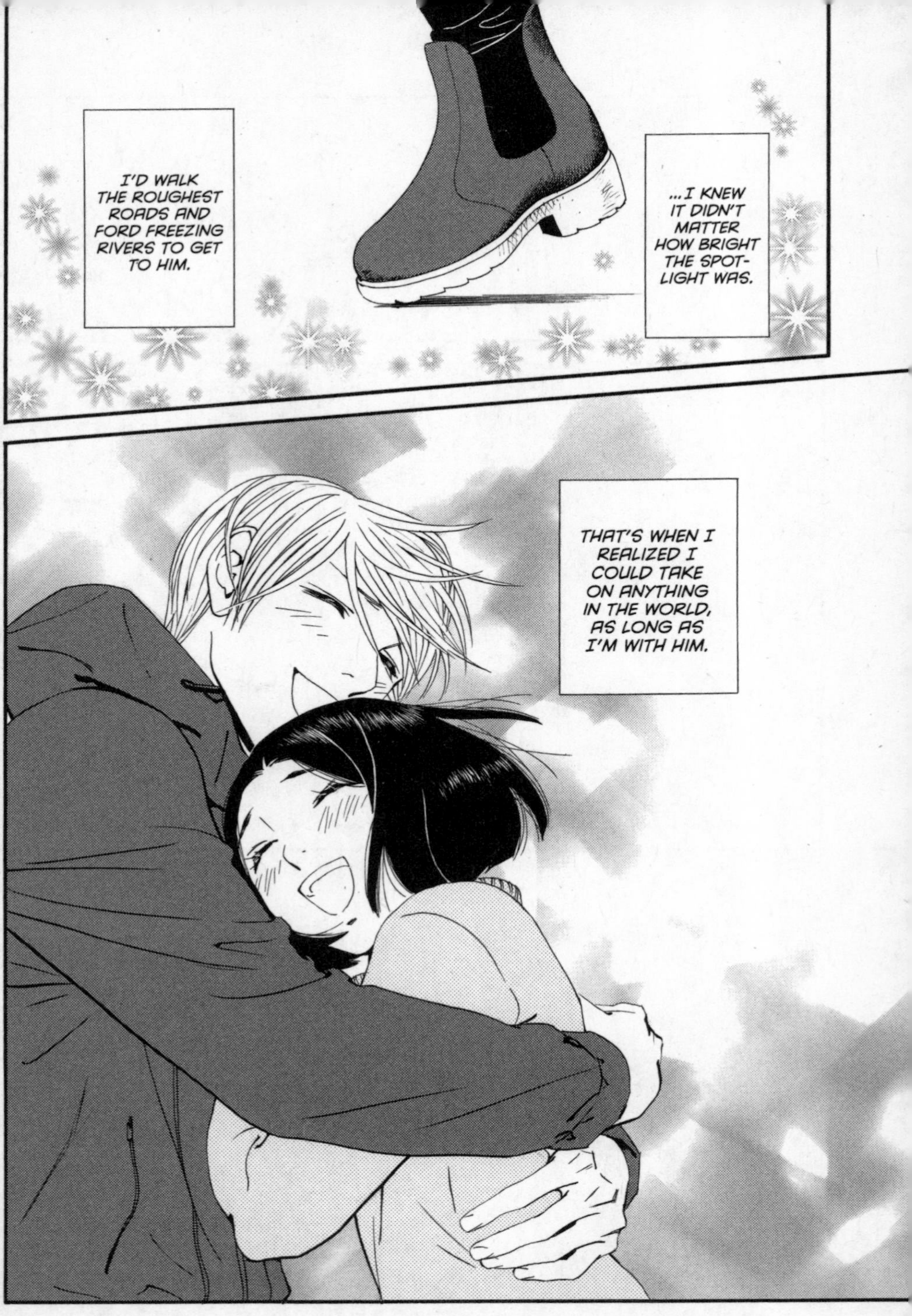
...I KNEW IT DIDN'T MATTER HOW BRIGHT THE SPOT-LIGHT WAS.
I'D WALK THE ROUGHEST ROADS AND FORD FREEZING RIVERS TO GET TO HIM.
THAT'S WHEN I REALIZED I COULD TAKE ON ANYTHING IN THE WORLD, AS LONG AS I'M WITH HIM.

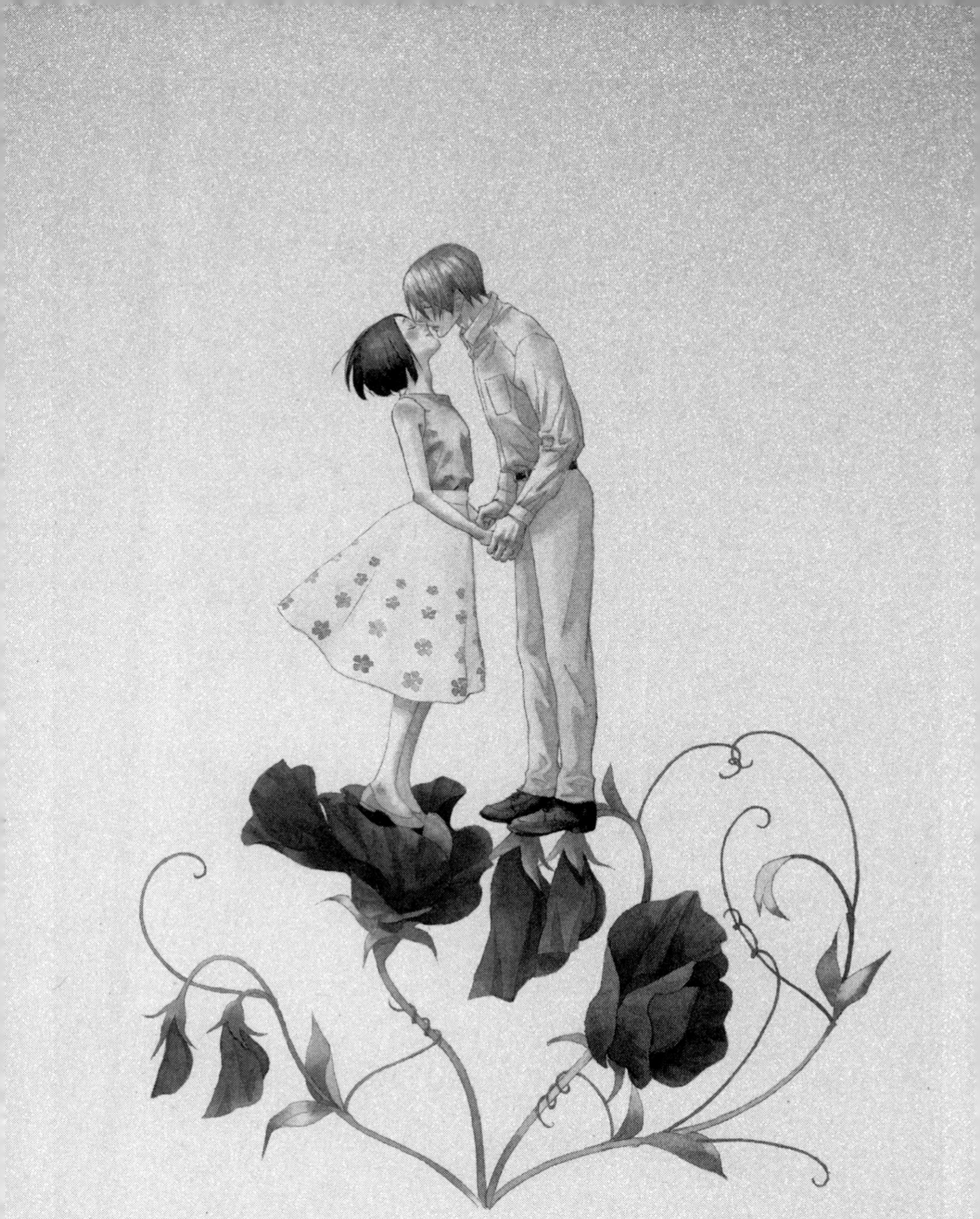

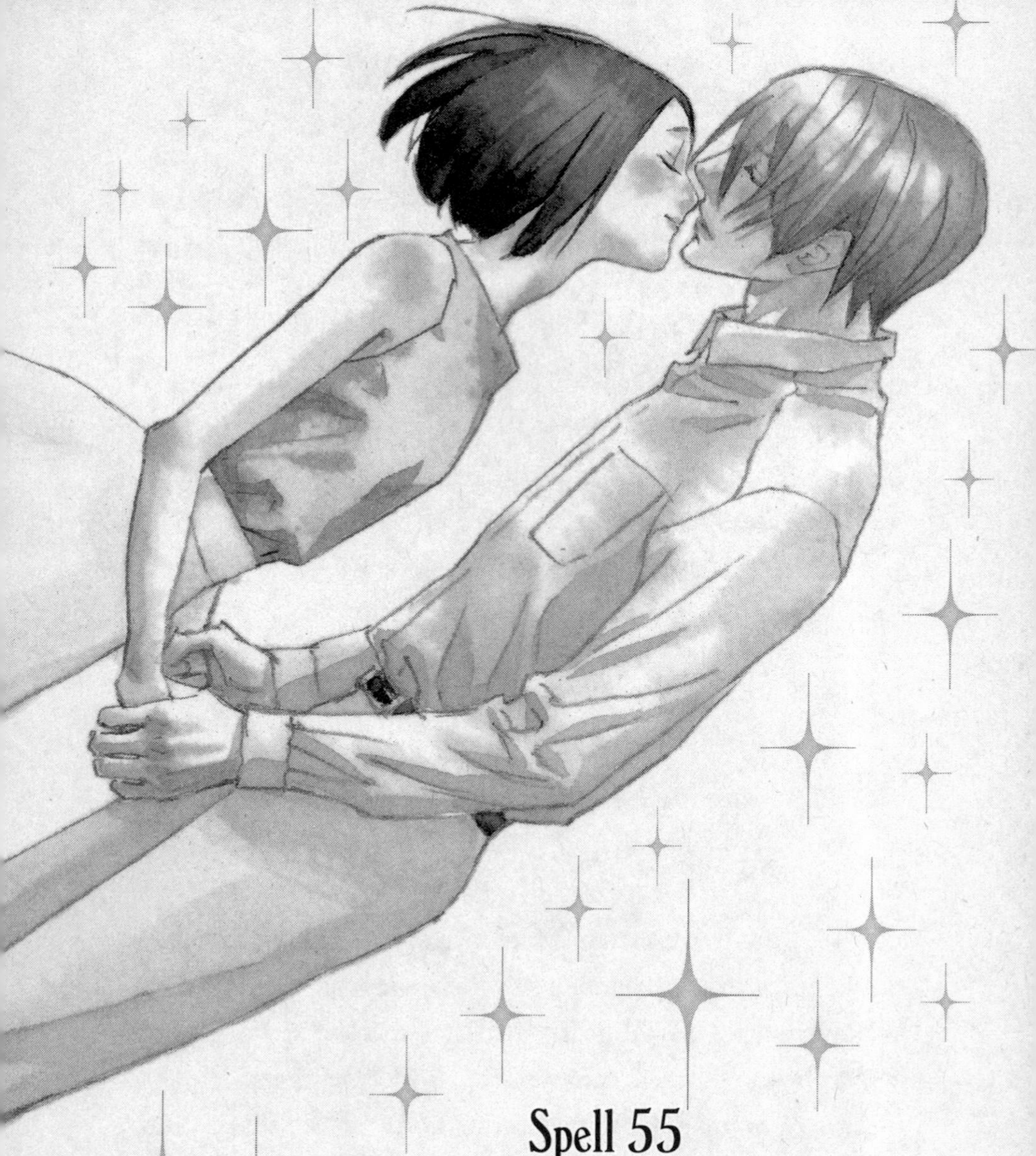

Spell 55

My Knight

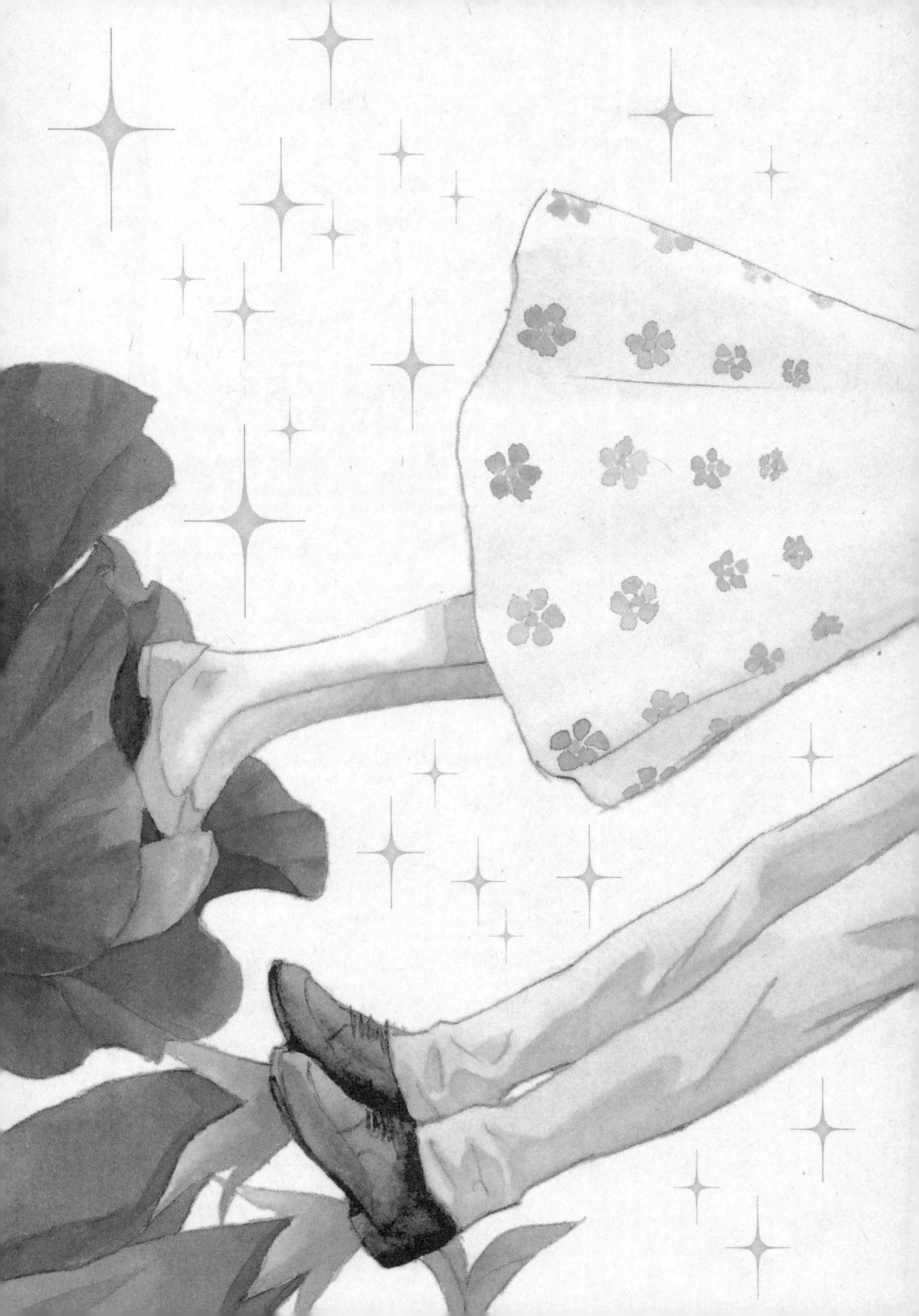

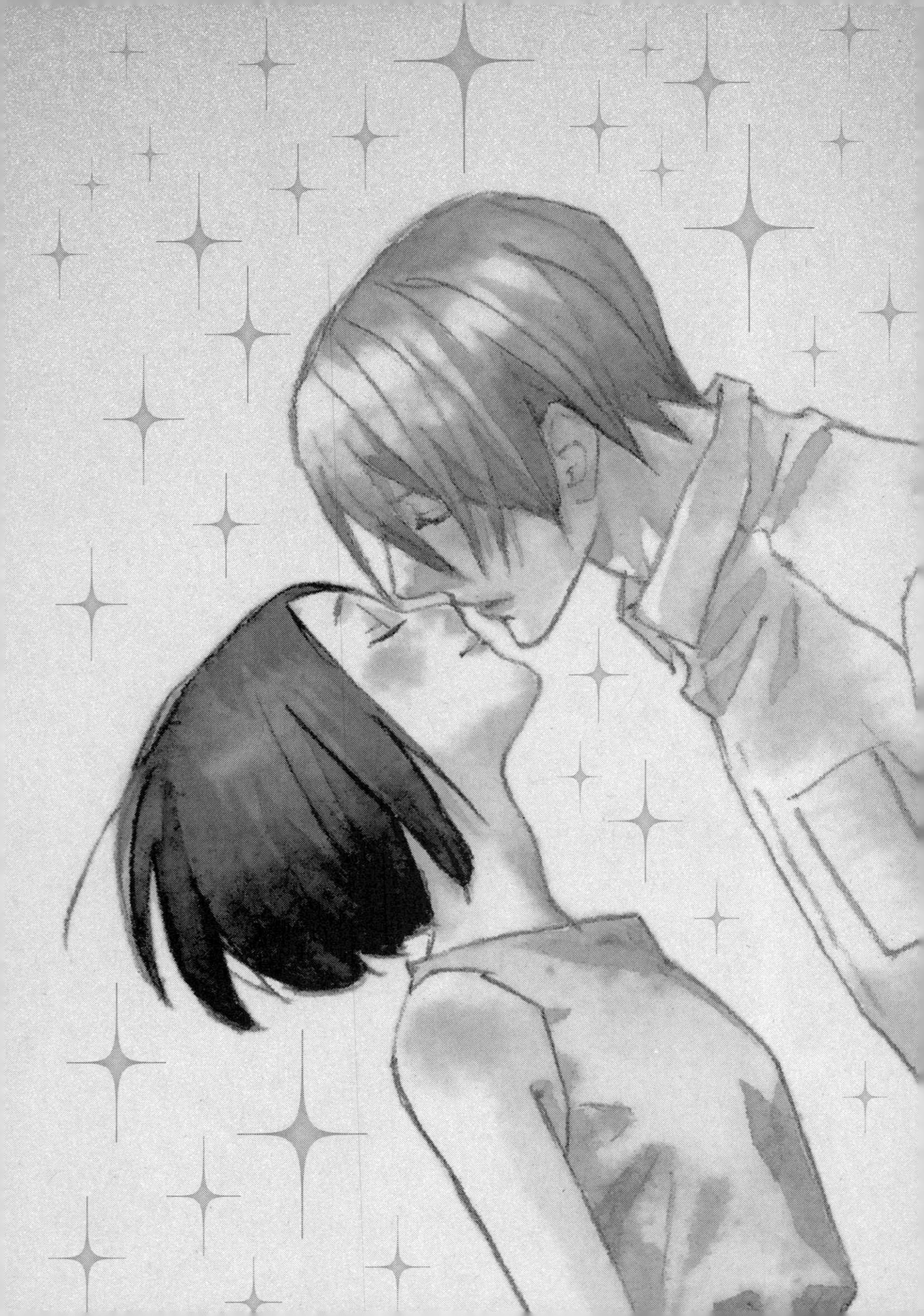

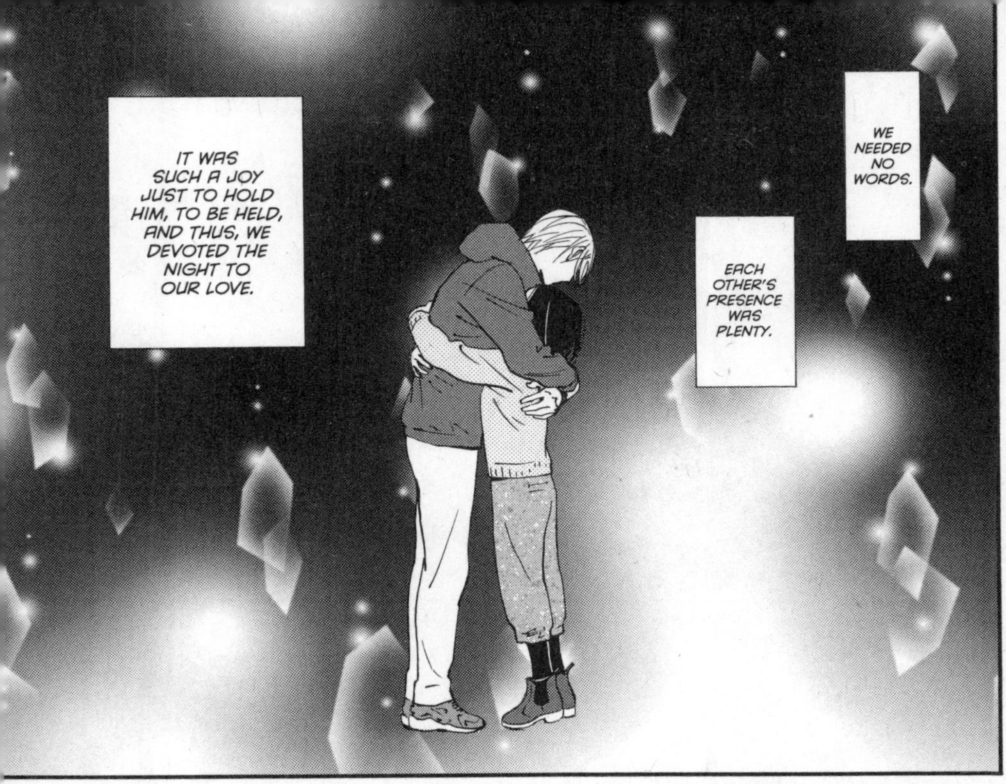
WE NEEDED NO WORDS.
EACH OTHER'S PRESENCE WAS PLENTY.
IT WAS SUCH A JOY JUST TO HOLD HIM, TO BE HELD, AND THUS, WE DEVOTED THE NIGHT TO OUR LOVE.
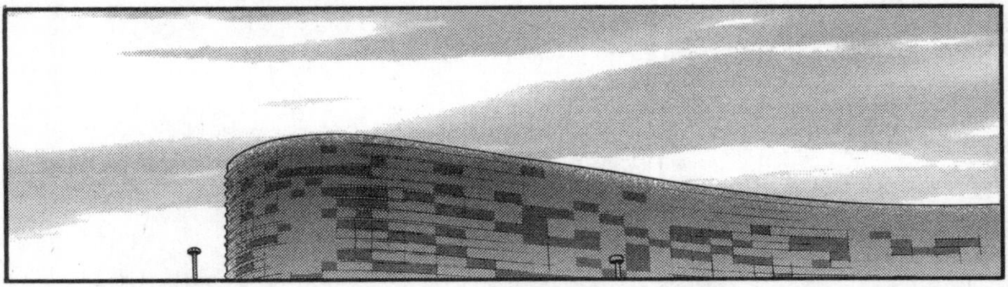
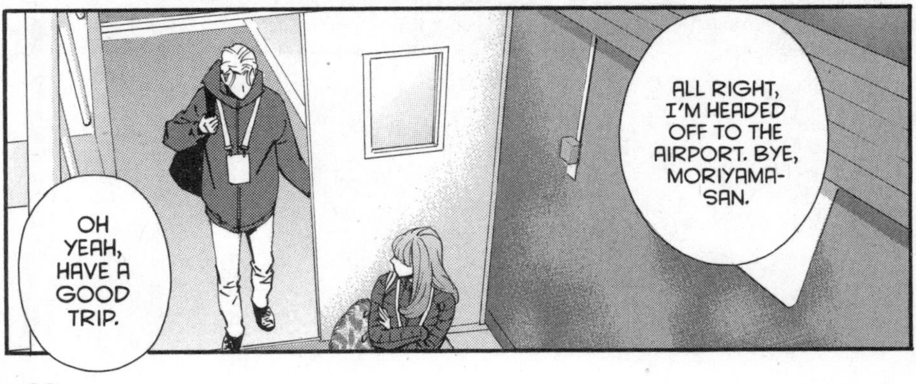
ALL RIGHT, I'M HEADED OFF TO THE AIRPORT. BYE, MORIYAMA-SAN.
OH YEAH, HAVE A GOOD TRIP.

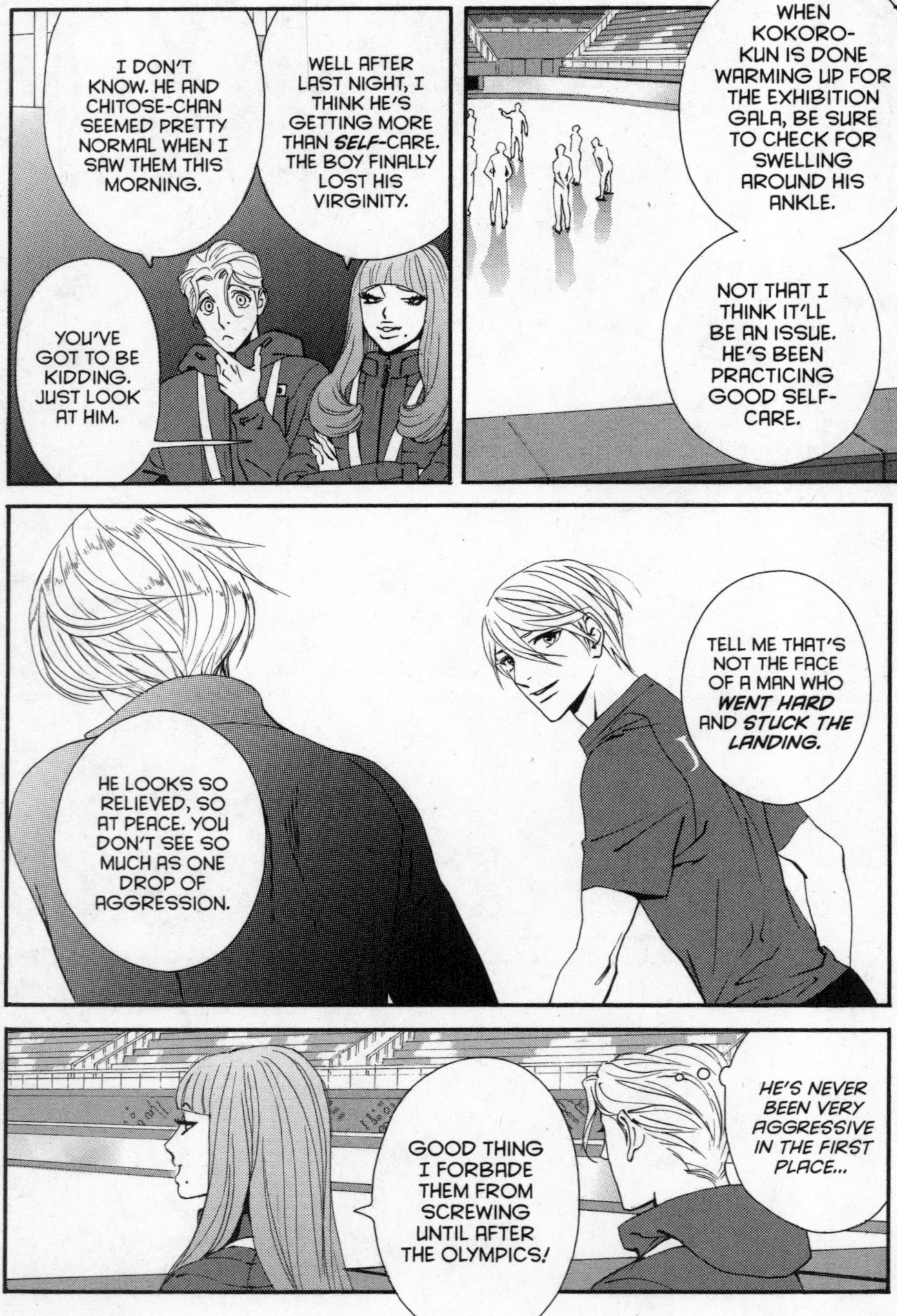
WHEN KOKORO-KUN IS DONE WARMING UP FOR THE EXHIBITION GALA, BE SURE TO CHECK FOR SWELLING AROUND HIS ANKLE.
NOT THAT I THINK IT'LL BE AN ISSUE. HE'S BEEN PRACTICING GOOD SELF-CARE.
WELL AFTER LAST NIGHT, I THINK HE'S GETTING MORE THAN *SELF*-CARE. THE BOY FINALLY LOST HIS VIRGINITY.
I DON'T KNOW. HE AND CHITOSE-CHAN SEEMED PRETTY NORMAL WHEN I SAW THEM THIS MORNING.
YOU'VE GOT TO BE KIDDING. JUST LOOK AT HIM.
TELL ME THAT'S NOT THE FACE OF A MAN WHO *WENT HARD* AND *STUCK THE LANDING.*
HE LOOKS SO RELIEVED, SO AT PEACE. YOU DON'T SEE SO MUCH AS ONE DROP OF AGGRESSION.
HE'S NEVER BEEN VERY AGGRESSIVE IN THE FIRST PLACE...
GOOD THING I FORBADE THEM FROM SCREWING UNTIL AFTER THE OLYMPICS!

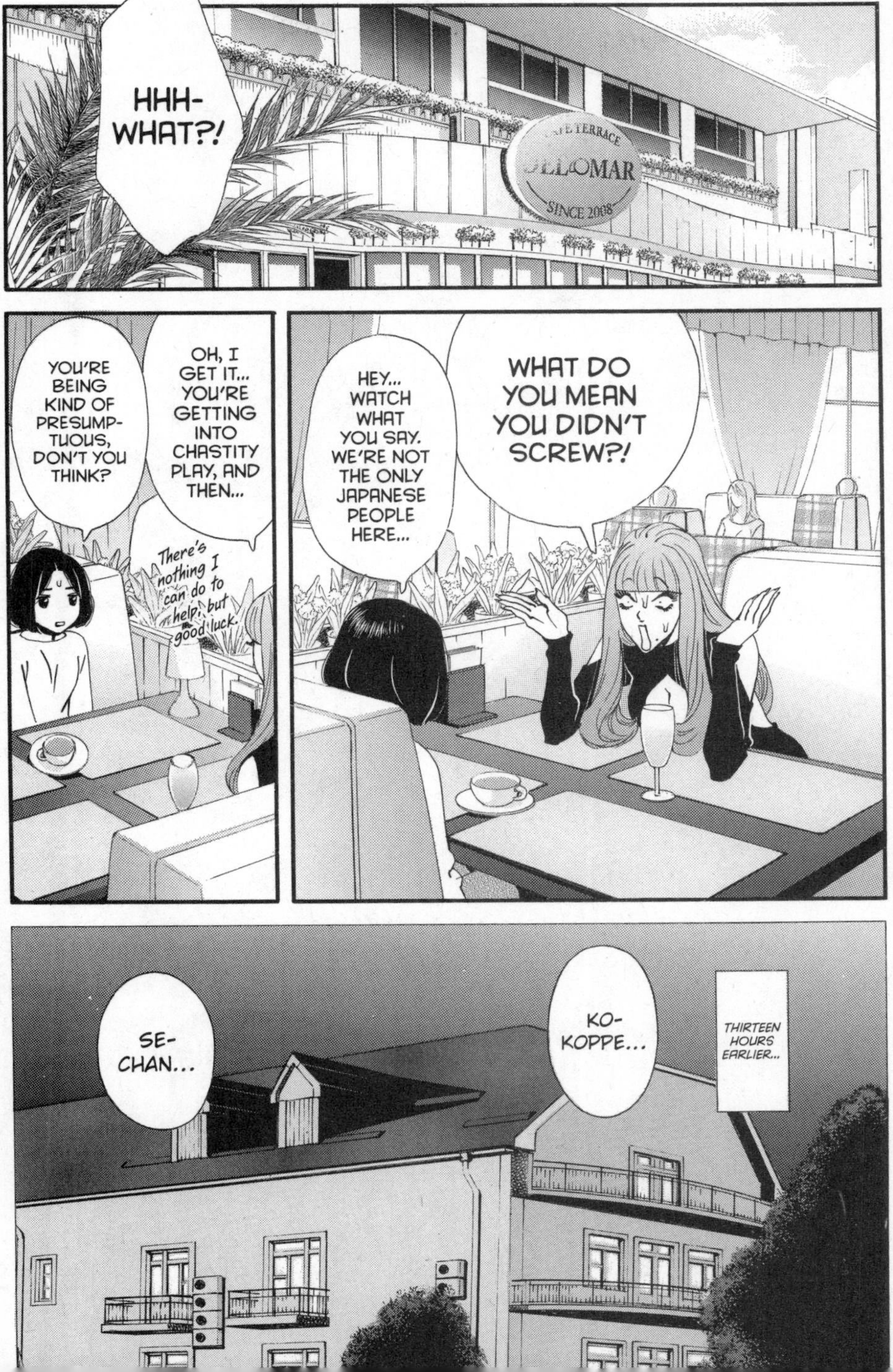
HHH-WHAT?!
SINCE 2008
WHAT DO YOU MEAN YOU DIDN'T SCREW?!
HEY... WATCH WHAT YOU SAY. WE'RE NOT THE ONLY JAPANESE PEOPLE HERE...
OH, I GET IT... YOU'RE GETTING INTO CHASTITY PLAY, AND THEN...
YOU'RE BEING KIND OF PRESUMPTUOUS, DON'T YOU THINK?
There's nothing I can do to help, but good luck.
THIRTEEN HOURS EARLIER...
KO-KOPPE...
SE-CHAN...

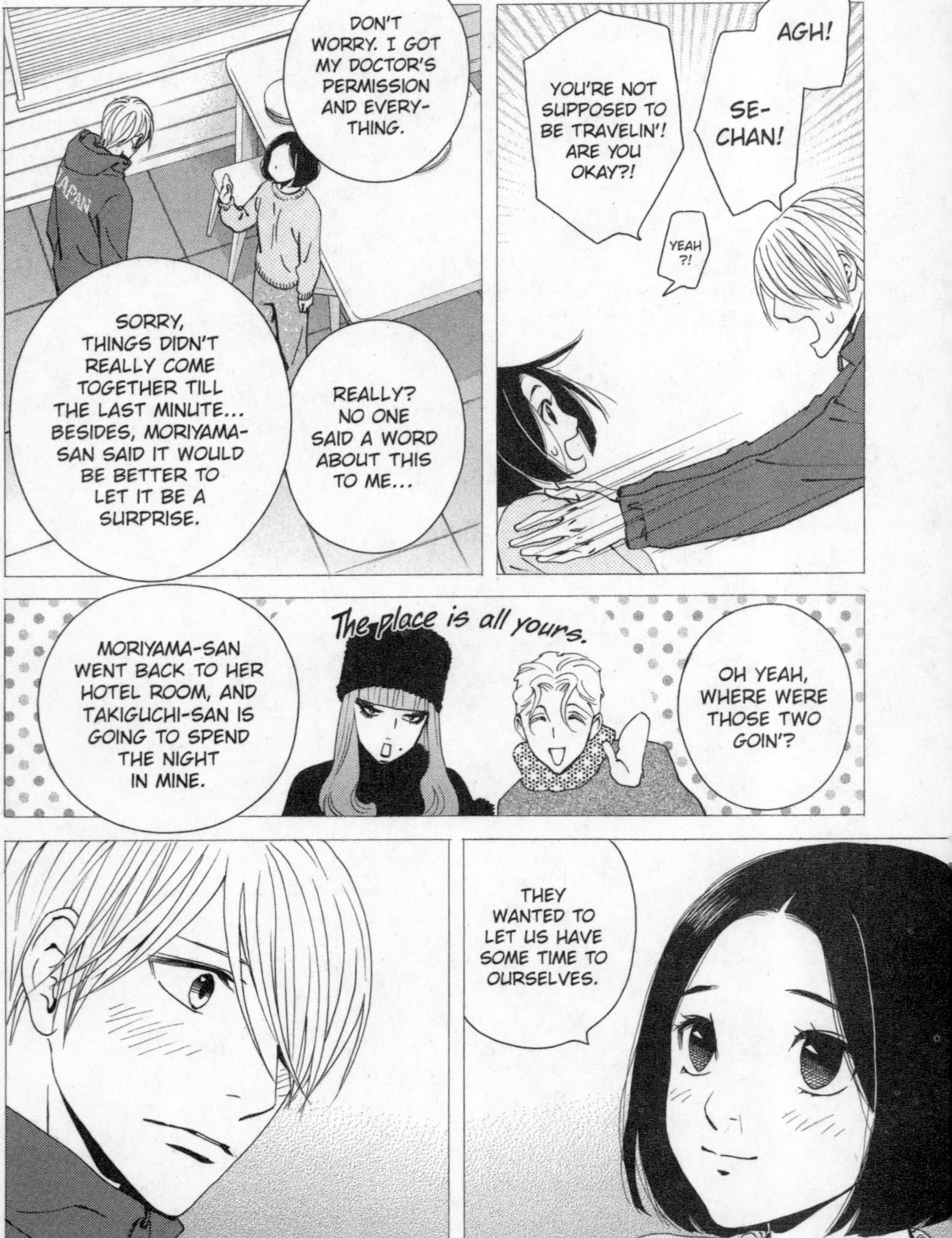
AGH!
SE-CHAN!
YOU'RE NOT SUPPOSED TO BE TRAVELIN'! ARE YOU OKAY?!
YEAH ?!
DON'T WORRY. I GOT MY DOCTOR'S PERMISSION AND EVERY-THING.
REALLY? NO ONE SAID A WORD ABOUT THIS TO ME...
SORRY, THINGS DIDN'T REALLY COME TOGETHER TILL THE LAST MINUTE... BESIDES, MORIYAMA-SAN SAID IT WOULD BE BETTER TO LET IT BE A SURPRISE.
OH YEAH, WHERE WERE THOSE TWO GOIN'?
The place is all yours.
MORIYAMA-SAN WENT BACK TO HER HOTEL ROOM, AND TAKIGUCHI-SAN IS GOING TO SPEND THE NIGHT IN MINE.
THEY WANTED TO LET US HAVE SOME TIME TO OURSELVES.

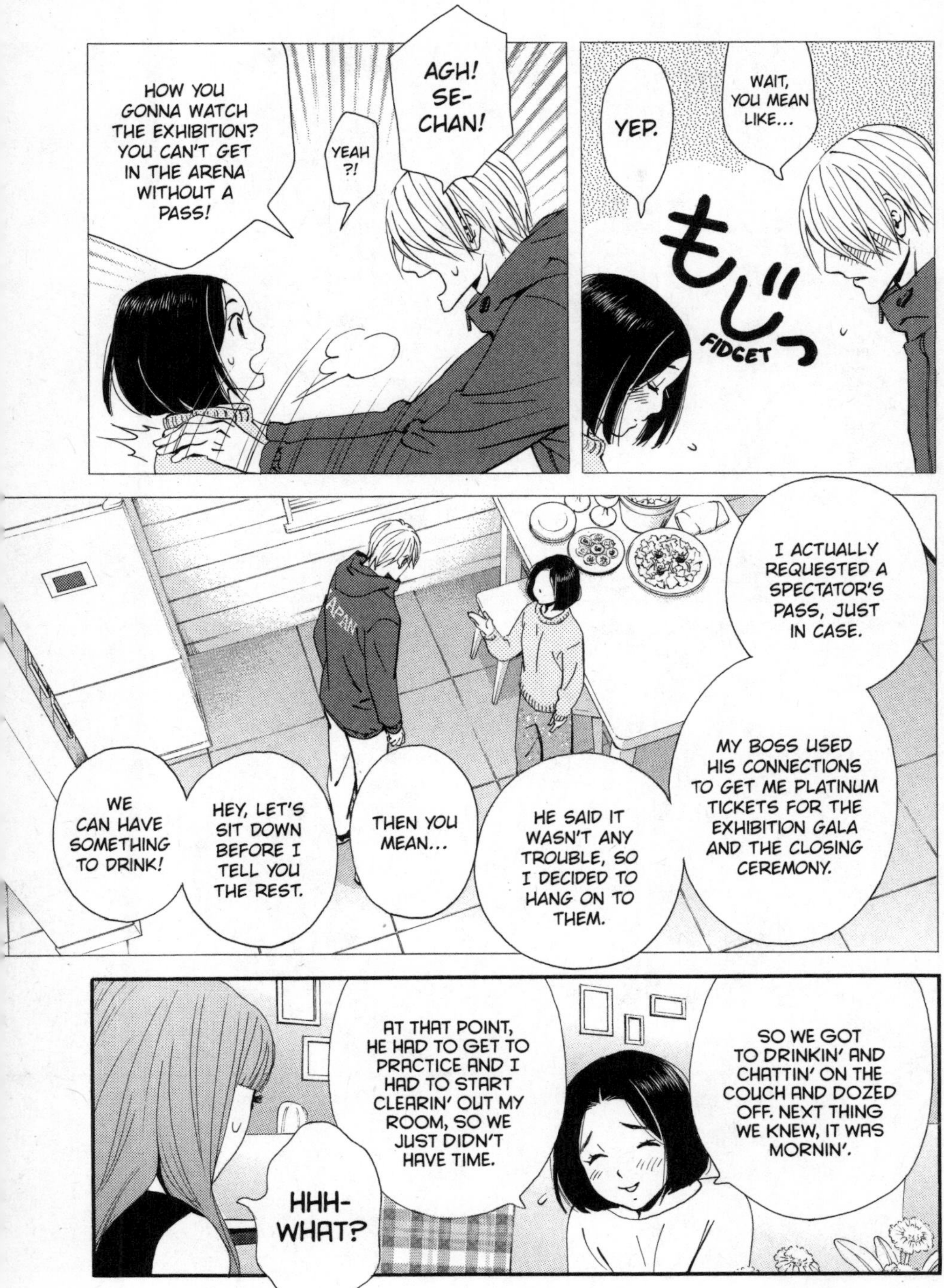
WAIT, YOU MEAN LIKE...
YEP.
もじっ
FIDGET
AGH! SE-CHAN!
YEAH ?!
HOW YOU GONNA WATCH THE EXHIBITION? YOU CAN'T GET IN THE ARENA WITHOUT A PASS!
I ACTUALLY REQUESTED A SPECTATOR'S PASS, JUST IN CASE.
MY BOSS USED HIS CONNECTIONS TO GET ME PLATINUM TICKETS FOR THE EXHIBITION GALA AND THE CLOSING CEREMONY.
HE SAID IT WASN'T ANY TROUBLE, SO I DECIDED TO HANG ON TO THEM.
THEN YOU MEAN...
HEY, LET'S SIT DOWN BEFORE I TELL YOU THE REST.
WE CAN HAVE SOMETHING TO DRINK!
SO WE GOT TO DRINKIN' AND CHATTIN' ON THE COUCH AND DOZED OFF. NEXT THING WE KNEW, IT WAS MORNIN'.
AT THAT POINT, HE HAD TO GET TO PRACTICE AND I HAD TO START CLEARIN' OUT MY ROOM, SO WE JUST DIDN'T HAVE TIME.
HHH-WHAT?

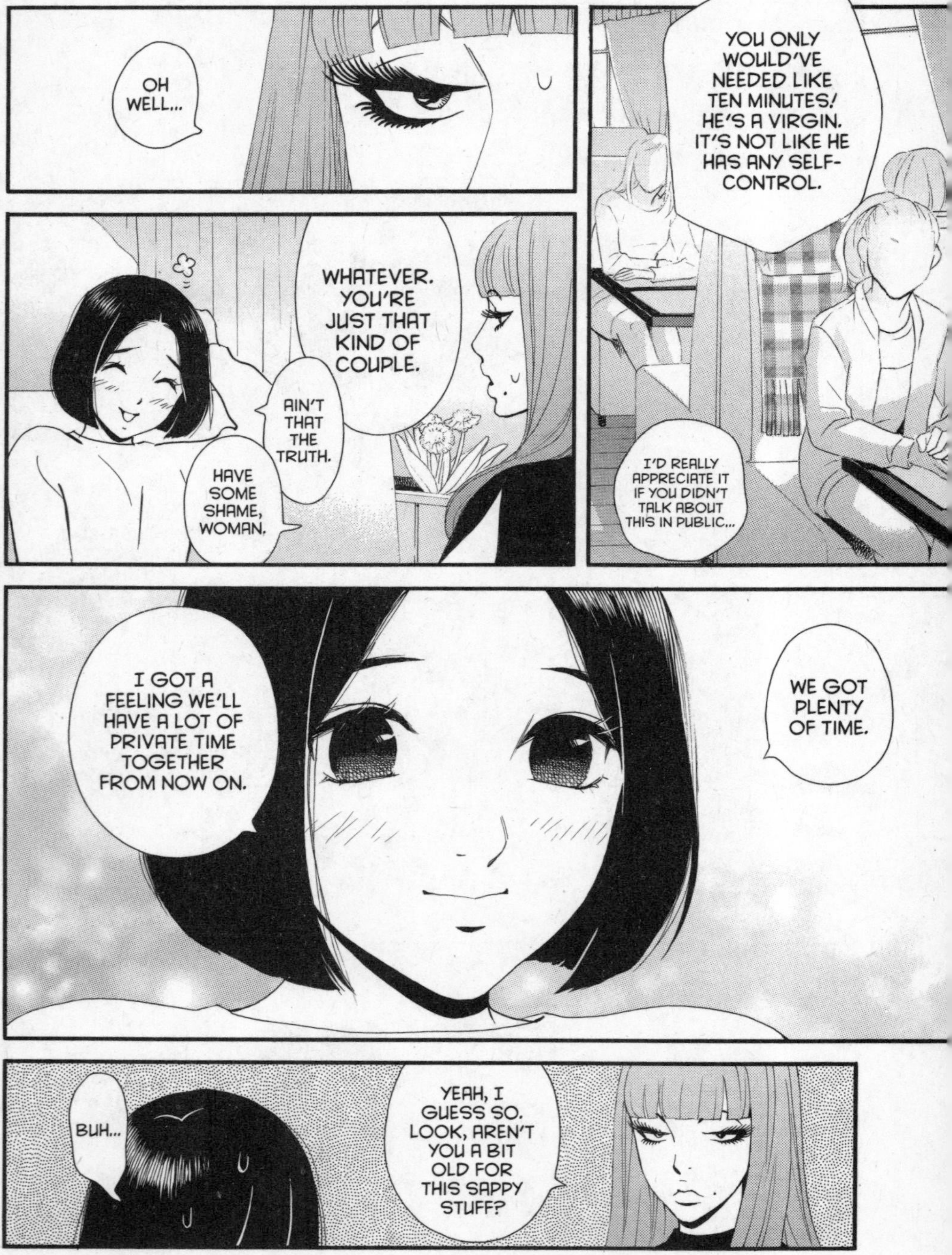
YOU ONLY WOULD'VE NEEDED LIKE TEN MINUTES! HE'S A VIRGIN. IT'S NOT LIKE HE HAS ANY SELF-CONTROL.
I'D REALLY APPRECIATE IT IF YOU DIDN'T TALK ABOUT THIS IN PUBLIC...
OH WELL...
WHATEVER. YOU'RE JUST THAT KIND OF COUPLE.
AIN'T THAT THE TRUTH.
HAVE SOME SHAME, WOMAN.
WE GOT PLENTY OF TIME.
I GOT A FEELING WE'LL HAVE A LOT OF PRIVATE TIME TOGETHER FROM NOW ON.
YEAH, I GUESS SO. LOOK, AREN'T YOU A BIT OLD FOR THIS SAPPY STUFF?
BUH...

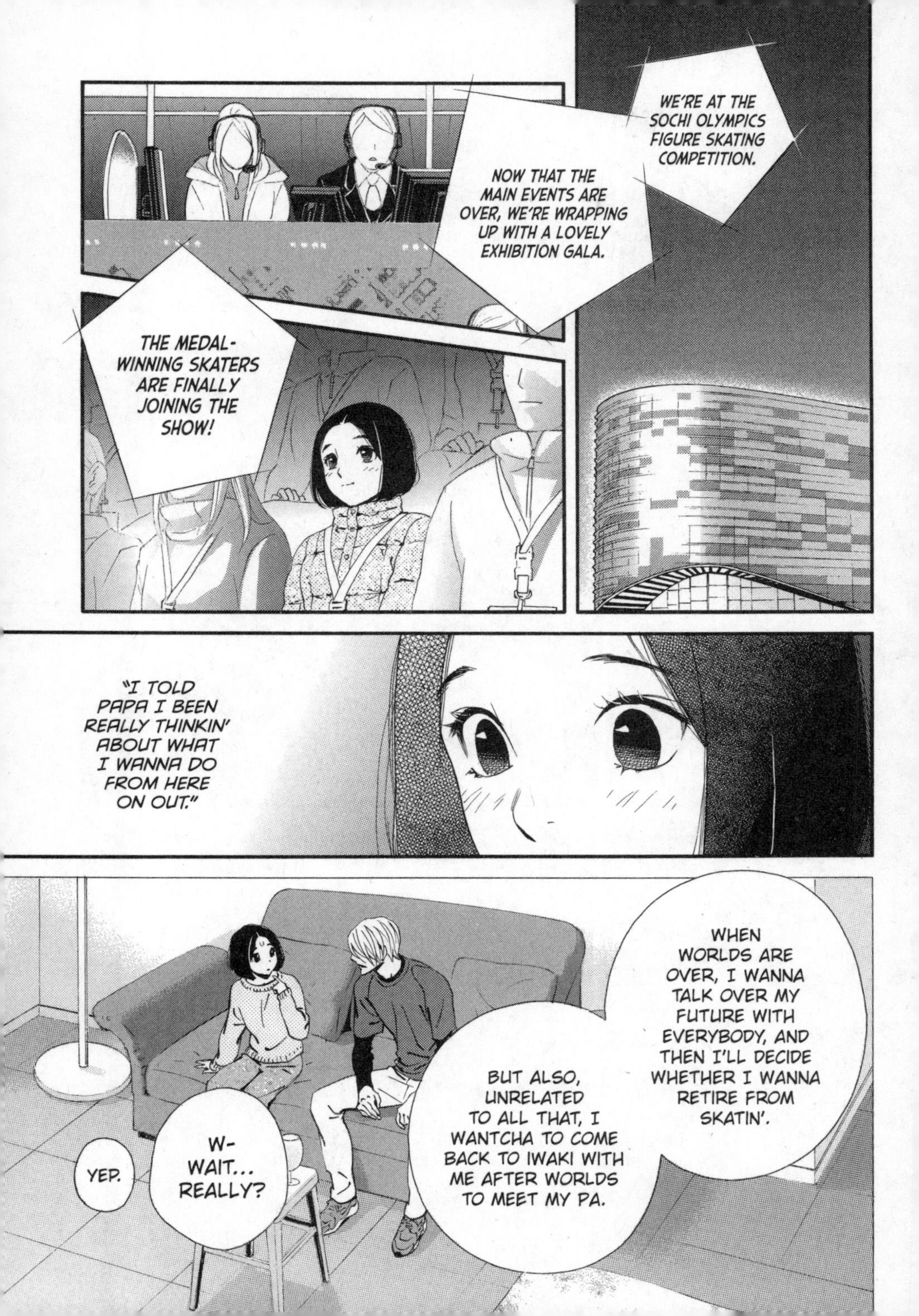
WE'RE AT THE SOCHI OLYMPICS FIGURE SKATING COMPETITION.
NOW THAT THE MAIN EVENTS ARE OVER, WE'RE WRAPPING UP WITH A LOVELY EXHIBITION GALA.
THE MEDAL-WINNING SKATERS ARE FINALLY JOINING THE SHOW!
"I TOLD PAPA I BEEN REALLY THINKIN' ABOUT WHAT I WANNA DO FROM HERE ON OUT."
WHEN WORLDS ARE OVER, I WANNA TALK OVER MY FUTURE WITH EVERYBODY, AND THEN I'LL DECIDE WHETHER I WANNA RETIRE FROM SKATIN'.
BUT ALSO, UNRELATED TO ALL THAT, I WANTCHA TO COME BACK TO IWAKI WITH ME AFTER WORLDS TO MEET MY PA.
W-WAIT... REALLY?
YEP.

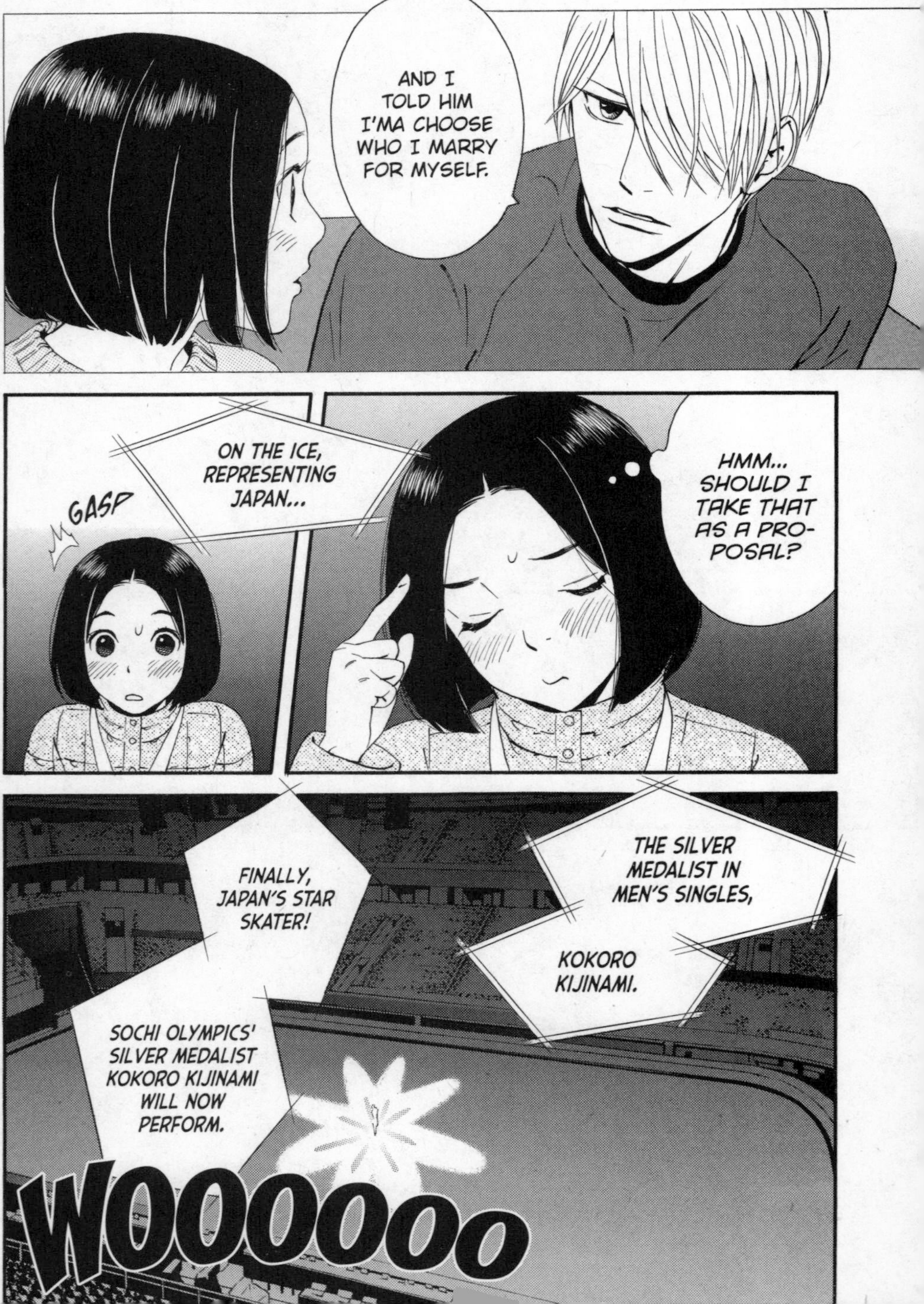
AND I TOLD HIM I'MA CHOOSE WHO I MARRY FOR MYSELF.
HMM... SHOULD I TAKE THAT AS A PRO-POSAL?
ON THE ICE, REPRESENTING JAPAN...
GASP
THE SILVER MEDALIST IN MEN'S SINGLES,
KOKORO KIJINAMI.
FINALLY, JAPAN'S STAR SKATER!
SOCHI OLYMPICS' SILVER MEDALIST KOKORO KIJINAMI WILL NOW PERFORM.
WOOOOOO

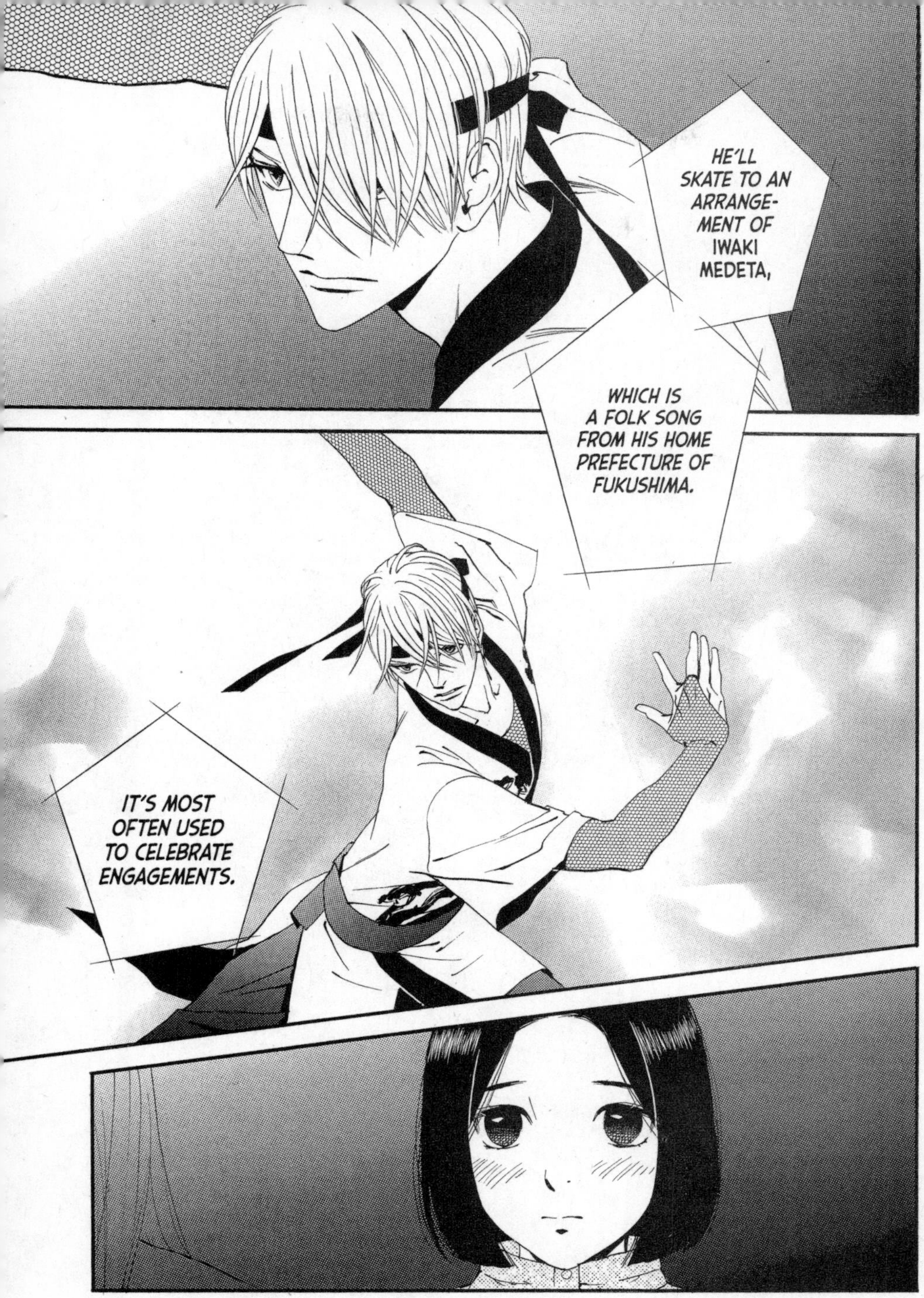
HE'LL SKATE TO AN ARRANGE-MENT OF IWAKI MEDETA,
WHICH IS A FOLK SONG FROM HIS HOME PREFECTURE OF FUKUSHIMA.
IT'S MOST OFTEN USED TO CELEBRATE ENGAGEMENTS.

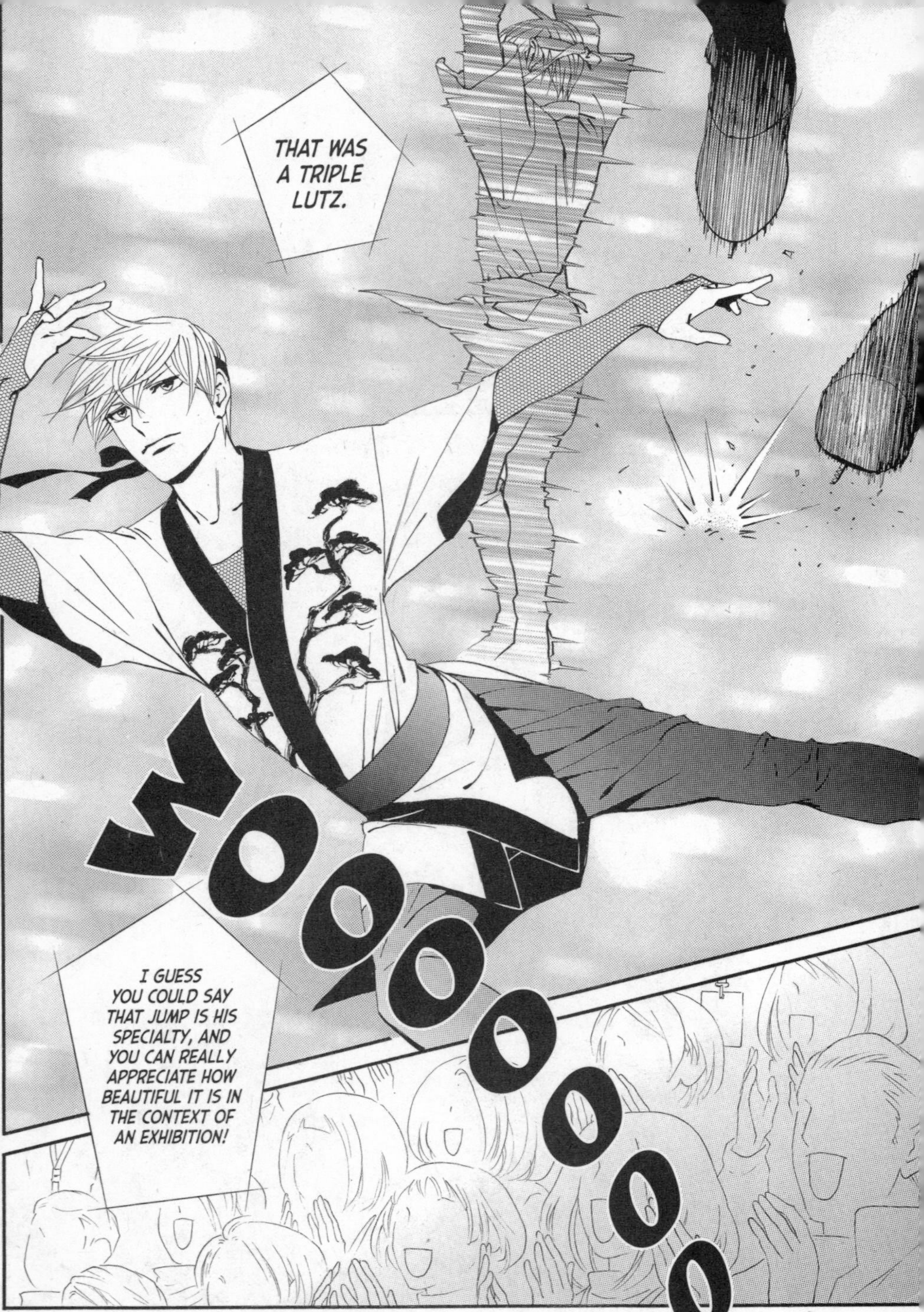
THAT WAS A TRIPLE LUTZ.
WOOOOOOOOO
I GUESS YOU COULD SAY THAT JUMP IS HIS SPECIALTY, AND YOU CAN REALLY APPRECIATE HOW BEAUTIFUL IT IS IN THE CONTEXT OF AN EXHIBITION!

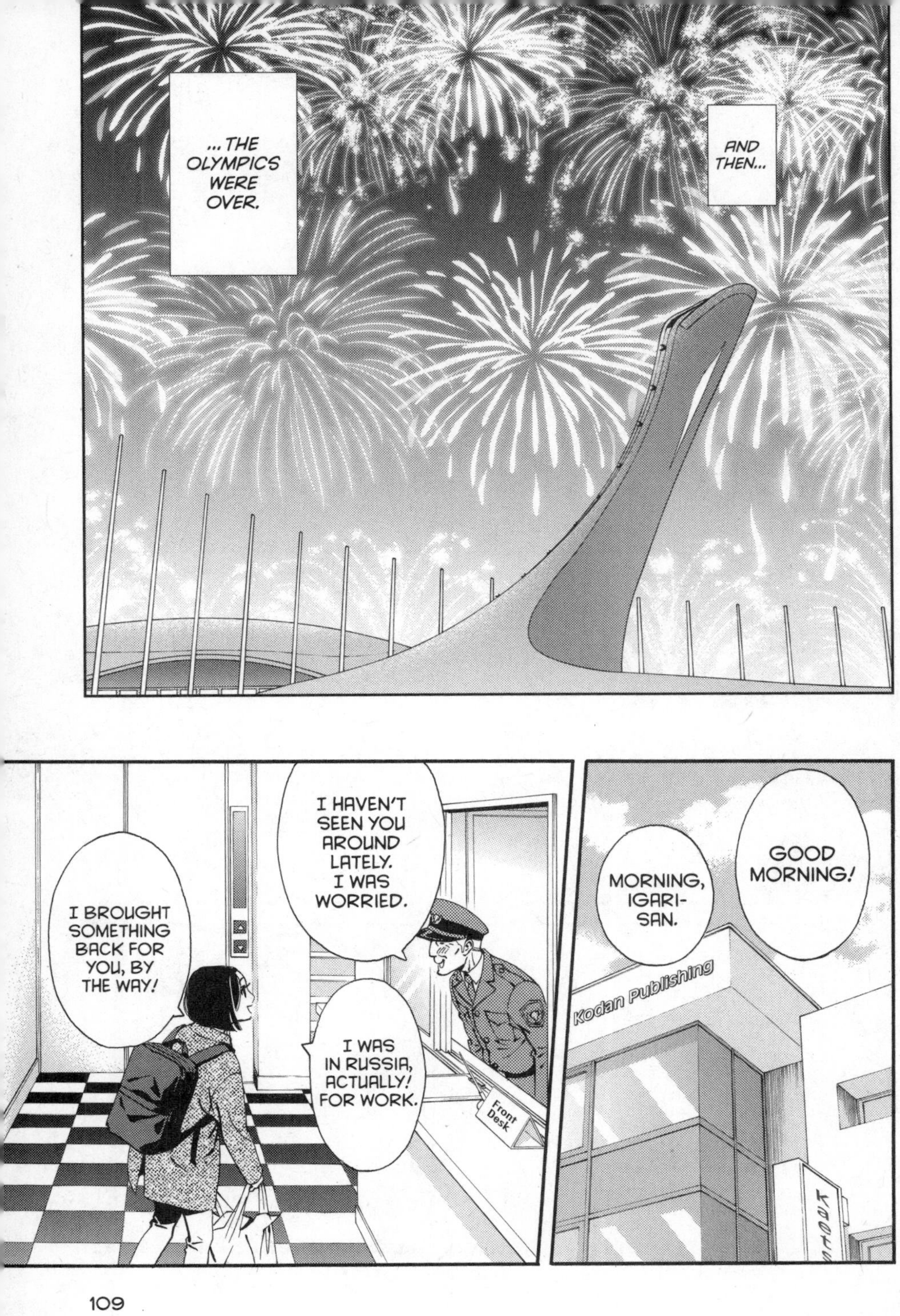
AND THEN...
...THE OLYMPICS WERE OVER.
GOOD MORNING!
MORNING, IGARI-SAN.
Kodan Publishing
I HAVEN'T SEEN YOU AROUND LATELY. I WAS WORRIED.
I WAS IN RUSSIA, ACTUALLY! FOR WORK.
I BROUGHT SOMETHING BACK FOR YOU, BY THE WAY!
Front Desk

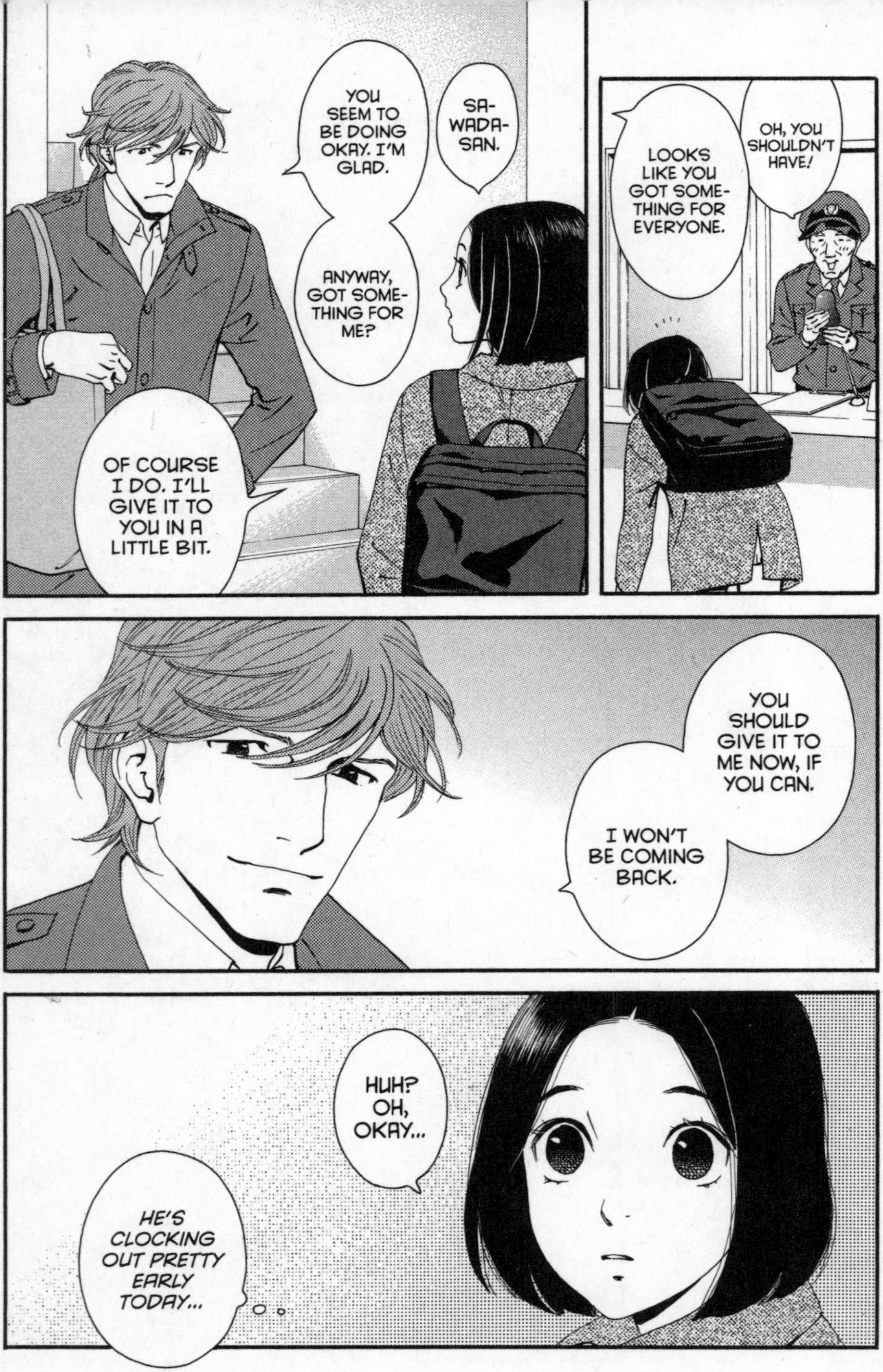
OH, YOU SHOULDN'T HAVE!
LOOKS LIKE YOU GOT SOME-THING FOR EVERYONE.
SA-WADA-SAN.
YOU SEEM TO BE DOING OKAY. I'M GLAD.
ANYWAY, GOT SOME-THING FOR ME?
OF COURSE I DO. I'LL GIVE IT TO YOU IN A LITTLE BIT.
YOU SHOULD GIVE IT TO ME NOW, IF YOU CAN.
I WON'T BE COMING BACK.
HUH? OH, OKAY...
HE'S CLOCKING OUT PRETTY EARLY TODAY...

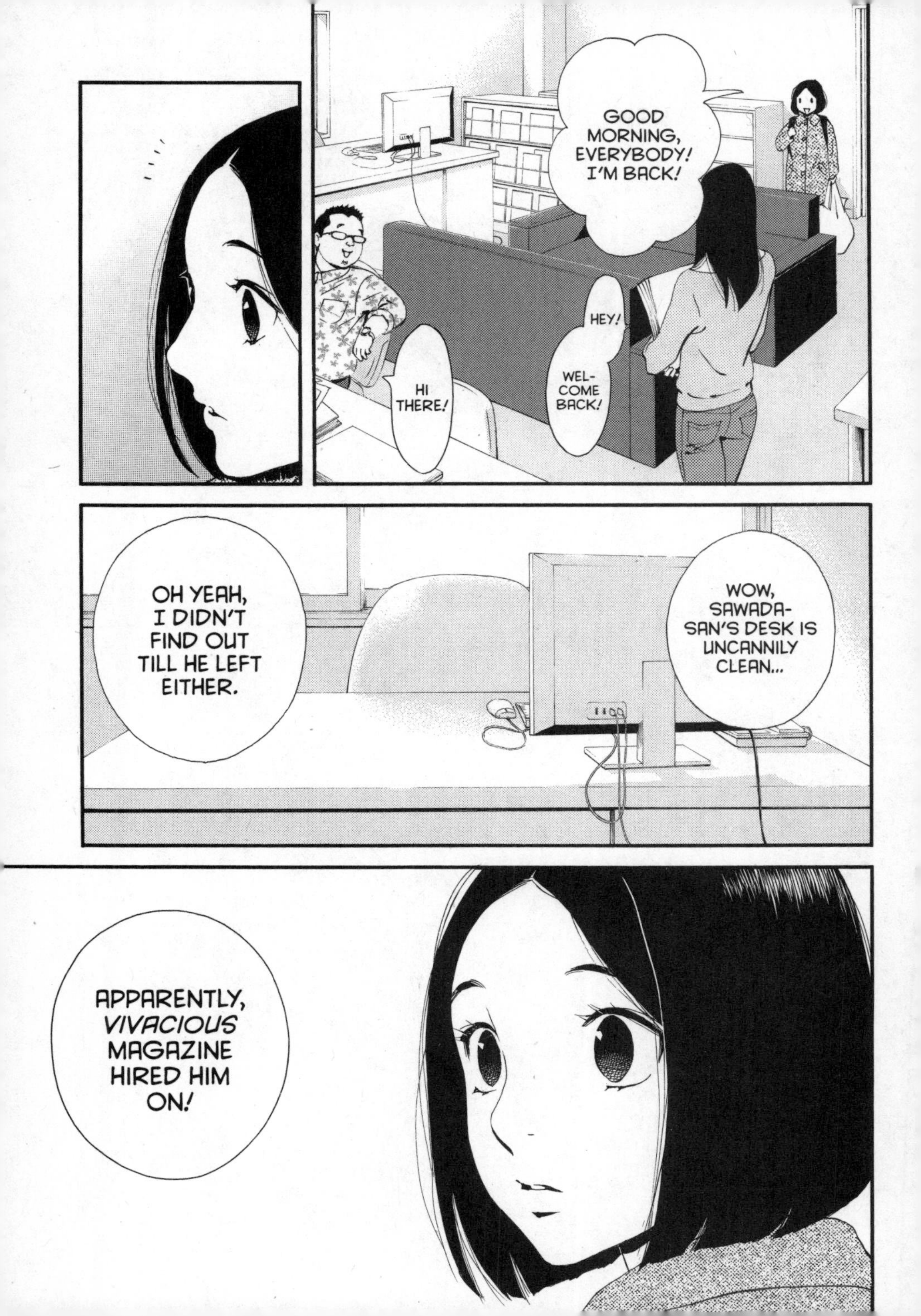
GOOD MORNING, EVERYBODY! I'M BACK!
HEY!
WEL-COME BACK!
HI THERE!
WOW, SAWADA-SAN'S DESK IS UNCANNILY CLEAN...
OH YEAH, I DIDN'T FIND OUT TILL HE LEFT EITHER.
APPARENTLY, *VIVACIOUS* MAGAZINE HIRED HIM ON!

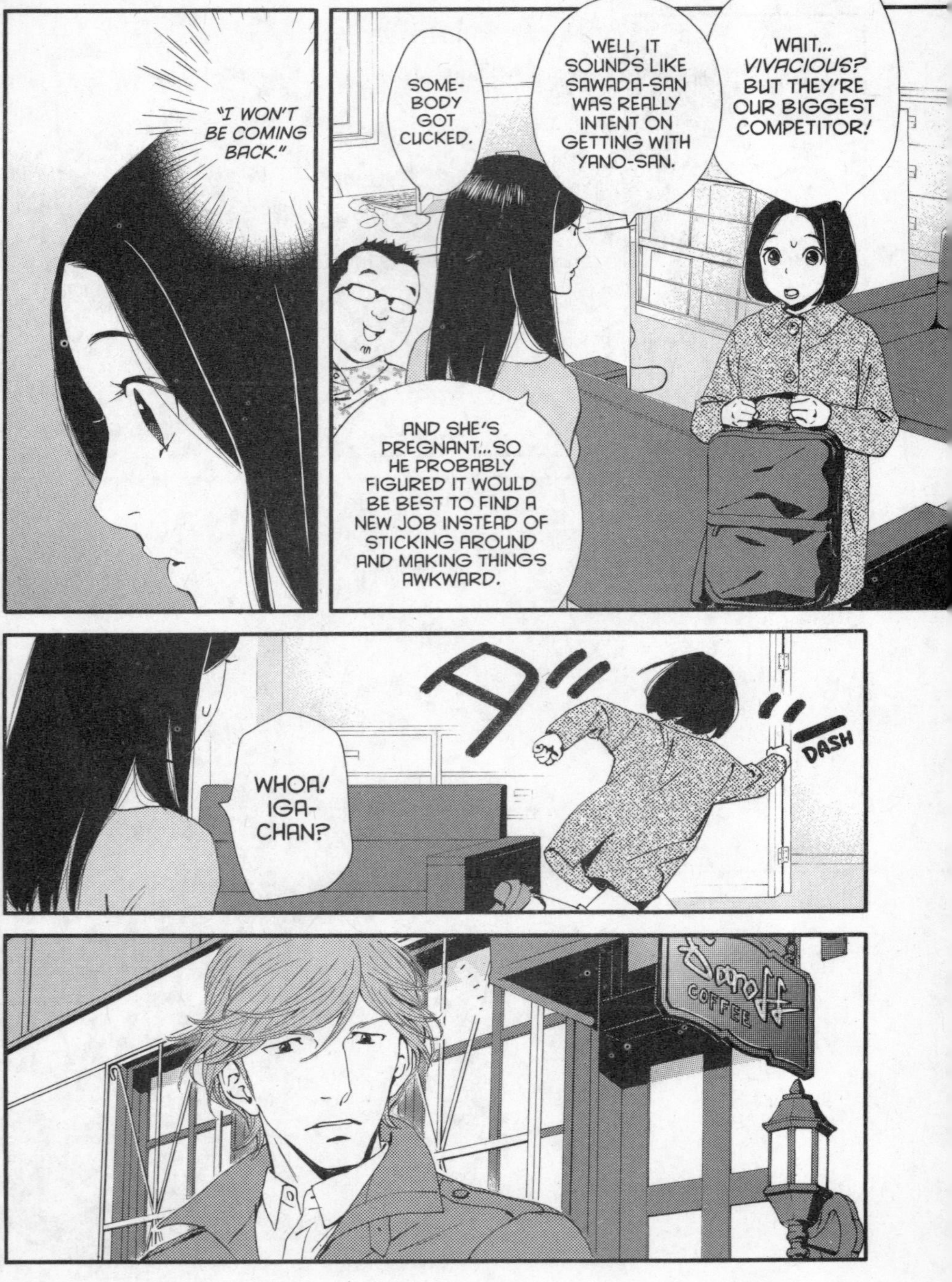
WAIT... VIVACIOUS? BUT THEY'RE OUR BIGGEST COMPETITOR!
WELL, IT SOUNDS LIKE SAWADA-SAN WAS REALLY INTENT ON GETTING WITH YANO-SAN.
SOME-BODY GOT CUCKED.
AND SHE'S PREGNANT...SO HE PROBABLY FIGURED IT WOULD BE BEST TO FIND A NEW JOB INSTEAD OF STICKING AROUND AND MAKING THINGS AWKWARD.
"I WON'T BE COMING BACK."
DASH
WHOA! IGA-CHAN?
COFFEE

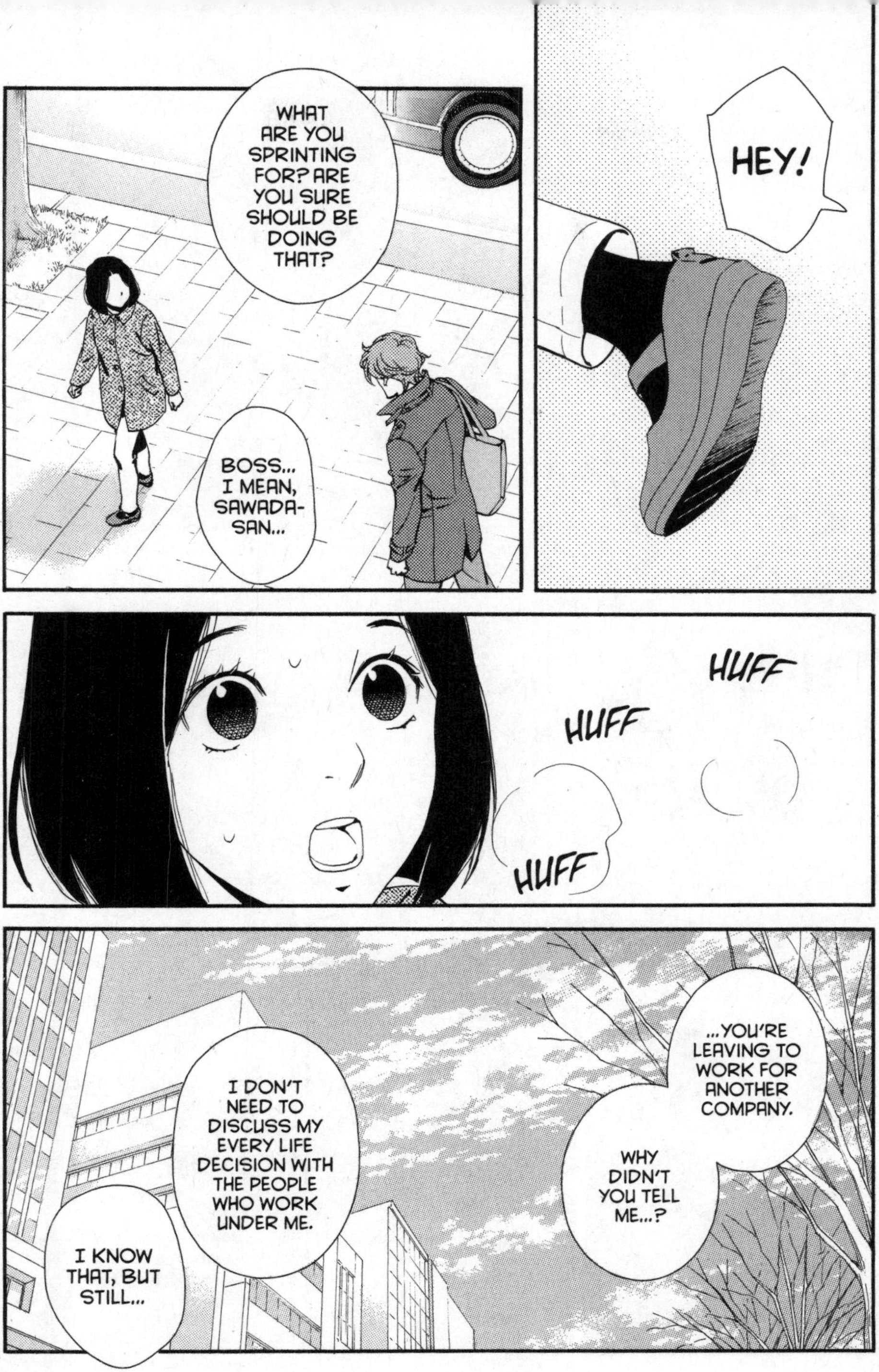
HEY!
WHAT ARE YOU SPRINTING FOR? ARE YOU SURE SHOULD BE DOING THAT?
BOSS... I MEAN, SAWADA-SAN...
HUFF
HUFF
HUFF
...YOU'RE LEAVING TO WORK FOR ANOTHER COMPANY.
WHY DIDN'T YOU TELL ME...?
I DON'T NEED TO DISCUSS MY EVERY LIFE DECISION WITH THE PEOPLE WHO WORK UNDER ME.
I KNOW THAT, BUT STILL...

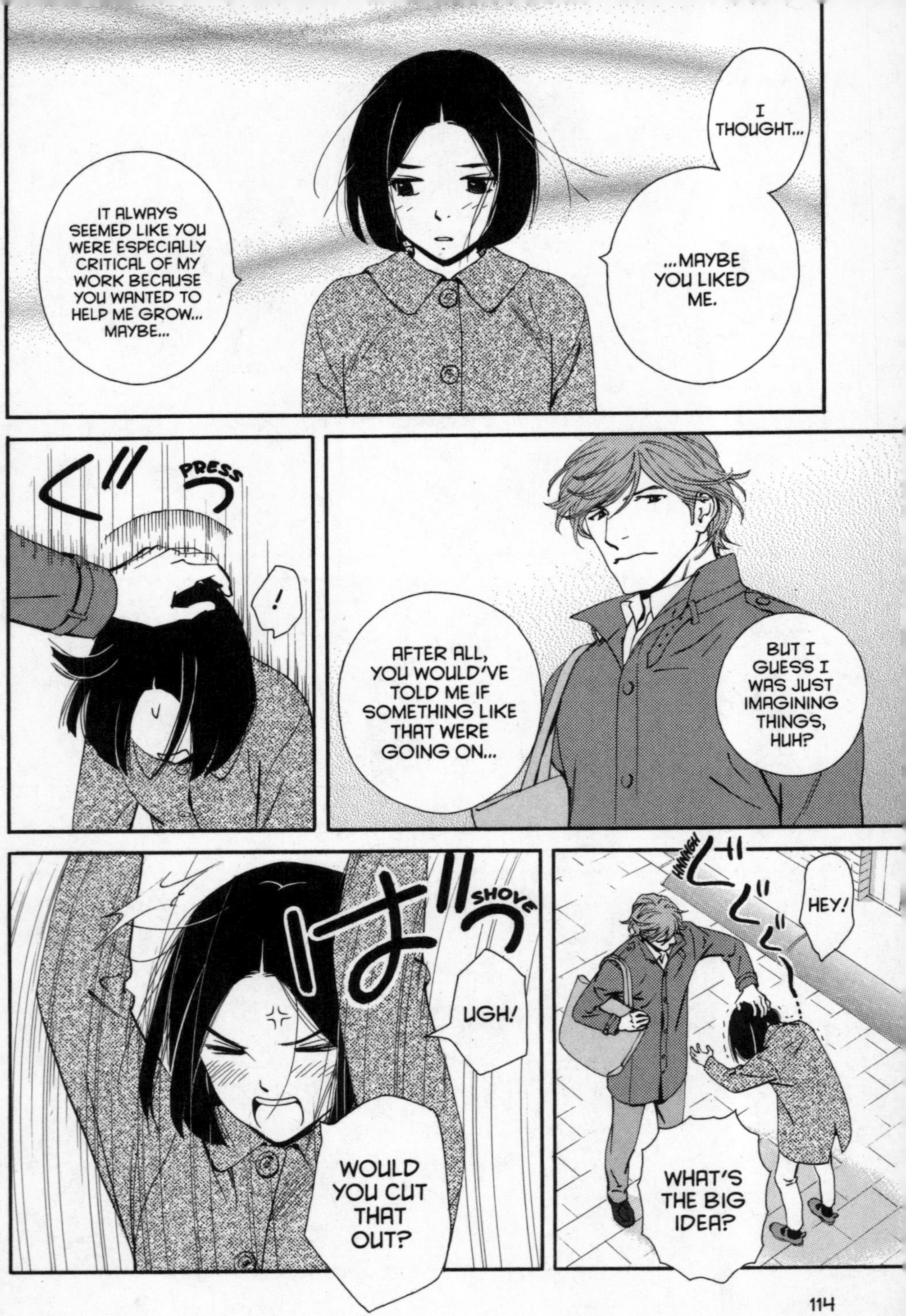
I THOUGHT...
...MAYBE YOU LIKED ME.
IT ALWAYS SEEMED LIKE YOU WERE ESPECIALLY CRITICAL OF MY WORK BECAUSE YOU WANTED TO HELP ME GROW... MAYBE...
BUT I GUESS I WAS JUST IMAGINING THINGS, HUH?
AFTER ALL, YOU WOULD'VE TOLD ME IF SOMETHING LIKE THAT WERE GOING ON...
PRESS
!
HNNNGH
HEY!
WHAT'S THE BIG IDEA?
SHOVE
UGH!
WOULD YOU CUT THAT OUT?

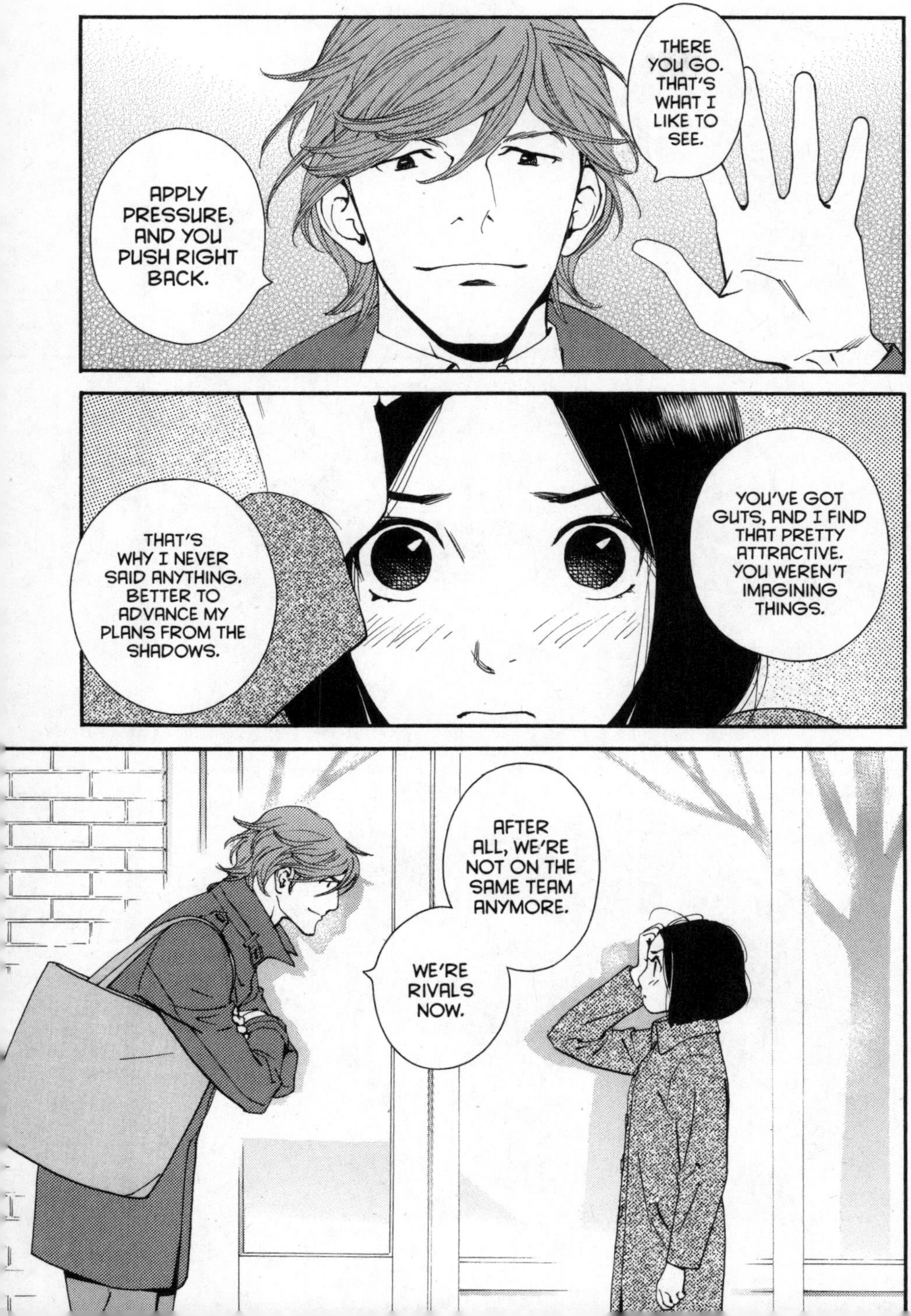
THERE YOU GO. THAT'S WHAT I LIKE TO SEE.
APPLY PRESSURE, AND YOU PUSH RIGHT BACK.
YOU'VE GOT GUTS, AND I FIND THAT PRETTY ATTRACTIVE. YOU WEREN'T IMAGINING THINGS.
THAT'S WHY I NEVER SAID ANYTHING. BETTER TO ADVANCE MY PLANS FROM THE SHADOWS.
AFTER ALL, WE'RE NOT ON THE SAME TEAM ANYMORE.
WE'RE RIVALS NOW.

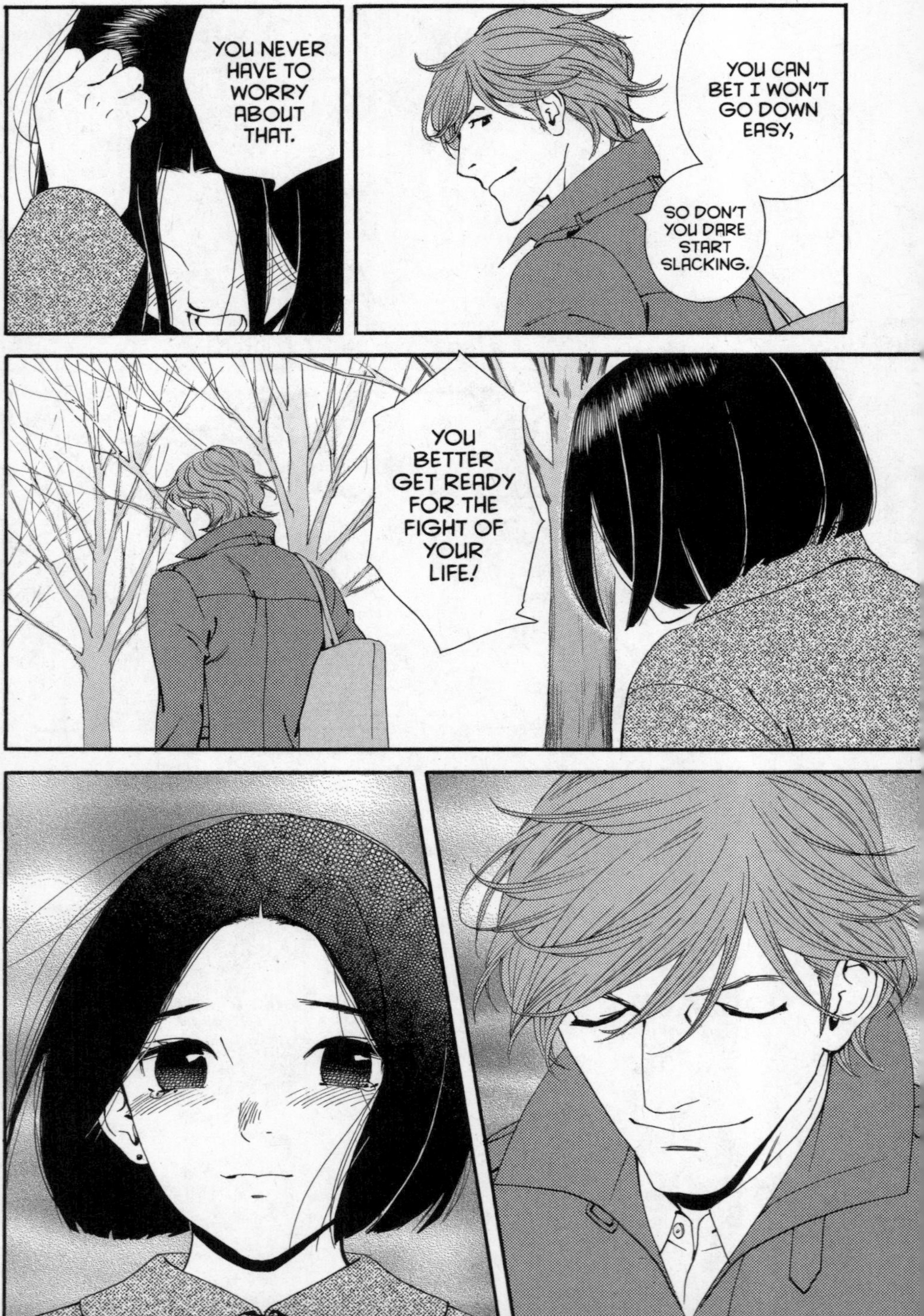
YOU CAN BET I WON'T GO DOWN EASY,
SO DON'T YOU DARE START SLACKING.
YOU NEVER HAVE TO WORRY ABOUT THAT.
YOU BETTER GET READY FOR THE FIGHT OF YOUR LIFE!

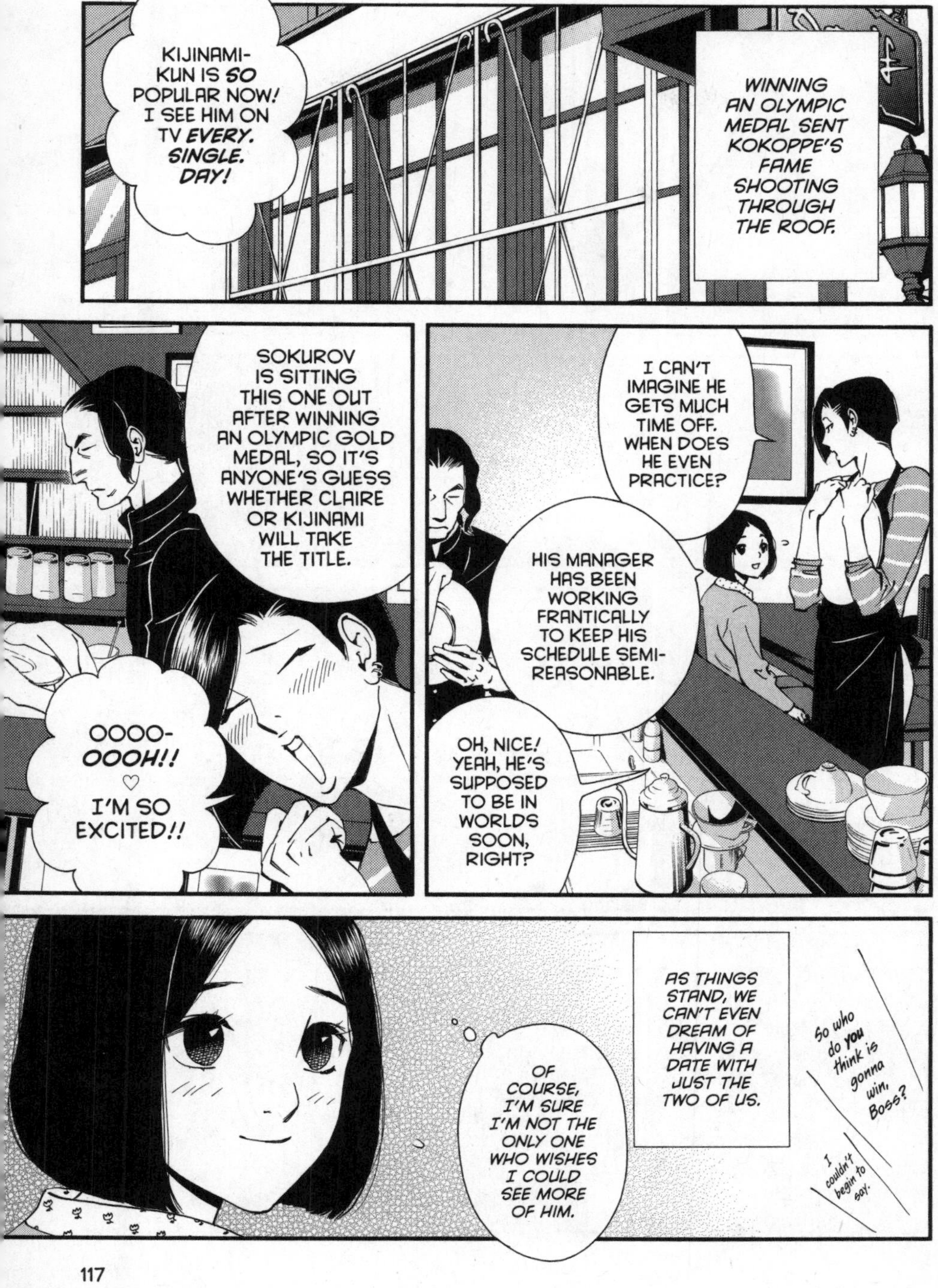
WINNING AN OLYMPIC MEDAL SENT KOKOPPE'S FAME SHOOTING THROUGH THE ROOF.
KIJINAMI-KUN IS *SO* POPULAR NOW! I SEE HIM ON TV *EVERY. SINGLE. DAY!*
I CAN'T IMAGINE HE GETS MUCH TIME OFF. WHEN DOES HE EVEN PRACTICE?
HIS MANAGER HAS BEEN WORKING FRANTICALLY TO KEEP HIS SCHEDULE SEMI-REASONABLE.
OH, NICE! YEAH, HE'S SUPPOSED TO BE IN WORLDS SOON, RIGHT?
SOKUROV IS SITTING THIS ONE OUT AFTER WINNING AN OLYMPIC GOLD MEDAL, SO IT'S ANYONE'S GUESS WHETHER CLAIRE OR KIJINAMI WILL TAKE THE TITLE.
OOOO-*OOOH!!* ♡ I'M SO EXCITED!!
So who do **you** think is gonna win, Boss?
I couldn't begin to say.
AS THINGS STAND, WE CAN'T EVEN DREAM OF HAVING A DATE WITH JUST THE TWO OF US.
OF COURSE, I'M SURE I'M NOT THE ONLY ONE WHO WISHES I COULD SEE MORE OF HIM.

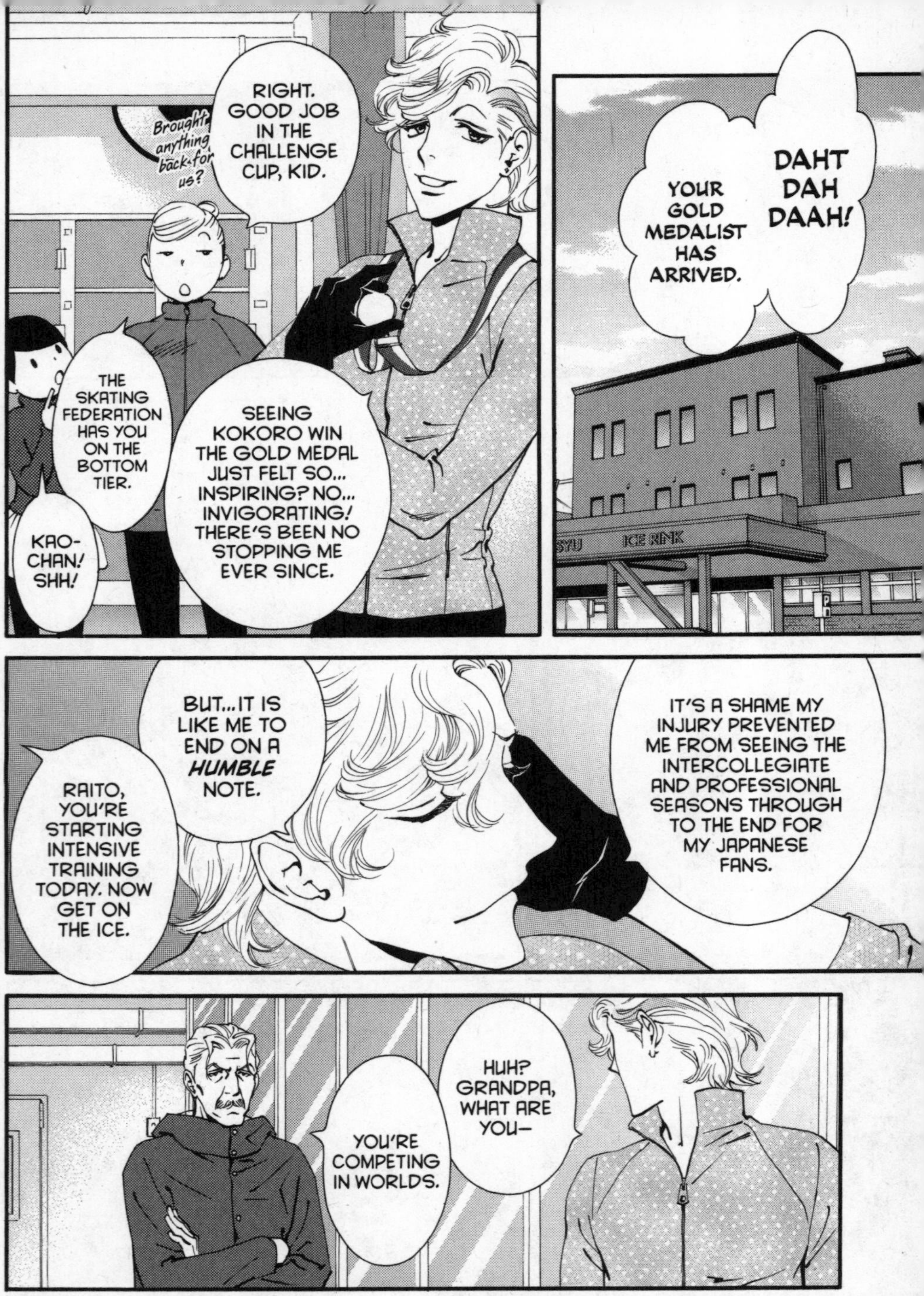
DAHT DAH DAAH!
YOUR GOLD MEDALIST HAS ARRIVED.
ICE RINK
RIGHT. GOOD JOB IN THE CHALLENGE CUP, KID.
Brought anything back for us?
SEEING KOKORO WIN THE GOLD MEDAL JUST FELT SO... INSPIRING? NO... INVIGORATING! THERE'S BEEN NO STOPPING ME EVER SINCE.
THE SKATING FEDERATION HAS YOU ON THE BOTTOM TIER.
KAO-CHAN! SHH!
IT'S A SHAME MY INJURY PREVENTED ME FROM SEEING THE INTERCOLLEGIATE AND PROFESSIONAL SEASONS THROUGH TO THE END FOR MY JAPANESE FANS.
BUT...IT IS LIKE ME TO END ON A *HUMBLE* NOTE.
RAITO, YOU'RE STARTING INTENSIVE TRAINING TODAY. NOW GET ON THE ICE.
HUH? GRANDPA, WHAT ARE YOU—
YOU'RE COMPETING IN WORLDS.

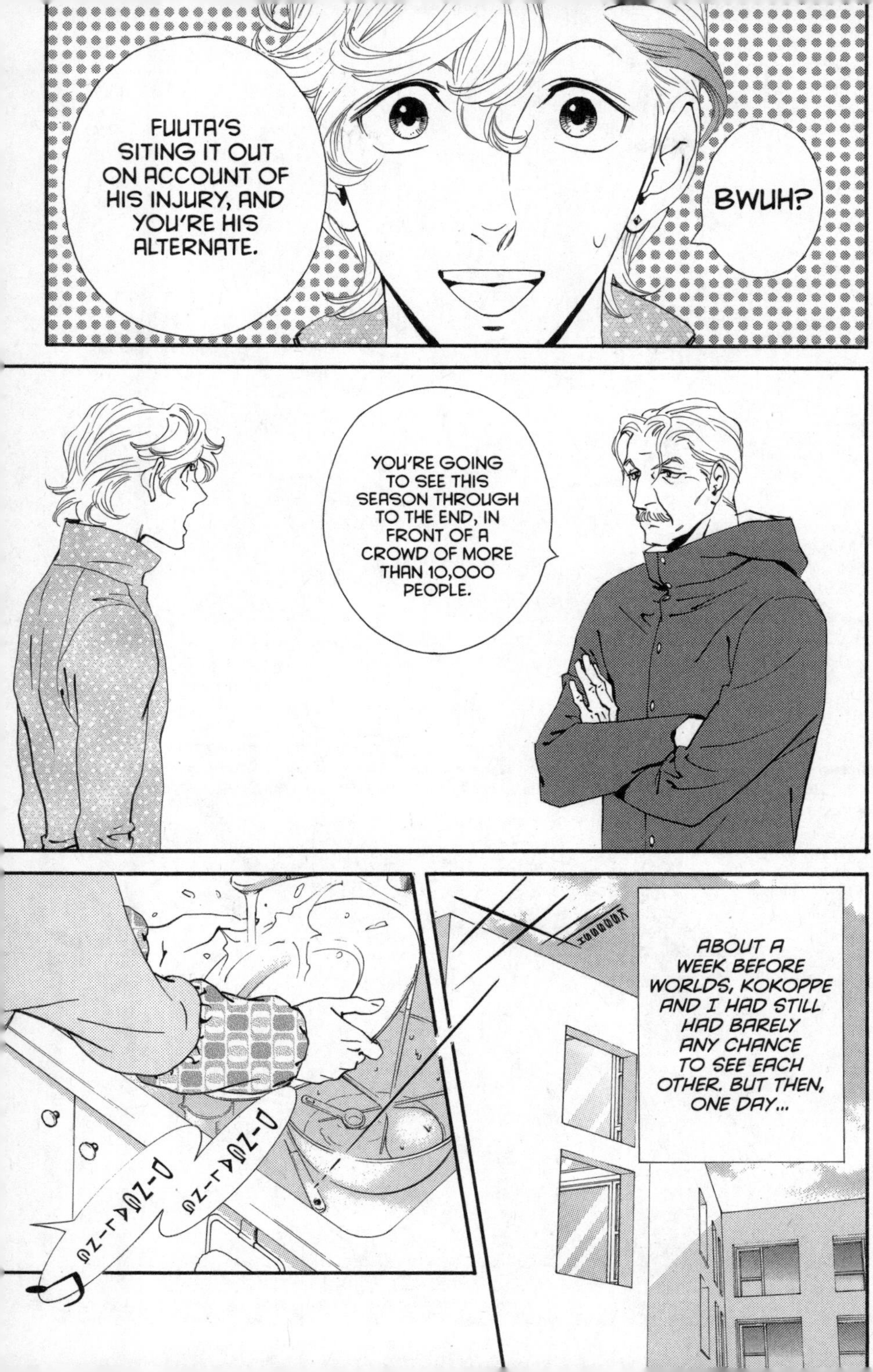
BWUH?
FUUTA'S SITING IT OUT ON ACCOUNT OF HIS INJURY, AND YOU'RE HIS ALTERNATE.
YOU'RE GOING TO SEE THIS SEASON THROUGH TO THE END, IN FRONT OF A CROWD OF MORE THAN 10,000 PEOPLE.
ABOUT A WEEK BEFORE WORLDS, KOKOPPE AND I HAD STILL HAD BARELY ANY CHANCE TO SEE EACH OTHER. BUT THEN, ONE DAY...

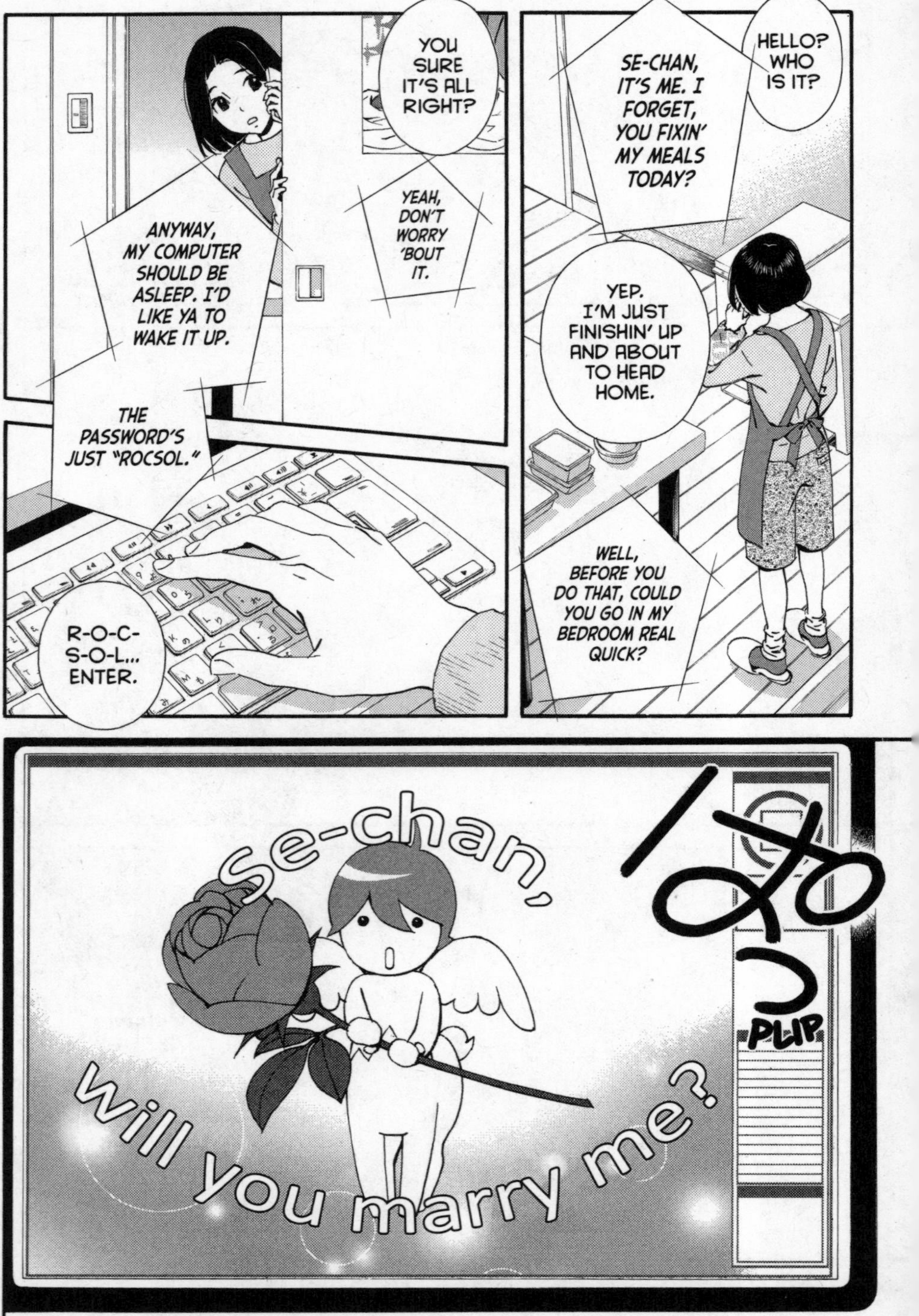
HELLO? WHO IS IT?
SE-CHAN, IT'S ME. I FORGET, YOU FIXIN' MY MEALS TODAY?
YEP. I'M JUST FINISHIN' UP AND ABOUT TO HEAD HOME.
WELL, BEFORE YOU DO THAT, COULD YOU GO IN MY BEDROOM REAL QUICK?
YOU SURE IT'S ALL RIGHT?
YEAH, DON'T WORRY 'BOUT IT.
ANYWAY, MY COMPUTER SHOULD BE ASLEEP. I'D LIKE YA TO WAKE IT UP.
THE PASSWORD'S JUST "ROCSOL."
R-O-C-S-O-L... ENTER.
ぬっ
PLIP
Se-chan, will you marry me?

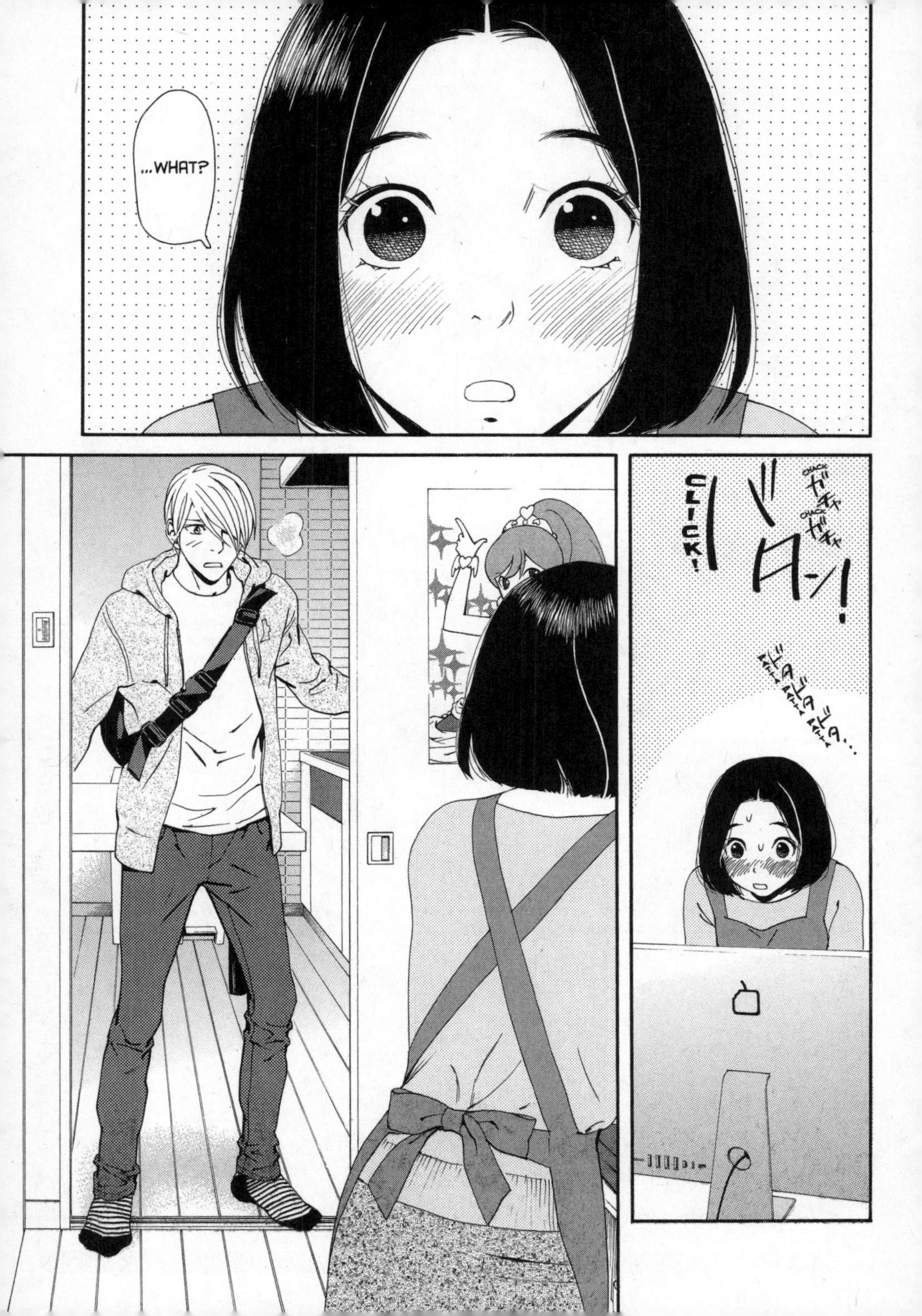
...WHAT?
CHACK ガチャ CHACK ガチャ
バターン!
CLICK!
ドタ ドタ ドタ...
RATTA RATTA RATTA

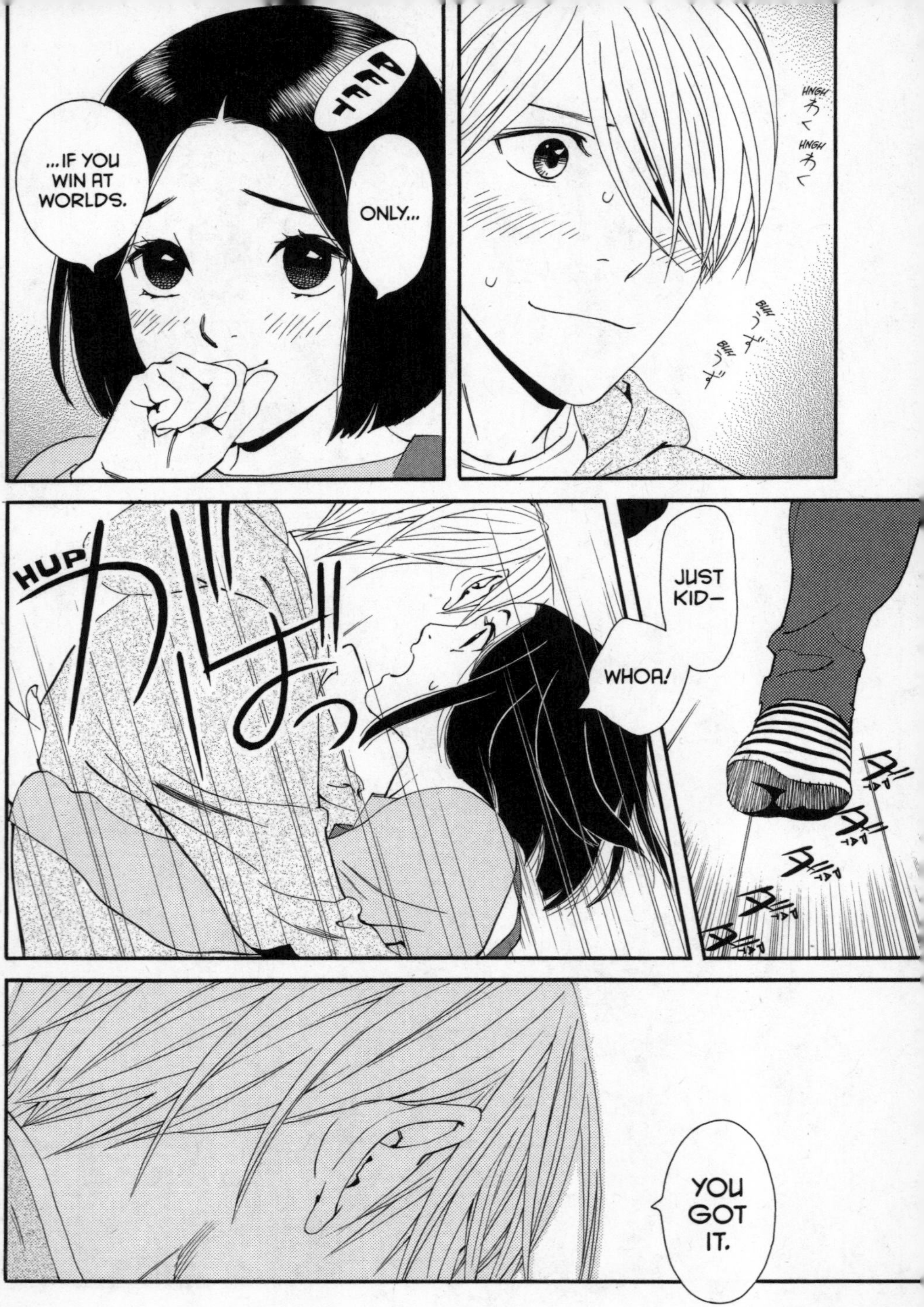
HNGH
HNGH
BUH
BUH
PFFT
ONLY...
...IF YOU WIN AT WORLDS.
JUST KID—
WHOA!
HUP
YOU GOT IT.

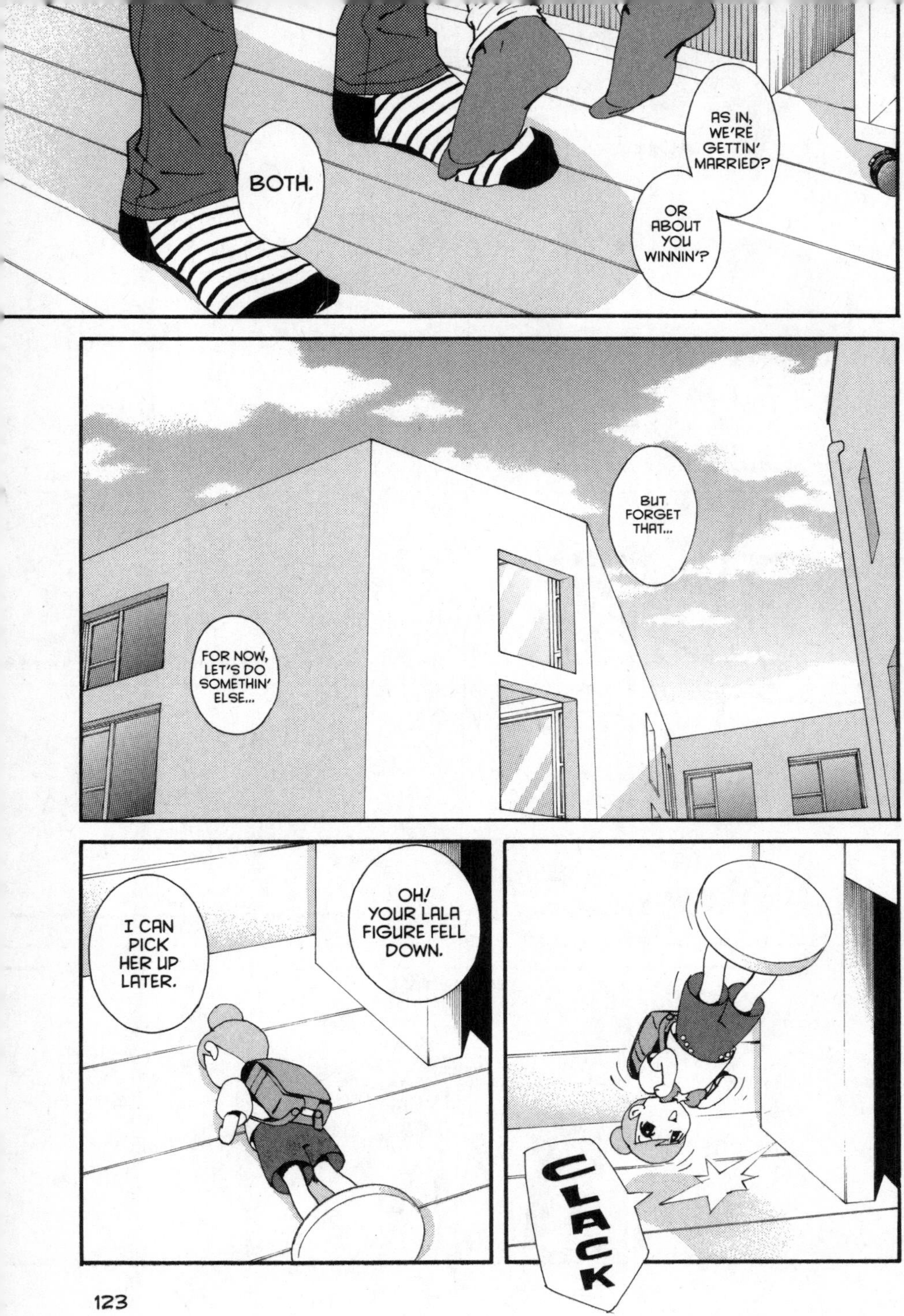
AS IN, WE'RE GETTIN' MARRIED?
OR ABOUT YOU WINNIN'?
BOTH.
BUT FORGET THAT...
FOR NOW, LET'S DO SOMETHIN' ELSE...
CLACK
OH! YOUR LALA FIGURE FELL DOWN.
I CAN PICK HER UP LATER.

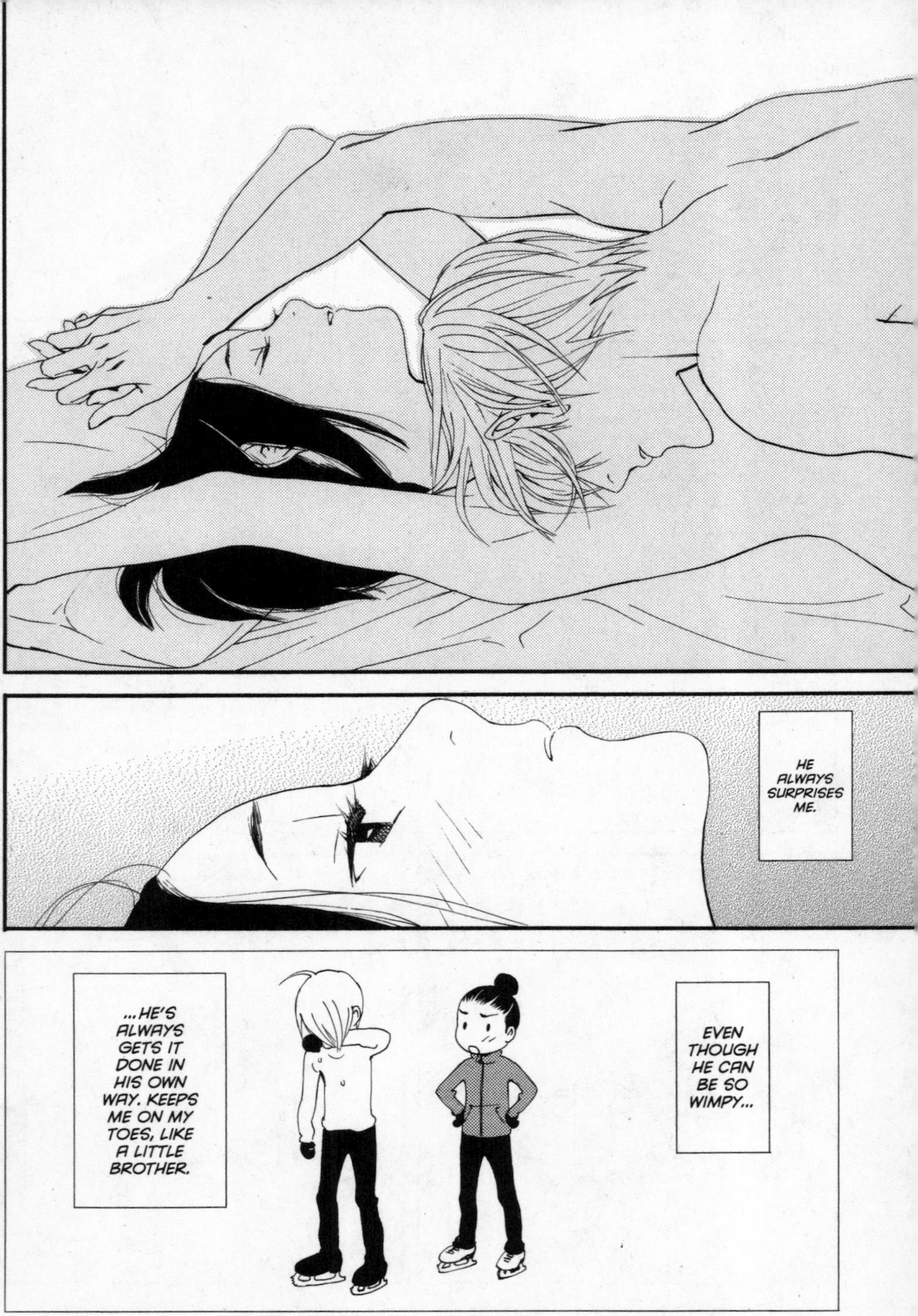
HE ALWAYS SURPRISES ME.
EVEN THOUGH HE CAN BE SO WIMPY...
...HE'S ALWAYS GETS IT DONE IN HIS OWN WAY. KEEPS ME ON MY TOES, LIKE A LITTLE BROTHER.

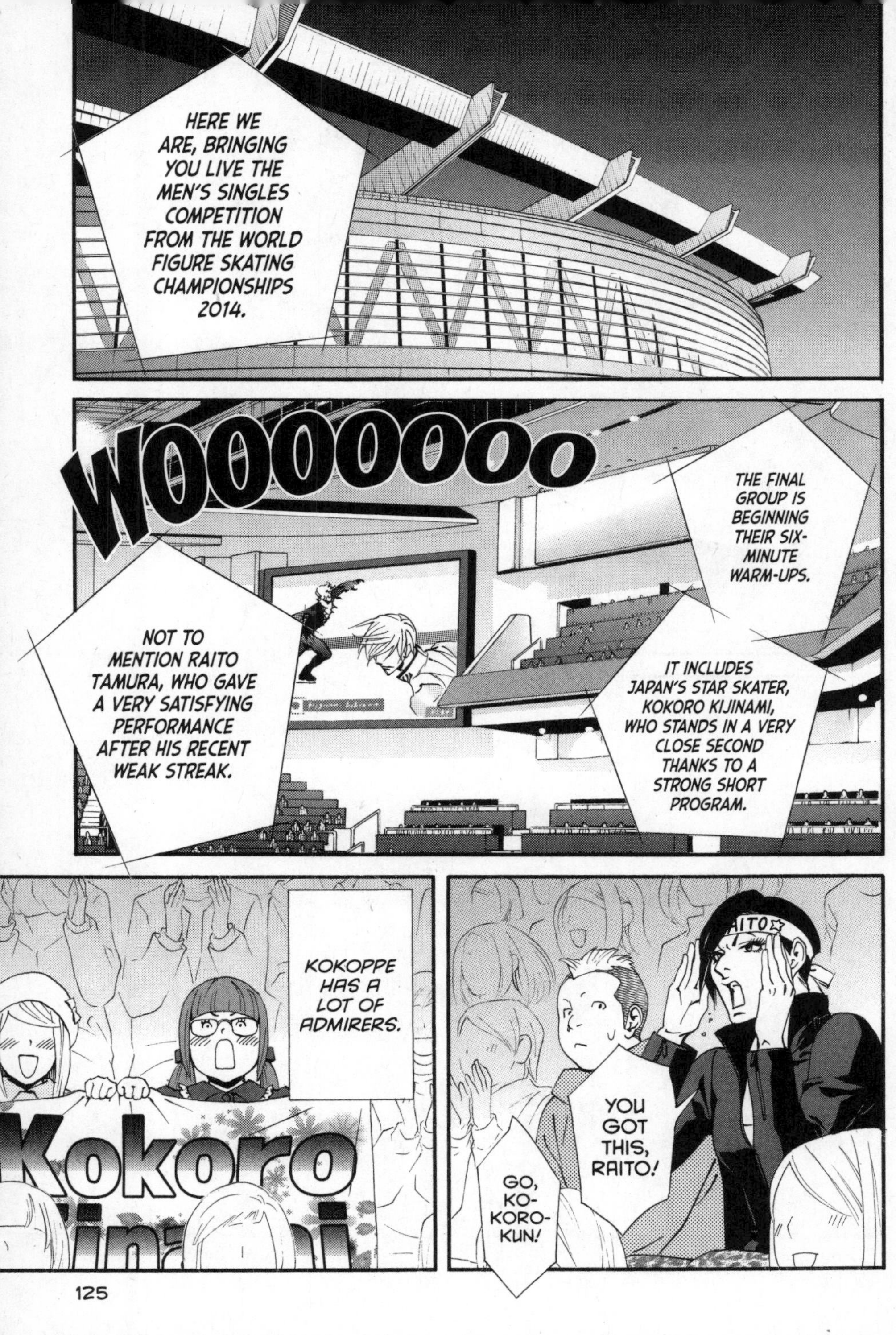
HERE WE ARE, BRINGING YOU LIVE THE MEN'S SINGLES COMPETITION FROM THE WORLD FIGURE SKATING CHAMPIONSHIPS 2014.
WOOOOOOO
THE FINAL GROUP IS BEGINNING THEIR SIX-MINUTE WARM-UPS.
IT INCLUDES JAPAN'S STAR SKATER, KOKORO KIJINAMI, WHO STANDS IN A VERY CLOSE SECOND THANKS TO A STRONG SHORT PROGRAM.
NOT TO MENTION RAITO TAMURA, WHO GAVE A VERY SATISFYING PERFORMANCE AFTER HIS RECENT WEAK STREAK.
RAITO
YOU GOT THIS, RAITO!
GO, KOKOROKUN!
KOKOPPE HAS A LOT OF ADMIRERS.
Kokoro

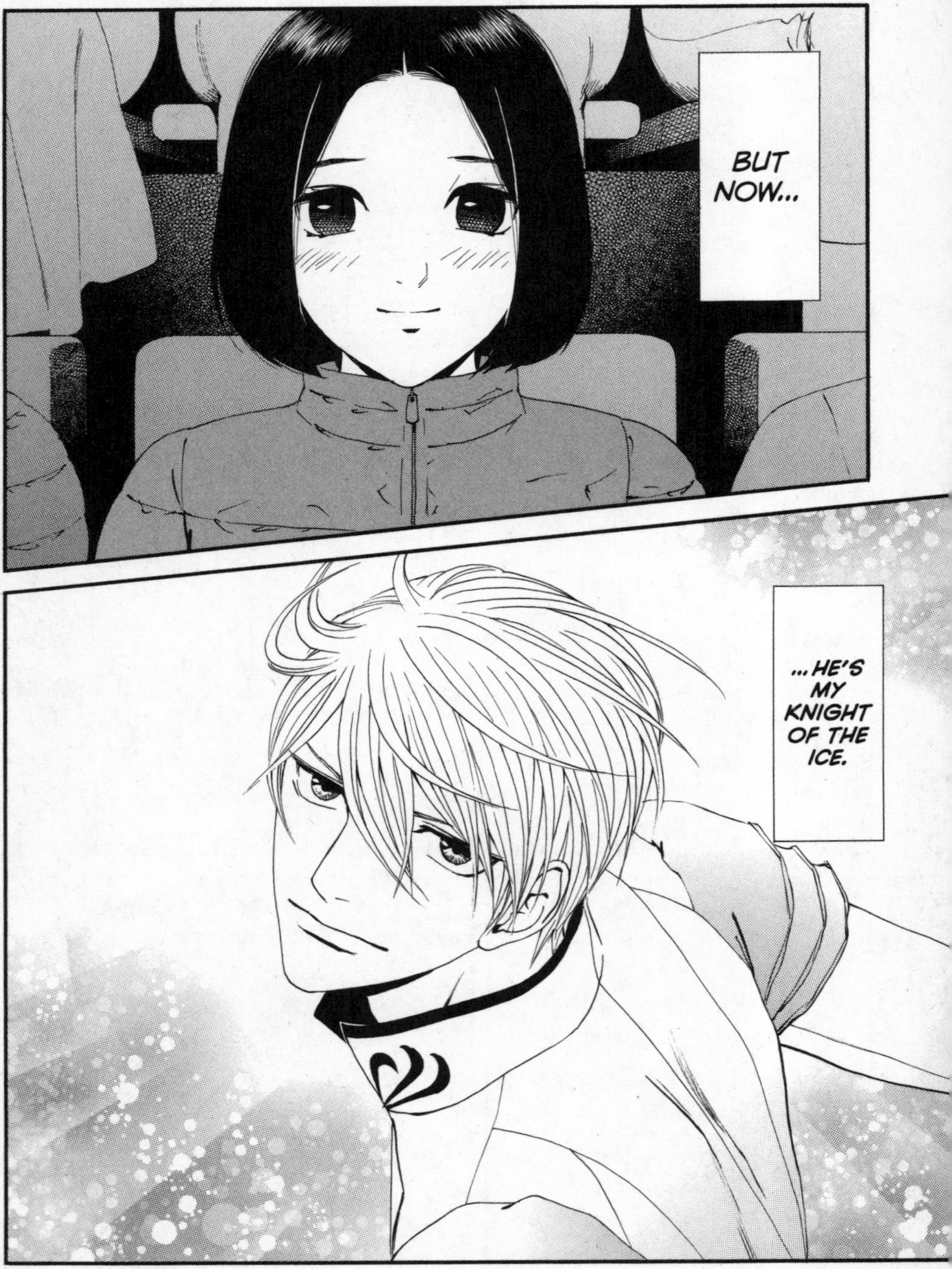
BUT NOW...
...HE'S MY KNIGHT OF THE ICE.

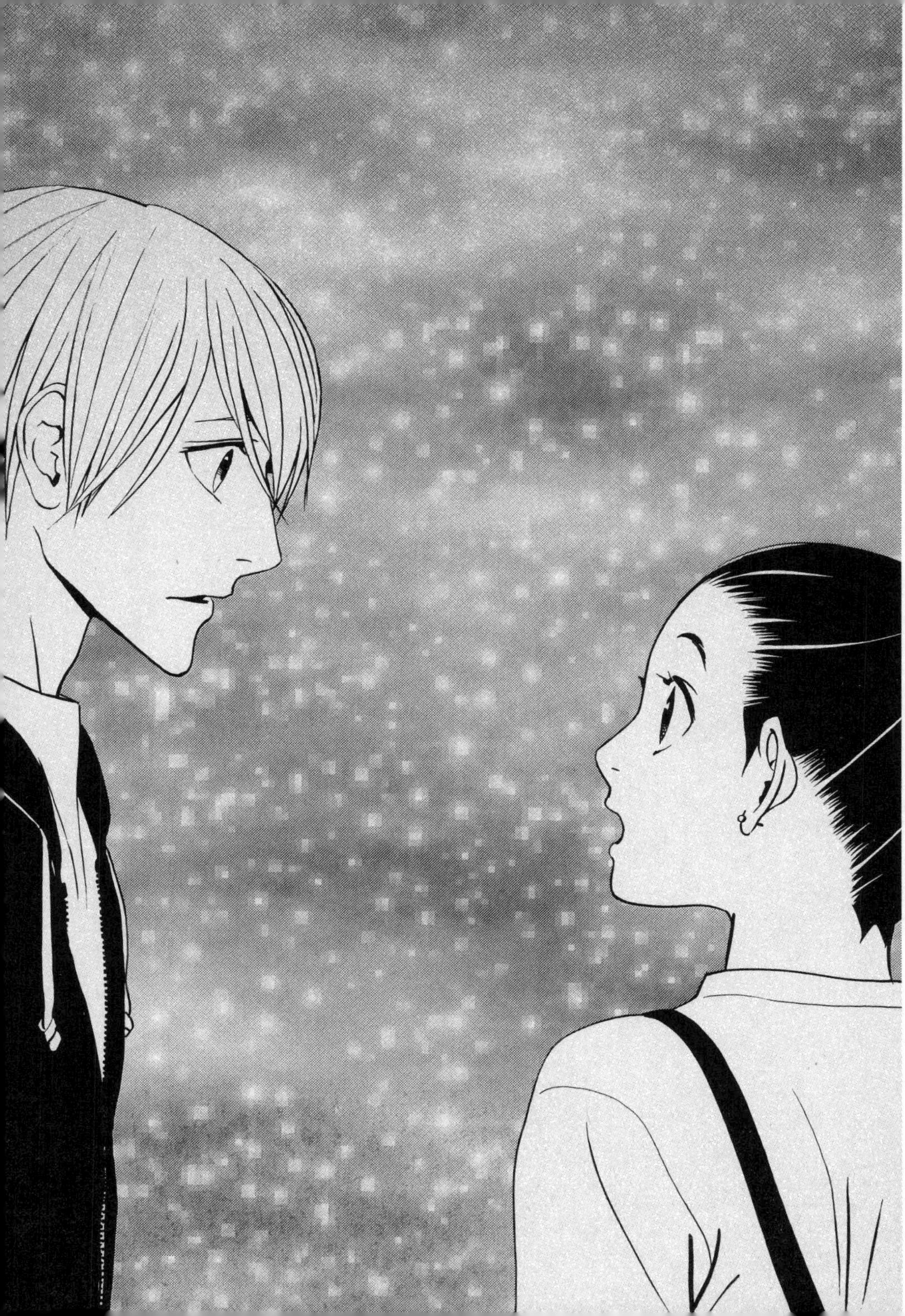

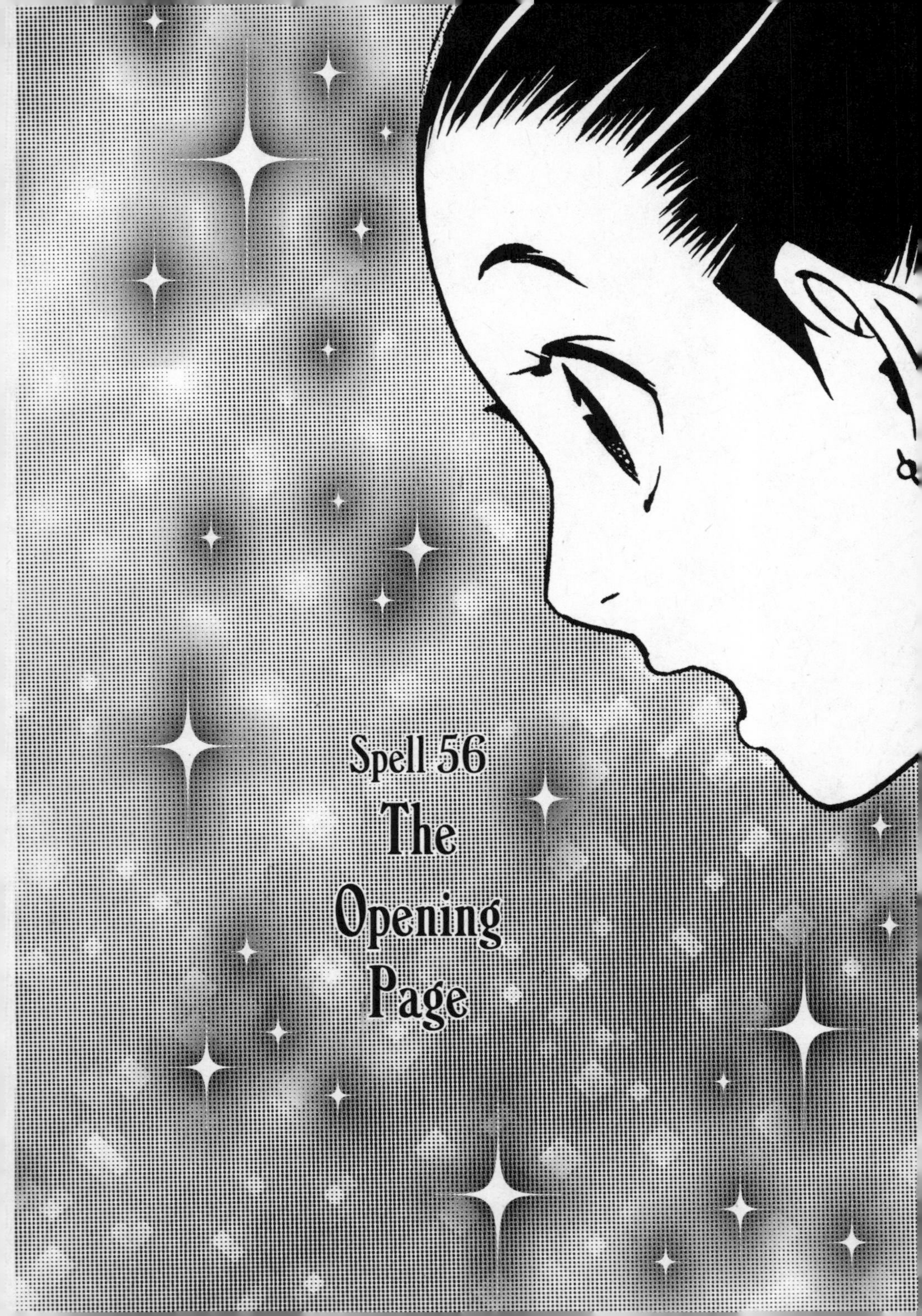
Spell 56
The Opening Page

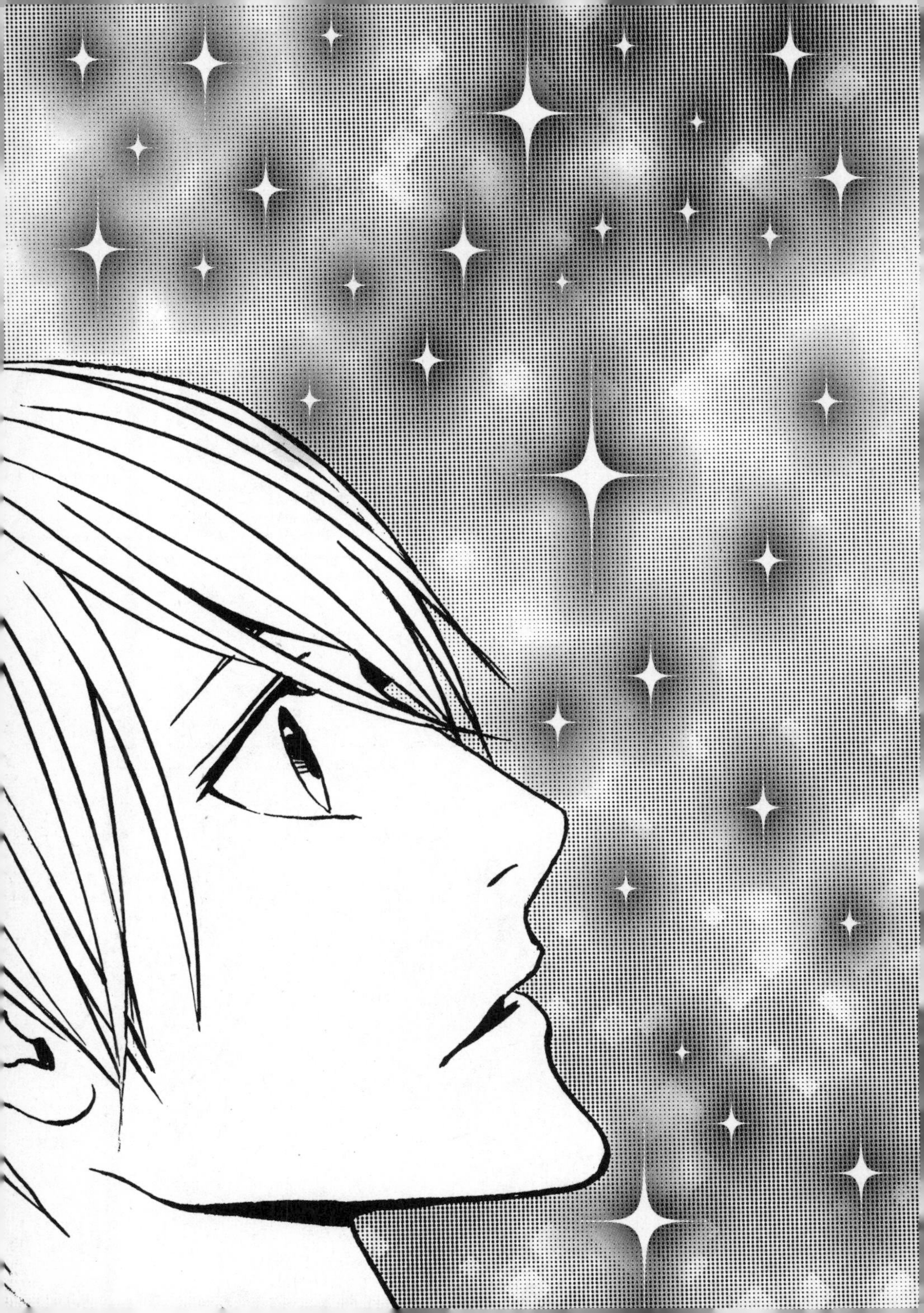

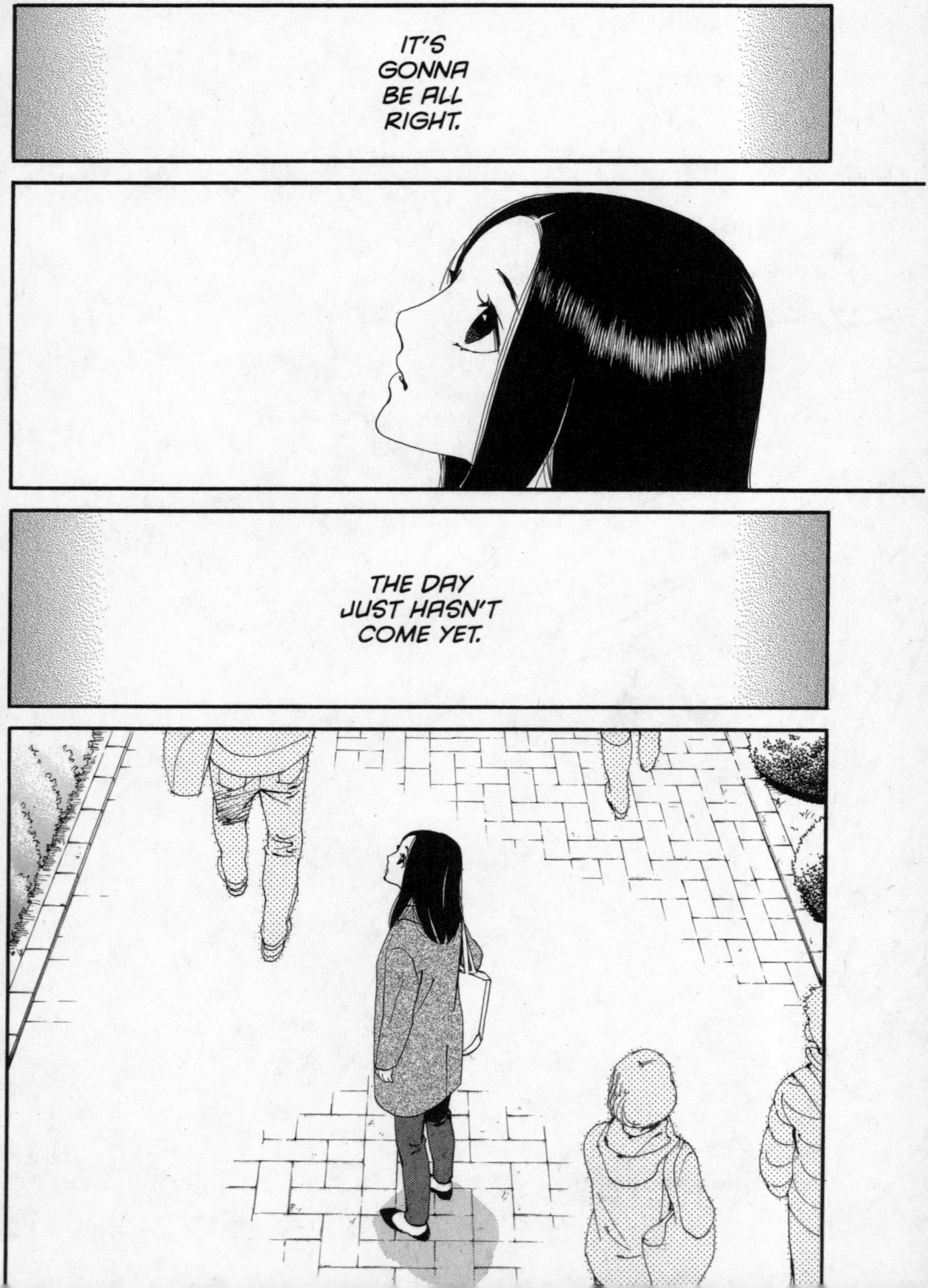
IT'S GONNA BE ALL RIGHT.
THE DAY JUST HASN'T COME YET.

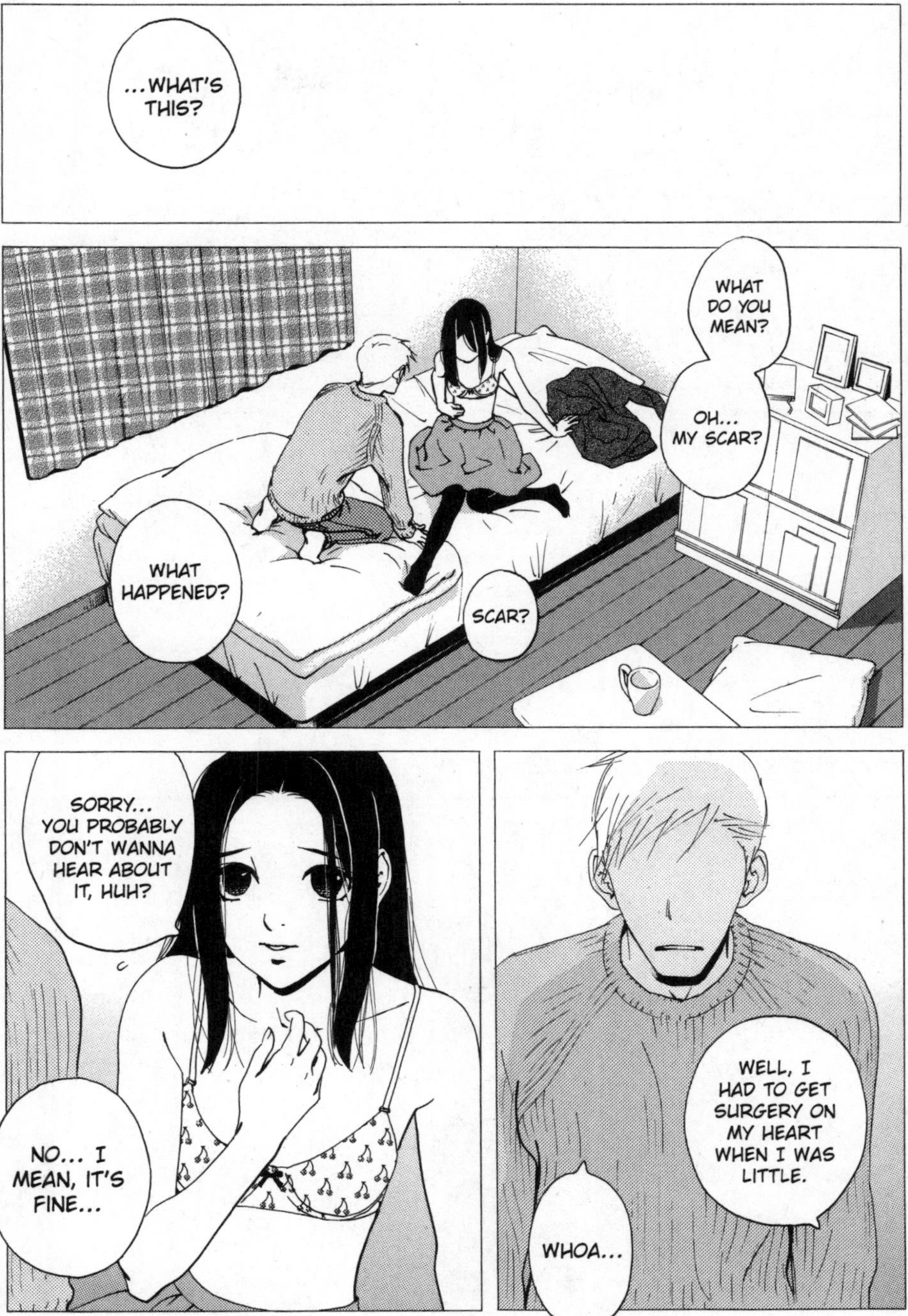
...WHAT'S THIS?
WHAT DO YOU MEAN?
OH... MY SCAR?
SCAR?
WHAT HAPPENED?
WELL, I HAD TO GET SURGERY ON MY HEART WHEN I WAS LITTLE.
WHOA...
SORRY... YOU PROBABLY DON'T WANNA HEAR ABOUT IT, HUH?
NO... I MEAN, IT'S FINE...

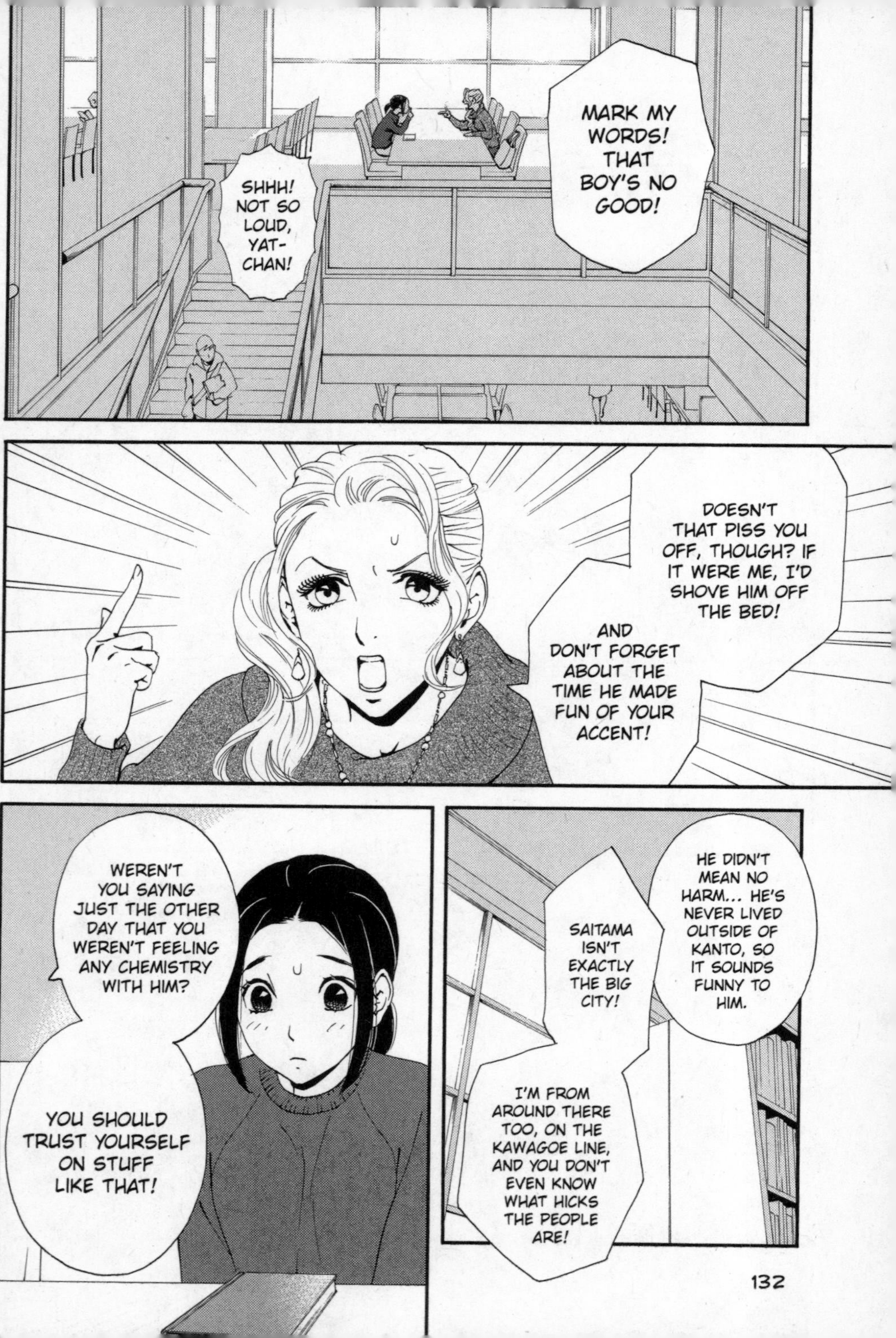
MARK MY WORDS! THAT BOY'S NO GOOD!
SHHH! NOT SO LOUD, YAT-CHAN!
DOESN'T THAT PISS YOU OFF, THOUGH? IF IT WERE ME, I'D SHOVE HIM OFF THE BED!
AND DON'T FORGET ABOUT THE TIME HE MADE FUN OF YOUR ACCENT!
HE DIDN'T MEAN NO HARM... HE'S NEVER LIVED OUTSIDE OF KANTO, SO IT SOUNDS FUNNY TO HIM.
SAITAMA ISN'T EXACTLY THE BIG CITY!
I'M FROM AROUND THERE TOO, ON THE KAWAGOE LINE, AND YOU DON'T EVEN KNOW WHAT HICKS THE PEOPLE ARE!
WEREN'T YOU SAYING JUST THE OTHER DAY THAT YOU WEREN'T FEELING ANY CHEMISTRY WITH HIM?
YOU SHOULD TRUST YOURSELF ON STUFF LIKE THAT!

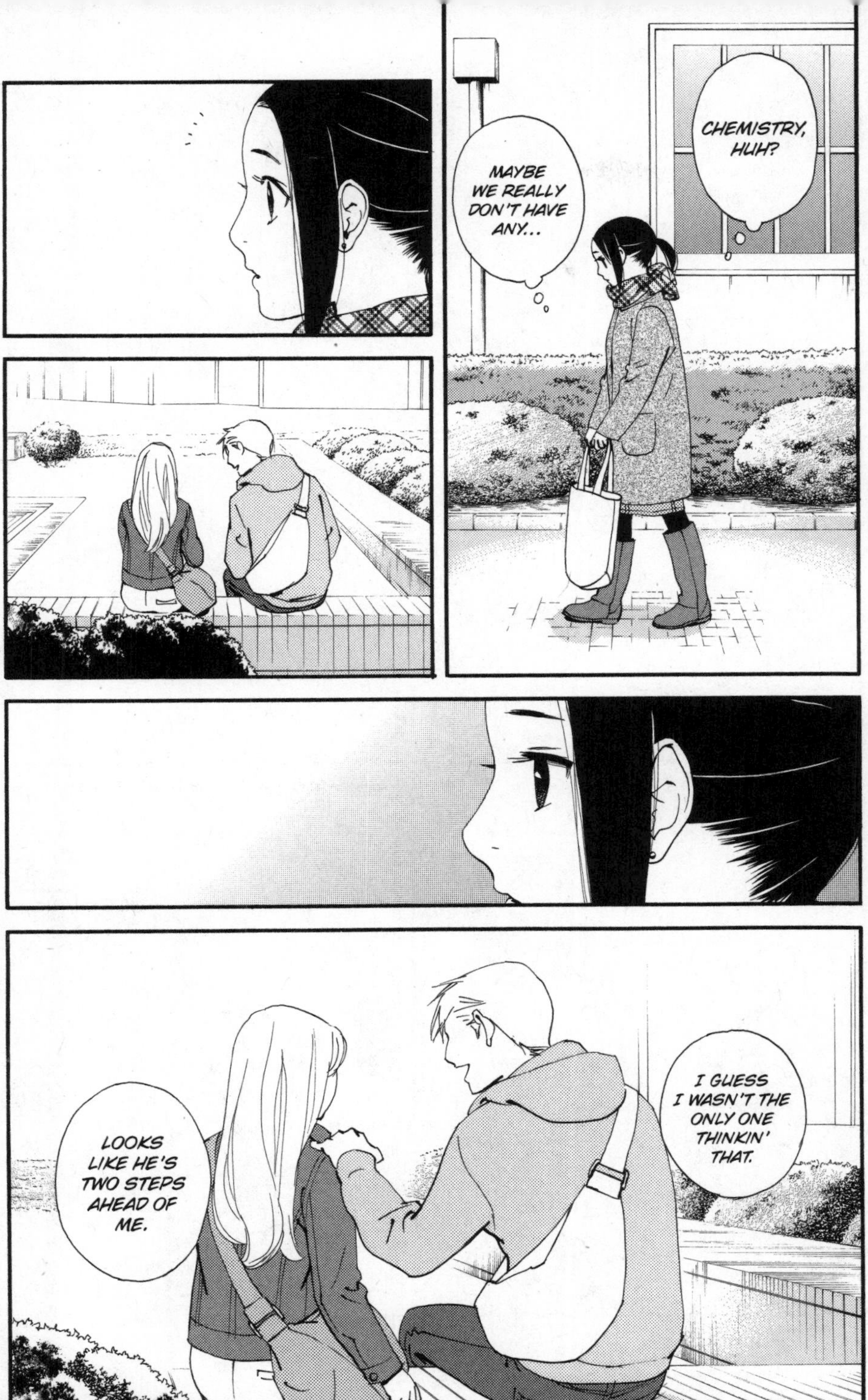
CHEMISTRY, HUH?
MAYBE WE REALLY DON'T HAVE ANY...
I GUESS I WASN'T THE ONLY ONE THINKIN' THAT.
LOOKS LIKE HE'S TWO STEPS AHEAD OF ME.

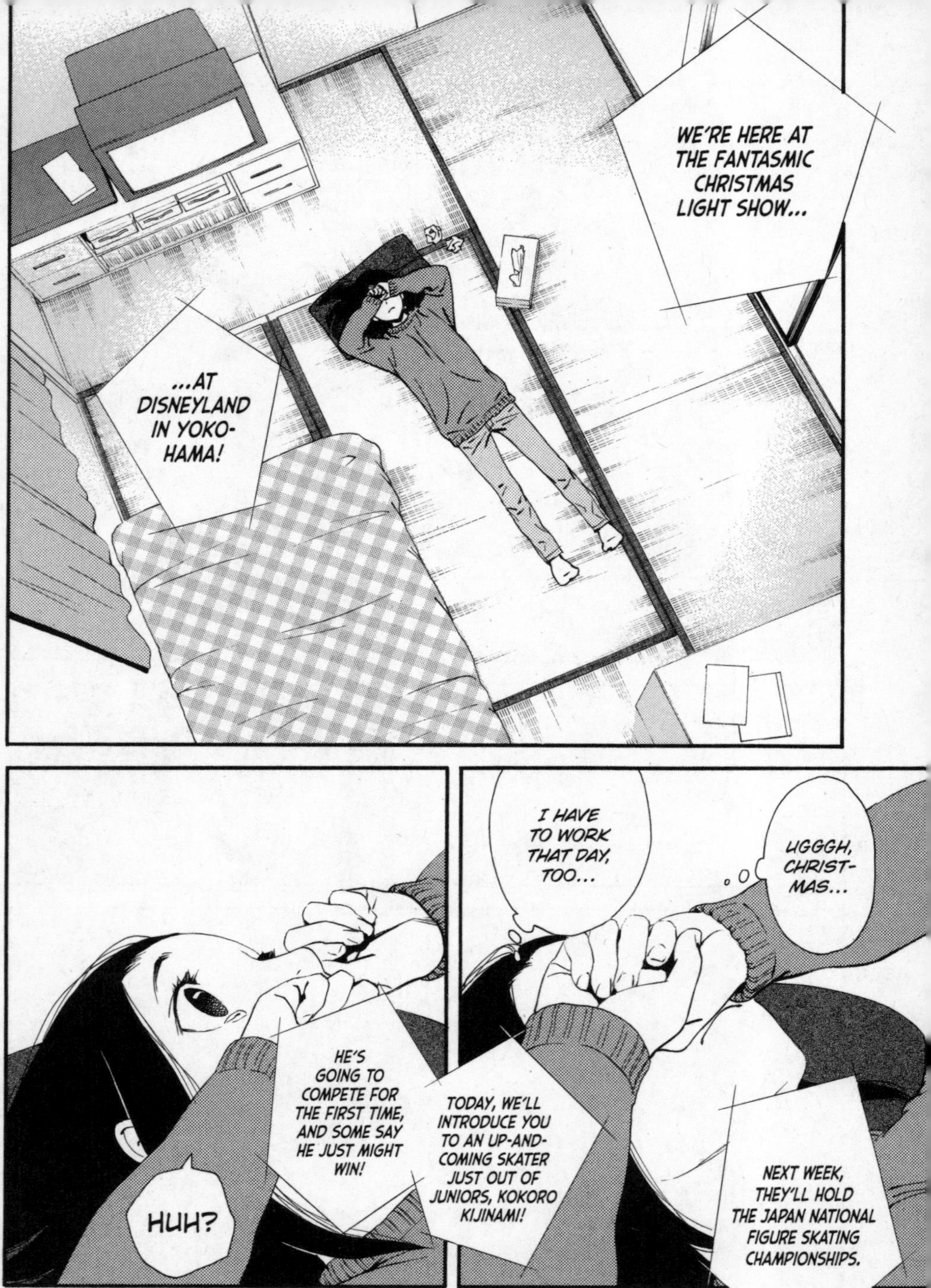
WE'RE HERE AT THE FANTASMIC CHRISTMAS LIGHT SHOW...
...AT DISNEYLAND IN YOKO-HAMA!
UGGGH, CHRIST-MAS...
I HAVE TO WORK THAT DAY, TOO...
NEXT WEEK, THEY'LL HOLD THE JAPAN NATIONAL FIGURE SKATING CHAMPIONSHIPS.
TODAY, WE'LL INTRODUCE YOU TO AN UP-AND-COMING SKATER JUST OUT OF JUNIORS, KOKORO KIJINAMI!
HE'S GOING TO COMPETE FOR THE FIRST TIME, AND SOME SAY HE JUST MIGHT WIN!
HUH?

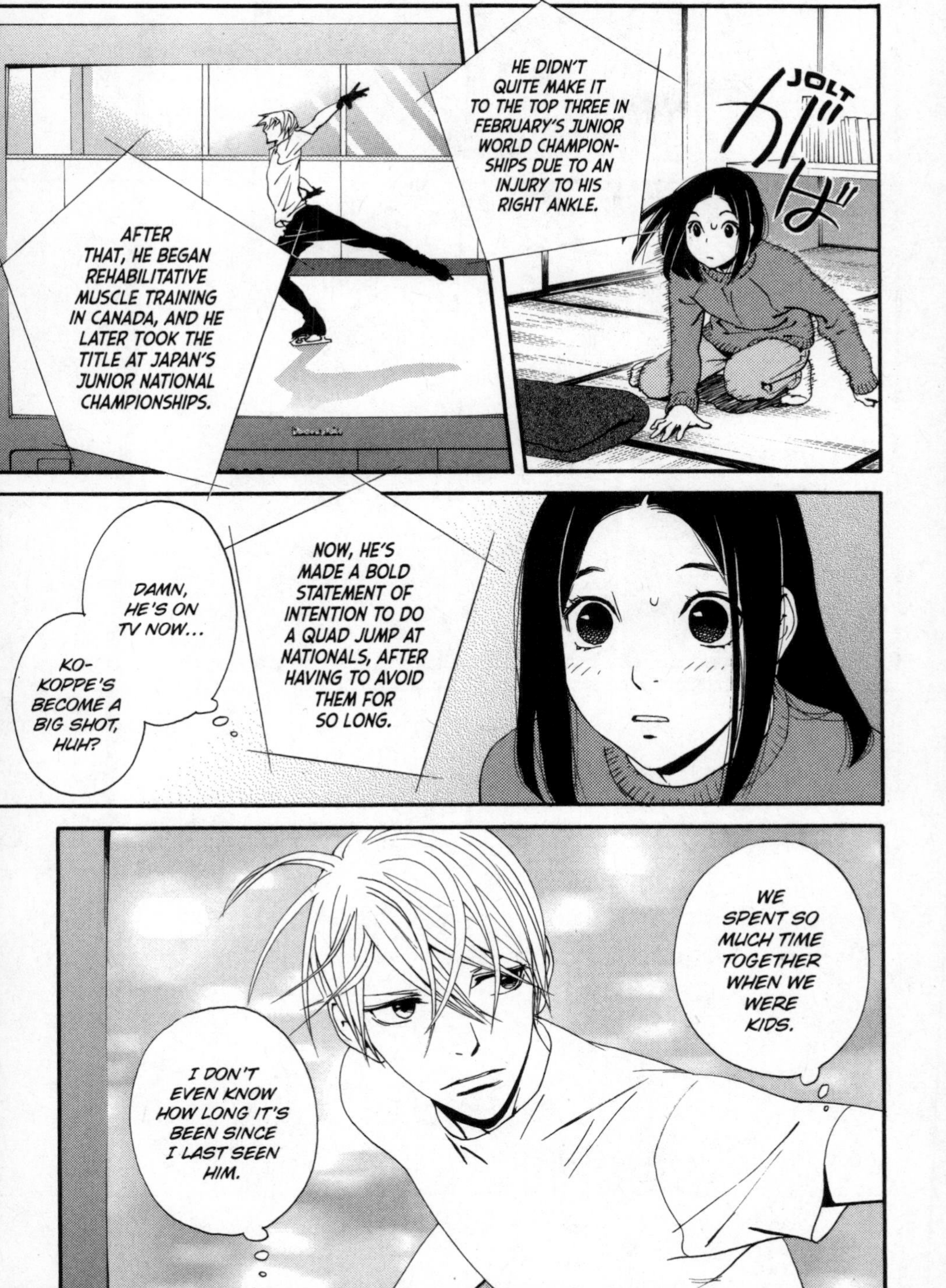
JOLT
がば
HE DIDN'T QUITE MAKE IT TO THE TOP THREE IN FEBRUARY'S JUNIOR WORLD CHAMPION-SHIPS DUE TO AN INJURY TO HIS RIGHT ANKLE.
AFTER THAT, HE BEGAN REHABILITATIVE MUSCLE TRAINING IN CANADA, AND HE LATER TOOK THE TITLE AT JAPAN'S JUNIOR NATIONAL CHAMPIONSHIPS.
NOW, HE'S MADE A BOLD STATEMENT OF INTENTION TO DO A QUAD JUMP AT NATIONALS, AFTER HAVING TO AVOID THEM FOR SO LONG.
DAMN, HE'S ON TV NOW...
KO-KOPPE'S BECOME A BIG SHOT, HUH?
WE SPENT SO MUCH TIME TOGETHER WHEN WE WERE KIDS.
I DON'T EVEN KNOW HOW LONG IT'S BEEN SINCE I LAST SEEN HIM.

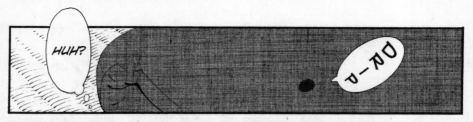

HUH?

d—a

WHAT'S MAKIN' ME FEEL SO SENTIMENTAL ALL OF A SUDDEN?

WHY AM I CRYIN'?

IT'S GONNA BE OKAY.

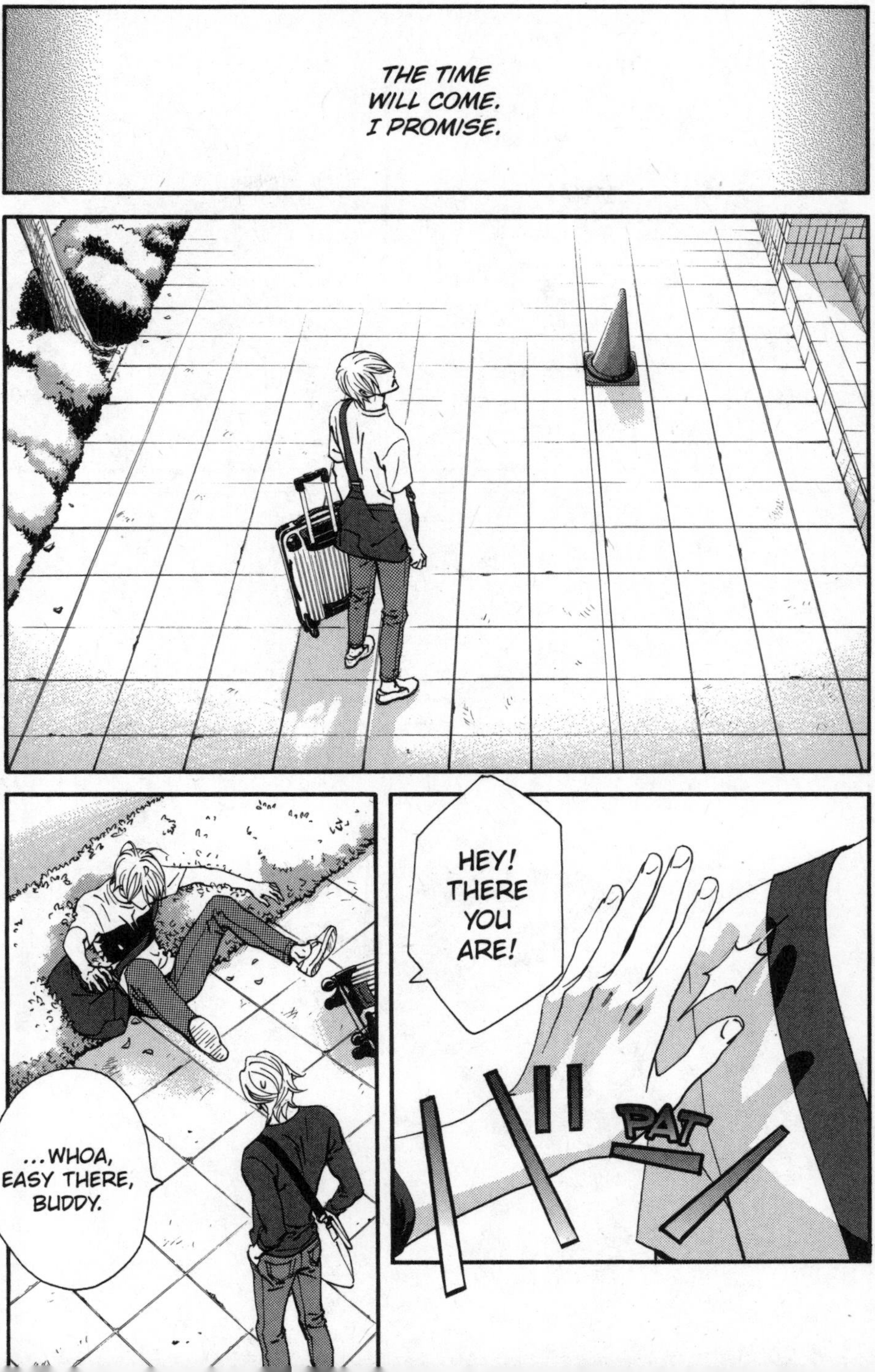
THE TIME WILL COME. I PROMISE.
HEY! THERE YOU ARE!
PAT
...WHOA, EASY THERE, BUDDY.

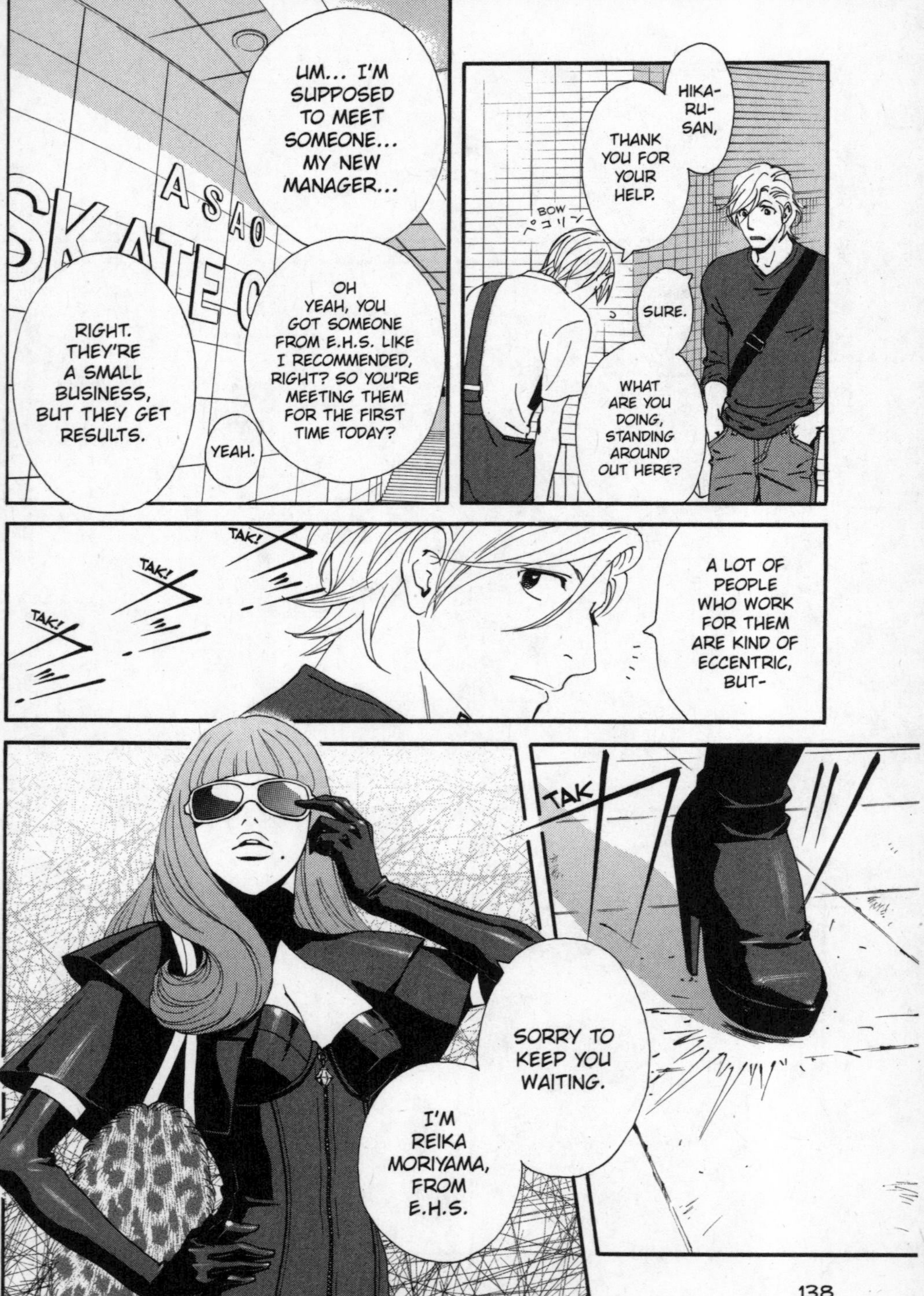
HIKARU-SAN,
THANK YOU FOR YOUR HELP.
BOW
SURE.
WHAT ARE YOU DOING, STANDING AROUND OUT HERE?
UM... I'M SUPPOSED TO MEET SOMEONE... MY NEW MANAGER...
ASAO SKATE C
OH YEAH, YOU GOT SOMEONE FROM E.H.S. LIKE I RECOMMENDED, RIGHT? SO YOU'RE MEETING THEM FOR THE FIRST TIME TODAY?
YEAH.
RIGHT. THEY'RE A SMALL BUSINESS, BUT THEY GET RESULTS.
A LOT OF PEOPLE WHO WORK FOR THEM ARE KIND OF ECCENTRIC, BUT-
TAK!
TAK!
TAK!
TAK
SORRY TO KEEP YOU WAITING.
I'M REIKA MORIYAMA, FROM E.H.S.

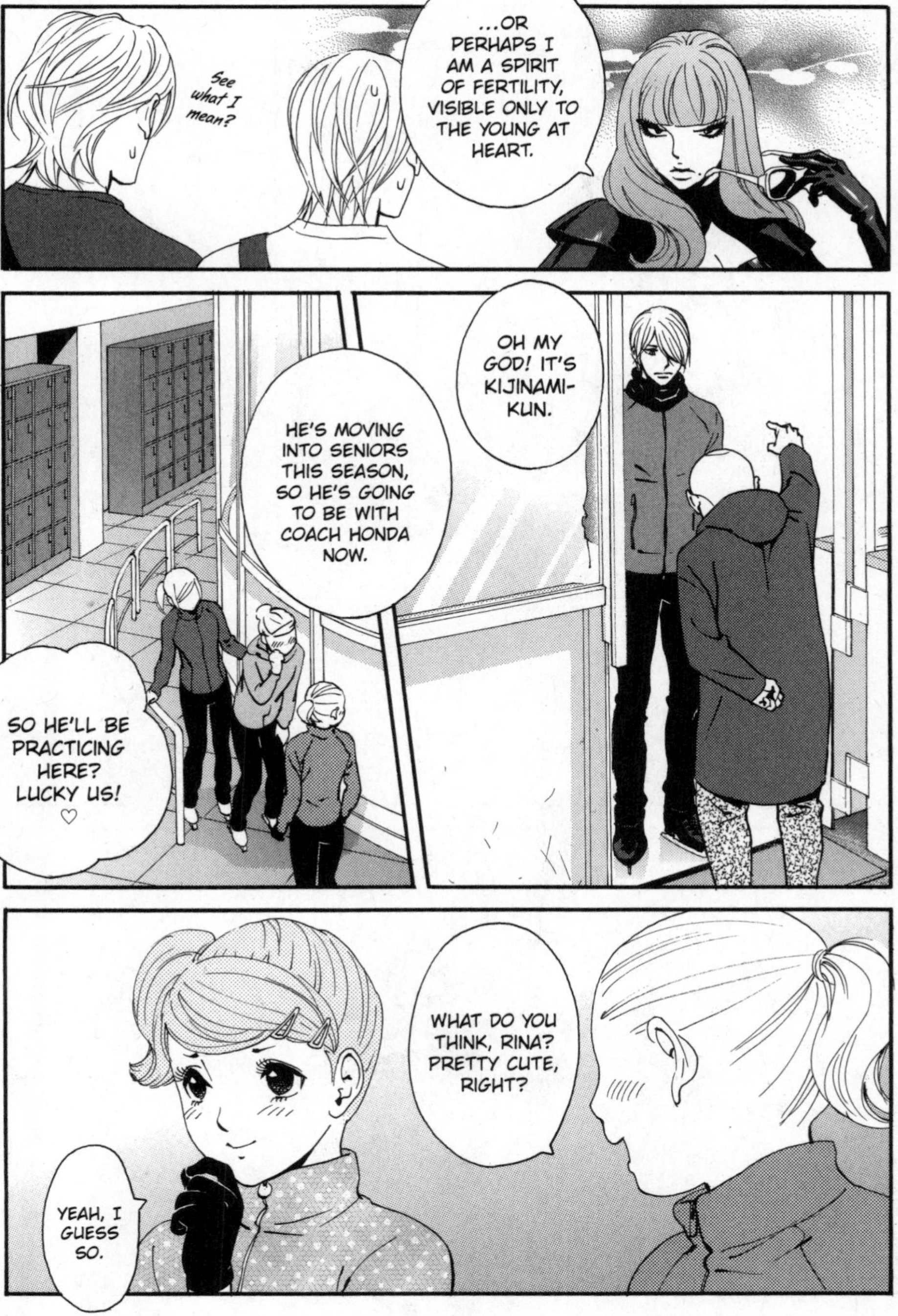
...OR PERHAPS I AM A SPIRIT OF FERTILITY, VISIBLE ONLY TO THE YOUNG AT HEART.
See what I mean?
OH MY GOD! IT'S KIJINAMI-KUN.
HE'S MOVING INTO SENIORS THIS SEASON, SO HE'S GOING TO BE WITH COACH HONDA NOW.
SO HE'LL BE PRACTICING HERE? LUCKY US! ♡
WHAT DO YOU THINK, RINA? PRETTY CUTE, RIGHT?
YEAH, I GUESS SO.

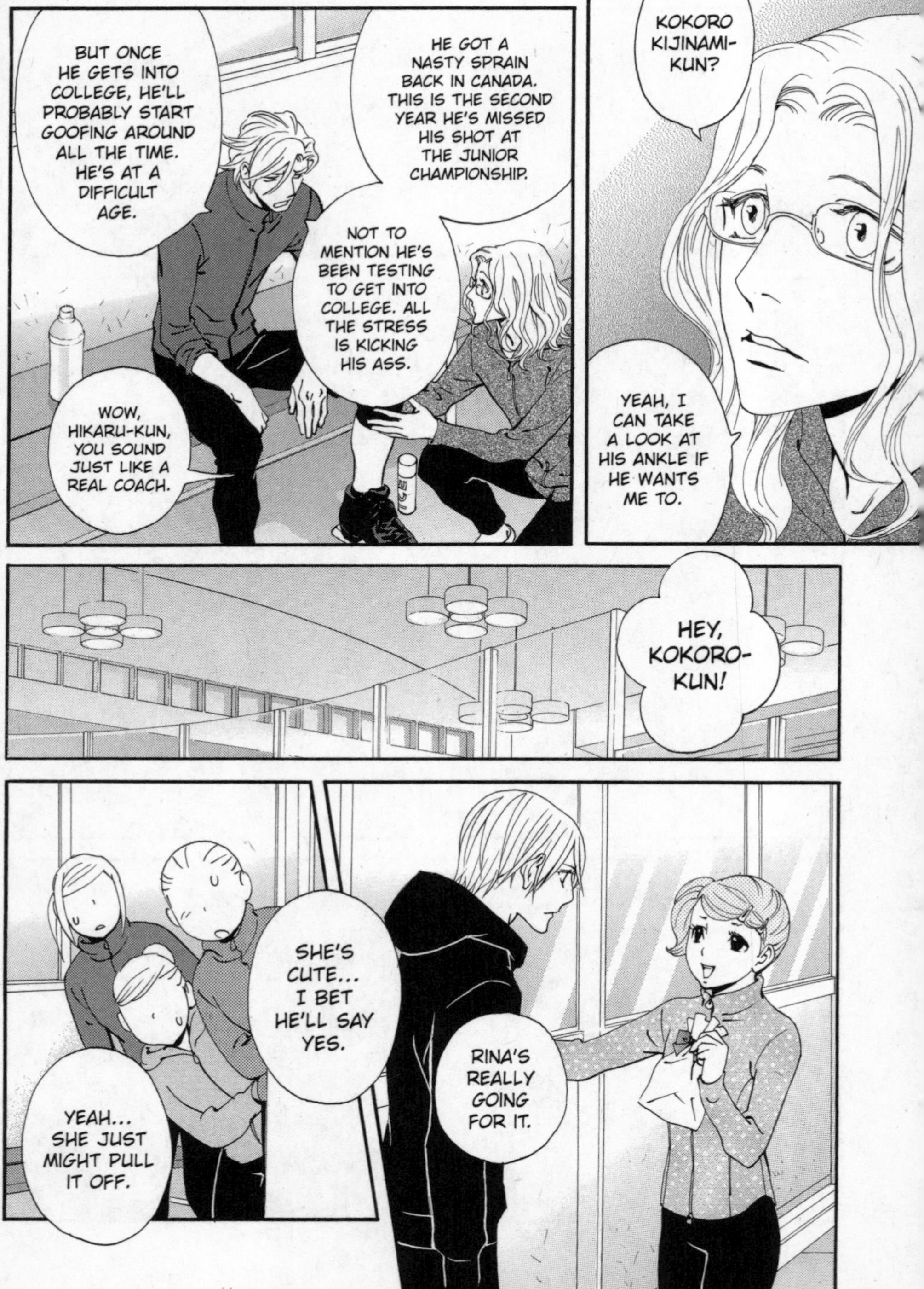
KOKORO KIJINAMI-KUN?
YEAH, I CAN TAKE A LOOK AT HIS ANKLE IF HE WANTS ME TO.
HE GOT A NASTY SPRAIN BACK IN CANADA. THIS IS THE SECOND YEAR HE'S MISSED HIS SHOT AT THE JUNIOR CHAMPIONSHIP.
BUT ONCE HE GETS INTO COLLEGE, HE'LL PROBABLY START GOOFING AROUND ALL THE TIME. HE'S AT A DIFFICULT AGE.
NOT TO MENTION HE'S BEEN TESTING TO GET INTO COLLEGE. ALL THE STRESS IS KICKING HIS ASS.
WOW, HIKARU-KUN, YOU SOUND JUST LIKE A REAL COACH.
HEY, KOKORO-KUN!
RINA'S REALLY GOING FOR IT.
SHE'S CUTE... I BET HE'LL SAY YES.
YEAH... SHE JUST MIGHT PULL IT OFF.

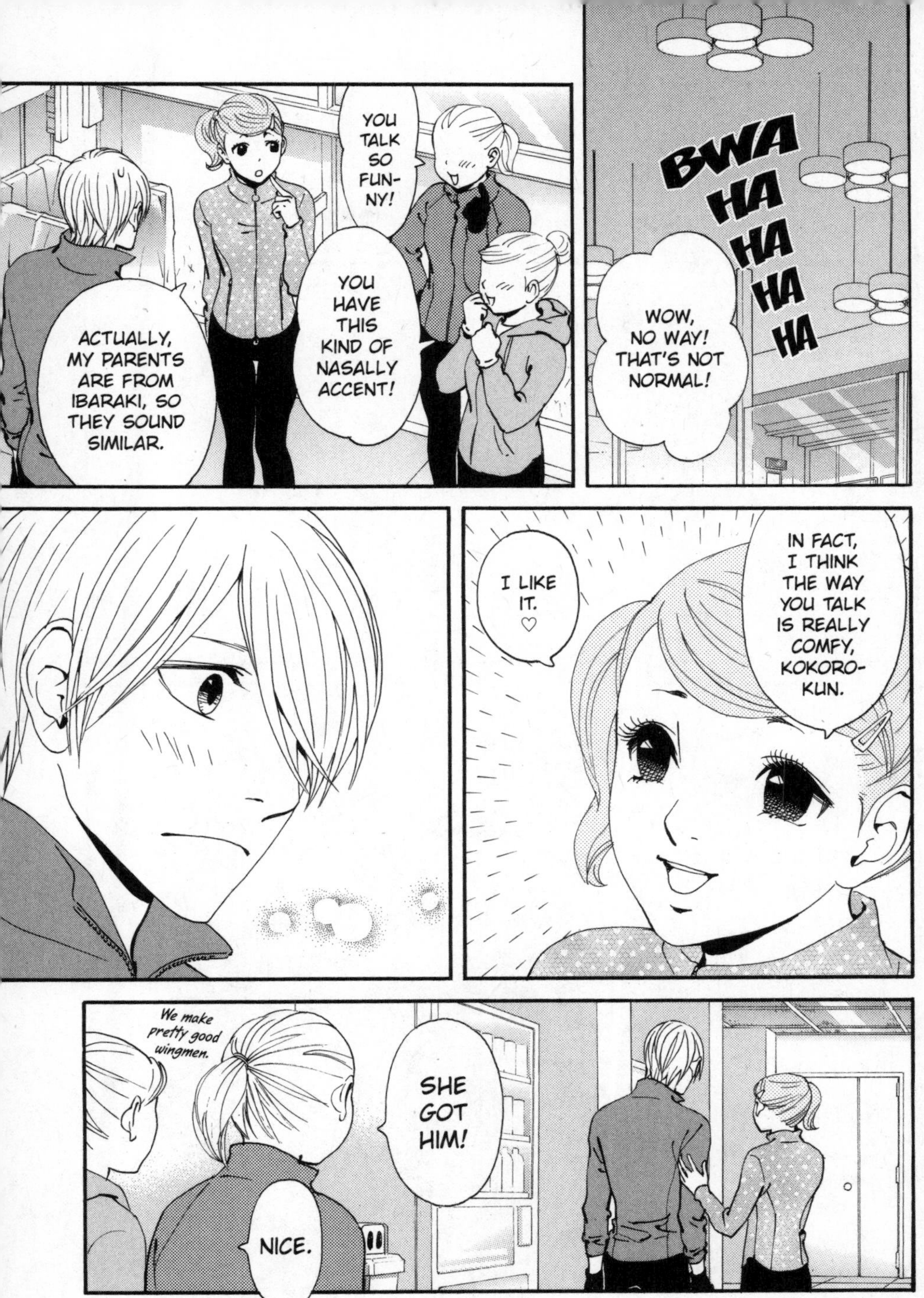
BWA HA HA HA HA HA
WOW, NO WAY! THAT'S NOT NORMAL!
YOU TALK SO FUN-NY!
YOU HAVE THIS KIND OF NASALLY ACCENT!
ACTUALLY, MY PARENTS ARE FROM IBARAKI, SO THEY SOUND SIMILAR.
IN FACT, I THINK THE WAY YOU TALK IS REALLY COMFY, KOKORO-KUN.
I LIKE IT. ♡
SHE GOT HIM!
We make pretty good wingmen.
NICE.

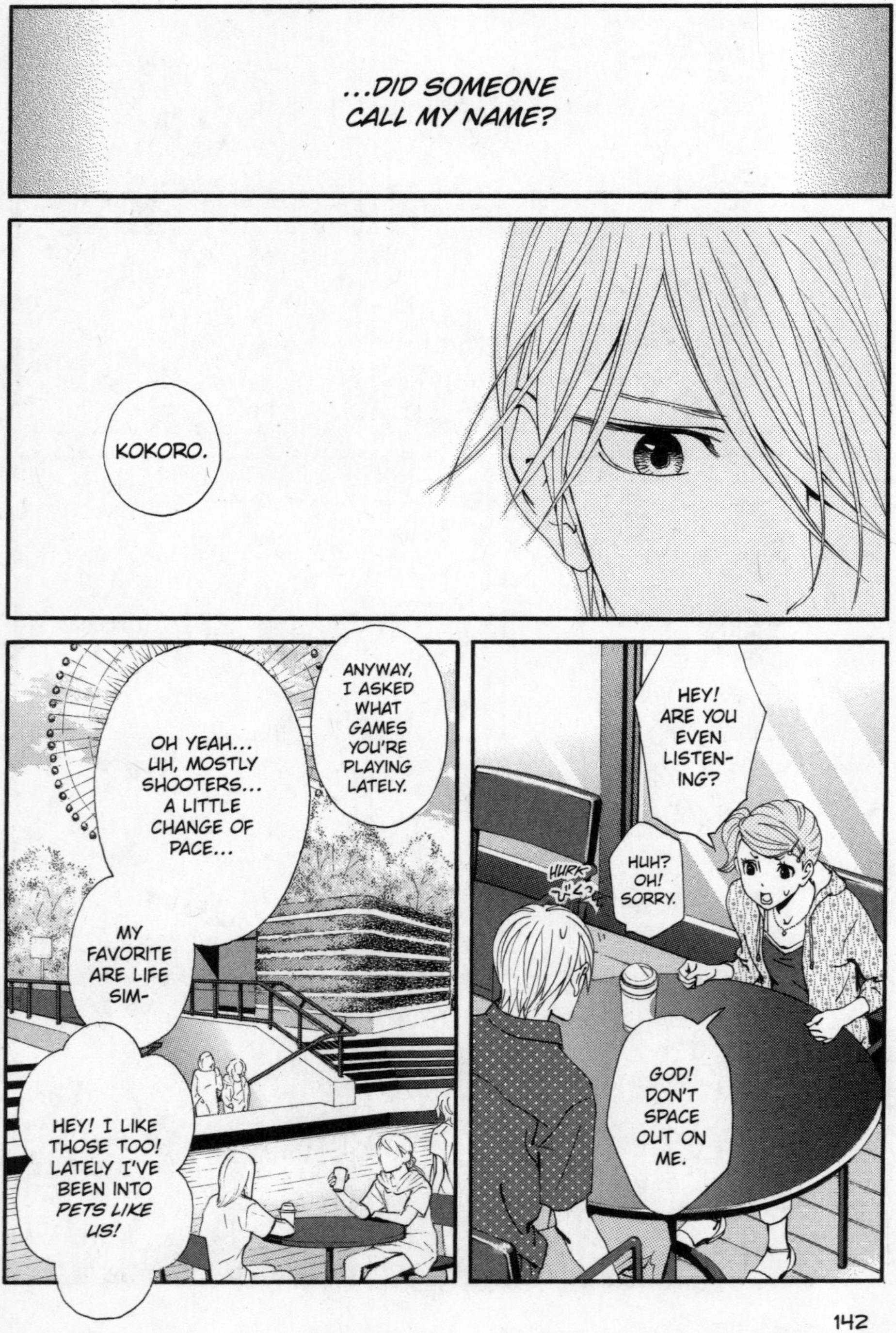
...DID SOMEONE CALL MY NAME?
KOKORO.
HEY! ARE YOU EVEN LISTEN-ING?
HURK
HUH? OH! SORRY.
GOD! DON'T SPACE OUT ON ME.
ANYWAY, I ASKED WHAT GAMES YOU'RE PLAYING LATELY.
OH YEAH... UH, MOSTLY SHOOTERS... A LITTLE CHANGE OF PACE...
MY FAVORITE ARE LIFE SIM-
HEY! I LIKE THOSE TOO! LATELY I'VE BEEN INTO PETS LIKE US!

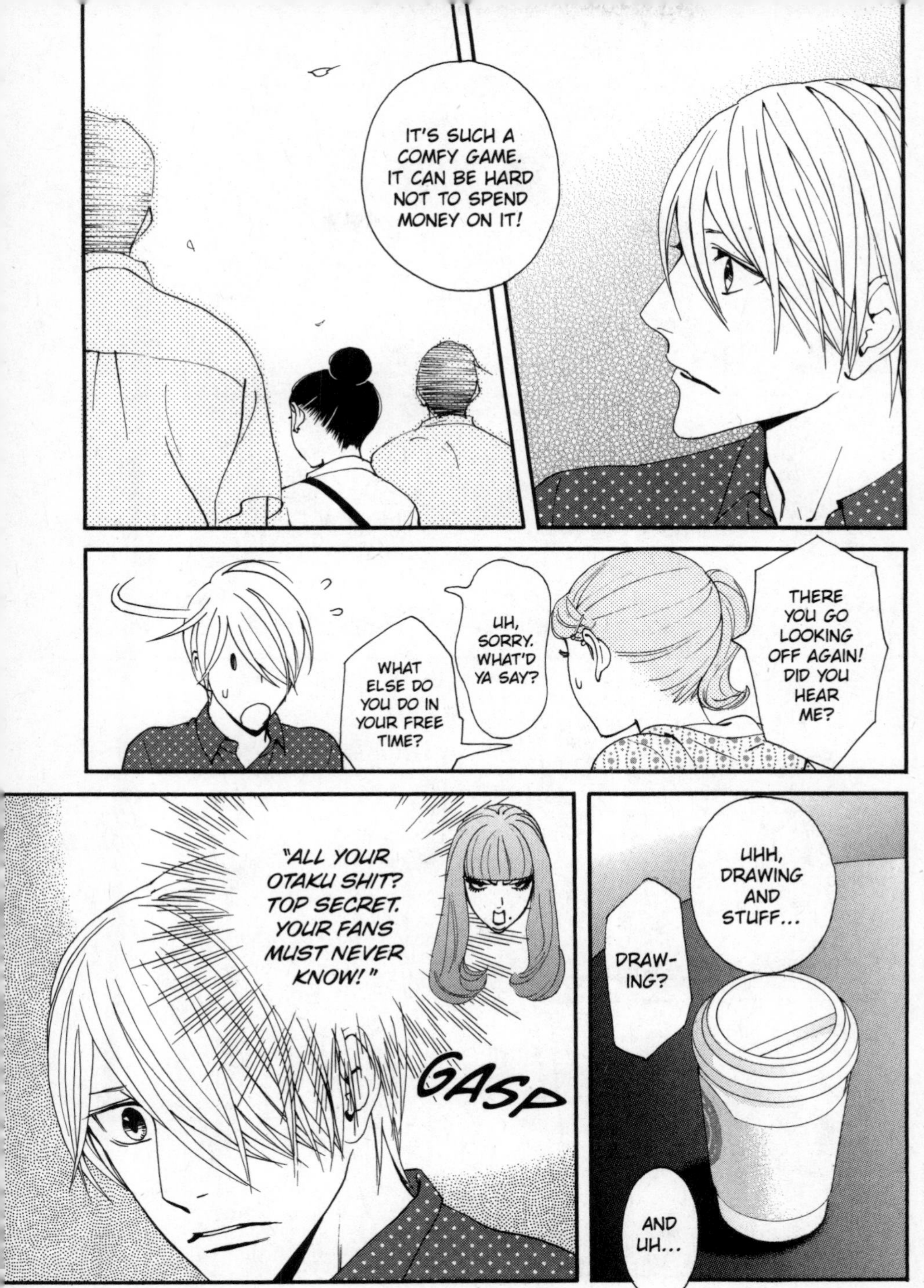
IT'S SUCH A COMFY GAME. IT CAN BE HARD NOT TO SPEND MONEY ON IT!
THERE YOU GO LOOKING OFF AGAIN! DID YOU HEAR ME?
UH, SORRY. WHAT'D YA SAY?
WHAT ELSE DO YOU DO IN YOUR FREE TIME?
UHH, DRAWING AND STUFF...
DRAWING?
AND UH...
"ALL YOUR OTAKU SHIT? TOP SECRET. YOUR FANS MUST NEVER KNOW!"
GASP

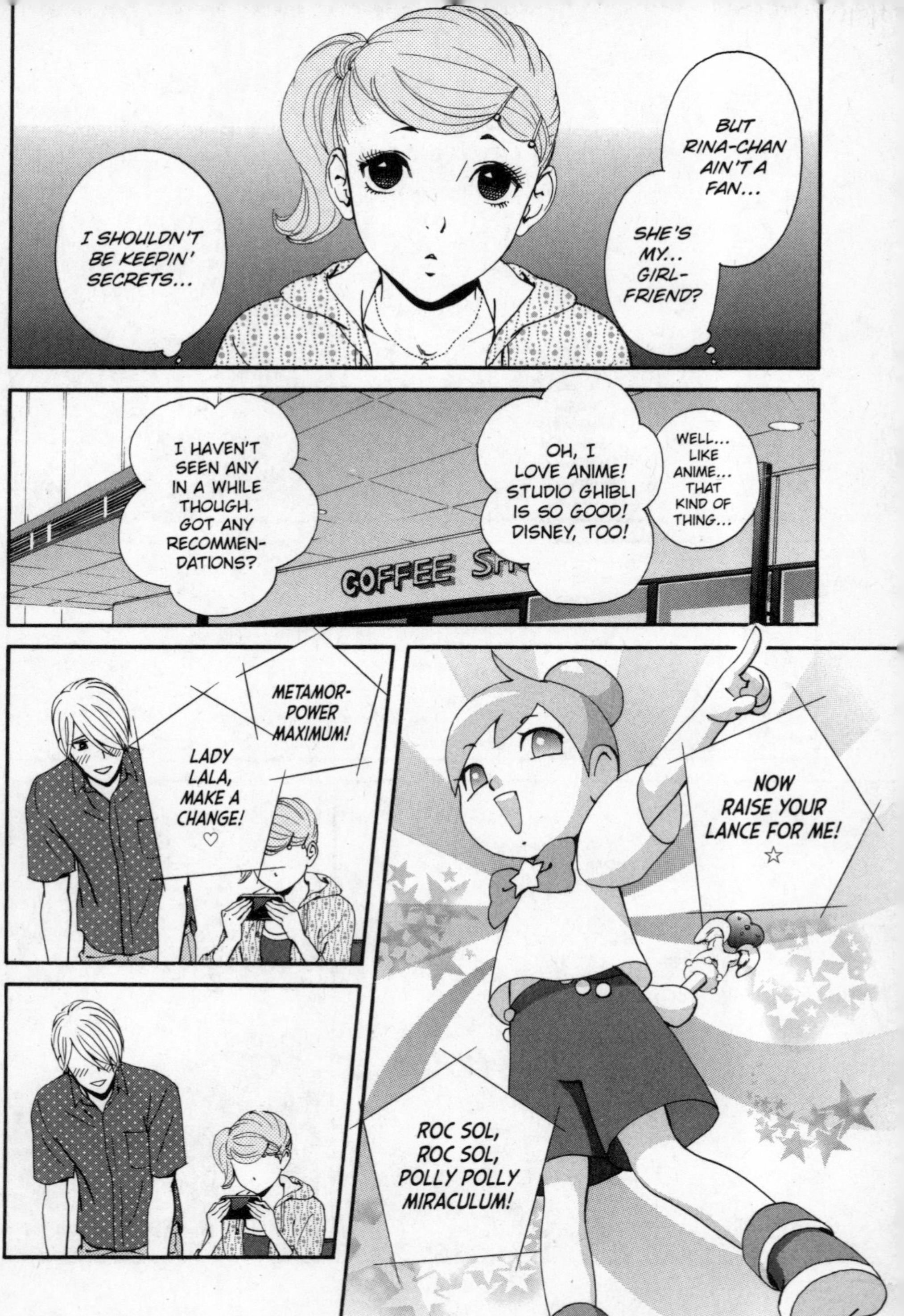
BUT RINA-CHAN AIN'T A FAN...
SHE'S MY... GIRL-FRIEND?
I SHOULDN'T BE KEEPIN' SECRETS...
WELL... LIKE ANIME... THAT KIND OF THING...
OH, I LOVE ANIME! STUDIO GHIBLI IS SO GOOD! DISNEY, TOO!
I HAVEN'T SEEN ANY IN A WHILE THOUGH. GOT ANY RECOMMEN-DATIONS?
NOW RAISE YOUR LANCE FOR ME! ☆
ROC SOL, ROC SOL, POLLY POLLY MIRACULUM!
METAMOR-POWER MAXIMUM!
LADY LALA, MAKE A CHANGE! ♡

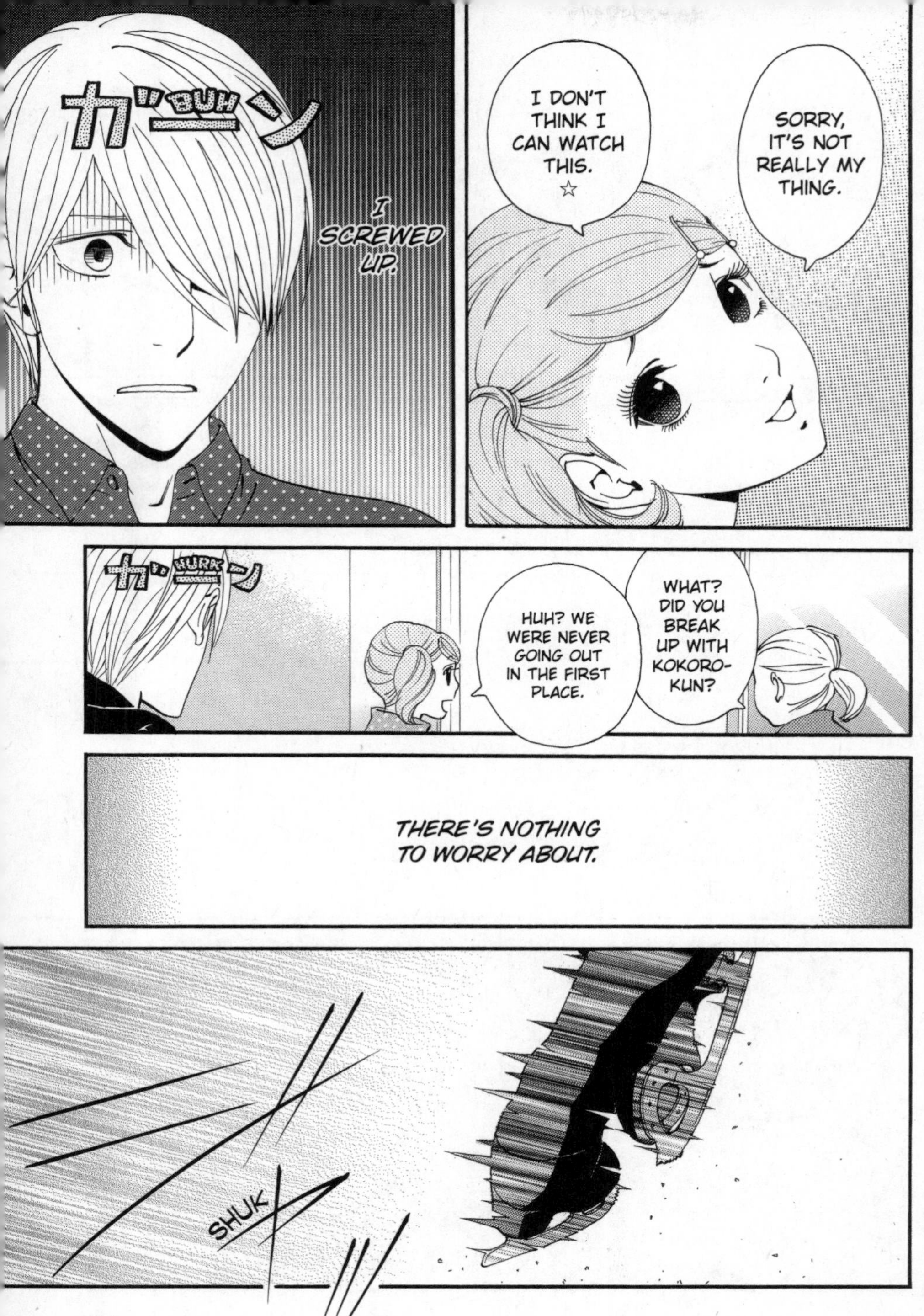
SORRY, IT'S NOT REALLY MY THING.
I DON'T THINK I CAN WATCH THIS. ☆
ガーン BUH
I SCREWED UP.
WHAT? DID YOU BREAK UP WITH KOKORO-KUN?
HUH? WE WERE NEVER GOING OUT IN THE FIRST PLACE.
ガーン HURK
THERE'S NOTHING TO WORRY ABOUT.
SHUK

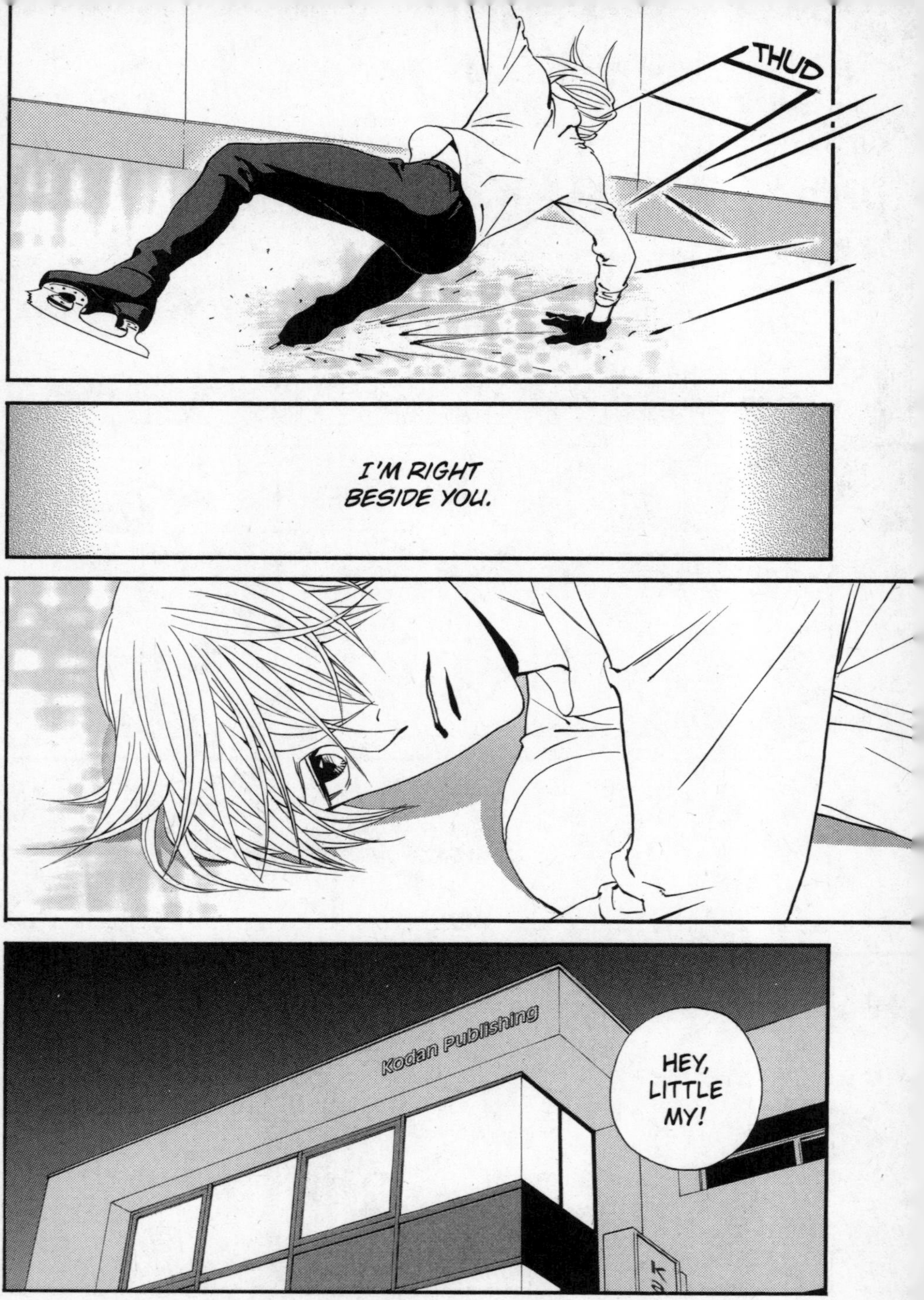
THUD
I'M RIGHT BESIDE YOU.
Kodan Publishing
HEY, LITTLE MY!

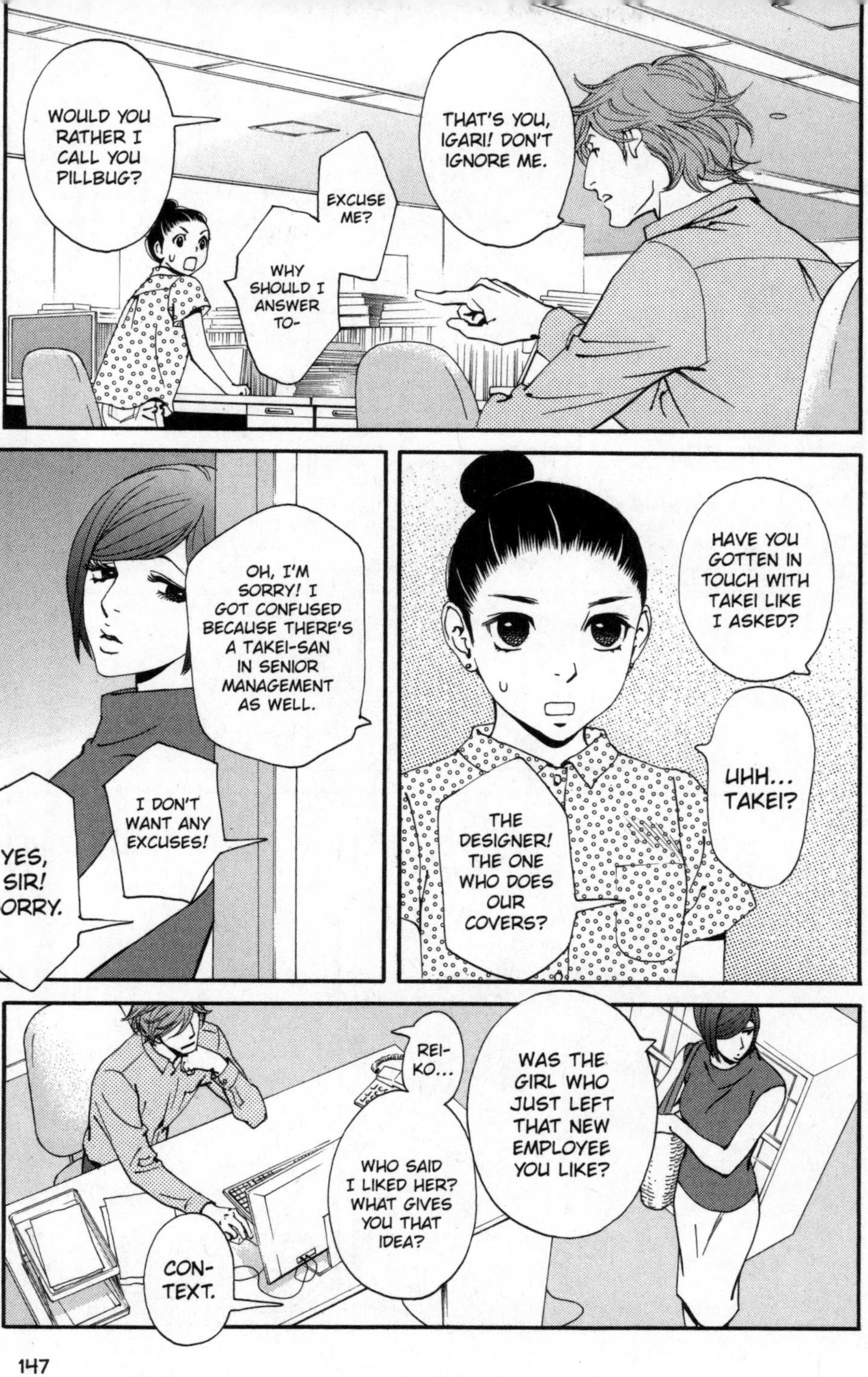
THAT'S YOU, IGARI! DON'T IGNORE ME.
EXCUSE ME?
WHY SHOULD I ANSWER TO-
WOULD YOU RATHER I CALL YOU PILLBUG?
HAVE YOU GOTTEN IN TOUCH WITH TAKEI LIKE I ASKED?
UHH... TAKEI?
THE DESIGNER! THE ONE WHO DOES OUR COVERS?
OH, I'M SORRY! I GOT CONFUSED BECAUSE THERE'S A TAKEI-SAN IN SENIOR MANAGEMENT AS WELL.
I DON'T WANT ANY EXCUSES!
YES, SIR! SORRY.
WAS THE GIRL WHO JUST LEFT THAT NEW EMPLOYEE YOU LIKE?
REI-KO...
WHO SAID I LIKED HER? WHAT GIVES YOU THAT IDEA?
CON-TEXT.

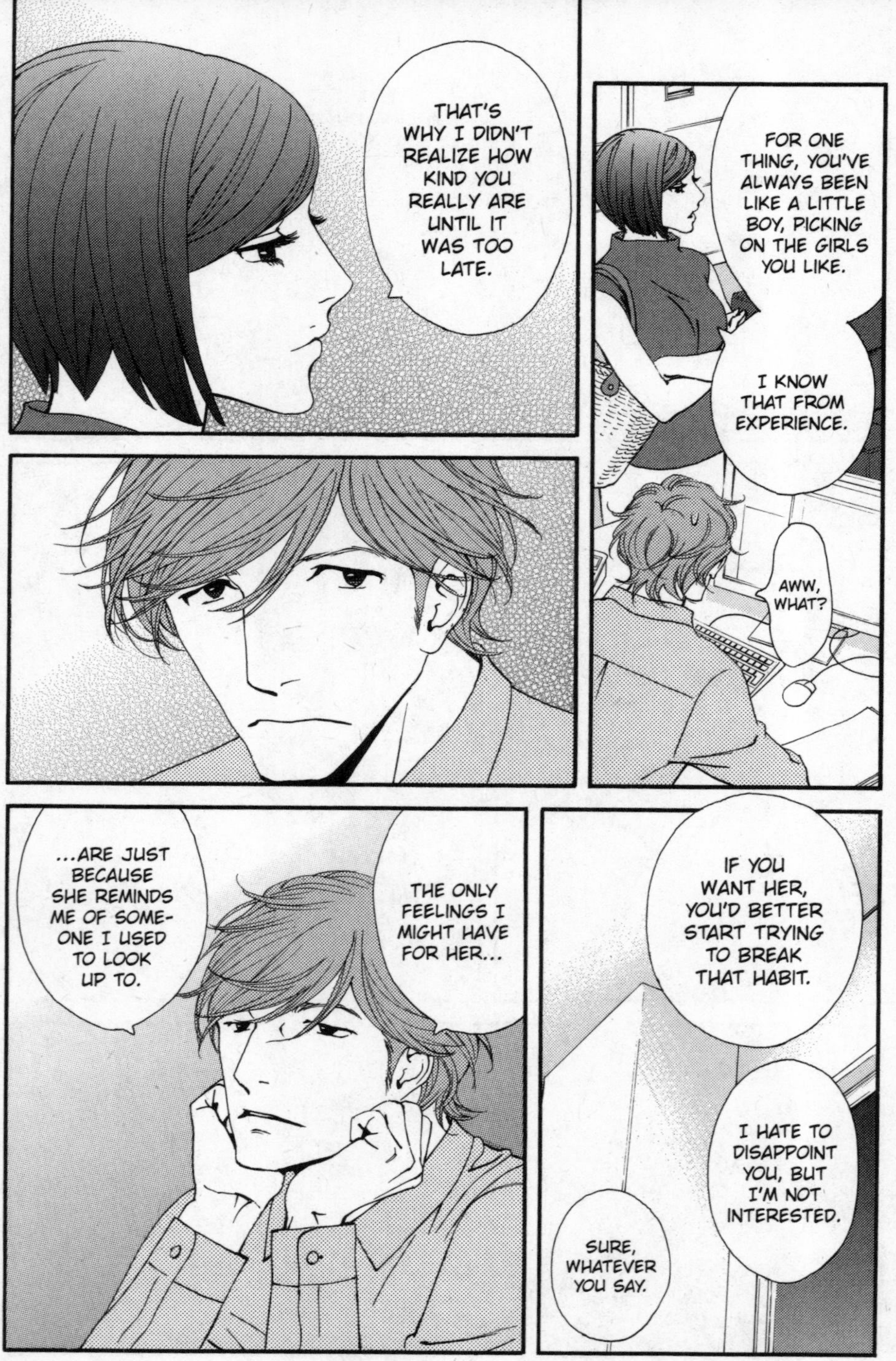
FOR ONE THING, YOU'VE ALWAYS BEEN LIKE A LITTLE BOY, PICKING ON THE GIRLS YOU LIKE.
I KNOW THAT FROM EXPERIENCE.
AWW, WHAT?
THAT'S WHY I DIDN'T REALIZE HOW KIND YOU REALLY ARE UNTIL IT WAS TOO LATE.
IF YOU WANT HER, YOU'D BETTER START TRYING TO BREAK THAT HABIT.
I HATE TO DISAPPOINT YOU, BUT I'M NOT INTERESTED.
SURE, WHATEVER YOU SAY.
THE ONLY FEELINGS I MIGHT HAVE FOR HER...
...ARE JUST BECAUSE SHE REMINDS ME OF SOME-ONE I USED TO LOOK UP TO.

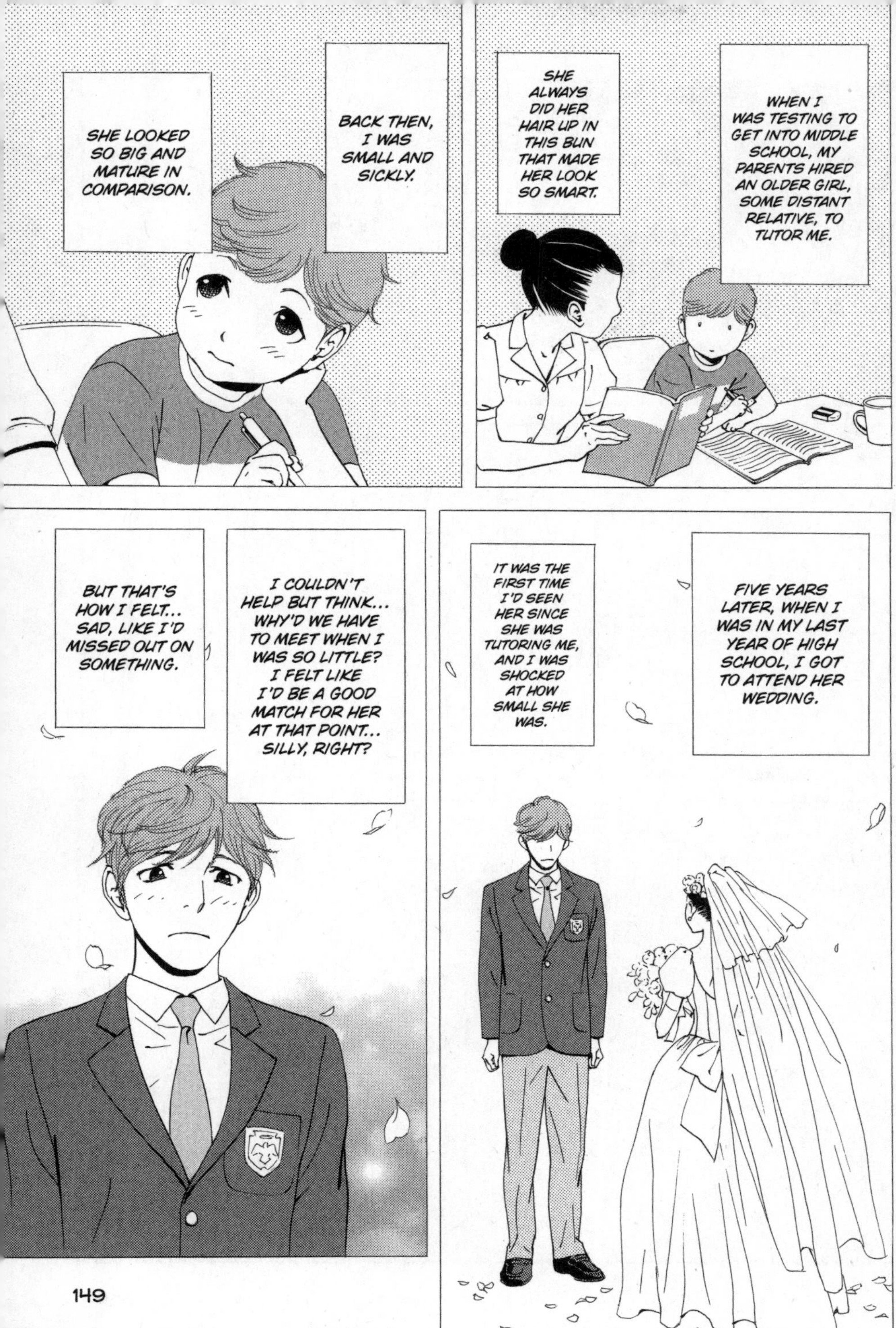
WHEN I WAS TESTING TO GET INTO MIDDLE SCHOOL, MY PARENTS HIRED AN OLDER GIRL, SOME DISTANT RELATIVE, TO TUTOR ME.
SHE ALWAYS DID HER HAIR UP IN THIS BUN THAT MADE HER LOOK SO SMART.
BACK THEN, I WAS SMALL AND SICKLY.
SHE LOOKED SO BIG AND MATURE IN COMPARISON.
FIVE YEARS LATER, WHEN I WAS IN MY LAST YEAR OF HIGH SCHOOL, I GOT TO ATTEND HER WEDDING.
IT WAS THE FIRST TIME I'D SEEN HER SINCE SHE WAS TUTORING ME, AND I WAS SHOCKED AT HOW SMALL SHE WAS.
I COULDN'T HELP BUT THINK... WHY'D WE HAVE TO MEET WHEN I WAS SO LITTLE? I FELT LIKE I'D BE A GOOD MATCH FOR HER AT THAT POINT... SILLY, RIGHT?
BUT THAT'S HOW I FELT... SAD, LIKE I'D MISSED OUT ON SOMETHING.

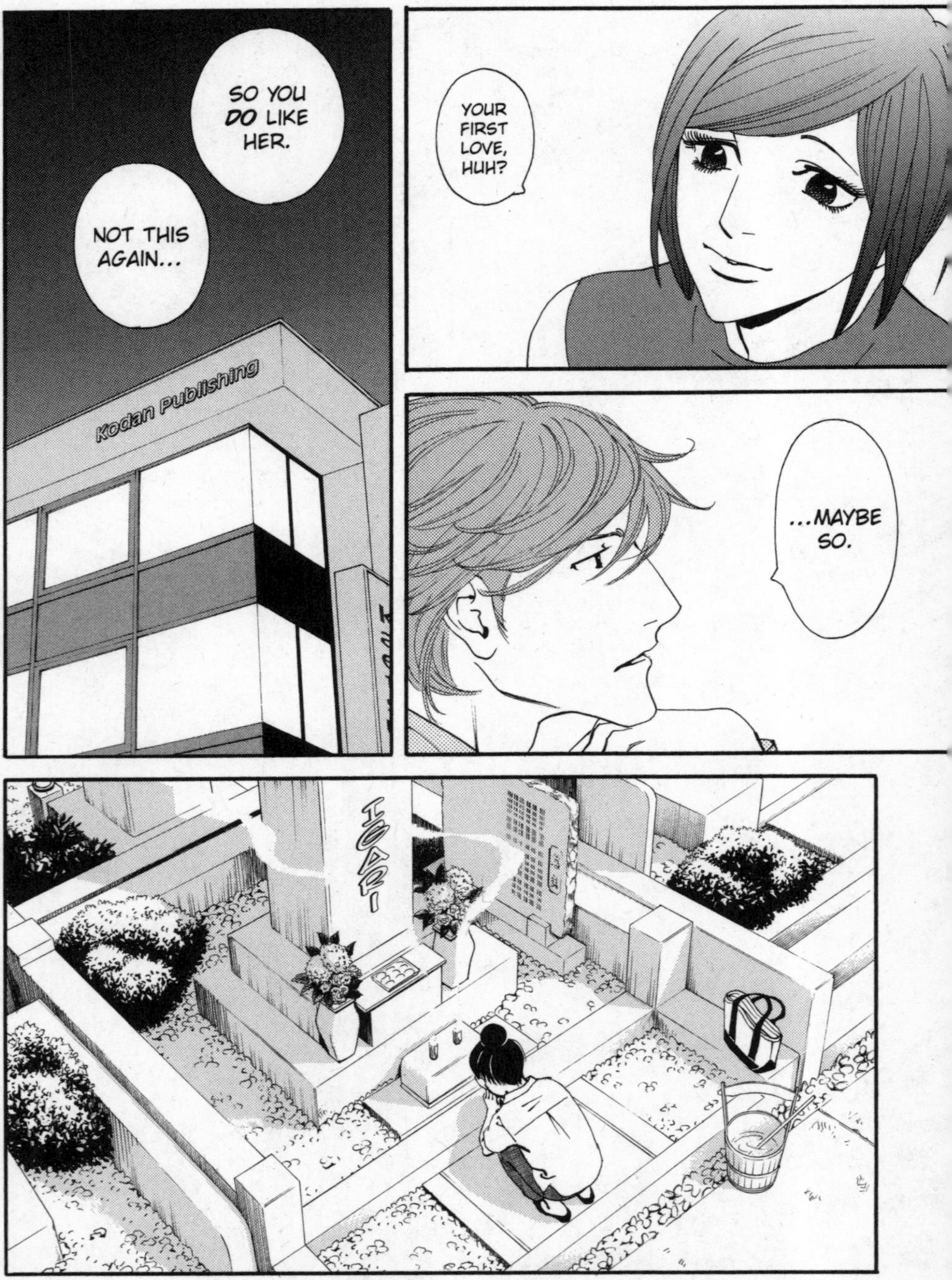
YOUR FIRST LOVE, HUH?
...MAYBE SO.
SO YOU DO LIKE HER.
NOT THIS AGAIN...
Kodan Publishing
IGARI

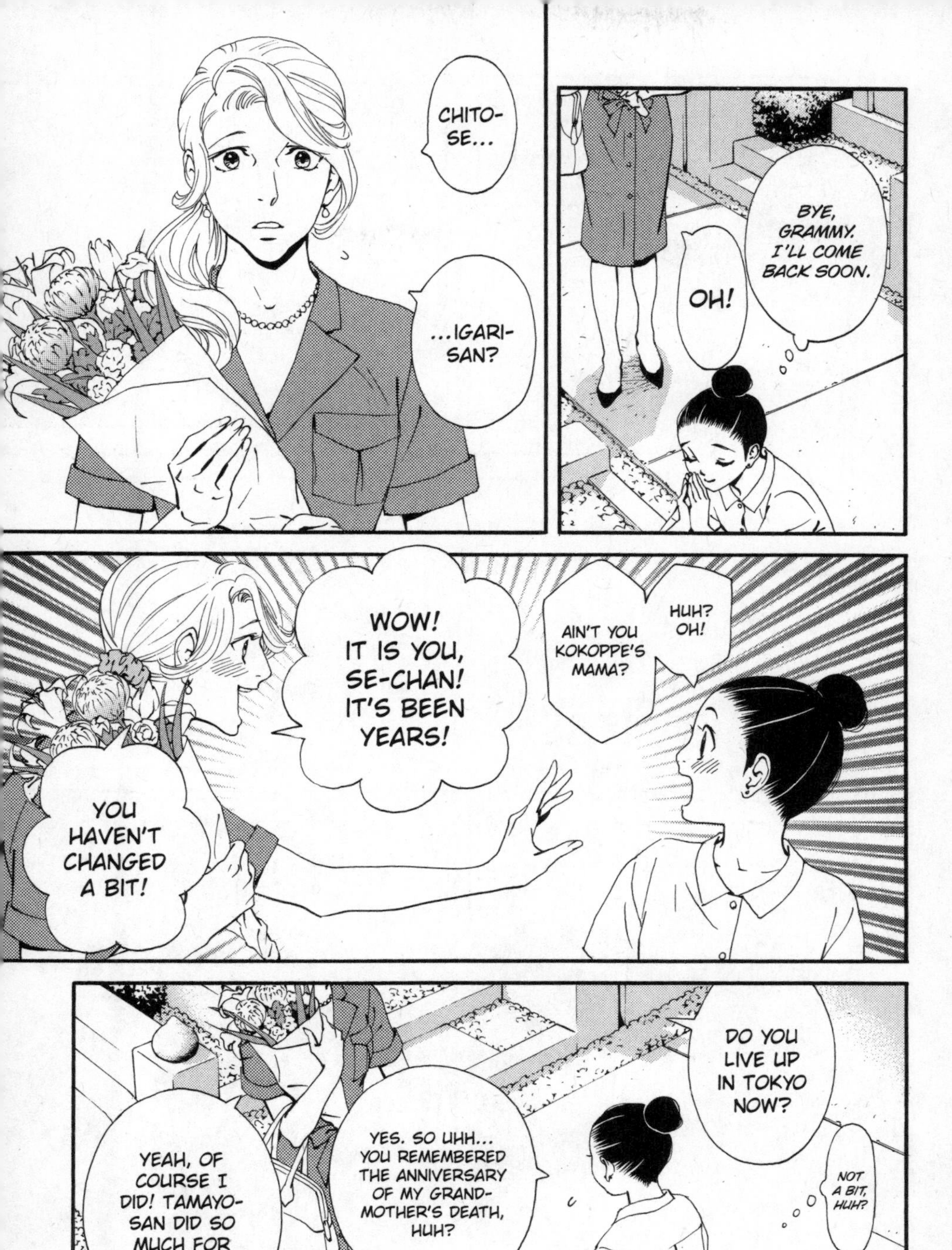

BYE, GRAMMY. I'LL COME BACK SOON.
OH!
CHITO-SE...
...IGARI-SAN?
HUH? OH!
AIN'T YOU KOKOPPE'S MAMA?
WOW! IT IS YOU, SE-CHAN! IT'S BEEN YEARS!
YOU HAVEN'T CHANGED A BIT!
NOT A BIT, HUH?
DO YOU LIVE UP IN TOKYO NOW?
YES. SO UHH... YOU REMEMBERED THE ANNIVERSARY OF MY GRAND-MOTHER'S DEATH, HUH?
YEAH, OF COURSE I DID! TAMAYO-SAN DID SO MUCH FOR MY FAMILY!

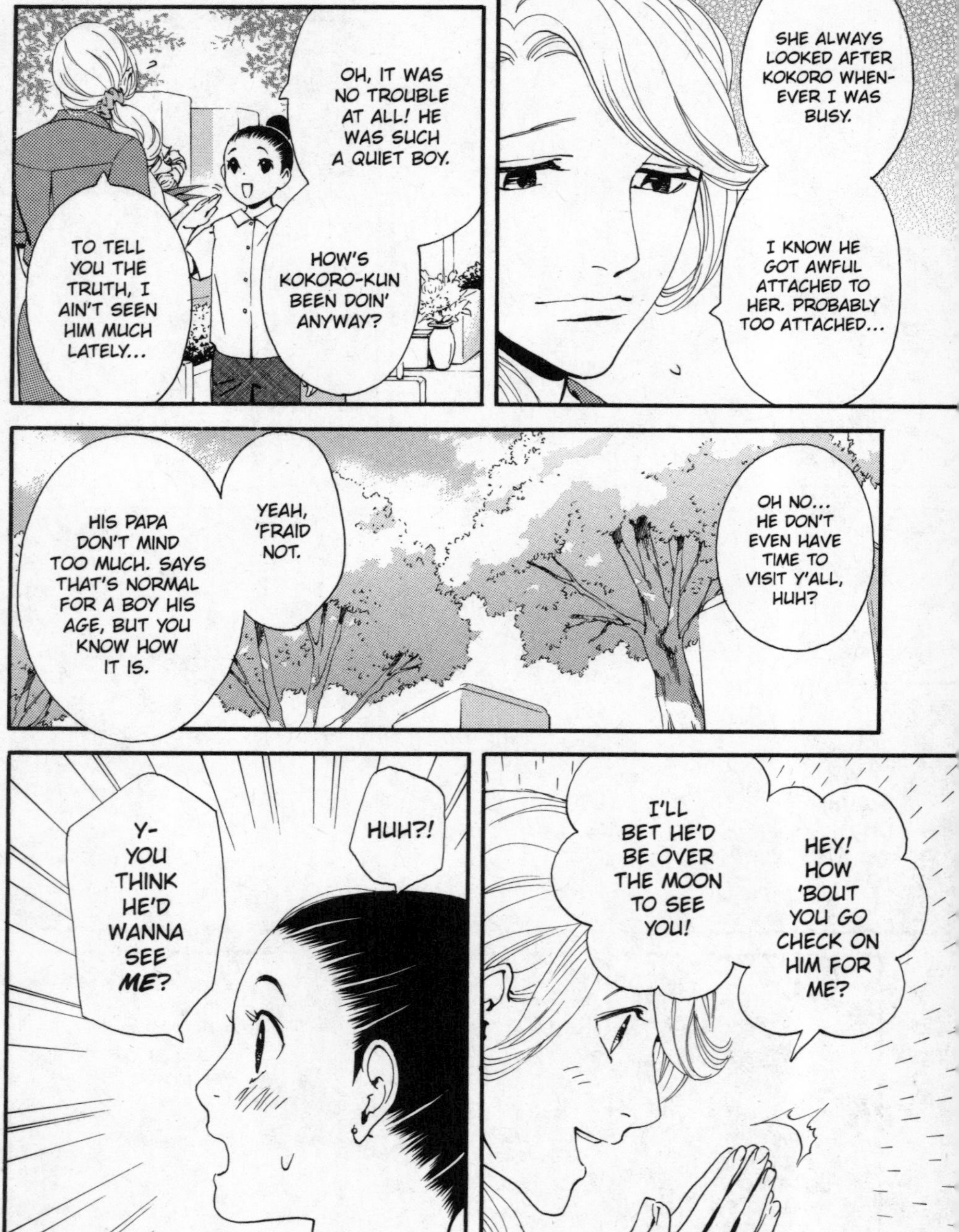
SHE ALWAYS LOOKED AFTER KOKORO WHEN-EVER I WAS BUSY.
I KNOW HE GOT AWFUL ATTACHED TO HER. PROBABLY TOO ATTACHED...
OH, IT WAS NO TROUBLE AT ALL! HE WAS SUCH A QUIET BOY.
HOW'S KOKORO-KUN BEEN DOIN' ANYWAY?
TO TELL YOU THE TRUTH, I AIN'T SEEN HIM MUCH LATELY...
OH NO... HE DON'T EVEN HAVE TIME TO VISIT Y'ALL, HUH?
YEAH, 'FRAID NOT.
HIS PAPA DON'T MIND TOO MUCH. SAYS THAT'S NORMAL FOR A BOY HIS AGE, BUT YOU KNOW HOW IT IS.
HEY! HOW 'BOUT YOU GO CHECK ON HIM FOR ME?
I'LL BET HE'D BE OVER THE MOON TO SEE YOU!
HUH?!
Y-YOU THINK HE'D WANNA SEE ME?

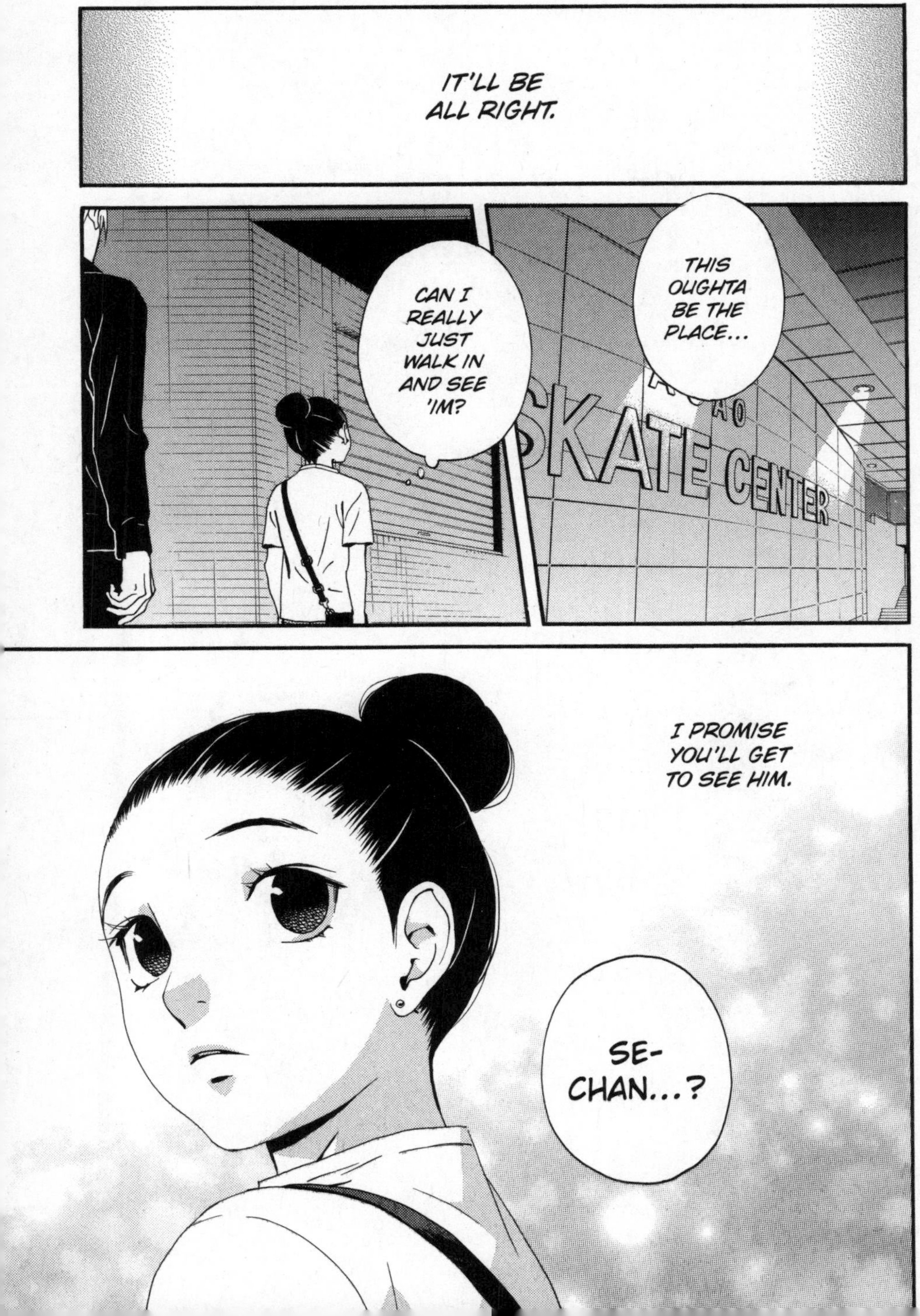
IT'LL BE ALL RIGHT.
THIS OUGHTA BE THE PLACE...
SKATE CENTER
CAN I REALLY JUST WALK IN AND SEE 'IM?
I PROMISE YOU'LL GET TO SEE HIM.
SE-CHAN...?

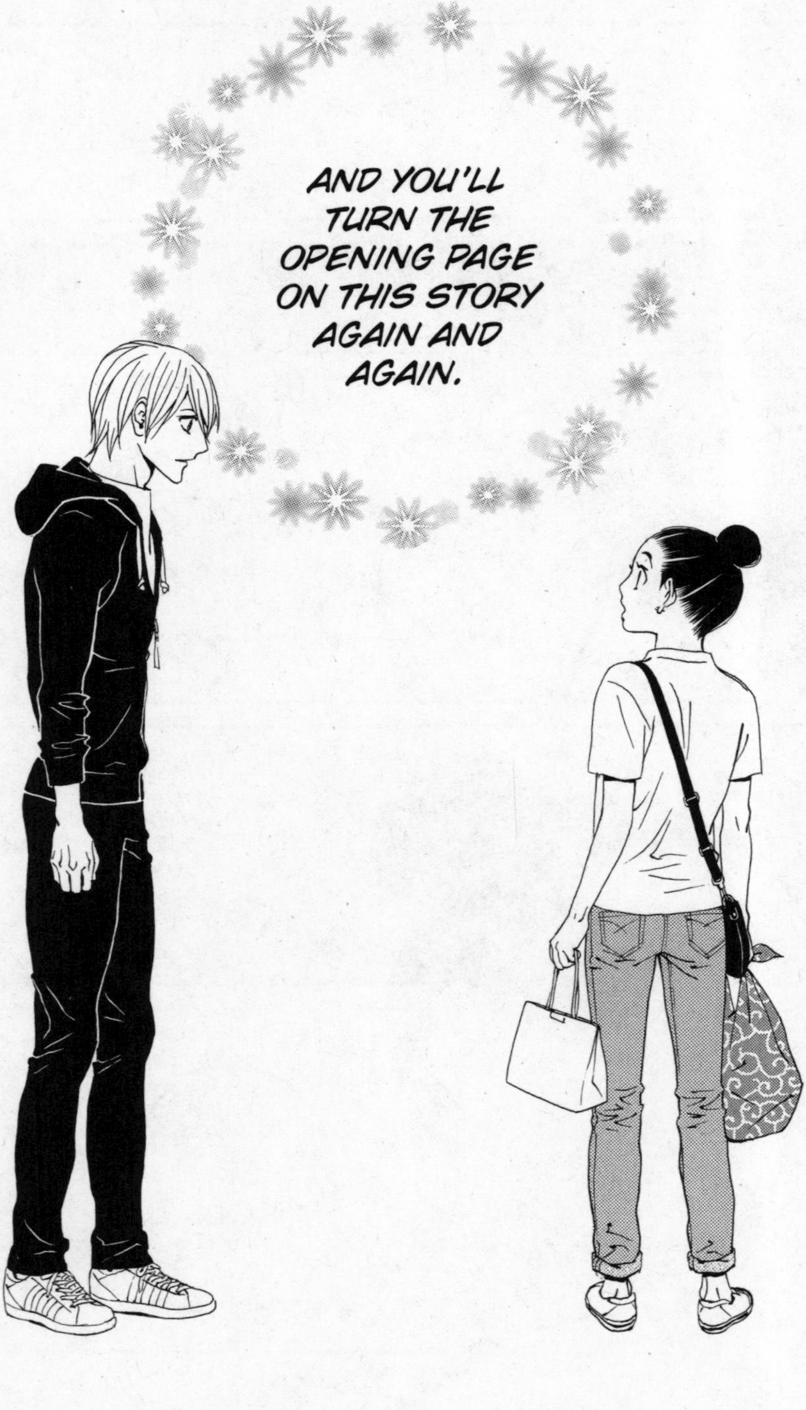
AND YOU'LL TURN THE OPENING PAGE ON THIS STORY AGAIN AND AGAIN.

KSSSSH

WHAT'S THE MATTER?

NOTH- IN'.

JUST THINKIN' ABOUT OLD TIMES.

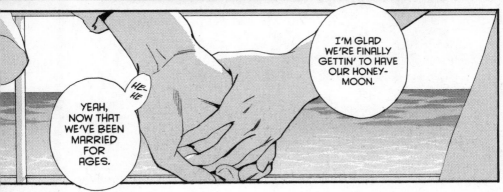

I'M GLAD WE'RE FINALLY GETTIN' TO HAVE OUR HONEY- MOON.

HE- HE

YEAH, NOW THAT WE'VE BEEN MARRIED FOR AGES.

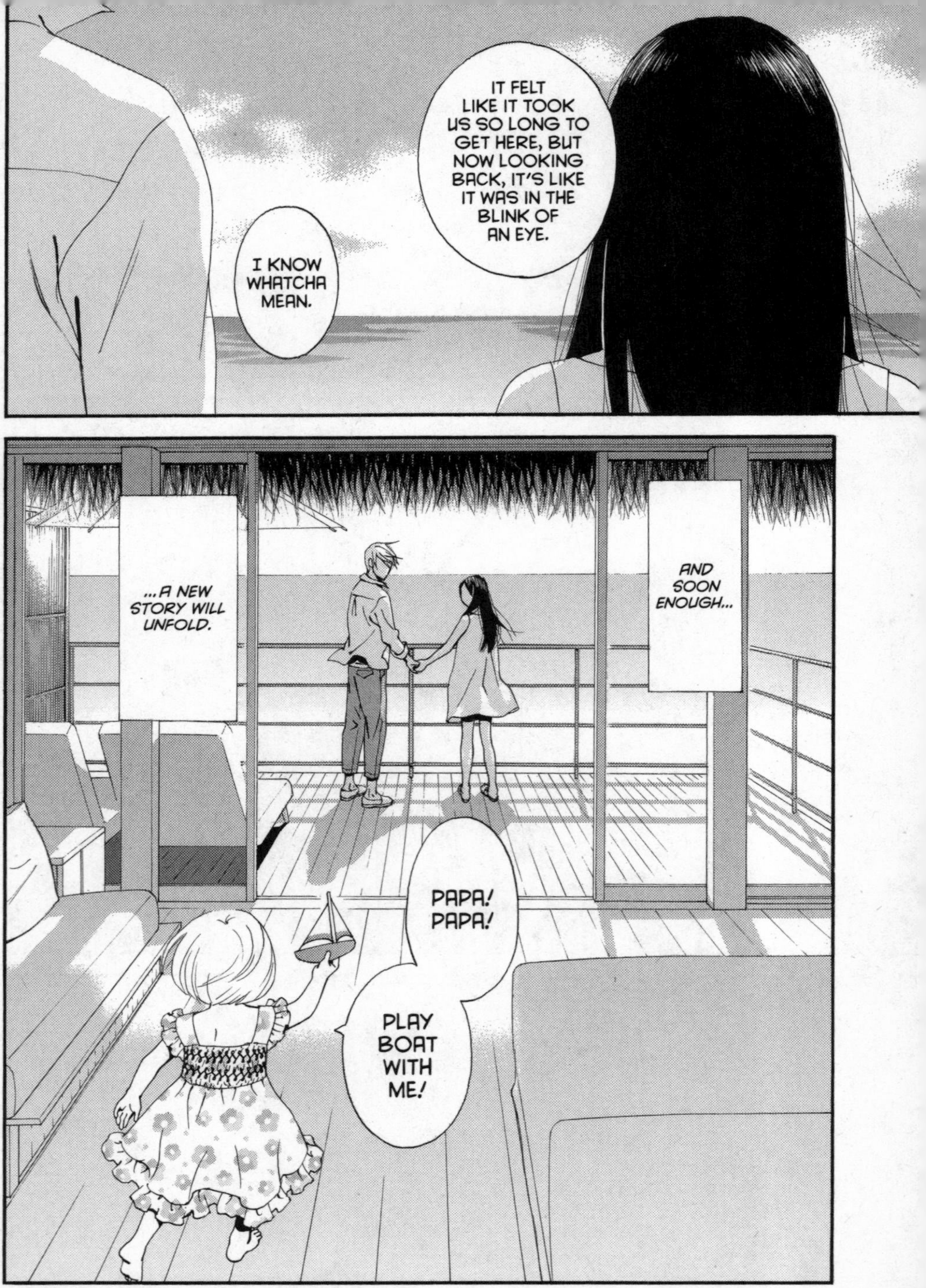
IT FELT LIKE IT TOOK US SO LONG TO GET HERE, BUT NOW LOOKING BACK, IT'S LIKE IT WAS IN THE BLINK OF AN EYE.
I KNOW WHATCHA MEAN.
AND SOON ENOUGH...
...A NEW STORY WILL UNFOLD.
PAPA! PAPA!
PLAY BOAT WITH ME!

The End

TRANSLATION NOTES

KANTO, PAGE 132
Not the Pokémon region! Kanto is actually the most populous region of Japan, and is where the city of Tokyo is located.

PETS LIKE US, PAGE 142
This is a reference to another manga by Yayoi Ogawa, *Tramps Like Us*. It's a romance between a single office lady and a younger man she finds in a box on the street, who she decides to adopt as her pet. Here, however, it appears to be the name of a fictional life simulation game in the vein of *Princess Maker*.

OTAKU, PAGE 143
Otaku is a Japanese word for a certain kind of hobby-obsessed nerd. It is often thought to emphasize the shut-in and socially dysfunctional nature of the people it describes, although some people today wear the label with pride.

Knight of the ICE

Glossary by Coach Akiyuki Kido

(based on January 2015 rules)

Free skate (page 8)
In the free skating competition, skaters get to choose what elements and moves to use. Still, to ensure a well-rounded program, there are rules about what jumps, spins, and steps are required, as well as restrictions on the number of them allowed. In women's singles, this segment lasts four minutes, and in men's singles, it lasts four minutes and thirty seconds.

Short Program (page 8)
The short program is a segment in which the skaters have up to two minutes and fifty seconds to perform eight predetermined elements, such as jumps, spins, or steps.

Quadruple Salchow (4S) (page 9)
A Salchow with four rotations. This jump is executed from the left foot's back inside edge by lifting the right foot forward and to the left. The way both feet face outward just before takeoff is a unique feature of the Salchow jump. It is typically considered an easy jump because its entrance from the back-inside edge makes rotating less difficult. Still, although they are rare, there do exist skaters who consider this their most difficult jump, often owing to personal difficulty skating on the back inside edge. It was named after the Swedish skater Ulrich Salchow.

Jumps in a program (page 10)
The six jumps in figure skating are the toe loop, Salchow, loop, flip, Lutz, and Axel. In the short program, the following jumps are required: 1) a triple-triple or triple-double jump combination, 2) a triple jump following a step, and 3) a double or triple Axel. In the free skate, the skater may perform up to eight jumps, one of which must be an Axel. No more than three jump combinations are allowed, and only one of those can consist of three jumps.

Quad Lutz (page 11)
A Lutz with four rotations. The Lutz is considered the second hardest jump after the Axel. It is named after the Austrian skater Alois Lutz, the first person to perform this jump. To perform this jump, a skater uses their right toe pick (the front of the skate's blade where it has teeth) to launch themself into the air from their left skate's back outside edge. Because of the difficulty of skating on this edge, many skaters make an edge error. Note that the roles of each foot are reversed for skaters who spin clockwise.

Under-spinning a jump (page 13)
Also known as under-rotation. Under-rotation is the failure to include the necessary number of revolutions in a jump. A jump that's under-rotated by half a revolution or more is downgraded and has the base value of a jump with one fewer revolutions.

Quadruple Toe Loop (4T) (page 14)
A toe loop with four rotations. The toe loop is considered the easiest jump. The skater uses their left toe to launch themself into the air from their right skate's back outside edge. To date, no one has managed to execute this jump with more than four revolutions, and only a select few skaters can do even that.

Program components score (PCS or presentation score) (page 16)
For this score, skaters are evaluated on the basis of five program components: skating skills, transitions, performance, composition, and interpretation. A skater's final score is the total of their program components score (PCS) and their technical score.
The technical score is determined by the technical elements included in the program and their quality. Jumps, spins, steps, and other elements each have a base value, which is modified by a grade of execution (GOE) to get the technical score. The GOE is the average of the modifiers assigned by the judges, excluding the highest and lowest. These modifiers have one of seven values between negative and positive three.

Jump Combination (page 16)

A jump combination is when a skater performs a jump and then immediately performs another from the foot they land on. Since jumps are landed on the right skate's back outside edge (or the left skate's if you're spinning clockwise), all jumps after the first in a combination are limited to either the toe loop or the loop jump. If the skater weaves footwork between their jumps, it's called a jump sequence instead.

Triple Axel (3A) (page 17)

There are six different jumps in figure skating. An Axel is the only one that begins with the skater facing directly forward (on the forward outside edge). It's the most difficult jump, and a triple Axel requires three and a half midair rotations. Midori Ito was the first woman in Japan to successfully execute this jump.

Choreographic sequence (page 20)

The choreographic sequence is a step sequence where the skater is allowed a great deal of freedom in choosing their components and is scored on the sequence as a whole.

Base score (page 39)

Each element—such as a step, a spin, or a jump—has a base value. Three people—the technical specialist, the assistant technical specialist, and the technical controller—work together to do things like identify elements, count jump rotations, and distinguish the level and type of each spin or step. These determinations result in the assignment of a base score.

Grade of execution (GOE) (page 40)

A skater's execution of each element is assigned a score modifier of between negative and positive three.

Triple Flip (page 45)

A flip with three rotations. To perform this jump, the skater rides the back inside edge of their left skate and uses their right toe to launch themself into the air. It is sometimes called the toe Salchow. Due to the relative difficulty of maintaining a vertical axis, this jump's base value is almost as high as that of the Lutz. Note that the roles of each foot are reversed for skaters who spin clockwise..

Loop (page 46)

To do a loop, the skater both takes off from and lands on only their right foot. With their left leg crossed in front of their right, they jump from the right skate's back outside edge.

Ice Dancing (page 85)

Alongside singles and pairs, ice dancing is a category of figure skating competition. Skaters participate in teams of one man and one woman. This unique style of skating that was inspired by ballroom dancing. Rhythm, musicality, and footwork are given priority in ice dancing, and there are those who argue that it requires the most skill of any kind of figure skating competition.

Exhibition gala (page 85)

After a competition, the winning skaters and other special guests may sometimes perform in a kind of ice show called an exhibition gala. This gives them an opportunity to skate without having to worry about rules, so they often do things like use props or play music with lyrics. It's also common for singers or other celebrities to participate as guests. (Editor's Note: Originally, skaters were not allowed to perform to music with lyrics. In 2014, the International Skating Union announced that they would allow skaters to perform to music with lyrics during figure skating competitions.)

World Championships (page 105)
The World Figure Skating Championships, also known as Worlds, is the biggest event of the skating season, excluding the Olympic season. The winner earns the title of world champion for that season.

Challenge Cup (page 118)
The International Challenge Cup is an ISU-recognized competition held annually in The Hague, Netherlands. It's often thought of primarily as an off-season diversion.

Japan National Figure Skating Championships (page 134)
The Japan Figure Skating Championships are held every year near the end of December to determine the best skater in Japan. The results of this competition largely determine who will represent Japan at the Olympics and World Championships.

Junior (page 134)
There are three age divisions in figure skating: novice, junior, and senior. The senior division includes skaters 15 or older, the junior division includes skaters ages 13 to 18, and the novice division is for skaters ages 10 to 13 (or sometimes 14). These ranges are based on the skaters' age on June 30th before the competition.

Season (page 139)
Each year's skating season begins in July and ends in June of the following year.

Coach (page 140)
Most coaches belong to the Figure Skating Instructor Association and teach at an ice rink. To work as a professional coach, even talented skaters are typically required to start by helping to teach beginners in a club or classroom setting.

Akiyuki Kido was born on August 28th, 1975. He represented Japan in ice dancing at the 2006 winter Olympics in Turin, Italy. He took fifteenth place, the highest Japan had ever placed in ice dancing at the time. Today, he works as a coach at the Shin-Yokohama Skate Center.

Knight of the ICE

Knight of the Ice Skater Profile 11

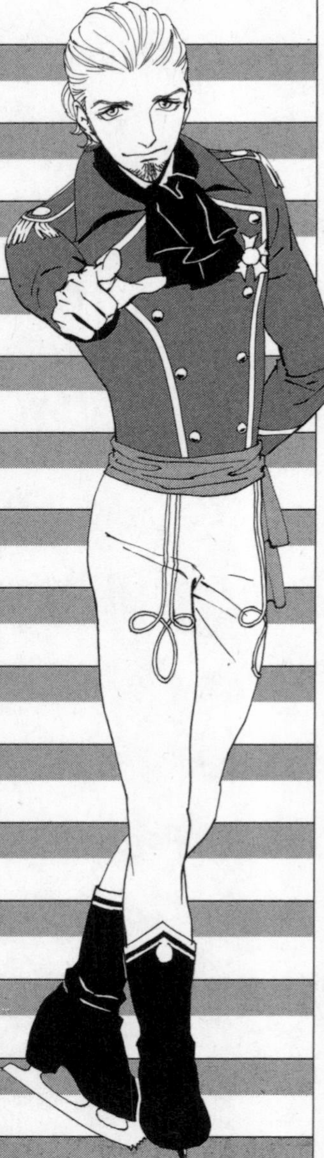

11 Hugues Desorges

Height:

169 cm

Blood type:

A

Birthday:

March 6th

Place of origin:

Lyon

Strongest element:

Steps

Strongest jump:

Lutz

Most difficult jump performed to date:

Quad toe loop

Strength:

The entertaining quality of his performances

Weakness:

He's a little stiff

Hobby:

Guitar

Talent:

Singing while playing guitar

Family composition:

His parents and two older brothers

Favorite food:

Duck confit

Least favorite food:

Green beans

Notes:

This guy pretty much never actually shows up, so I went ahead and gave him this outfit. If you recognize it, please just laugh and move along... Yeah, I think Napoleon is cool...

Dress-up Doll

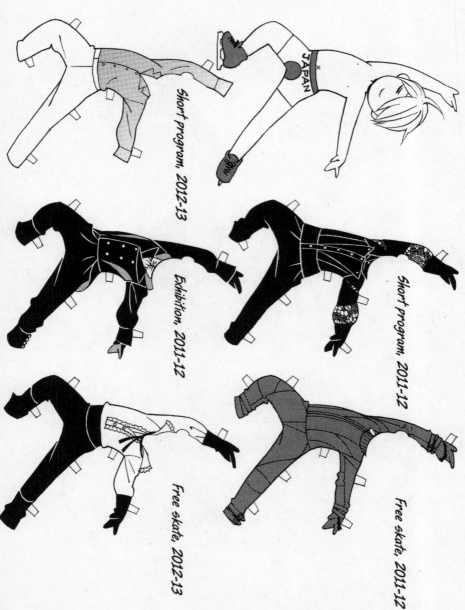

Short program, 2012-13

Exhibition, 2011-12

Short program, 2011-12

Free skate, 2012-13

Free skate, 2011-12

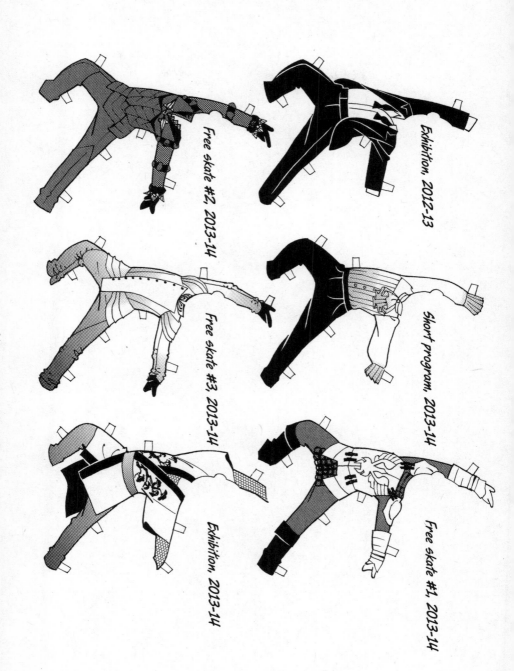

Free skate #2, 2013-14

Exhibition, 2012-13

Free skate #3, 2013-14

Short program, 2013-14

Exhibition, 2013-14

Free skate #1, 2013-14

A SMART, NEW ROMANTIC COMEDY FOR FANS OF *SHORTCAKE CAKE* AND *TERRACE HOUSE*!

A romance manga starring high school girl Meeko, who learns to live on her own in a boarding house whose living room is home to the odd (but handsome) Matsunaga-san. She begins to adjust to her new life away from her parents, but Meeko soon learns that no matter how far away from home she is, she's still a young girl at heart — especially when she finds herself falling for Matsunaga-san.

THE SWEET SCENT OF LOVE IS IN THE AIR! FOR FANS OF OFFBEAT ROMANCES LIKE *WOTAKOI*

VOL. 1

SWEAT AND SOAP

KINTETSU YAMADA

Sweat and Soap © Kintetsu Yamada / Kodansha Ltd.

In an office romance, there's a fine line between sexy and awkward... and that line is where Asako — a woman who sweats copiously — meets Koutarou — a perfume developer who can't get enough of Asako's, er, scent. Don't miss a romcom manga like no other!

KC
KODANSHA
COMICS

PERFECT WORLD

Rie Aruga

A TOUCHING NEW SERIES ABOUT LOVE AND COPING WITH DISABILITY

An office party reunites Tsugumi with her high school crush Itsuki. He's realized his dream of becoming an architect, but along the way, he experienced a spinal injury that put him in a wheelchair. Now Tsugumi's rekindled feelings will butt up against prejudices she never considered — and Itsuki will have to decide if he's ready to let someone into his heart...

"Depicts with great delicacy and courage the difficulties some with disabilities experience getting involved in romantic relationships... Rie Aruga refuses to romanticize, pushing her heroine to face the reality of disability. She invites her readers to the same tasks of empathy, knowledge and recognition."
—Slate.fr

"An important entry [in manga romance]... The emotional core of both plot and characters indicates thoughtfulness... [Aruga's] research is readily apparent in the text and artwork, making this feel like a real story."
—Anime News Network

KC
KODANSHA COMICS

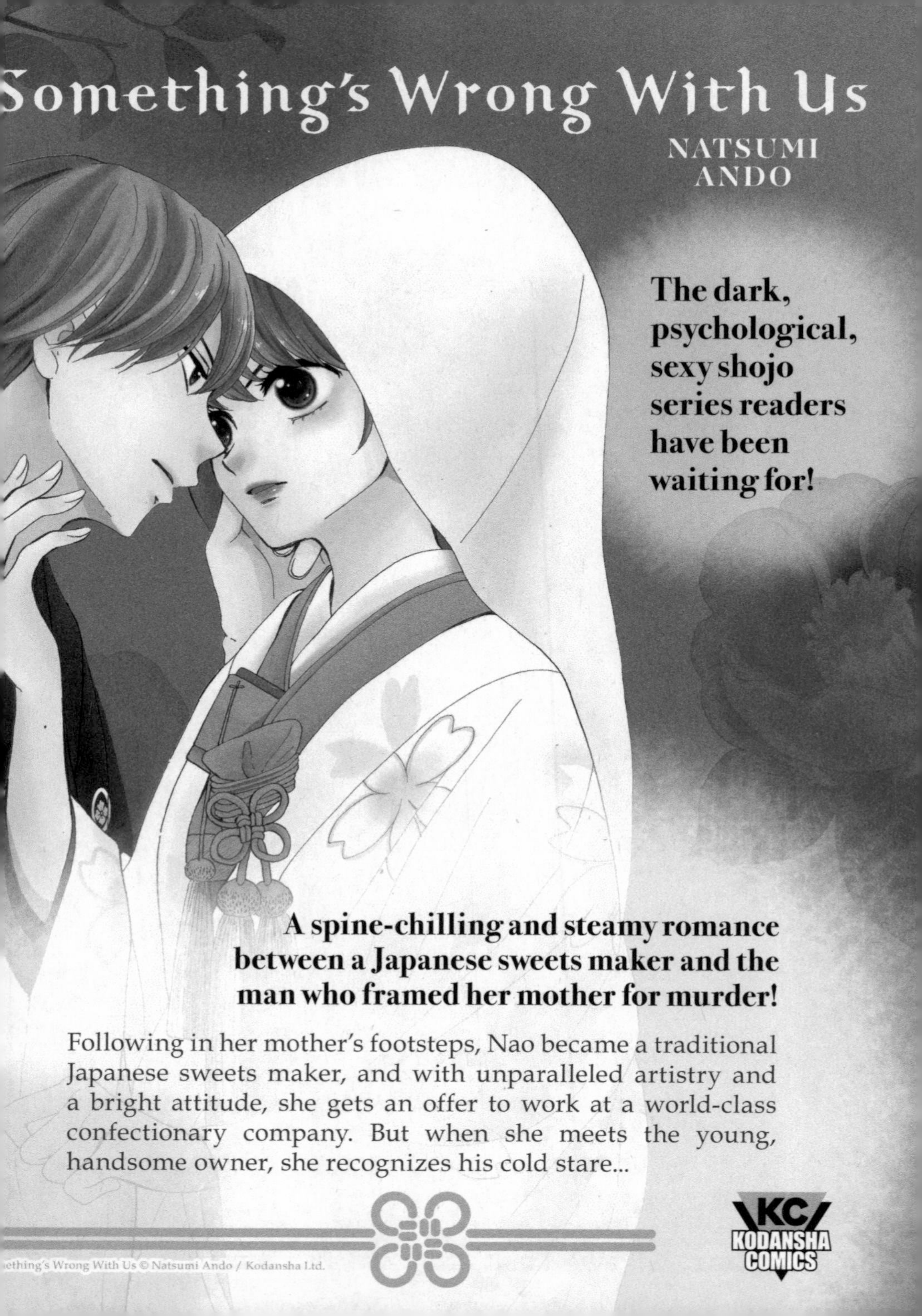
Something's Wrong With Us
NATSUMI ANDO
The dark, psychological, sexy shojo series readers have been waiting for!
A spine-chilling and steamy romance between a Japanese sweets maker and the man who framed her mother for murder!
Following in her mother's footsteps, Nao became a traditional Japanese sweets maker, and with unparalleled artistry and a bright attitude, she gets an offer to work at a world-class confectionary company. But when she meets the young, handsome owner, she recognizes his cold stare...
KC KODANSHA COMICS
ething's Wrong With Us © Natsumi Ando / Kodansha Ltd.

Young characters and steampunk setting, like *Howl's Moving Castle* and *Battle Angel Alita*

Beyond the Clouds © 2018 Nicke / Ki-oon

A boy with a talent for machines and a mysterious girl whose wings he's fixed will take you beyond the clouds! In the tradition of the high-flying, resonant adventure stories of Studio Ghibli comes a gorgeous tale about the longing of young hearts for adventure and friendship!

The adorable new odd-couple cat comedy manga from the creator of the beloved *Chi's Sweet Home*, in full color!

Sue & Tai-chan

Konami Kanata

Sue is an aging housecat who's looking forward to living out her life in peace... but her plans change when the mischievous black tomcat Tai-chan enters the picture! Hey! Sue never signed up to be a catsitter! *Sue & Tai-chan* is the latest from the reigning meow-narch of cute kitty comics, Konami Kanata.

KC
KODANSHA
COMICS

CUTE ANIMALS AND LIFE LESSONS, PERFECT FOR ASPIRING PET VETS OF ALL AGES!

YUZU THE PET VET

1

BY MINGO ITO

In collaboration with NIPPON COLUMBIA CO., LTD.

Yuzu the Pet Vet © Mingo Ito / NIPPON COLUMBIA CO., LTD./ Kodansha Ltd.

For an 11-year-old, Yuzu has a lot on her plate. When her mom gets sick and has to be hospitalized, Yuzu goes to live with her uncle who runs the local veterinary clinic. Yuzu's always been scared of animals, but she tries to help out. Through all the tough moments in her life, Yuzu realizes that she can help make things all right with a little help from her animal pals, peers, and kind grown-ups.

Every new patient is a furry friend in the making!

Knight of the Ice 11 is a work of fiction. Names, characters, places, and incidents are the products of the author's imagination or are used fictitiously. Any resemblance to actual events, locales, or persons, living or dead, is entirely coincidental.

A Kodansha Comics Trade Paperback Original

Published in the United States by Kodansha Comics, an imprint of Kodansha USA Publishing, LLC, New York.

Publication rights for this English edition arranged through Kodansha Ltd., Tokyo.

First published in Japan in 2017 by Kodansha Ltd., Tokyo as *Ginban kishi*, volume 11.

ISBN 978-1-64651-088-7

Printed in the United States of America.

www.kodansha.us

9 8 7 6 5 4 3 2 1
Translation: Rose Padgett
Lettering: Jennifer Skarupa
Editing: Aimee Zink
Kodansha Comics edition cover design by Phil Balsman

KC
KODANSHA
COMICS

Publisher: Kiichiro Sugawara

Director of publishing services: Ben Applegate
Director of publishing operations: Dave Barrett
Associate director of operations: Stephen Pakula
Publishing services managing editors: Alanna Ruse, Madison Salters
Production manager: Angela Zurlo